World of Art

James A. Doyle, an archaeologist and curator, is a leading scholar on the art and architecture of the Indigenous Americas and has published and lectured widely on the ancestral peoples of the Mesoamerican and Isthmo-Colombian areas. He is Director of the Matson Museum of Anthropology, Research Professor of Anthropology, and Affiliate Professor of Art History at the Pennsylvania State University. In addition to scholarly publications including the book *Architecture and the Origins of Preclassic Maya Politics* (2017), he has also organized and participated in multiple award-winning, critically acclaimed exhibitions for the public such as *Lives of the Gods: Divinity in Maya Art* (2022–23), *Arte del Mar: Artistic Exchange in the Caribbean* (2019–21), and *Golden Kingdoms: Luxury and Legacy in the Ancient Americas* (2017–18). His work has been supported by, among others, the National Gallery of Art, Dumbarton Oaks Research Library and Collection, the National Endowment for the Humanities, the Institute for Museum and Library Services, the National Science Foundation, and the Wenner-Gren Foundation. He obtained his M.A. and Ph.D. degrees in Anthropology from Brown University, and his B.A. in Anthropology from Vanderbilt University.

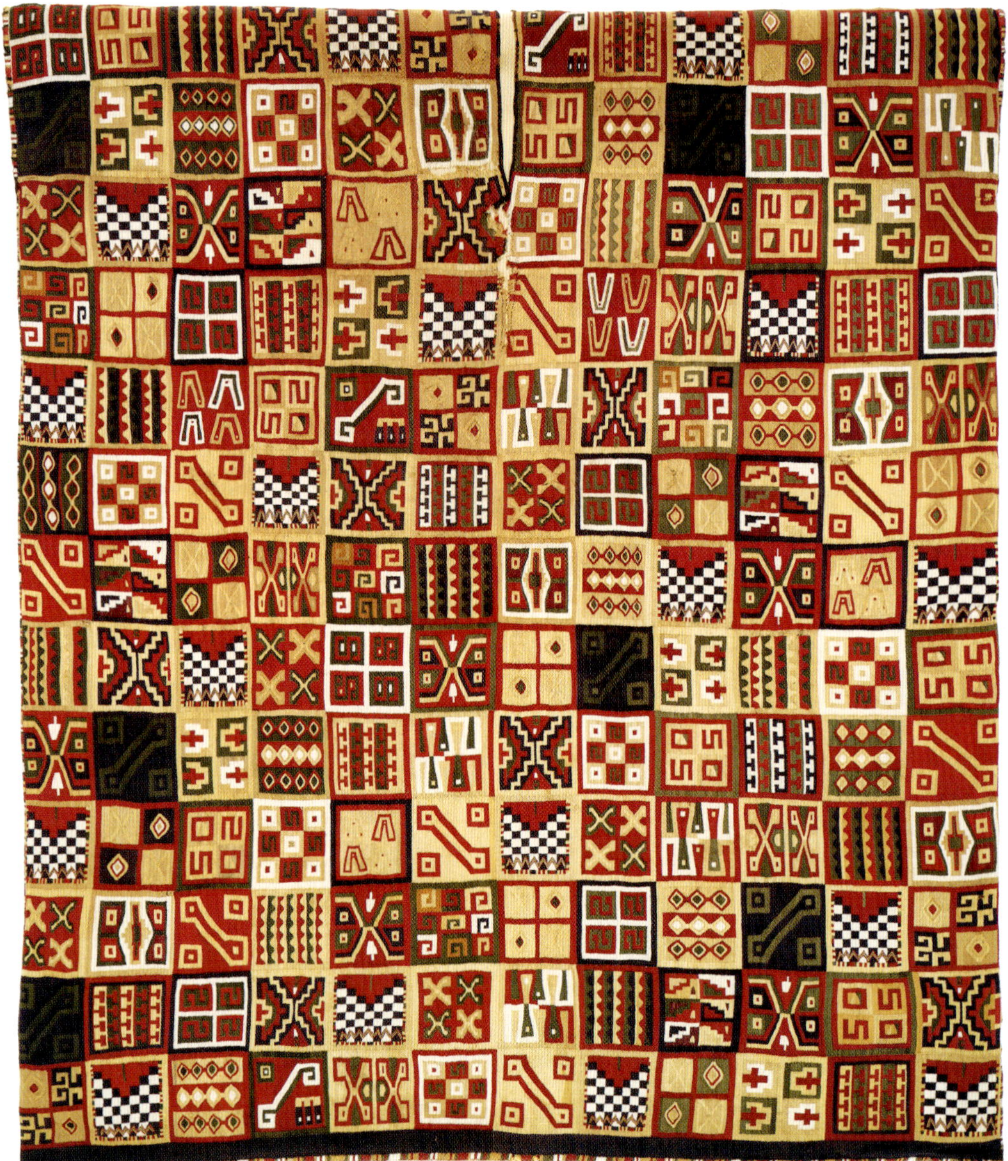

1 Royal Tunic, 1450–1540

World of Art

Arts of the Ancient Americas

James A. Doyle

T&H

To Pablo (and Misi)

All dates are CE unless stated otherwise.

First published in the United Kingdom in 2026 by
Thames & Hudson Ltd, 6–24 Britannia Street,
London WC1X 9JD

First published in the United States of America in 2026 by
Thames & Hudson Inc., 500 Fifth Avenue, New York,
New York 10110

Art direction and series design by Kummer & Herrman
Layout by Adam Hay Studio

EU Authorized Representative: Interart S.A.R.L.
19 rue Charles Auray, 93500 Pantin, Paris, France
productsafety@thameshudson.co.uk
interart.fr

A CIP catalogue record for this book is available from
the British Library

Library of Congress Control Number 2024950046

ISBN 978-0-500-20503-7
01

Printed and bound in China through Asia Pacific
Offset Ltd

MIX
Paper | Supporting
responsible forestry
FSC® C136333
FSC
www.fsc.org

Contents

6 Preface

11 **Introduction: Art Born from Mountains**

Part I
30 **Early Art in the Americas**

Chapter 1
33 **In the Shadow of the Andes: Chavín, Cupisnique, Paracas, and Nasca (1200 BCE–600 CE)**

Chapter 2
53 **Monumental Origins in Mesoamerica: The Olmec (1800–400 BCE)**

Part II
74 **Royal Patrons and Their Artists**

Chapter 3
77 **Mountains of Mud Brick: Moche (300–800 CE) and Their Successors**

Chapter 4
98 **Mountain Pyramids: The Ancestral Maya (100 BCE–1300 CE)**

Chapter 5
127 **Extracting Brilliance: The Northern Andes, Central America, the Amazon, and the Antilles (100 BCE–1500 CE)**

Part III
148 **The Art of Cities**

Chapter 6
151 **Volcanic Authority: Teotihuacán and its Successors (100–1500 CE)**

Chapter 7
173 **High-Altitude States: Tiwanaku and Wari (100–1000 CE)**

Chapter 8
192 **East and West of the Rockies: Ancestral Native North America (200–1600 CE)**

Part IV
210 **The Arts of Empires**

Chapter 9
213 **Harnessing the *Wak'a*: Chimú and Inka (1000–1532 CE)**

Chapter 10
235 ***Altepetl*, the Water Mountain: Mexica (1000–1521 CE)**

Chapter 11
256 **Epilogue: Final Considerations**

270 Suggested Reading
284 List of Illustrations
290 Index

Preface

This book tells the story of creative expression in North, Central, and South America over several millennia. To do proper justice to all the makers, their patrons, and the cultural or spiritual contexts of their works of art in what is known as the ancient Americas, however, is impossible. Fortunately, recent advances in the understanding of Indigenous concepts of the landscape and creativity allow this book to present a fresh take on this important part of the global history of art by telling the rich stories of iconic objects and their creators. We can now see how diverse ancient American societies immortalized their ancestors, their histories, and their core origin stories through artistic representation, enshrining systems of values and social meanings in tangible materials. In some cases, as with the ancient Maya, we now know how artists identified themselves and described sculpture and painting in the first millennium CE. It is now possible to question what ancient people thought about what is known as art, because we can now reconstruct how it was produced and received by past audiences. The main objective of the present volume is to demonstrate how foundational elements of artistic expressions emerged, fractured, and recombined throughout the history of the Americas, from the deep past to the time of European invasion.

Anyone curious about the global past will recognize shared themes from world history in these case studies from the Americas, where disparate peoples were connected by politics and migration throughout ancestral North, Central, and South America. Raging conflicts between feuding royal families strained power relations just as they did in other parts of the world that might be more familiar. Empires led by dynasts with a divine mandate, such as the Mexica *huey tlatoani* (emperor) and his counterpart in Peru, the Sapa Inka (emperor), controlled vast swaths of territory just as similar emperors did in the Mediterranean, Asia, and Africa. Thriving land and sea trade routes within the Americas itself—for moving gold, silver, turquoise, marine shell, textiles, and even tropical bird feathers—connected people between parts of all the modern nations of the Western Hemisphere and along the coasts of the Atlantic, Pacific, and the Caribbean Sea. When the Spanish invaders walked or rode horses into the major cities of the Americas in the sixteenth century, they wondered if this previously unknown but analogous world was all just a dream. Europeans soon coopted ancient trade routes to funnel luxury materials from the Americas to their homelands and distribute people throughout the so-called "new" world. The Americas were not, in fact, new to Europeans at all; Norse settlers had briefly explored and settled what is now the Canadian coast several centuries before Spanish arrival. Here I present the histories from the Americas that ran parallel to events that occurred in ancient Egypt, the Roman or Mongol Empires, or even the European Renaissance.

This introductory book proceeds roughly from early to late, in four main parts. Where possible, the prose avoids overly technical time periods or ceramic phases used by scholars that tend to vary over time or between regions. Instead, overarching themes—the earliest art making, royal patrons and their artists, the arts of cities, and imperial arts—unite chapters addressing roughly contemporaneous case studies from across the Americas. Each chapter focuses on a regional investigation, placing different related traditions in conversation with comparative examples from other cultural areas. The goal of this thematic organization is to move away from strict geographical understandings of art traditions (divided by locations such as Mesoamerica, the Andes, etc.) that tend to isolate rather than celebrate commonalities. The chapters thus stand alone or spark connections with the others in each part. Each chapter addresses universal components of world art such as architecture, color, materiality, regalia, luminosity, performance, and visual parables, among others, to expand our understanding of what ancient American art was and who the creators were in these regions. Overall, *Arts of the Ancient Americas* hopefully provides readers an updated consensus on important visual cultures employing interdisciplinary scholarship of archaeology, art history, epigraphy, and related fields. Although many earlier scholars have united the continents under one visual narrative—notably Pál Kelemen (*Medieval American Art*, 1943), G. H. S. Bushnell in this very series (*Ancient Art of the Americas*, 1965), and Esther Pasztory (*Pre-Columbian Art*, 1998)—recent hemispheric treatments have been limited to particular museum collections or special exhibitions (see Suggested Reading).

Several historical factors that influenced the previous treatment of the arts of the ancient Americas deserve mention here, such as the aforementioned imperial and settler colonial enterprises of the Spanish, and later English, French, Portuguese, and others. The violent oppression of Indigenous peoples that began in the late fifteenth century and continues until today, compounded with campaigns against Indigenous religious traditions and political retaliation, created devastating losses to cultural traditions, ecosystems, and Indigenous lifeways—and the corpus of artwork. Colonial thoughts and attitudes still color the interpretation of the works of ancient art that were not lost to destruction or transformation. In anthropology and archaeology, the Americas has suffered from an overemphasis on social evolution as an explanatory model. For example, since the first comparative studies of world civilizations and ancient cities, case studies coming from the Americas have confounded scholars searching for broad theories on the rise of social complexity and artistic expression. This has caused whole disciplines to relegate the ancient Americas as counterexamples or cases that show less "complexity," a nebulous term that has little utility in making broad analogies.

The disciplines of anthropology and art history have historically been limited in discerning the patterns and meanings of art of the ancient Americas from the third millennium BCE to the colonial period in the sixteenth century. The historical research on such works instead tended to marginalize the material as "ethnographic" or "primitive," characterizations that ultimately permeated mainstream opinion until the late twentieth century, and even today. Such pejorative designations live on, perhaps under different names, at large art museums across the world that group Africa, the Pacific, and the ancient and Indigenous Americas under one department and in adjacent galleries. Popular television shows and conspiracy-fueled online musings have also proliferated, spreading speculation and assigning agency for some of the creations described in this book to extraterrestrial powers or heretofore undiscovered ancient civilizations, for which no evidence currently exists.

Some have even questioned the applicability of the term *art* at all: the creators of much, if not most, of the works in this book may not have even thought of their products as art in the modern analytical sense. The arbitrary, neat divisions in the discipline of ancient Western art history such as paintings, sculpture, and fine or decorative arts, are simply not appropriate. Many of the illustrated places or objects here would have been pleasing to their ancient viewers but, perhaps conversely, some were created to repel. A notable feature of art in the ancient Americas is that such realistic approaches as naturalism, in which artists approximate observed subjects, and such tactics as geometric abstraction, in which artists break subjects apart, could be deeply intertwined and not mutually exclusive. As the subsequent chapters will show, the artists' adherence to faithful representation of spatial or human reality was culturally relative and context specific, and not at all bound by time periods.

Perhaps the largest issue confronting the study of the arts of the ancient Americas today is the simple fact that many works exist outside of their countries of origins, including thousands upon thousands of objects in museum collections around the world, having been looted and trafficked. These illicit activities have contributed to a great loss of archaeological data about these objects that would have enriched the biographies of the artists and patrons involved in their creation. The extraction of sculptures, paintings, regalia, and sacred objects from their original contexts has physically damaged sites of cultural patrimony and created a cognitive disconnect between these ancestral materials and their descendant communities. Meaningful and sustained consultations are beginning to address this gap.

Imperialist and colonialist attitudes toward Indigenous peoples' conceptualization of their own past have also impeded the study of archaeological materials. A new generation of Indigenous scholars—as well as collaborative art historians, archaeologists, anthropologists, epigraphers, linguists, activists, and other stakeholders—are working to chart a new path forward in studying and producing knowledge about materials from the ancient Americas. As such, Indigenous community members and culture bearers will be true partners in generating new directions, encouraging the creation of a truly collaborative, multidisciplinary, and multivocal window into the past. Such collaboration is critical to the future of the disciplines of archaeology and art history, and especially to such institutions as museums.

As the narrator of this book, I build on the work of many greats in the fields of art history, archaeology, ethnohistory, linguistics, and especially the Indigenous collaborators who are leading research today or who have documented their traditions to outsiders since the fifteenth century. Many people have contributed to my own evolving perspective in the last two decades, especially my dear mentor and friend Stephen Houston. Conversations with Pablo Suárez Becerra over many years have elevated my own approach to reaching general readers with scientific and humanistic findings in both English and Spanish. Several dear colleagues have served as crucial interlocutors in the development of the structure and content of this volume; these include Caitlin Earley, Lisa Trever, Claudia Brittenham, Sarahh Scher, Melanie Kingsley, Alicia Boswell, Amara Solari, Annabeth Headrick, Simon Martin, Julia McHugh, Hillary Olcott, Caitlin Mahony, Orlando Hernández Ying, and Andrew Hamilton. Early opportunities to engage in trans-regional conversations and site visits that built my own knowledge considerably were organized by Colin McEwan of Dumbarton Oaks and Joanne Pillsbury and Kim Richter as part of the game-changing exhibition in 2017–18, *Golden Kingdoms: Luxury and Legacy in the Ancient Americas*. Helpful suggestions for new directions in inclusive images and bibliographies came from Tahnee Ahtone, Traci Ardren, Davide Domenici, Jamie Forde, Emiliano Gallaga, Zac Hruby, Joseph Kopta, Jake and Isabelle Holland-Lulewicz, John Hoopes, Bryan Keene, Elizabeth Klarich, Bertrand Lobjois, Jon Lohse, Kyle Marini, Jeffrey Quilter, Lawrence Waldron, and Marcony Lopes Alves, among many others. All potential errors in interpretation or summation remain solely my own.

For the orthography of cultures, sites, and concepts throughout I have tried to be consistent with the spellings most commonly found in recent literature, while including new readings or transliterations when helpful. Wherever possible, I have privileged the Indigenous terms (e.g. Mexica vs. Aztec) in order to encourage this when teaching and publishing. There are considerable differences of opinion on the proper spellings of terms in Nahuatl (e.g. Moteuczoma), Quechua (e.g. Wari, Tiwanaku), or Indigenous loan words into Spanish and English (e.g. zemí vs. cemí). The hope is that this volume presents a balance between such academic uncertainties and an overall clarity so that general readers can easily follow along the journey through time.

My gratitude also extends to the team at Thames & Hudson, especially editors Roger Thorp and Mohara Gill for stewarding the project, editor Mary Christian, and picture researcher Nikos Kostopoulos. The publisher's dedication to producing high-quality illustrated books in this series is commendable, and it is truly a privilege for me to continue in that legacy.

Introduction: Art Born from Mountains

A foundational concept of this project is the connectedness of ancient American creativity through human social relations and movement. People and ideas flowed throughout the American continent for thousands of years, from the densest corners of the rainforests to the dry altiplanos (elevated plains). The arrival of ancestors from Paleolithic Eurasia with shared social trajectories incited a history rooted in the uniquely American landscape; the intersections between geography and culture inspired work by makers in their newly formed communities. Artists made very distinct choices at different places and different times within the Americas, and those creative preferences were made wholly independently from those made in other parts of the ancient world. Despite the eventual physical separation from Eurasia, intriguing parallels between different contexts exist in types of architecture, such as pyramidal buildings or palatial royal courts, and methods of expression, such as fresco mural painting or lost-wax gold casting, as the following chapters elucidate. The underlying thread of many artistic traditions here is that both the subjects and the raw materials emerged from the American landscape itself. The stony outcrops and hills forming the limestone spine of mountains from Canada to Chile became beings in their own right that shaped peoples' cognition of the environment and inspired epic narratives, physical buildings, and transformative works of art. This introduction outlines the earliest art-making periods and describes the different source materials highlighted in subsequent chapters.

The palaces, temples, and plazas of American societies owe their roots to the nomadic groups who first crossed the Bering Land Bridge. The motivations of the first Americans, who had arrived by at least 13,500 years ago, are largely unknown to us as they walked over time, presumably following food and fairer weather. They carried what they could on their backs. They were skilled in hunting, cooking, and creating temporary shelters wherever their destinies led them. They also carried with them ingrained worldviews and cultures, symbolic thought and behavior, and what can be thought of as art. For thousands of years, their ancestors had already been transforming natural materials into colors, fibers, regalia, representations of themselves and supernatural beings, and things that make sound. These multivalent objects incorporated aesthetic systems and symbolic meanings. Could the concept of beauty, which bears legacies of Eurocentrism and individual subjectivities, be useful in this context? How the beholders of these early works perceived them as attractive—whether through their symmetries, colors, spiritual references, or tactile experiences—is currently inaccessible to modern peoples. The study of ephemeral arts like clothing or body painting from between the early crossing to the fourth millennium BCE also remains speculative.

People who crossed into the Americas were curious about newly encountered natural surroundings; they likely sang and
2 laughed as they traveled. They stood in awe at the massive ice floes and snow-capped peaks they encountered in ancient Alaska and British Columbia. Offshore currents created some of the most diverse marine environments in the world at the base of this chain of high peaks. Some mountains were at once comforting as natural defensive vantage points, providing shelter and sustenance, and others, such as volcanoes, could be threatening as shaking, shifting, erupting forces. They guided human movement along the coastlines southward with their imposing peaks but beckoned adventurous spirits eastward over the difficult alpine passes with crisp, chilled breezes. Seasons of wet, dry, cold, and warm shaped how these early settlers worked together to prosper in the newly encountered world. Peoples carried with them their own stories about their heritage, but each day in their new world caused them to form new foundational identities in once unfamiliar places. The human-made products that were derived from mountains' veins reminded the artists who made them and patrons who used them about the natural origins of things on the new landscape.

Mountains were, and still are in many places, the conceptual center of communities, whether physical or spiritual. Throughout the Americas, peoples who lived in the shadow of these mountains re-created them through symbolism and representation, bringing them to a human scale that made them tangible and malleable. Even those who lived far away from mountains deified the peaks and mythologized them as distant, yet imminent powers. Pilgrimages, even continuing among Indigenous communities until the present

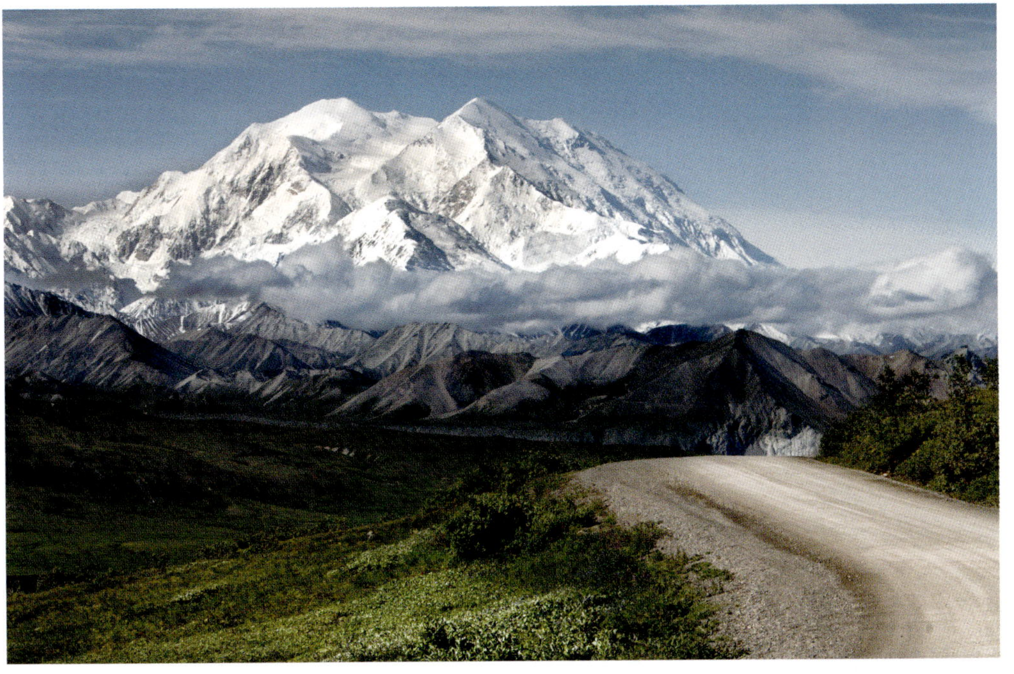

2 Denali National Park and Preserve, Alaska

day, allowed them to honor mountains as mythic ancestors. As highlighted in the following chapters, Indigenous makers often made mountains present as living beings for their respective societies. The sources of creativity, underlying inspiration, and raw material for artworks of all media, mountains were, along with other landscape features, the inspirational anchors of art in the ancient Americas.

The Arts of Weaponry: Clovis Points and Bannerstones

The mobile lifeways of the first Americans have left archaeologists with little material culture to study for the first millennia after humans entered the continents. Some of the earliest evidence of human creative expressions were spear points, delicately chipped to be aerodynamic and presumably lethal, but also aesthetically pleasing in their own way. Through trial and error, early American men and women created works they might have considered beautiful out of the mountains and volcanoes themselves, utilizing such materials as chert, flint, or obsidian. The skilled hands of artists with a deep practical knowledge of stone exacted dozens or even hundreds of knap strikes that created a fluted point. Early Americans followed big

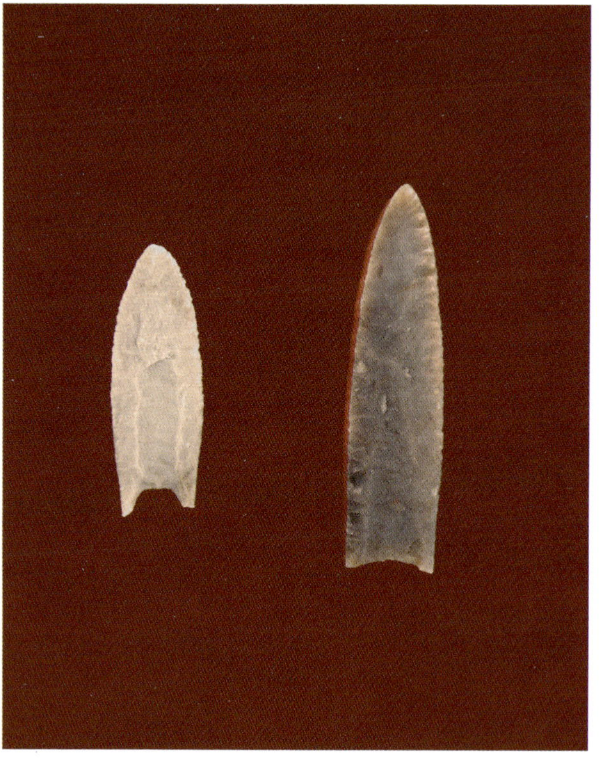

3 LEFT Fluted Projectile Points, 9000–8500 BCE
4 OPPOSITE Bannerstone, 3000–1000 BCE

game, including Pleistocene megafauna such as the American mastodons or bison, which no longer roam the arid plains.

3 After their discovery at the site of Clovis, New Mexico, "Clovis culture" objects are the earliest clues to an ancient American art tradition, distinct from the rest of the world. Clovis-style spear points do not exist in Paleolithic Asia. There were likely earlier peoples living across the Americas, but Clovis points, dating as early as 11,500 BCE, are the first widespread evidence that early Americans shared a common creative bond through craft and the practice of symbolic expression. The burial of an infant at the Anzick site, Montana, about 12,990 to 12,840 years ago, using Clovis-period tools and antlers covered with red ocher pigment, gives an insight into the value and honor afforded to a lost loved one. Over time, a combination of overhunting and climatic shifts eliminated certain species of large mammals that necessitated new tactics and new tools. Later peoples created points between 8550 BCE and 7550 BCE, such as those known as Hell Gap points, after the site in Wyoming, out of distinct non-local raw materials. These

variations in point making signal both the long-distance movement of goods and a great diversity of early artistic styles yet to be discovered and documented.

Beginning possibly as early as the fifth millennium BCE, before evidence of intensive agriculture or monumental architecture, sculptors in the Eastern United States also sought out special stones and honored them by turning them into cherished hunting implements, known today as bannerstones. They used materials not available closer to home, such as brightly colored or veined, slaty hard stones, which they flaked, pecked, and ground into symmetrical shapes. First, though, they drilled a hole through the center of the source stone. They are made to be mounted onto something perishable, either wood or fiber. Most show no wear and tear on the surface, or other evidence that they were used, although they have been interpreted as hunting paraphernalia, perhaps counterweights for spear throwers used to launch pointed darts. Spearthrowers, known by the term *atlatl* in Nahuatl (the language of the Mexica, see chapter 10), are wooden hooked instruments that extend the reach of a hunter's arm in order to create more force, distance, and accuracy when throwing pointed projectiles. These useful stones radiate creativity with their flourishes in

4

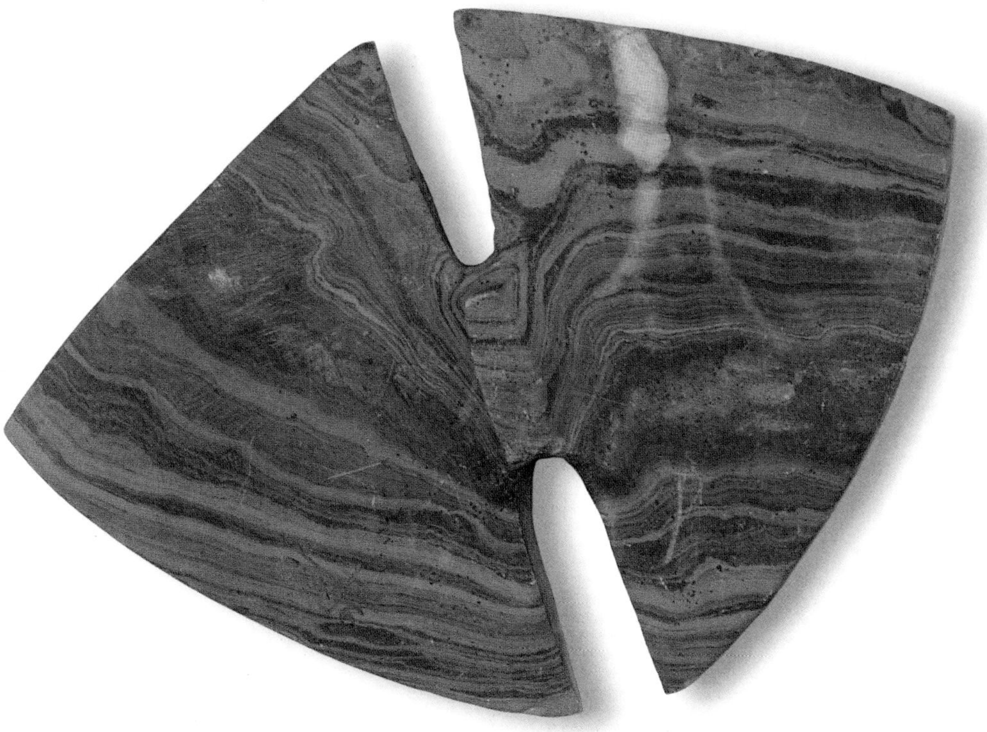

form, although the worldview of their creators remains difficult to reconstruct in such a remote past. A similar class of stone sculptures, known collectively as birdstones, represents stylized avian figures and also could have been hafted to perishable staffs to create spearthrowers or alternatively worn as regalia.

Whether the so-called bannerstones and birdstones are parts of a weaponry toolkit or not, they are undoubtedly evidence of a change in the collective American consciousness. Perhaps the journey to collect these special stones—banded slate or ferruginous quartz—from specific spots on the landscape was a rite of passage. That the stones' sources were not local like those used to make earlier points also reveals a more important truth about peoples: they had set down roots at least for part of the year, if not year-round, by the third millennium BCE. That is, the entire community probably did not travel to collect the source stones, so that those who went on such journeys knew where to return. Or, perhaps, even long-distance trade networks in such raw materials had already been established to connect makers to the rare stones.

Seasonality of villages and of social relations, however, prevailed in many places. Certain societies made specific choices throughout centuries to participate in non-urban, non-permanent residences, for example, in the Arctic region. Weather patterns and mammal migrations conditioned
5 how often and where people gathered. They created hunting implements—harpoon points, toggles, and counterweights—for use in procuring game or ceremonies. These objects were often highly decorated, and, along with figural sculptures, were interred with the owners as grave goods by their descendants, underscoring the symbolic importance as possessions of the deceased. Presumably their impermanent dwellings were considered both practical and beautiful, although these vernacular architectures have been lost to time and the elements.

The Arts of Shelter: Rock Art and Early Architecture

Before they constructed platforms and buildings, people in the Americas retreated to nature's architecture: rock shelters, caves, overhangs, and other geological formations. Rock walls were constants, practically eternal, if changing very slowly. In these early homes, there remain some non-portable creative expressions such as petroglyphs and pictographs, as they were affixed to the natural rock. Although difficult to place on a chronological timeline through scientific means, cave paintings and geoglyphs dot the darkened inner walls of

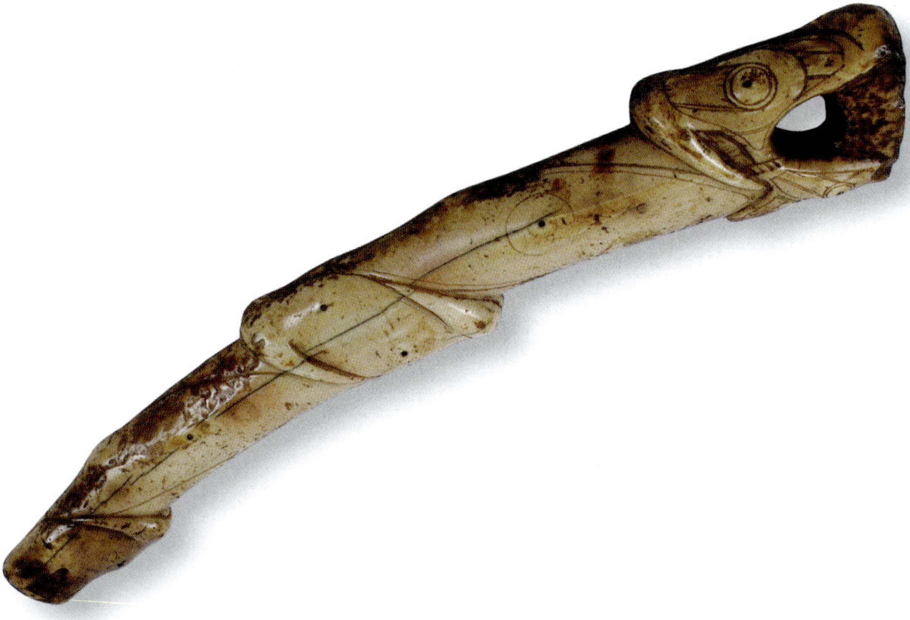

5 Zoomorphic Adze Handle, 100–500

caves from Brazil to the Southwest United States. The refuge they provided might have prompted celebration, but often the commemoration of human presence is only visible in negative
6 spaces: handprints, whose outlines were created by blowing pigments toward one's hand pressed against the wall, testify to the long-lost personalities of the people who made them. Places such as the Cueva de las Manos in Argentina, in use for centuries between about the eighth and first millennia BCE, became ancestral destinations for pilgrims and artists to visit and create new layers to the generational paintings. Many hidden and inaccessible paintings and earthworks were probably meant for supernatural eyes only (see chapter 1 for information about the Nasca lines, perhaps the most famous example of manipulation of geology in the ancient Americas). Rock art across time is deeply significant throughout the ancient Americas.

Ancient American philosophies on space and landscape shifted toward collective understandings that were made manifest in community construction projects, representing

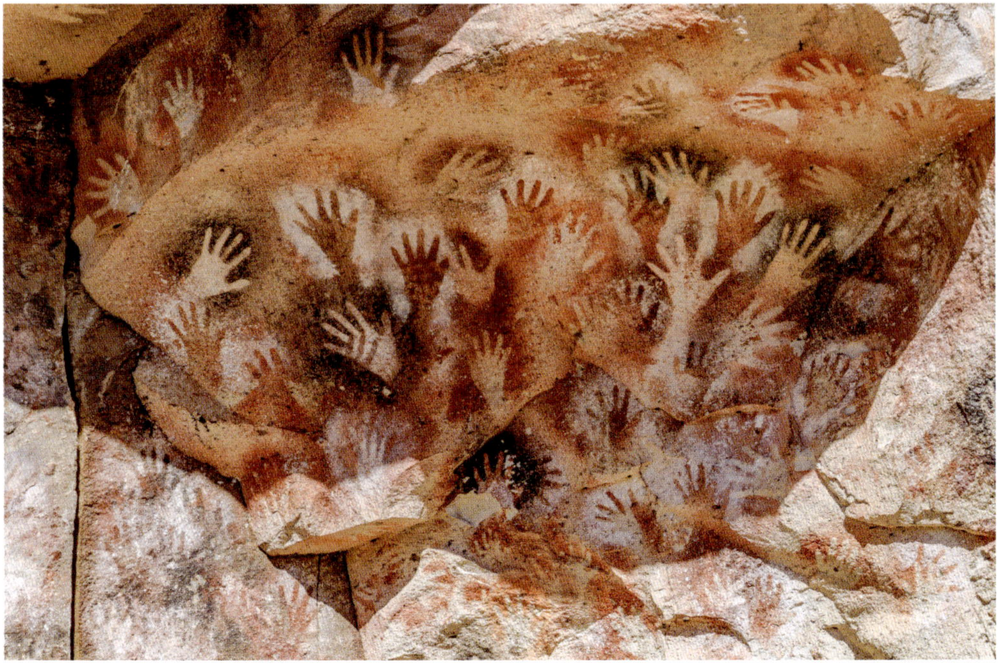

6 Cueva de las Manos, Argentina

the culmination of centuries of marking rocks and moving earth for a non-human audience. As early as 3500 BCE, groups of people cooperated to create monumental mounds, perhaps to re-create mountains known only in legend by that time, in the tributaries of the Mississippi Delta, for example at Watson Brake, Louisiana. At such places, it seems that no one was residing permanently, but instead engaging in seasonal or episodic bursts of building. Big building projects imply the cooperation of many hands, but also suggest that a small group or individuals may have wielded influence over the efforts. The desire to transform the earth itself and build mounds speaks to an early impetus to elevate residences and ceremonial spaces, especially by the second millennium BCE. Poverty Point, a massive site, also in Louisiana, dating to the
7 second millennium BCE, contains large mounds, causeways, and massive arcs of raised earthworks that surround the bend of the local tributary. The crescent focused peoples' attentions on the large plaza next to the water. Political power or a major collective effort to move so much earth in the sultry swamp is also implied. The motivations of Poverty Point residents to build big things, however, remain opaque to modern observers.

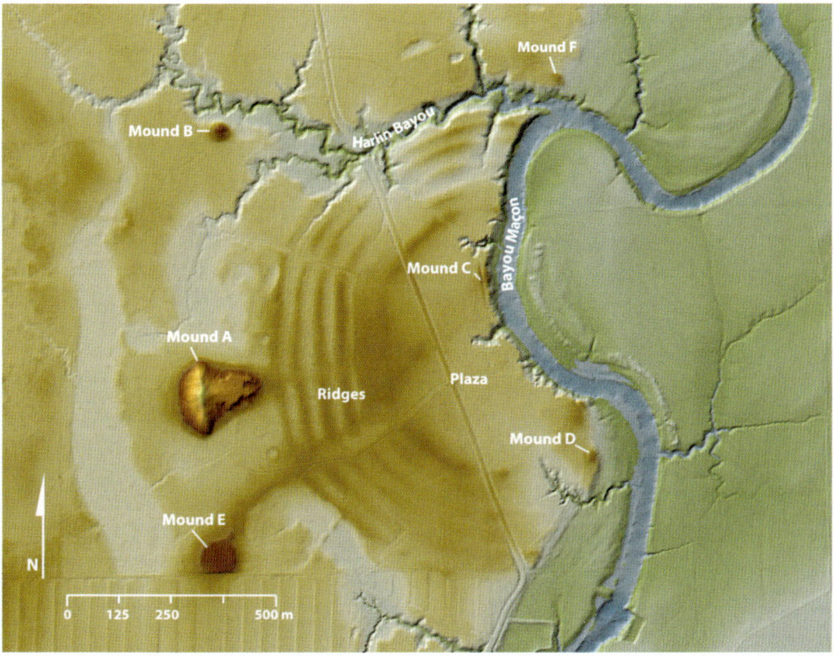

7 LiDAR Image of Poverty Point, Louisiana

The seasonality of building permanent places while maintaining an impermanent, mobile lifeway at many sites in North, Central, and South America is a fundamental difference between the rise of civilizations in the Americas and other parts of the world. In Mesoamerica, the region from Central Mexico to Central America united by shared cultural traits, research has identified the earliest monumental architecture, scraped directly out of the bedrock of the natural geology, created by people who were still practicing a mobile lifestyle. In other words, there was a shared idea, a very big idea, that motivated cooperation on a grand scale. Exciting new technologies such as LiDAR (Light Detection and Ranging), a type of laser remote sensing that allows high-resolution scans of the topography even through dense vegetation, are revealing more and more large platforms and monumental architecture throughout the Americas. By 1000 BCE, peoples at places like Aguada Fénix, in Tabasco, Mexico, constructed mega-scalar platforms as they defined the centers of their communities.

The impulse for peoples to erect early monumental ceremonial places before the third millennium BCE is paralleled in South America, culminating in constructions such as those found at the Peruvian site of Caral, in the shadow of the Andes. In this area, people who were farming cotton in the inland Supe Valley traded with those who were harvesting seafood from the rich coastal waters of Peru. The residents of Caral and surrounding communities constructed giant places, characterized by pyramidal buildings and open plazas, for ritual performance. People used their talents for producing and weaving cotton fibers to create containers, garments, and beaded adornments for their bodies. Music filled the air at Caral as well; people made flutes out of bird bones for celebrations. A big idea there, too, caught on and compelled communities to invest in themselves and future generations. Architectural complexes were centripetal forces; they became larger settlements over time as people craved interaction and proximity to each other and social activities. Precursors to what we now think of as cities, though in many different forms, soon began to outnumber the mobile communities that thrived before architecture in many regions, engendering urbanization across the Americas (see part III).

The Dramatic Arts: Song, Dance, and Storytelling

Ideas that congealed into rich creation narratives and humorous morality tales were acted out and shared orally by these early peoples, and were passed down through generations. Across the ancient Americas—from Louisiana to Mexico to Honduras to Peru—the earliest communal constructions essentially created giant, level performance stages. Unlike dramas from other cultures in the ancient Mediterranean world, some of which survived through written histories recorded and retold in different languages centuries later, the great stories that Indigenous American communities shared orally in early ceremonies slipped away from the common memory, for the most part. In addition to early instruments like those of Caral, some of the earliest artworks depict impersonation, regalia, gestural communications, individual and group dance performances, and other traces of a rich tradition of Indigenous American performing arts.

Music and singing appear in early representations of performance, and ancient artists made musical instruments from a variety of media. Details about site-specific arts and performances from ancient times survive only in rare instances, such as through the decipherment of Maya hieroglyphic texts. The ancient Maya depicted and narrated the acts of mortals impersonating ancestors and deities while creating song and dance. Rich texts recorded by the invading Europeans in the sixteenth century are most often religious and limited in their ethnographic detail; some only hint at the lively poetic and sonic lives of peoples who lived long before. Maya and Mexica lyric or epic poems represent separate traditions from the time, perhaps providing the clearest insight into what would have been a widespread tradition of poetry expressing metaphysical thought. Oppositional couplets as metaphors, or synecdoche, in which the part represents the whole, express abstract concepts that certainly had a deep antiquity in the Americas. In most cases, the only clues are material remains in the form of regalia and instruments used in the daily performative lives of ancestral Americans.

The Art of Containers: Gourds and Pottery

Stone made impractical, heavy containers for early American people leading mobile lifeways. They instead used the lightweight hollowed shells of gourds to hold water. In addition to such perishable containers as leather waterskins, these dried fruit skins enabled ancient Americans throughout centuries to wander farther than previously possible on a given journey for days or even weeks. Some of the earliest gourds that survive were decorated with painting or a technique known as pyrogravure, scorching the surface with burning wood. These hard objects, born of pure utility, became some of the New World's first canvases for creative expression. Some of the earliest manmade pottery vessels mimicked the vegetal form of these primordial containers.

The true visionary power of the arts of the Americas can be seen in creations that came straight from the long-eroded and softened bones of the mountains themselves: clays. The earliest manipulations of clay after about 4000 BCE took the form of figurines depicting females with elaborate hairstyles and exaggerated features. Valdivia artists from Ecuador created
8 these feminine images out of baked clay, molded and incised or impressed to adorn the bodies and large hairstyles. They sometimes are depicted carrying children. Life was hard for mothers in the pre-industrial world and the preoccupation with creating a new generation arguably inspired these first figurative sculptures. Sometimes the Valdivia characters have two heads: what ancient idea prompted the representation of such a conjoined twin or dual-identity character?

The power of baked and painted clay to create human representations and watertight containers became of great value to innovators from Pacific Mexico to Peru by the second millennium BCE. The care that early potters took in crafting their wares was extraordinary. One would expect to see the earliest pottery assemblages including rough attempts at

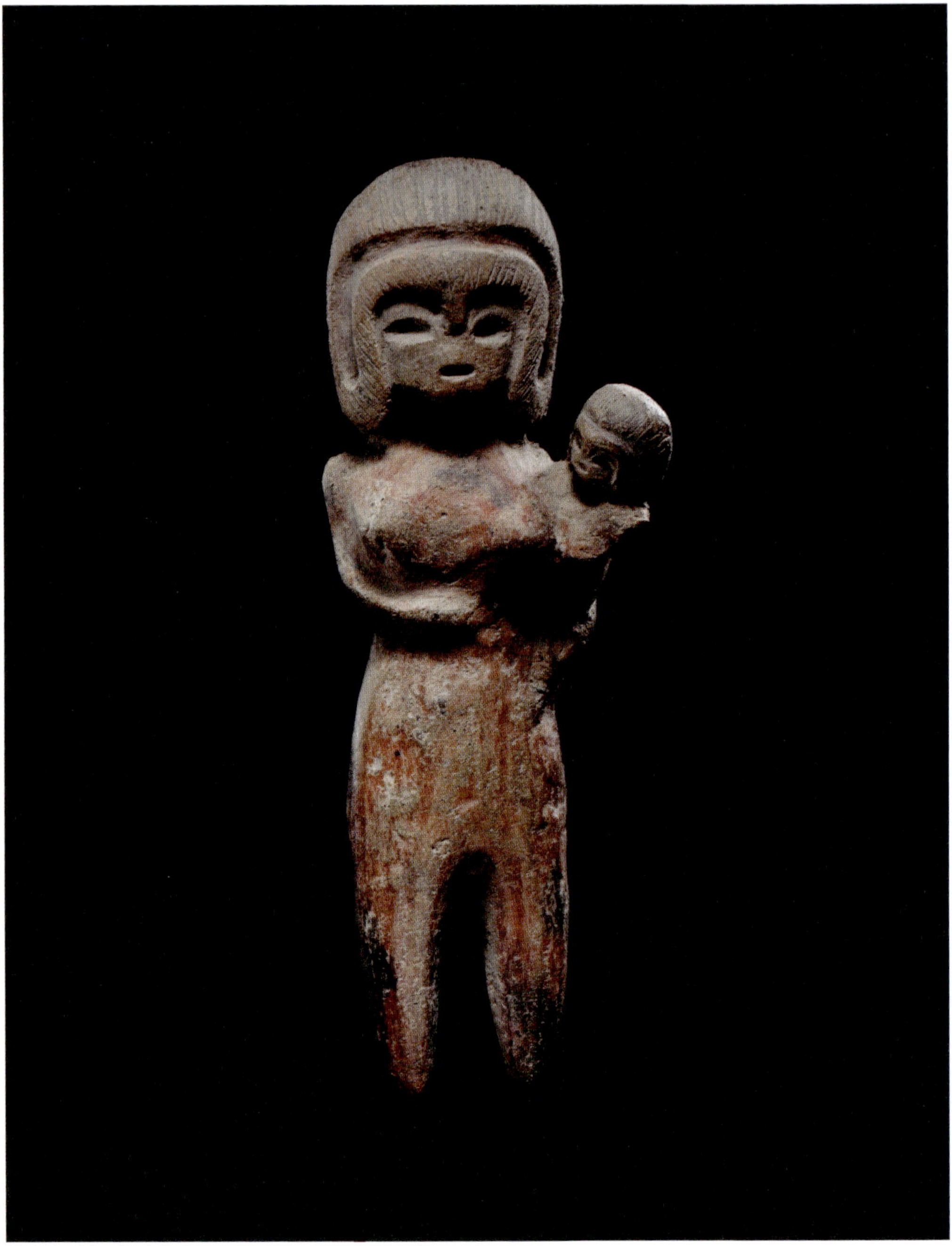

8 Anthropomorphic Figurine, 4000–1500 BCE

crude works, or at least far cruder than polished objects, but this does not seem to be the case. The drive of early potters was probably to prepare luxurious containers for large group events, feasting for special occasions. The gatherings held at the early community or performance spaces inspired the creativity leading to sculptural vessels with representational aspects. It is important to emphasize that all Indigenous pottery in the Americas was constructed entirely by hand before the sixteenth century, signifying an intimate personal relationship between each pot and its maker. Although molds were prolific and simple turning mechanisms may have been used, devices such as a potter's wheel were only later introduced by Europeans.

On the Pacific coast of Chiapas, Mexico, and Guatemala, for example, artists captured the essence of plant containers with clay and embellished them with a creative palette of earth-toned mineral slips (pigments dispersed in water) beginning about 1800 BCE. These earliest ceramics in Mexico underscore how important vessels became for aesthetic expression in the Americas. Ceramic eating and drinking objects were the canvases of the arts of the ancient Americas, and even these early examples contain symbolic content that hints at the abstract thoughts of their makers and users. They also speak to the creativity and social standing of the potters. Access to the best kinds of raw clays, tempers (additions to the clay), and pigments for slips was crucial to producing a masterwork container. These potters may have dedicated most of their time to learning and perfecting their skills, suggesting an early recognition of talent as a driver of social mobility.

Over time, pottery also became the preferred medium for artists to use when sculpting living family members and deceased ancestors. Because most of such works were produced as burial offerings, the target beholders for this artwork comprised a non-living, perhaps supernatural audience. Lively earthenware scenes from western Mexico, especially the modern state of Nayarit, show festivities in houses and community centers. These clay scenes rendered in a reduced scale were placed in shaft tombs, so the deceased lay for eternity with their families and homes. Ancestral pairs, delicately modeled and painted to represent male-female progenitors, also ensured the spiritual audience that the descendant family would live on, even in the absence of the deceased.

The Arts of Flora and Fauna: Fibers, Wood, Bone, and Shell

Perhaps the most spectacular of all ancient American expressions occurred because of the complex and ongoing intersections between people and the natural world. Cotton,

independently domesticated in the Americas, originally grew in the ancient neotropical lowlands but people soon realized its utility and its cultivation spread over great distances. Spinning and weaving engendered new techniques of hunting and fishing, as seen on some of the earliest mural paintings in the Americas at Ventarrón, Peru. There, fear-stricken deer are shown after having been trapped in nets, just as fish had been trapped for centuries prior. Textiles also quickly became arts in themselves as weavers employed different patterns and colors to transmit complex ideas. The earliest textiles also testify to the cognition and symbolic vocabulary of early artists. When archaeologists began excavating the site of Huaca Prieta on the north coast of Peru in the 1940s, they quickly realized the important implications of textile production in the absence of ceramics. Artists at Huaca Prieta mastered techniques such as twining (twisting two fibers around each other or another thread to create an interlaced structure), weaving (interlacing fibers to those perpendicular to them to create a structure), and netting (knotting fibers together) to enhance their haul from the ocean but also inscribe their worldview. Through dyed cotton threads, designs of condors, humans, serpents, and crustaceans appear on these early textiles made to be worn as
9 garments or filled as bags. Later cotton and camelid fibers were tapestry woven and embroidered to create a startling visual universe with a diverse cast of non-human characters.

That an elaborate tradition of fiber arts developed independently in the Americas is unsurprising. A vast wealth of grasses abounded in the plateaus and watersheds. Ancient Americans, however, took basketry and vegetal mat

9 Mantle, 450–175 BCE

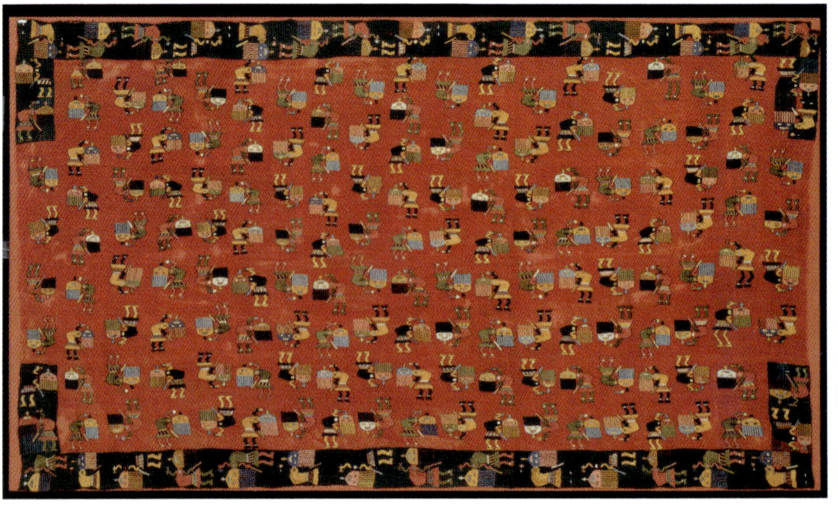

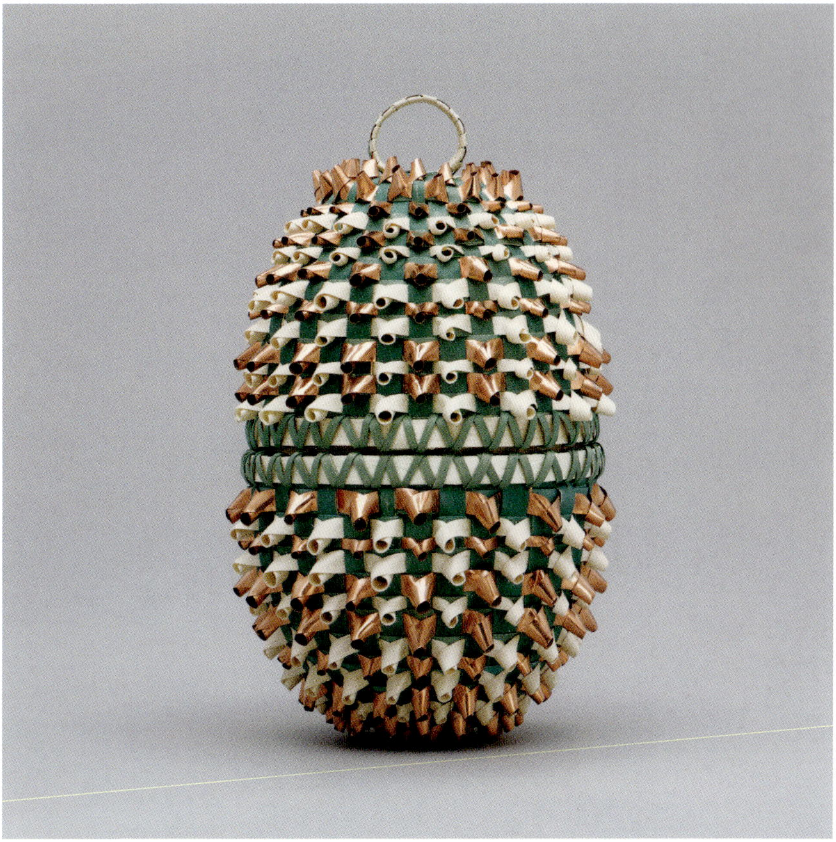

10 Kelly Church, *Sustaining Traditions—Digital Teachings*, 2018

creation to new heights, on par with the skill level of some of the best examples from the global past. The weaving of baskets continues to be an honored practice among
10 Indigenous communities in the Americas today, even using contemporary materials and technologies. Containers and clothing notwithstanding, tall grasses gave shape to throne coverings and even boats that crisscrossed Lake Titicaca, the highest navigable lake on earth. Although often the first things to rot away, woven containers exhibit designs, motifs, and symbols that their artists—very often women—encoded into these masterworks.

Wood was also a preferred medium from the earliest times until the present among Indigenous American sculptors. Wooden sculptures, most now lost to the ravages of time, moisture, and insects, range from large-scale monuments

and architectural features to portable and wearable images of
11 important people and concepts, such as ancestors or deities.
Shaping trees and shrubs was intricately linked with hunting
and conflict; spearthrowers, arrows, and clubs facilitated the
procurement of meat and pelts. It also signals the prevalence
of violent conflict among competitive peoples from early times.
Symbols of war were later embedded into warriors' wooden
weapons.

Ancient peoples collected prized materials from wild fauna,
mostly in the form of the bones, feathers, pelts and teeth of
mammals, birds, fish, and reptiles. The four-legged and winged
creatures that the first Americans encountered captured their
imaginations, perhaps fulfilling expectations of a populated
environment that they carried from their former homelands. By
integrating animal products into ritual regalia and other works,
ancient American artists harnessed their qualities for their own
purposes. Weavers and feather workers even transformed the
109 inside of buildings into feathered walls. Ethnographic research
from South America showing deep cosmologies centered
on the human relationship with the natural world provides
tantalizing frameworks for analogy with past cultures. For
example, Amazonian peoples, inheritors of ancient traditions,
have provided ethnographers who observed their worlds with
exciting insights into what is known as "perspectivism." This
term describes the cognitive differences in humans' perception
of the vital forces of the landscape, ancestors, the natural world,
supernatural characters, celestial phenomena, etc., and how
these beings see themselves or humans. Such frameworks help
interpret representations of such beings in ancient artworks.

Inspiration from the landscape also came from the watery
realms of the seas, islands, and coasts. In fact, some of the
earliest bodily adornments in the Americas were composed of
worked marine shell, which held special value for all ancient
American peoples throughout time, similar to other cultures
around the world. Different types of mollusks, such as conchs
and *Spondylus* bivalves, were collected and traded very long
distances to adorn the bodies of important people or form
musical instruments. Often associated with the power of water
and abundance, shells represented primordial fertility when
11 worked and worn. Shell inlays vivified other media such as stone
and wood, as nacreous eyes and teeth shone out from sacred
sculptures.

Metal Arts: Gold, Silver, Copper, and Platinum

Natural outcrops in the American mountains also provided metals through placer mining, which is separating out minerals

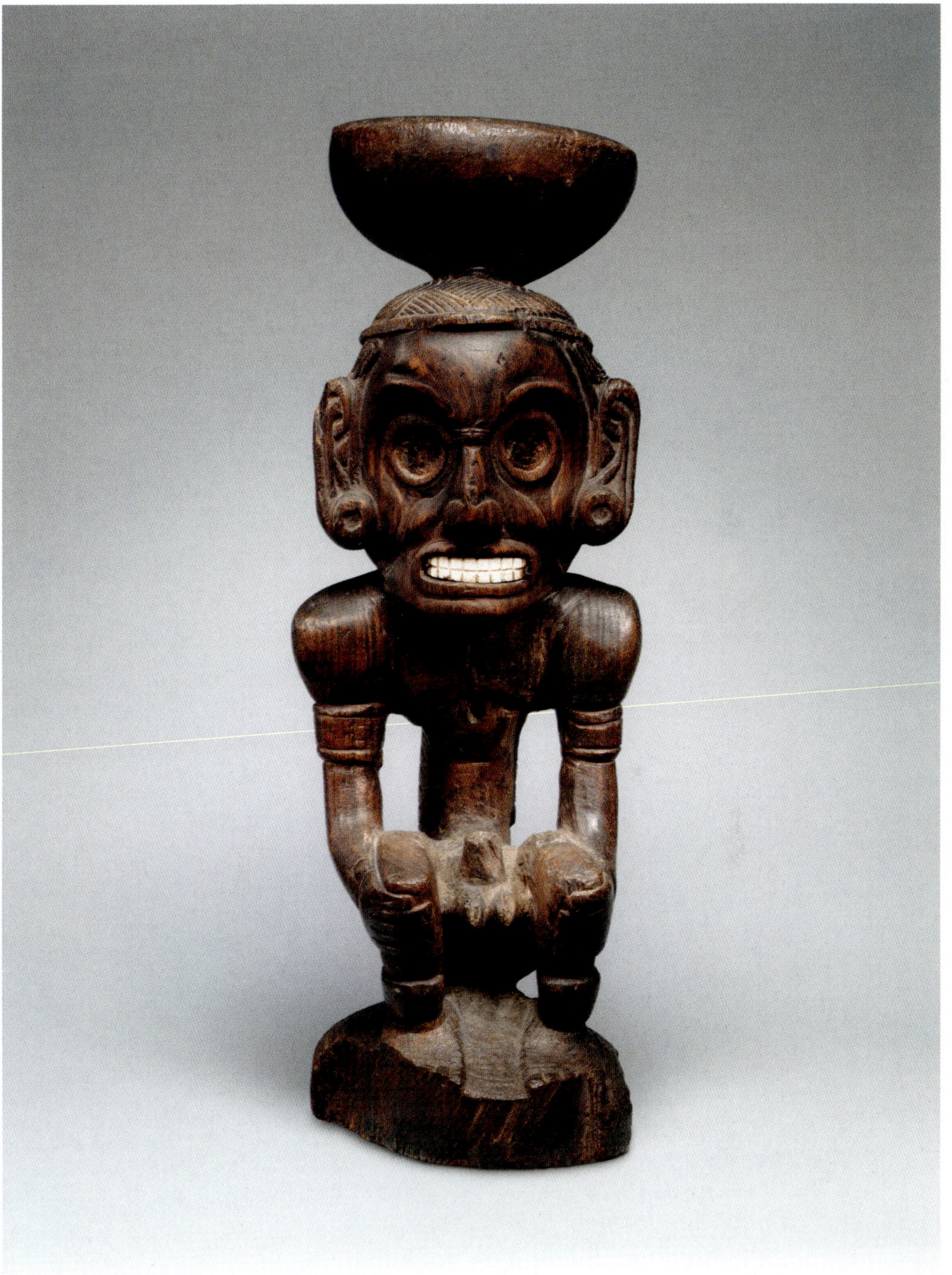

11 Zemí Cohoba Stand, 974–1020

from stream bed deposits. Metalworking in the Americas was invented in South America around the second millennium BCE to create luxurious adornment, similar to other parts of the world, but largely not employed to create tools, weapons, or money. Early in the Andes, artists began extracting and shaping the brilliance of the mountains for their patrons to wear it. These rulers, such as those buried with gold masks and crowns at Kuntur Wasi, Peru, between 800 BCE and 550 BCE, incorporated metals into bodily performance and influenced
20 their beholders' perception of themselves in dazzling displays.
Gold and silver, widely symbolic of the sun and the moon, respectively, as well as copper, became important parts of artists' toolkits.

By doing so, metal artists changed the course of art history as metallurgical practices traveled with ideas and goods northward into the Isthmus of Panama and, many centuries
12 later, into what is now Mexico. Hammered and cast objects
quickly became coveted luxury goods, worn in life by leaders who later carried them into the afterlife in their lavish burials. As the Spanish invaders reached Mexico, Peru, and Colombia in the sixteenth century, rumors of golden cities known as El Dorado fueled the foreigners' march across the unfamiliar American landscape. They melted down the masterpiece metal objects adorning people and things and sent the transformed commodity back to fuel the Europeans' imperial ambitions.

12 Crowns, 800–500 BCE

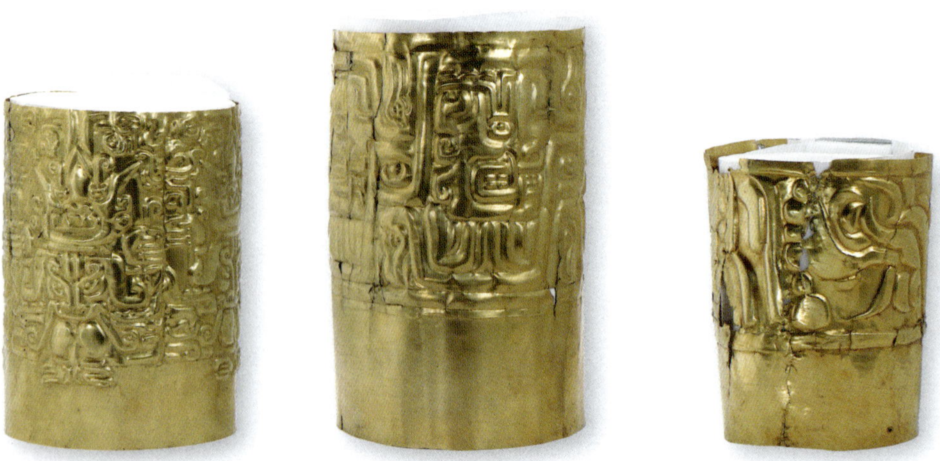

The identities of the ancient American makers themselves are most often unknown today. Some of the interpretive challenges that emerge from a lack of documentation about the career of an artist, for example, include the inability to judge works of art as indicative of different levels of skill between different people or the trajectory of one's work over a lifetime. With decorative techniques such as painting, modern observers can observe different degrees of ability through comparison of color production, line work, brush strokes, and composition with a corpus of similar examples. Some evidence from the ancient Maya context suggests that makers may have worked in an atelier structure, with one or two experienced creators guiding a group of skilled hands in a workshop. The methods of instruction and the mechanisms for passing down learning through generations, however, are not well known in most time periods. Nor did the creators themselves explicitly depict the act of artistic production in most contexts, leaving researchers to draw analogies from across time and space. The following chapters highlight major hubs of art making, and while not comprehensive, they demonstrate the range of creativity that flourished in the ancient Americas.

Part I

Early Art in the Americas

This section explores some of the earliest widespread art-making traditions in the Andes and ancient Mesoamerica. Although representational art had existed earlier, at least by the second millennium BCE (see introduction), peoples all over the Americas began infusing their belongings with imagery related to both the natural world and other realms populated by supernatural beings. Iconic works of monumental sculpture and delicate ornamentation tell the tales of these important innovators and their patrons. This was an era of big ideas bringing people together for communal purposes. Large settlements engendered a sense of belonging, and these places cultivated artists who worked clay, stone, metal, shell, bone, and other materials with their skilled hands. Artistic choices are evident in how faithfully people made their representations of individuals, plants, and animals to how they appeared in reality; in most cases, naturalism was not the objective.

This early slice of time also saw the beginnings of complex political organization, likely with powerful leaders at the helm of incipient city-states. In other words, the rulers pictured in the colossal heads of the Mexican Gulf Coast, or the important individuals buried with gold regalia in highland Peru at the same time, may have held influence over their neighbors. In that sense, from the beginning, art was also political. Art played a key role in the ability of individuals or important families to reinforce claims over other people and their local landscape. The access of only certain elite peoples to luxury materials, such as jade and shell, also underscores the growing inequality around the turn of the first millennium BCE. While the names of rulers and their dynasties remain opaque at present, their tombs or depictions as divine characters signal new forms of social organization that centered around powerful families.

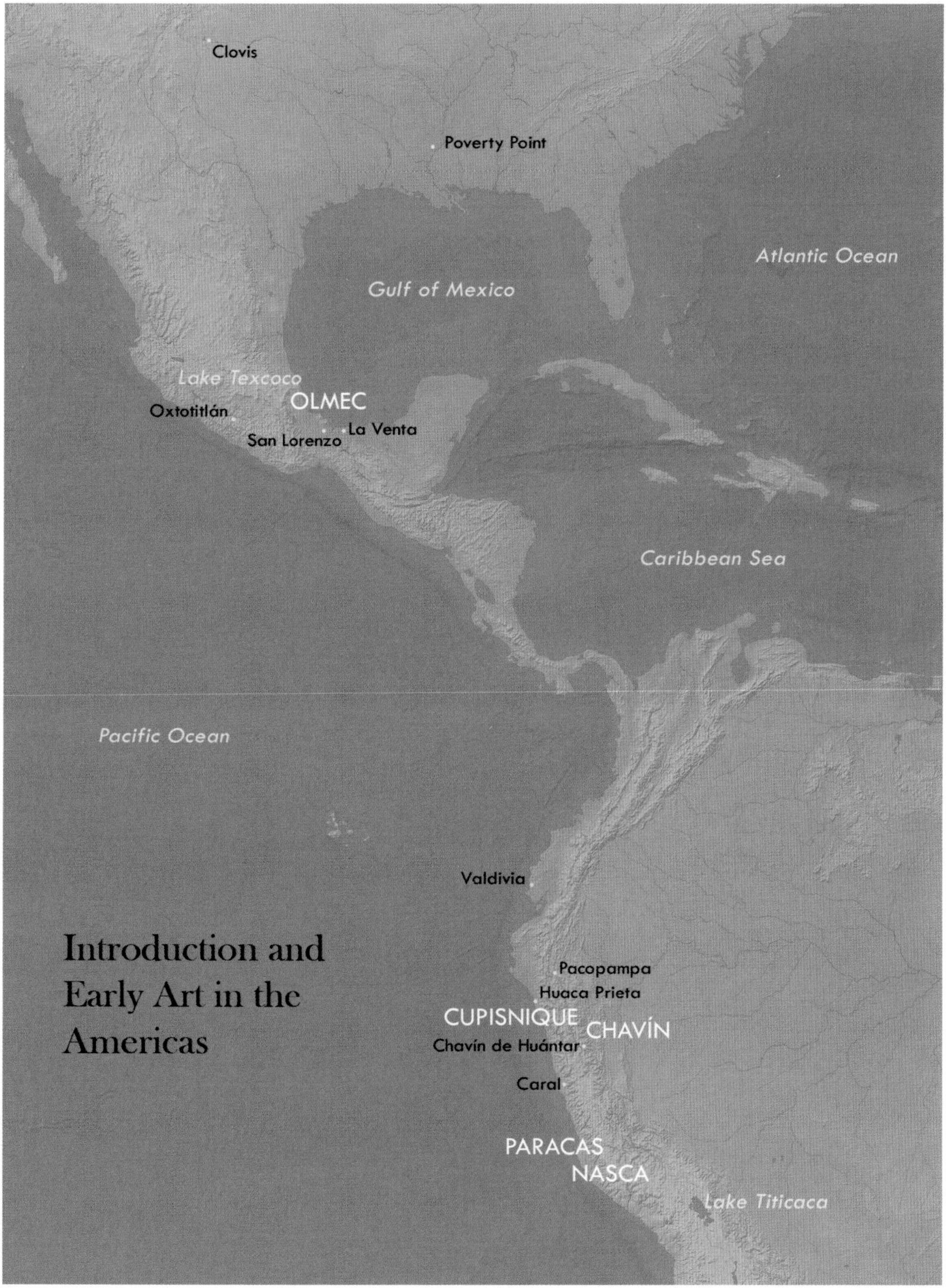

Introduction and Early Art in the Americas

Evidence suggests that the development of artistic communities of practice in the Americas occurred in different places and different times, and styles ebbed and flowed over centuries. For these early case studies, the absolute chronology, such as that based on radiocarbon dating, is not currently refined enough to talk about individual patrons or artists. New archaeological research from Mexico and Peru, however, is shedding more light on these important creative groups. Perhaps most notably, these early visual cultures had lasting legacies. The traces of these traditions—known as Chavín in South America and Olmec in Mesoamerica—appear in later creations, a testimony to the power of those first enduring images. The images of descendant peoples, discussed in subsequent chapters, harkened back to these pioneering images, consciously or unconsciously, acknowledging and celebrating works of their predecessors.

Chapter 1
In the Shadow of the Andes: Chavín, Cupisnique, Paracas, and Nasca (1200 BCE–600 CE)

Chavín de Huántar (1200–200 BCE)

The western region of South America, where the early site known as Chavín de Huántar is located, is a land of contradictions. The high mountains of the Andes rise sharply out of the ocean where the fish-rich currents collide with the desert coast of what is now Peru. The air that rides those same ocean currents flows up the peaks, leaving the western slopes dry and cracked, showering the eastern side of the mountains with rain, eventually coming together to form the Amazon drainage. Highland rains and melting glaciers feed the numerous rivers that cut west through the Peruvian desert. The fertile river valleys created ideal places for managed cultivation of plants and animals, and eventually sophisticated agricultural irrigation to produce crops such as maize, beans, squash, and especially cotton, which was essential for textiles. For thousands of years, Andean peoples have thrived in these resource-rich zones, trading with each other. There were those specialized in marine fishing, cotton farmers, and highland pastoralists herding llamas and alpacas. There was diversification within groups and they all lived in an interdependent network of cooperative populations. This interchange of peoples, ideas, and prestige materials created some of the most important visual cultures of the ancient world.

Woven textiles in the Andes were created by some of the earliest populations known from Peru. Early uses of indigo as a dye have been confirmed at the coastal site of Huaca Prieta, where fiber artists were creating woven fabrics with the twining technique without looms by at least the fourth millennium BCE, if not before (see introduction).

The discovery of indigo-dyed fibers suggests that coastal populations were harvesting or cultivating plants for their visual properties very early. Using the different colored threads, these early twining weavers created complex designs with faunal imagery, such as birds, snakes, and marine creatures. Certain conventions in Andean art were already established in these early works, such as the technique known as contour rivalry, in which an image can be interpreted in different ways depending on the viewer's position. In other words, the image confronts the viewer with complementary viewing possibilities. For example, a creature in frontal
18 view with a headdress when viewed at 180 degrees creates a different being with the original face as the headdress. By around 1500 BCE, weavers were using backstrap looms, a portable loom looped around the body and attached to a fixed post, to form plain-weave cotton garments that also allowed for crucial innovations in textile arts.

This time before about 1800 BCE is known to specialists as "pre-ceramic," because artists focused creative energy on fiber arts, the carving of gourd or wooden containers, working bone and shell into personal regalia, and monumental stone architecture. Some buildings were adorned with reliefs made of adobe, sun-dried clay mixed with organic materials. When builders and sculptors began to create elevated platforms and sunken plazas, such as at Caral mentioned in the introduction, one guiding principle was the play of light as the sun passes over the community. The orientation of buildings to the path of the sun and other celestial bodies signals the foundational role of celestial light in spiritual and visual production in the Andes. In fact, this is a common thread throughout the cultures represented in this book: people combined observations of the sky with the local landscape to build their communities, even down to the level of individual households. These religious ideas and motifs that were surely present in oral tradition began to take tangible form in architectural sculpture, in both low and high relief. Some sculpted images relied on light to activate them, such as those present at the site of Cerro Sechín, which developed centuries before Chavín de Huántar near the coast to the north of Lima. There, artists depicted possible warfare events in low relief with incised details on some of the earliest stone monuments from the Andean region.

Other foundational concepts of a distinctly Andean worldview appear in early art and form enduring interpretive frameworks for later cultures. A pervasive concept is that of duality, meaning that a whole concept or image is composed

of two interrelated but distinct parts. Duality can be formal, in which compositions are split into two opposing or complementary halves; material, in which two different materials are used or represented; or conceptual, referencing complementary duos such as male/female, sun/moon, mortal/supernatural, and so on. A related formal quality, known in the later Quechua language spoken by the Indigenous peoples of highland Peru as *tinku*, is the confluence of two things
21, into one, such as two tributaries uniting to form a river, or
47–50 two spouts on a bottle combining together. Another Quechua concept, that of *wak'a* (or huaca), which can be sacredness or a sacred thing, place, or person, seems to have a deep antiquity in the Andes. People undertook pilgrimages through certain paths to reach *wak'a*s. Another formal aspect of Andean art is that it is often meant to be seen from multiple viewpoints, in what has been termed anatropic or anamorphic imagery, containing a sort of complex rotational geometry as artists bend the perspective of the beholder. Materials of value and luxury pigments and dyes that characterize Andean art styles also emerged in artistic practice during this early period.

14 The highland site of Chavín de Huántar is one of the most important ceremonial centers in the ancient world, comparable with contemporaneous places in the Mediterranean or ancient Western Asia. The site consists of large platforms, mega-scalar masonry buildings with interior above-ground and subterranean passages decorated with ornate stone sculptures, wide plazas, and material and visual culture that indicates broad influence and exchange throughout the central Andes and Amazon. Light was integral to the design of buildings, and the different access to sunlight, shadow, and even torchlight in the depths of built chambers played a role in reinforcing the political power of the buildings' patrons in this early gathering place. Chavín culture flourished for several centuries, beginning in the late second millennium BCE at this important place, located at the confluence of the Río Mosna and one of its tributaries, which provided both a strategic position situated between the Amazon and the Pacific Coast and a symbolic location as a *tinku*. Although research on the Chavín style is ongoing, the general consensus is that builders and artists there originated or elaborated a set of iconographic conventions and shared visual elements that characterized the early period of art making in the Andes.

A series of sunken plazas and grand stone temples defines the core of the site. One circular plaza forms a focal point of the largest platformed structure at the site, which seems to

13 RIGHT Richard Burger and Luis Caballero, Drawing of the Lanzón
14 BELOW Chavín de Huántar, Peru

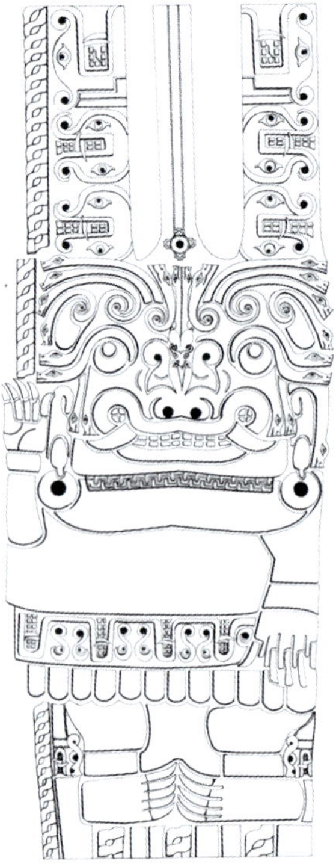

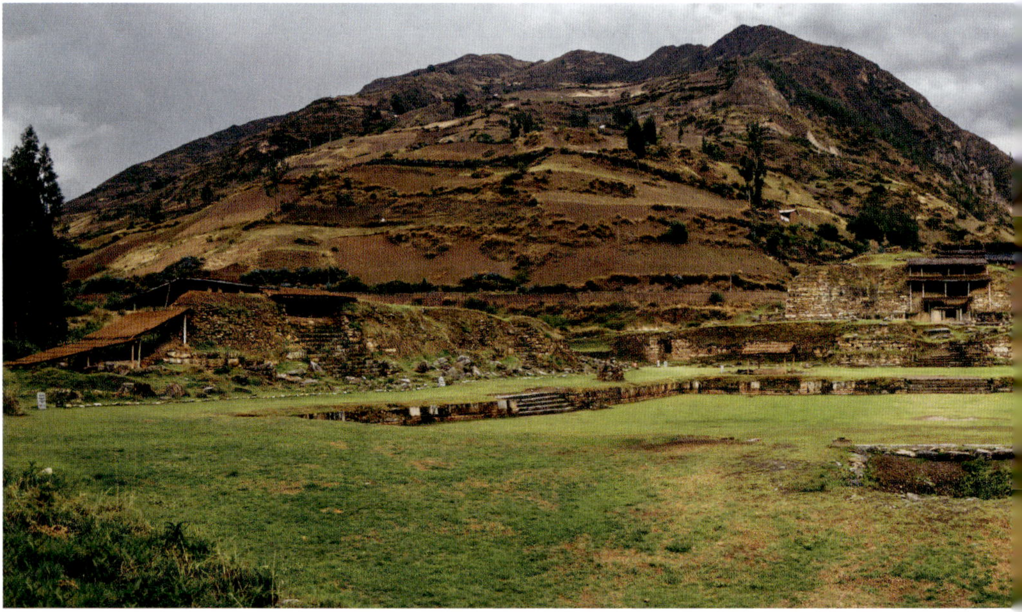

have been built around it and expanded away from it. In this temple, Chavín architects created a series of subterranean galleries, possibly between thirty-one and thirty-six individual chambers connected by a series of ducts or passageways. One such passageway, in a building off of the circular plaza, holds one of the most enigmatic works in ancient Andean art, a megalithic sculpture known as the Lanzón. The creators of the
13 granite stela wrapped the image of a standing supernatural figure around the triangular, almost prismatic form of the stone. The figure displays crocodilian and feline features, serpents emerging from the head, and wears jewelry from humanlike features and a belt or skirt. It raises one hand and lowers the other in a gesture of significance addressing the viewers, the meaning of which is now lost. This fanged entity appears throughout the relief sculpture of the site and has been interpreted to be a principal deity that formed a focus of ceremonial activities there. The chamber above the Lanzón may have served as an oracle, a pilgrimage destination for residents from around the central Andes.

15 Adorning the facades of the temples at Chavín were numerous so-called tenoned heads. These stone sculptures were created to be inserted into the intricate facade of blocks so that only the three-dimensional head protruded, and the cantilevered horizontal post sustained the weight of the head.

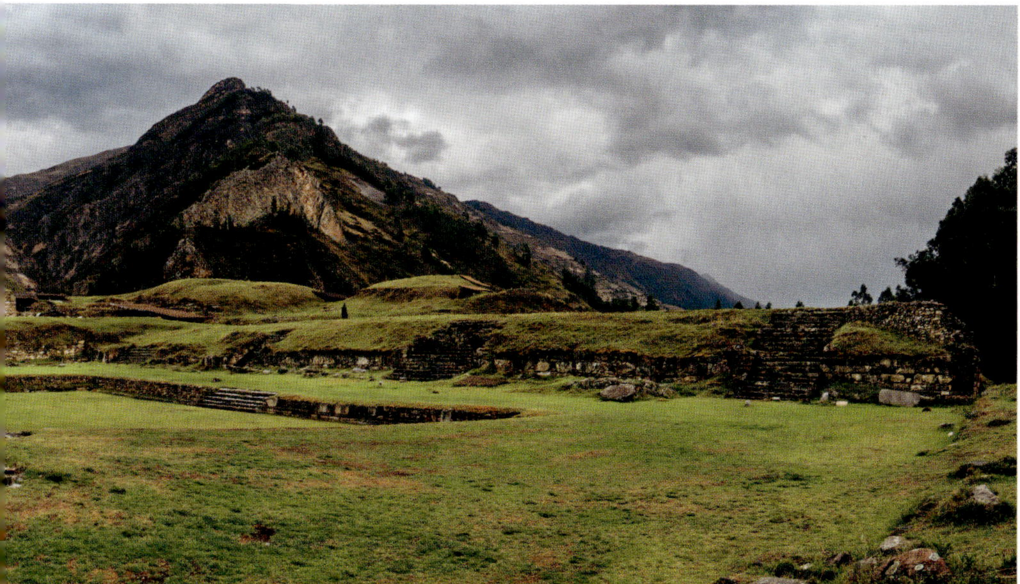

The heads themselves varied widely in composition, some having humanlike features, feline attributes, reptilian details, or various combinations of the above. Sculptors purposely marked many humanlike faces with wrinkles and exaggerated eyes or noses, allowing these visages to be viewed from afar. When visitors to the buildings approached them, the heads also interacted with stones in the upper cornice of the temples that were carved in low relief on their undersides. As the sun's course changed throughout the day, the cornice stones could have made the heads seem to be emerging from the darkness of the shadowed facade.

Evidence of intense ritual activity comes from archaeological excavations in the galleries around the circular plaza and items in museum collections. The residents of the city obtained
16 conch shells from long-distance trade and transformed them into powerful trumpets. Artists imbued the instruments with sacred identities by incising delicate deities or other figures into their exterior surface. This example of a conch-shell trumpet was recovered from a gallery known as the Caracolas Gallery, in which Chavín residents deposited twenty complete instruments directly on the gallery floor. The erosion of the surface of the engraved design suggests a long history of repeated performances, and some fragments of broken trumpets found in the deposit were so valuable that they had been reworked with imagery. Acoustics and sound were clearly important to those who designed and used these buildings. Other galleries had ritual human burials, and one gallery, nicknamed the Gallery of the Inhalers (Galería de los Inhaladores), had small tubes made out of bird bones, likely for the ingestion of ritual materials.

The ceremonial use of psychoactive substances made from tropical plants and the native San Pedro cactus, which elicit altered states of consciousness, was an important part of spirituality at Chavín de Huántar. Ritual practitioners commissioned elaborate spoons through which such sacred substances would have been inhaled or swallowed, such as an extraordinary bimetallic Chavín spoon, reportedly from the
17 fourth to third century BCE, in the form of a conch-shell player squatting on a circular woven or wooden stool. The spoon, stool (which contains pellets to function as a rattle), and figure are all made of gold, while the conch-shell trumpet is made of silver. The contrast of the two metals represents an early example of this mineral duality, conceptually related to the shine of the sun and the glow of the moon, present in subsequent traditions of Andean art. The spoon has perforations so it could be worn as a pendant and, remarkably, the metalworker included a

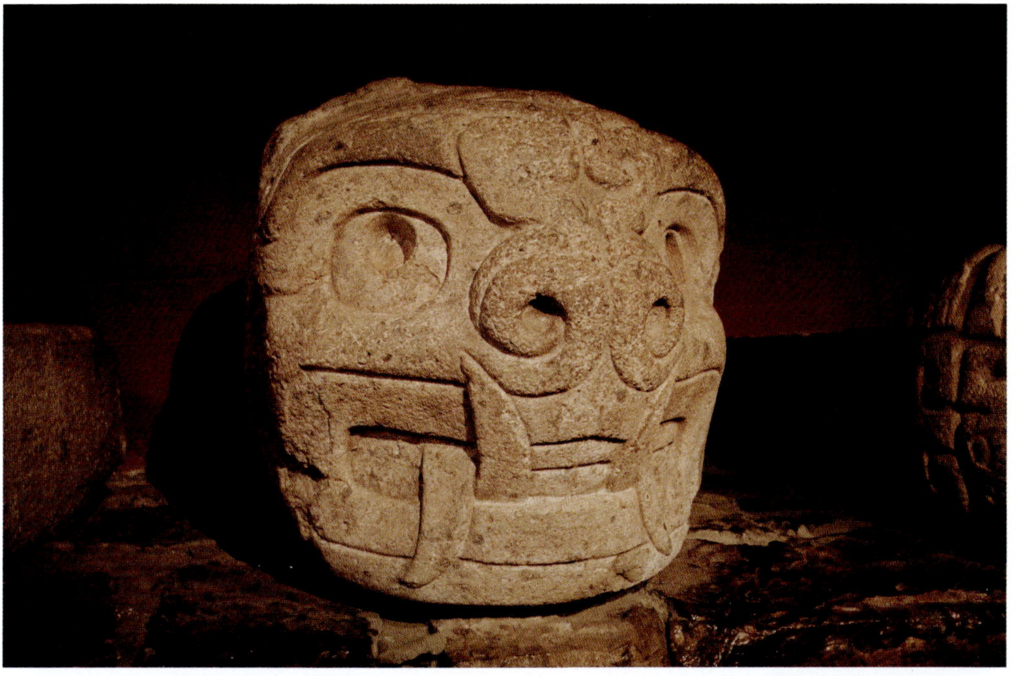

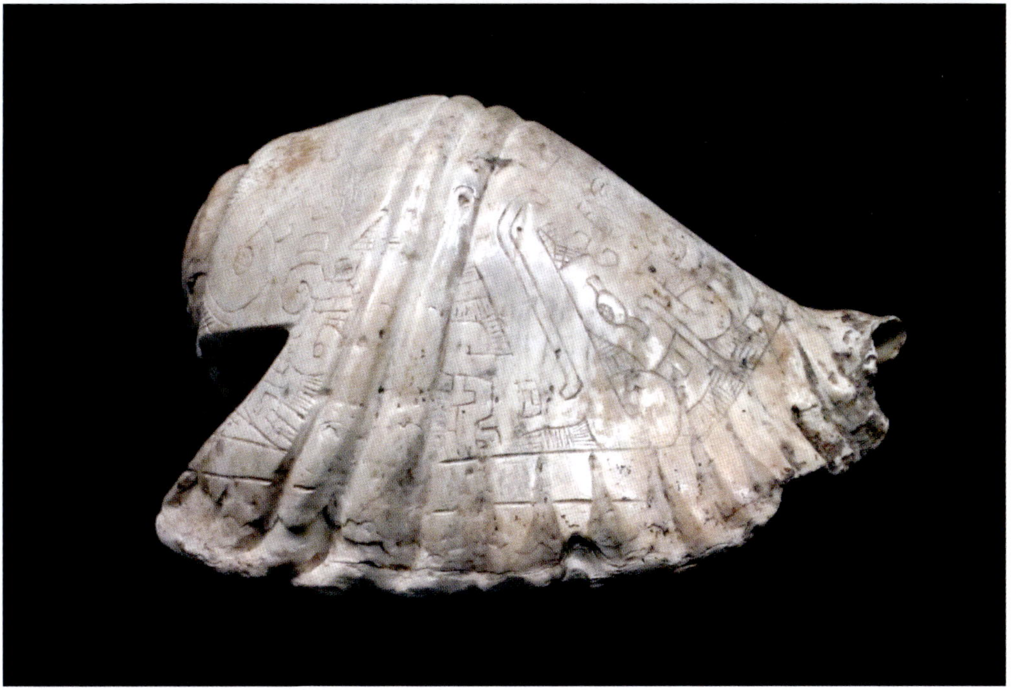

15 TOP Tenoned Head, 1200–500 BCE
16 ABOVE Shell Trumpet, 1200–500 BCE

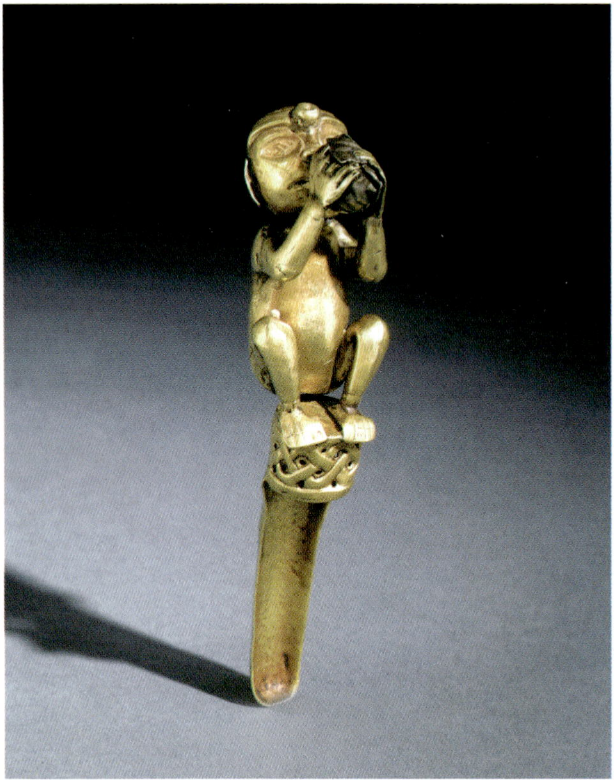

17 Bimetallic Effigy Spoon, 400–200 BCE

hidden anthropomorphic image on the underside of the stool, so that it would be only visible to those using the spoon at close range.

Artists at Chavín emphasized species found further east from the city itself, including aspects of Amazonian apex predators of air, land, and water, such as harpy eagles, jaguars and other large felines, and crocodilians such as caimans. Sculpture in the round also featured supernatural felines and reptilian characters. The skill level of these artists is also quite evident, so the lack of any realism is notable, in that they chose to work in a non-naturalistic style. Stone carvers often played with two and three dimensions, creating what is known as double profiles, in which two images in profile come together to create a frontal image, making the sculptures change their visual message as the beholders shifted their position, as mentioned above. Not until centuries later did makers begin to approach naturalistic representations of humans and animals. Although speculative, perhaps during the principal occupation

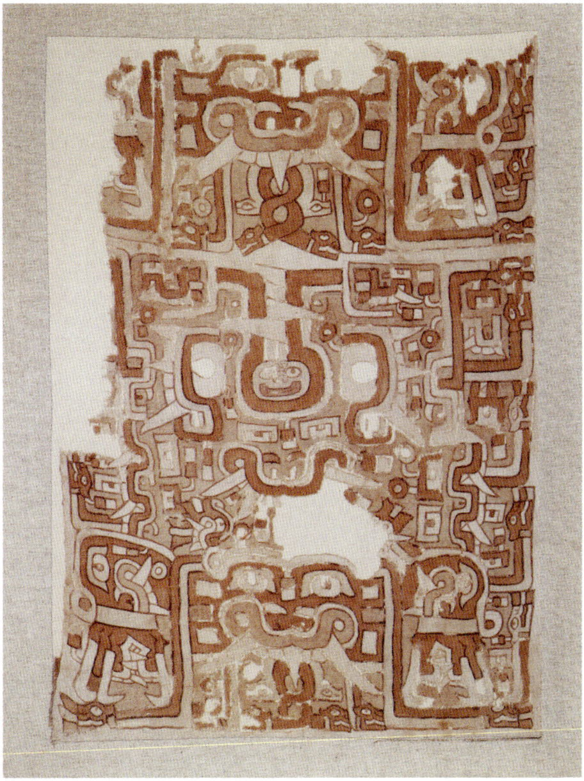

18 Textile,
800–700 BCE

of Chavín de Huántar, images of humans were believed to be too powerful or, alternatively, not important enough, to be rendered in stone.

The design innovation in which images sometimes had multiple, rather than fixed, frames of orientation is a hallmark of later Chavín culture. These conventions were especially
18 present in the works of textile artists at this time, who created plain-weave cotton textiles that were then painted with elaborate images. The light weight and portability of textiles allowed for the imagery of Chavín artists to travel far from the pilgrimage center itself, spreading the accompanying beliefs and sacred narratives that underpinned the powerful divine beings. This example from the eighth century BCE is reportedly from near Callango, Peru, in the lower Ica Valley, and a fragment of the fangs missing in the lower right portion of the image was recovered inside a cloth bag in a tomb from Coyungo, dozens of kilometers away, in the Nasca drainage. The fragmentation of the textile may have been intentional,

and it underscores the power of Chavín paintings, in which there are stacked images of fanged caimans in frontal view with menacing claws in outstretched hands, interspersed with serpents and other caimans in profile view.

The art of Chavín was meant to be experienced not just by local residents but also by pilgrims from far and wide, who brought ideas, raw materials, and finished products from their homelands and took home Chavín objects and ideas. The effects of the visual culture originating at Chavín were felt also far from the temples themselves, where local artists and builders throughout the Andes created unique but interconnected architectural spaces and aesthetic modes in the late second millennium BCE. Several days' walk north of Chavín lies a site from this period called Pacopampa in the
19 Cajamarca region. A standing monument from the site, dating to between 1200 BCE and 500 BCE, is a unique depiction of a supernatural female figure carved in low relief. The sculptor played with asymmetry in the outline of the monument, by making the left side of the figure's head slightly shorter than the right side, referring to a duality represented in the different vertical halves. The otherwise symmetrical figure in frontal view has an outsized head with stylized, squared features, including a fanged mouth from which emerges a tongue or fluids. The figure displays a *vagina dentata*, in which the female reproductive organs take the form of fanged jaws, a motif also seen in sculpture at Chavín.

In early Andean art, supernatural figures often display the features of arachnids or avian creatures, and the Pacopampa female displays appendages radiating from her central torso that recall the paired legs of orb weaver spiders or wings. A rhomboid shape is highlighted in relief at the very center of the composition, with a spiral motif that may be linked to a mollusk, such as the conch-shell trumpets mentioned above. Serpentlike volutes also emerge to either side of the figure's waist. The tomb of a high-status female was found in 2009 at Pacopampa, suggesting that the depiction of a powerful supernatural goddess was connected to the role of women in the ritual life or governance of this community. While evidence of rulers at Chavín de Huántar itself is scant, it seems that regional centers had clearer funerary practices involving important figures.

This is perhaps best seen at the site known as Kuntur Wasi, located to the northwest of Chavín de Huántar, where an
20 extraordinary early tomb contained the remains of an elderly male adorned with fine hammered gold nose ornaments and a crown, all embossed with supernatural beings. The ruler

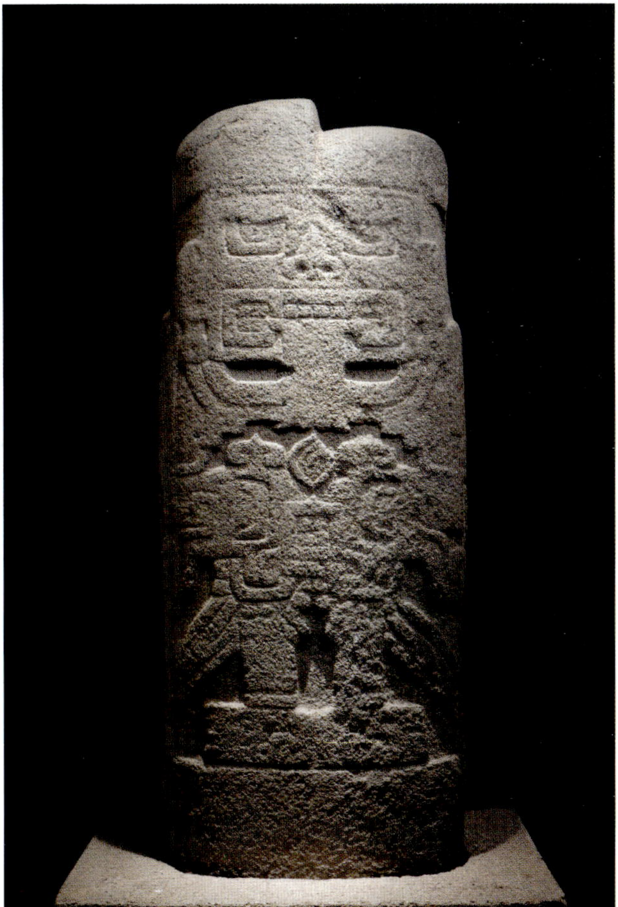

19 Stela, 1200–500 BCE

lived between 800 BCE and 550 BCE and presumably would have worn the nose ornament that masked the lower half of his face, projecting the image of a fanged deity reaching out and grasping two figures to either side. The principal figure
13 is similar to the deity on the Lanzón and other monuments from Chavín. These smaller figures seem to be grimacing in agony as the impressive snarling feline character grips them by their upper back. The presence of figural danglers, sheet-metal elements attached by wire, would have enhanced the ruler's presence, whether seen from up close or afar, as the mouth mask shimmered in motion and created rhythmic sound.

12 Metalworkers from this northern region excelled at transforming gold into objects for displaying supernatural

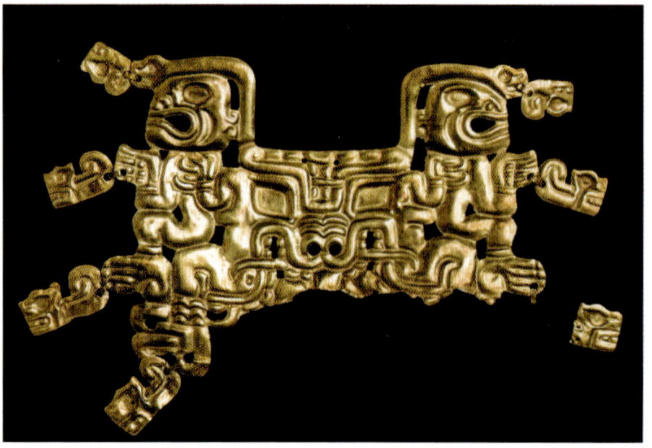

20 Mouth Mask, 800–550 BCE

imagery on human bodies. The time, skill, and procurement of raw materials involved in this process, combined with the discovery of tombs celebrating individual ancestral figures, suggest that there were political leaders at these places. While evidence leads toward individual rulers, it is possible that other forms of civic organization, such as collective rule or council governance, could have also been present. There are interesting anthropological implications of a leader or ruling family directing the social roles and community goals of these places. For example, were these rulers the ones who accumulated some sort of wealth or social status, or did the wealth and status come as by-products of other inherited or bequeathed qualities? Future studies of art and archaeology in this region have the potential to contribute greatly to global conversations about the origins of political complexity and the relationship between spirituality and sovereignty.

Along the northern coast of Peru, artists created monumental adobe architecture with decoration that recalls Chavín style. In this region, the style has become known as Cupisnique, named after the coastal region between the modern cities of Chiclayo and Trujillo, Peru, between the Jequetepeque and Chicama river valleys. Potters in this region created elaborate jars, bowls, and bottles that combined different modeling and finishing techniques to depict flora, fauna, and supernatural beings. Artists paid special attention to predators such as felines and serpents, some highlighted with pigments painted onto the surface or incised lines interplaying with modeled relief. Some of these compositions also exhibit the Andean shifting perspectives, so that, for example, the rotation of a ceramic vessel produces different experiences that enhance its visual and social impact.

Many Cupisnique works reflect one of the key tenets of
21 early Andean style: duality. An example from near Trujillo,
Peru, typifies the enduring form of ceramic bottles known as
"stirrup spout," which artists produced for many centuries in
the coastal Andes. The stirrup shape may have been functional,
reducing evaporation of liquids and providing a means to
which to attach or carry the bottle, as well as symbolic, a form
of *tinku*. The pottery portrays a severed head on the body
of the vessel that is divided into two halves with a vertical
separation. To the viewer's right is a stylized face that includes
a prominent eye, ridged brow, zoomorphic nose, and a squared
mouth from which emerges a creature, possibly a serpent. The
artist sculpted the other side to represent a more supernatural
fanged being in profile. The two halves do not quite intersect,
suggesting a transformation from one form to the other or a
conflict between the two identities represented in each half,
19 similar to the slight asymmetry in the Pacopampa stela.

Early rulers and related artists also proliferated in the central
coastal area, now located near Lima's metropolitan area,
22 such as at a site with a group of temples known as Garagay,
dating from 1200 BCE to 600 BCE. There sculptors composed a
polychrome frieze out of modeled adobe. The imagery depicts
two fanged supernatural beings, perhaps referencing a feline

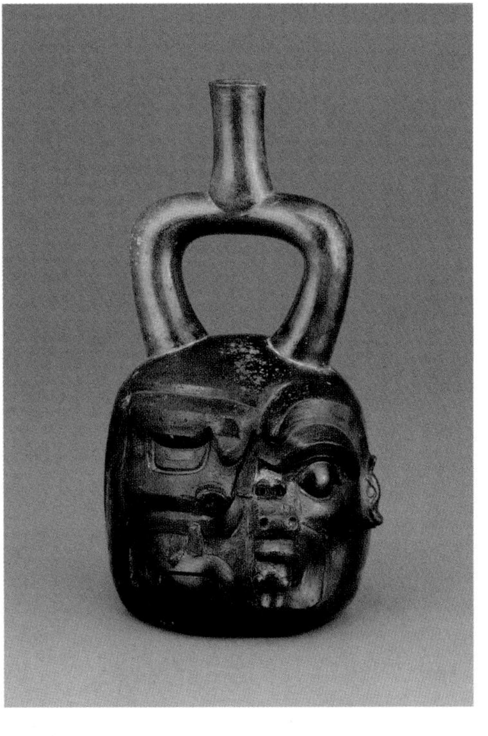

21 Stirrup-spout Bottle,
1200–500 BCE

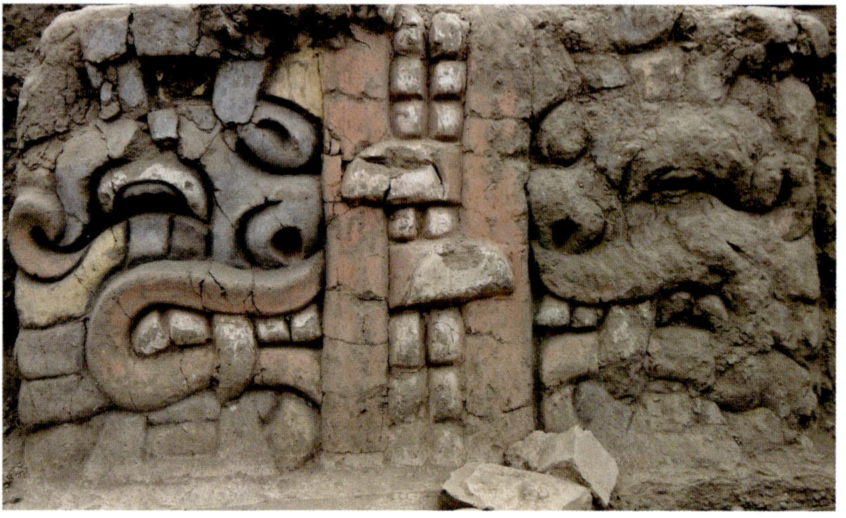

22 Frieze, 1200–600 BCE

or crocodilian similar to the creatures at Chavín de Huántar, facing each other across a vertical motif of red lip bands punctuated by rows of teeth and horizontal crossed fangs. The artists highlighted the supernatural beings with blue, yellow, red, and white pigment, vivifying the facade of this building. The inclusion of the vertical mouth band, which is also found in architectural sculpture and monuments at Chavín, adds a dimension of identity to the building itself, as if at any time it could open its jaws and engulf the residents of Garagay. The interior of the temple, then, could have been perceived as the cavelike interior of a supernatural creature. This represents one key example in which residents far from Chavín employed the site's imagery in a distinct style using local materials. This aesthetic strategy of depicting deities, perhaps the same ones
13 pictured on Chavín monuments, is also found at such sites in the region as Cardal in the Lurin River Valley. In later cultures, for example the Moche on the northern coast (see chapter 3) or the Paracas peoples on the southern coast, the visual influence of Chavín de Huántar lived on through both divine subjects and sculptural or painting techniques.

Paracas

Other early art traditions, especially those focused on ceramic modeling, textile production, and developing unique styles and materials, emerged in the southern coast of Peru centuries after the decline of Chavín de Huántar. Jutting out into the Pacific

Ocean, the Paracas peninsula forms a distinct landmark on the southern coast of Peru near the modern city of Ica. After the discovery of spectacular necropolis deposits at the sites known as Wari Kayan and Cavernas in the 1920s, international scholarly attention turned to the high quality of the woven and embroidered textiles wrapped around the deceased ancestors. Current consensus is that the south-central coast, where the societies known as Paracas flourished, consisted of a series of polities that constructed related settlements, cultivating weavers and potters that innovated local material
9 cultures reflected in the funerary assemblages. The elaborate rectangular funerary mantles with embroidered imagery also hint at the rich spiritual world populated with humanlike figures with aspects of felines and other fauna.

Paracas artists exhibited an extraordinary ability to manipulate camelid fibers into spectacular compositions of color, figures, and geometry. In a departure from earlier weavers, they perfected strategies for embroidering the surfaces of textiles rather than weaving or painting patterns and motifs.
23 Well-preserved examples show striking fields of black, red, and yellow, with a center field composed of alternating bands and two embroidered, fringed borders bracketing the long edge. From a distance, the motifs appear to be interlocking S-scrolls, but closer inspection reveals a complex interplay of serpents and felines embroidered in the borders and central bands. The rich textile and its linear form of embroidery represents the power of Paracas weavers and embroiderers to create sumptuous garments for their patrons, which were miraculously preserved in the desert sands for over two thousand years.

The elaborate textiles wrapped around the deceased Paracas ancestors also speak to the social complexity present by the end of the first millennium on the south coast. Some mummy bundles contained dozens of embroidered and plain cloths, food offerings, gold and shell regalia, and other offerings such as sacrificed animals, feathered garments, and pottery. The amount of time represented in just one large mantle—which could have numbered more than one thousand work hours in choosing and spinning fibers, dyeing threads, weaving grounds, and embroidering images with mathematical precision—suggests a well-established community of practice devoted to the fiber arts in Paracas societies. The more linear compositions represent fauna and supernatural beings in embroidered outlines that make the figures appear to be fused with the ground. In the more fluid style, embroiderers used blocks of color to define supernatural figures that have attributes of humans and other beings.

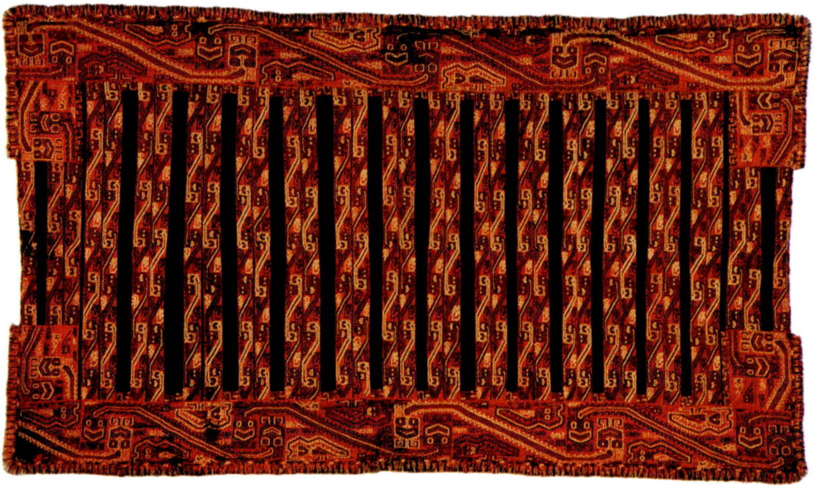

23 Mantle, 450–175 BCE

Much like Chavín artists, creators of the Paracas textiles chose to represent the human figure in a flat, abstracted style. In figure 9, for example, the central field is covered with free-floating images of individuals in contorted positions with their heads thrown back, hair falling or blown back, an element on the chin that may represent a beard, and holding ritual implements. The figures alternate orientations and some of them are depicted as smiling or grimacing, which has been interpreted as evidence that they represent ritual practitioners during states of altered consciousness. The most important people in Paracas societies wore these elaborate garments in life, and special care was taken to ensure that they were accompanied by these luxury goods for eternity.

Paracas makers also excelled at the plastic arts, creating fine hand-modeled ceramics with distinct forms and surface decorations. One particular Paracas technique that stands out is the application of post-fire paint to pottery vessels. This involved incising images into the wet clay. Then, after firing the vessel, a paint mixture, composed of an organic binder and a pigment, was applied to the baked clay's surface. The palette of Paracas ceramic painters include rich colors of brown, red, yellow, greens, and blues. The different pigments collected and used by artists in this region sometimes come from far and wide, such as cinnabar or copper-based green pigments like azurite.

Some Paracas potters utilized imagery known from the Chavín culture, for example the way of depicting eyes or the

shapes of serpents, which may indicate shared ideas or beliefs
24 about similar supernatural beings. One example depicts a fanged supernatural being with snakes protruding from its head. This bottle has two spouts, although one is non-functional and modeled in the shape of a bird, connected by an arched bridge. The globular chamber of the vessel is flattened on the bottom, and the stylized deity peers out in profile from below the bird spout. The bright yellow and red post-firing hues highlight the motif from the dark brown ground, likely created with a slip, a combination of minerals and water, before firing. Such bottles with narrow spouts would have been difficult to fill, and there is no consensus from scientific analysis about what they were used to carry. The form would have allowed for portability of water and storage for longer durations, reducing evaporation in the arid desert climate. Other forms of ceramic containers such as bowls, jars, and vessels with handles would have presumably been used as containers for foods and beverages before being placed in the tombs as offerings.

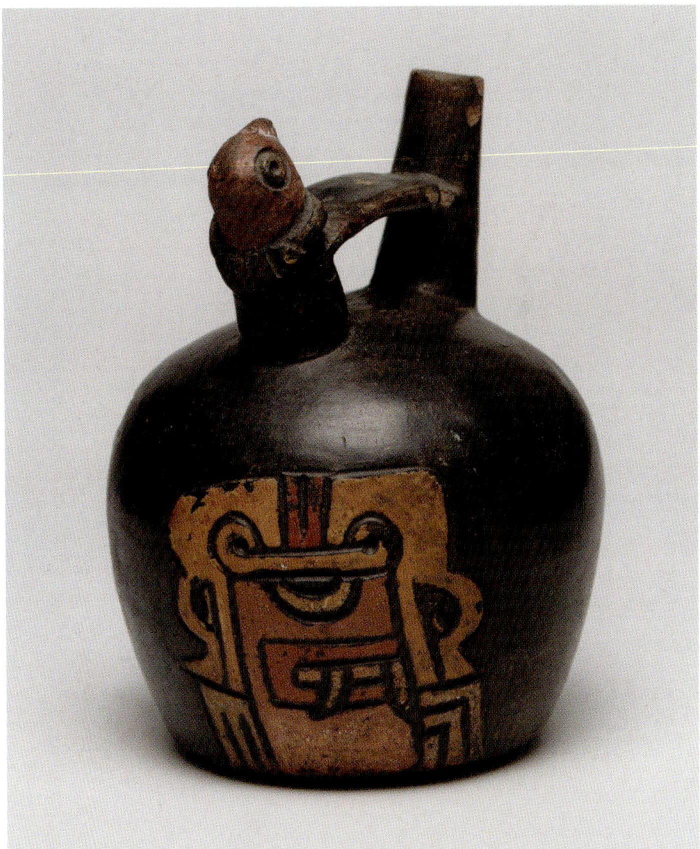

24 Vessel, 600–500 BCE

Nasca

The cultural florescence known as Nasca in southern Peru is
25 perhaps best recognized for the large-scale manipulations of stone to create geoglyphs known as the Nasca Lines. These designs of animals, people, and geometric patterns are only visible in their entirety from the height of modern aircrafts, but their symmetry and execution suggest elaborate planning on the part of the artists, perhaps similar to creation of large textiles. Some may have been less about their aesthetic impact and more about the physical journey it took as one paced alongside or atop the lines themselves, although their exact function as pathways is not well documented. Walking in spirals on the tail of a monkey or along the outline of a monumental hummingbird could have been an important route to take in some sort of spiritual moment or ceremonial occasion. Perhaps just as peoples traveled far and wide to partake in the ritual life of Chavín de Huántar, they journeyed to Nasca to walk the lines as a rite of passage.

The lines are located near the large center of Cahuachi, where archaeologists have recovered elaborate adobe architecture and burials of important individuals, but little evidence of full-time domestic spaces. This suggests that people gathered there periodically, perhaps for special occasions. Musical instruments and their depictions at Cahuachi suggest grand performances, and the finding of broken pottery near the lines themselves suggests ceremonies or offerings in which drinking was involved. Regalia in Nasca societies was similar to those found in Paracas funerary assemblages, including hammered metal ornaments. Perhaps the people wearing such luxury goods were members of powerful families or even individual rulers, who could have been responsible for commissioning lines over many generations in conjunction with pilgrimage activities.

Nasca pottery is finely made with relatively thin walls and decorated using slips, which were painted on the clay surface and highly burnished before firing, creating a glossier surface appearance than the matte texture favored by Paracas artists using post-fire paint. Like the earlier forms, Nasca potters made bridge-and-spout bottles, bowls, large jars, drinking vessels, and musical instruments such as drums and panpipes. Subjects include plants, with playful modeling of tubers or ears of corn, and animals, such as a stylized killer whale or delicate hummingbirds sipping at a flower. The creative interplay between naturalism and abstraction is a hallmark of Nasca ceramics, and the complex compositions of some pottery vessels are also found on painted plain-weave textiles from this

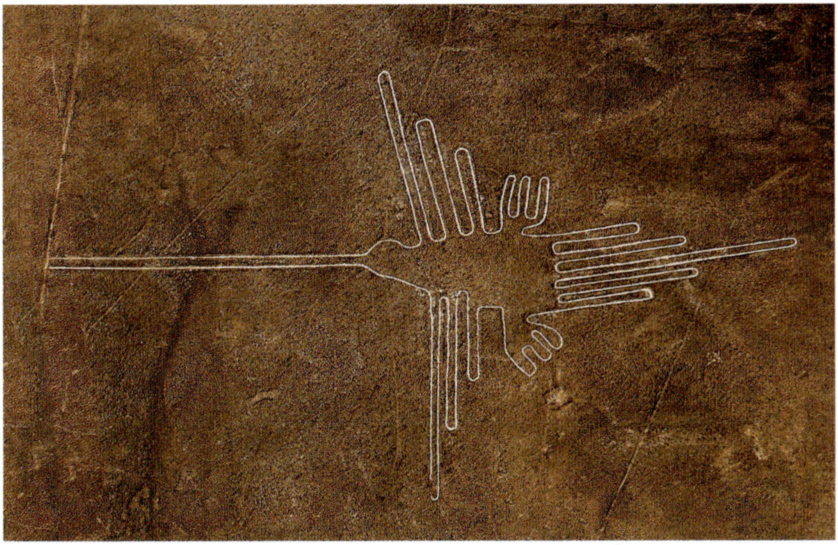

25 Hummingbird Geoglyph

era. Nasca potters' use of mineral slips allowed the vessels to be burnished to a high shine that still remains polished today.

The ceramic painters cultivated by Nasca societies excelled at the complex use of two-dimensional surfaces on three-dimensional spaces, naturalism versus abstraction, bold lines of even width, and vibrant fields of color that make the images
26 seem vivified, such as this example of a stylized female vessel. The individual's head forms one end of the bridge opposite the spout, and the bell-shaped body of the vessel evokes the woman's wide, flaring skirt. Her facial features are delicately modeled in clay and emphasized with flesh-toned, brown, and red slips. The person is at once stylized and individualized, with a distinct hairstyle flowing onto the globular upper body of the vessel. No limbs are indicated on the reddish-brown torso part of the bottle. The lower part of the bottle contains supernatural creatures seemingly floating horizontally as they travel counterclockwise around the cream-colored ground. The composite creatures have features of reptiles, insects, and humans, hinting at a rich narrative world that would have accompanied the drinking of liquids poured from such a vessel.

Nasca art includes portraits of people wearing regalia that approach realistic depictions, who may have been political leaders. One potential aspect of Nasca governance may have been conquest, or the threat thereof, evidence of which is found in images of ritualized violence in the form of head

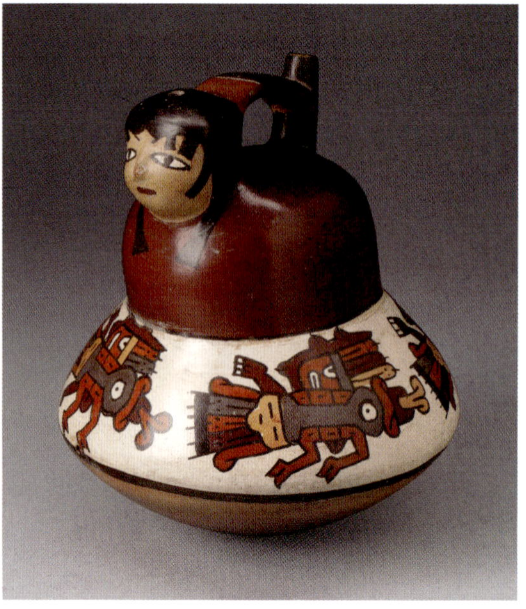

26 Vessel, 350–500

taking. This practice, which presumably was the result of violent conflicts leading to the taking of captives who were subsequently decapitated, is evidenced by severed heads found in archaeological contexts and imagery from ceramics. These trends suggest a shift both in Andean aesthetic values and social norms. How does this early first-millennium visual culture presage movements in subsequent centuries? In chapter 3 we see how similar impulses to violence and artistic competition played out in the contemporaneous north-coast political milieu known as the Moche. Chapters 7 and 9 will outline the later Andean visual cultures that valued abstraction to serve imperial strategies, and luxury materials made of gold and silver produced at an almost industrial scale.

Chapter 2

Monumental Origins in Mesoamerica: The Olmec (1800–400 BCE)

Olmec Style: San Lorenzo and the Highlands

When Mexican and foreign researchers began unearthing
27, 28 colossal basalt heads from archaeological explorations at Olmec sites on the Gulf Coast in the nineteenth century, those unique works spawned a host of questions. Who produced these massive sculptures? Where did the stones come from and how were they transported? Perhaps more importantly, who were the individuals depicted in these realistic portraits? This last question remains largely unanswered. Although scholarly consensus is that they were created over time by different hands, the monumental heads as a group challenged art-historical narratives of supposed progress from conventionalized to naturalistic depictions. This chapter addresses the Olmec, considered to be the earliest widespread visual culture in Mesoamerica, which is the cultural region between Mexico and Honduras united by shared languages, scripts, and practices.

People in the Gulf Coast region began to construct large settlements in the second millennium BCE, and those social gatherings and communal projects inspired makers to create large- and small-scale representational art for the first time. Sculptors, potters, and painters began to fuse flora and fauna from the biodiverse environments with humans to depict supernatural beings, as previously seen in the contemporaneous Chavín tradition (see chapter 1). Works in both volcanic and imported precious stones, such as basalt and jadeite or other greenstones, were used to represent concepts of a sacred landscape, including mythologized and personified forms of maize, the staple crop. The subjects of Olmec works, often human beings wearing elaborate regalia, also hint at novel forms of political leadership centered around individual rulers claiming connections with the supernatural.

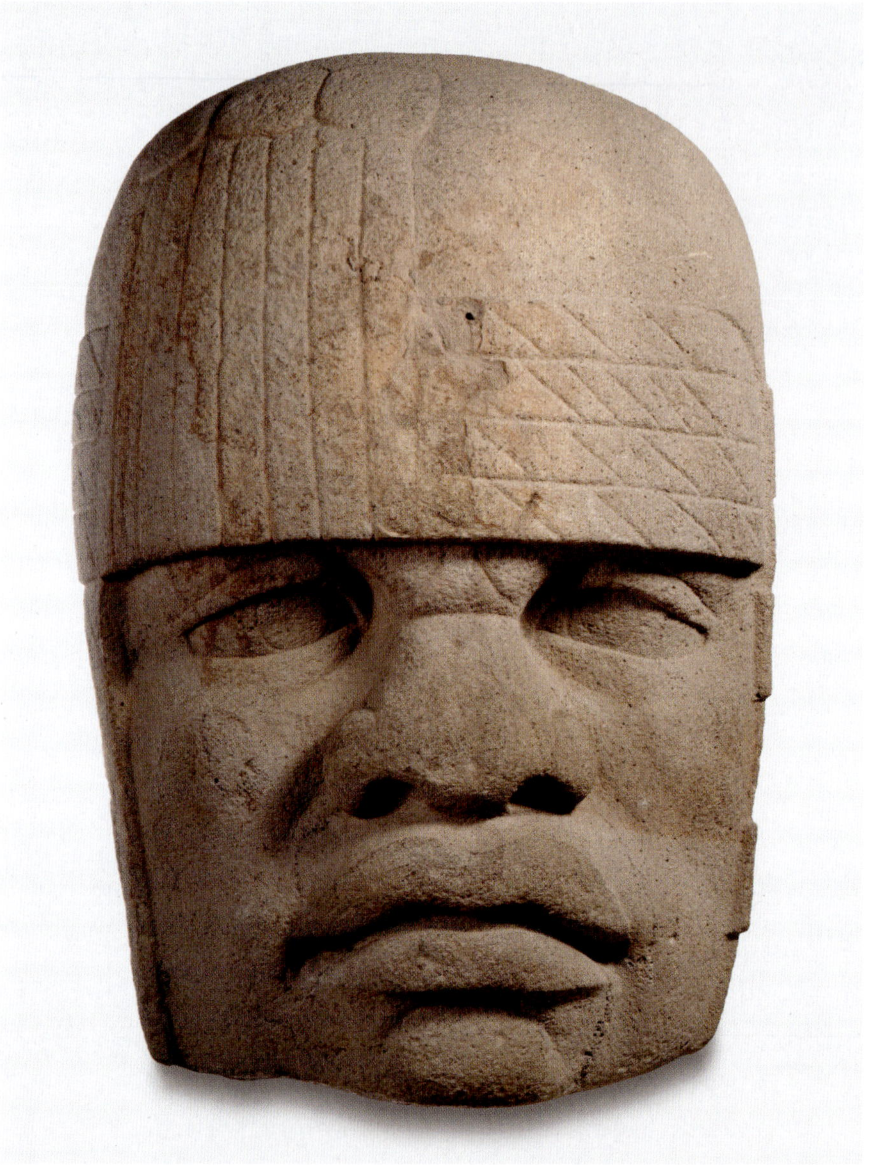

27 ABOVE Colossal Head Number 4, 1200–900 BCE
28 OPPOSITE Colossal Head Number 8, 1200–900 BCE

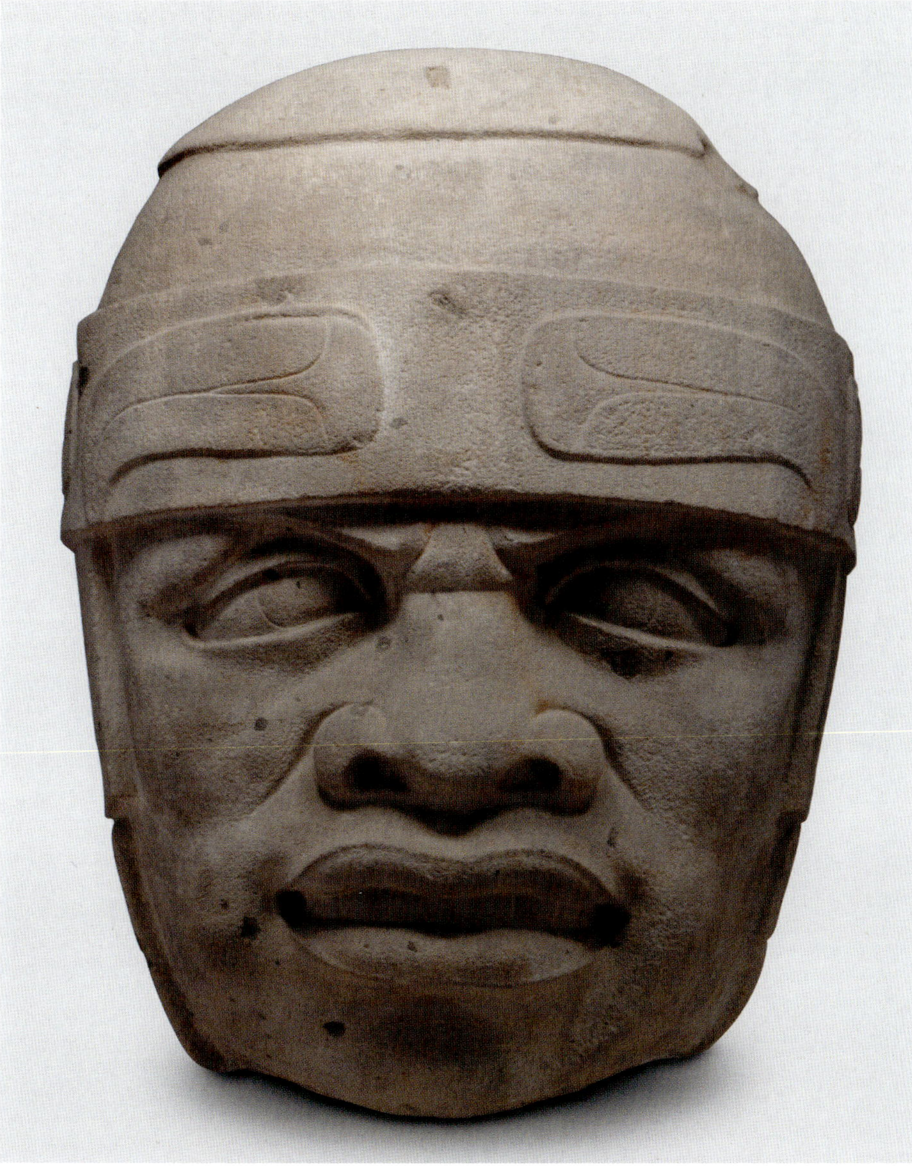

The first true scripts, symbols that recorded speech, developed during this time, laying a foundation for subsequent historical monument-making traditions in both central-southern Mexico and the Maya area. During this time period, Indigenous scribes also began creating written histories for the first time in the Americas.

Furthermore, these artists known from Olmec sites such as San Lorenzo, La Venta, and Tres Zapotes established what can be considered the first widespread style in Mesoamerica. This style is characterized by depictions of humans and animals with such realism as found in the portrait heads, simultaneously with geometric abstraction, as well as other forms of visual expression reserved for supernatural beings. Archaeology demonstrates that Olmec art and monumental building projects also accompanied increased social inequality and differential access to luxury goods through newly established routes of exchange for obsidian, cacao, rubber, greenstone, iron ore, and cinnabar. Exchange also spurred innovation in Olmec visual culture. Olmec style eventually spread from the Gulf Coast to the highlands of Mexico and southward to what is now El Salvador and Honduras.

During this time period, foundational concepts of a Mesoamerican worldview came together, differentiating it from other culture areas such as those in the Andes discussed in chapter 1. Both settlement planning conventions and artistic compositions demonstrate a rectangular, planar geometry at the core of Olmec aesthetics, epitomized by the cardinal and intercardinal directions defined by the sun's movement. The quincunx shape, the arrangement of elements at four corners and the center, such as the number 5 on a pair of dice, was consistently included on large-scale monuments and at a smaller scale on houses, bodies, and objects. The relationship of early maize agriculture and artistic creation is also borne out in Olmec color aesthetics. Deep blue-green hues are directly equated to the color of precious water and young maize sprouts. Artists also established a long-lasting tradition of employing representations in which an icon stands in for a whole concept, such as signifying a supernatural crocodilian with just a flame-shaped eyebrow or a gaping maw, or a maize deity with just a V-shaped cleft, symbolizing the hole in the earth where the seed was planted.

The site known as San Lorenzo rises above the floodplain of the Coatzacoalcos River in modern-day Veracruz. Between about 1800 BCE and 1000 BCE, residents built a monumental platform, forming a manmade plateau, which held residences and ceremonial buildings and spaces. There builders created massive earthen buildings; laborers moved and shaped enormous boulders from the faraway Tuxtla Mountains in the forms of thrones and colossal heads; and engineers designed sophisticated waterworks to tame the powerful runoff of torrential seasonal rainfall. The monumental sculpture speaks to the mythological universe in the minds of artists and their patrons. Although opaque in meaning to modern observers, Olmec art frequently represents anthropomorphic beings, felines, and feathered serpents, which all seem to be playing out parts of important primordial events. The incipient governmental institutions of Mesoamerican leadership presumably counted on such myths as foundational to claims of political power.

Other stone sculptures at San Lorenzo and related sites testify to the rich religious life of the societies in which these patrons, who were often depicted in monuments with elaborate regalia, commissioned such works in service of incipient political institutions. The disembodied colossal heads and anthropomorphic sculptures from San Lorenzo demonstrate several shared principles in Mesoamerican art. The heads of sculptures, from the monumental to the tiny, are often outsized in relation to figures' bodies (or the only element represented), signaling to modern observers that the Olmec idea of the locus of what makes us human resides in the head. Sculptures and the images they contained were agentive and sometimes needed to breathe as well. Figures and masks also often contain representations of breath elements, and makers often went to extra lengths to ensure that the beings represented had nasal passages. Bilateral symmetry and verticality were of great importance in sculptures in the round—unlike the contour rivalry seen in Andean traditions—yet Olmec artists also excelled at representing figures in profile in low relief, as did their southern counterparts (see chapter 1). Certain iconographic elements present in the corpus of art from San Lorenzo, such as crossed bands, U-shaped brackets, maize plants, celts, and feathers, outlast the monumental center itself in compositions created by artists in subsequent societies.

Other societies thrived elsewhere during the heyday of San Lorenzo. If one were to see the location of modern Mexico City from the top of the nearby snow-capped volcano of Popocatépetl, the view at that time would have been drastically different from that of today. Smoke rising from villages would have signaled the diverse lifeways along the shores of one of five great ancient lakes—Lake Texcoco, now under urban sprawl—that formed an important core of the social and cultural life of Central Mexico in the late second millennium

BCE. Life in the village known as Tlatilco, as it was in the related towns now called Tlapacoya and Las Bocas, revolved around farming the nearby fields in the shadows of the volcanoes. These three village sites are well known for their distinctive artistic portrayals of the human body through ceramic figurines, as well as the importation of works from other parts of Mesoamerica. Archaeologists have documented that the ancient residents in these Central Mexican villages had intense ties to powerful rulers of such major ceremonial centers as San Lorenzo, far to the east on the Gulf Coast.

The scale of political integration in these communities was different than in their counterparts in the Olmec heartland, however, where richly adorned nobles undertook big building programs and were surrounded by sculptors and potters. In fact, ceramic artists from San Lorenzo itself produced such high-quality vessels that they began to be exported to the area around Lake Texcoco. The quantity of goods that moved around suggest an insatiable demand for "Olmec" things among highland Mexican peoples. It is impossible to know if the impeccable works of art meant the same to the Tlatilco-, Las Bocas-, or Tlapacoya-era societies as they did to the San Lorenzo Olmec. The artistic creations of the Gulf Coast artists, however, became prized possessions and valued funerary offerings for family ancestors in Central Mexico. This glimpse into Mexico's first art market, of sorts, offers tantalizing clues into the role of art in the formation of Mesoamerican civilizations.

With the influx of gouged and incised pottery designs from the east, Tlatilco artists ventured into new creative territory. They depicted the feathered serpent, perhaps an early embodiment of the sun, or other creatures as a snarling face with flame eyebrows. Experimentation allowed them to express serpents and crocodiles with abstracted techniques in which excised or stylized parts represented whole beings or concepts. Just the bracketed gums of the reptile, for example, signaled to the pots' owners where they came from or who made them. A wing wrapped around the body of a delicate bottle signaled to its owner that it was imbued with a mythological higher power. Perhaps the works most emblematic of the creativity of Olmec style are the masterpieces in which sculptors simultaneously used naturalistic and highly stylized representations of people and animals.

One work of a skilled potter, in the form of a human figure
29 displaying infantile characteristics, exemplifies this highland Olmec-period style. The artist of this hollow baby figure worked in a fine, white clay decorated with a white slip and red pigment. Usually without marked gender and seated with splayed legs

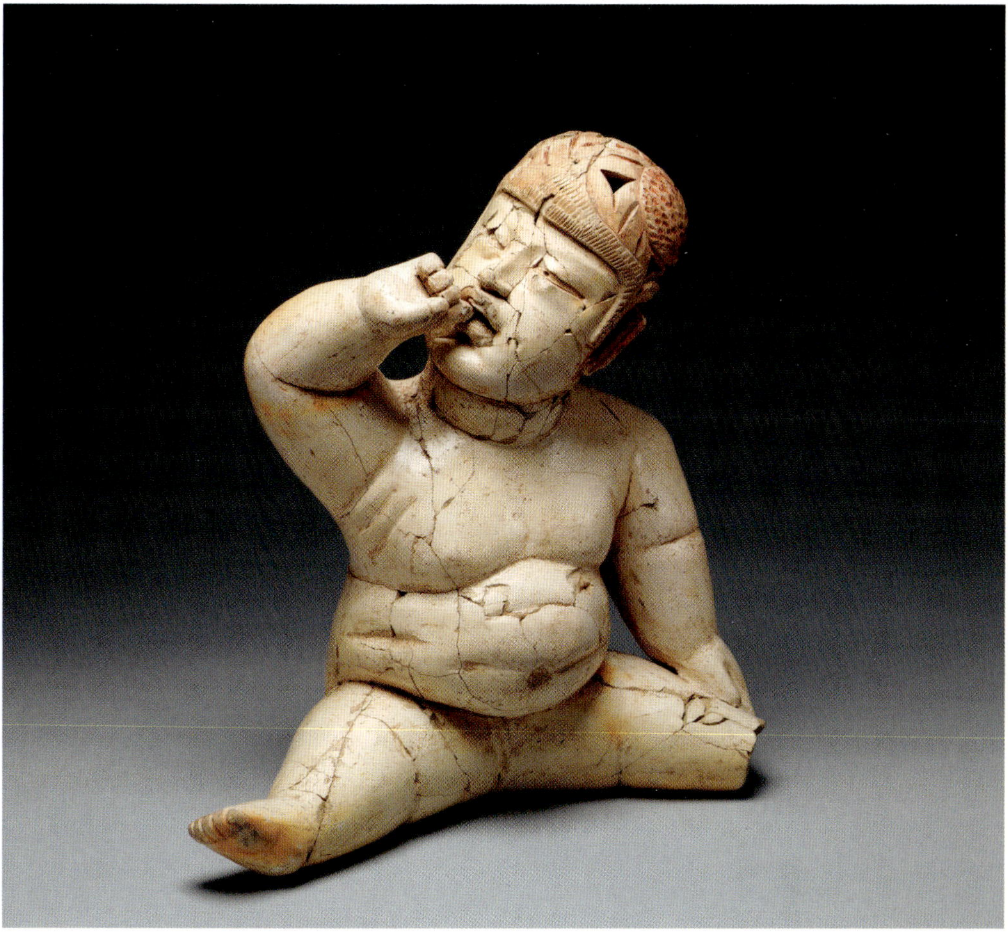

29 Seated Figure, 1200–900 BCE

and hands on thighs, these baby figures have the posture, body proportions, and fleshiness of human babies, although some are embellished with symbolic designs on their bodies and wear distinctive headdresses, such as the one here. From the neck up, the baby displays conventionalized features that are associated with the depictions of supernaturals in Olmec art. The left side of the baby's back is decorated with modeled iconographic elements, including an X, vertical bands, and a crosshatched pattern, signaling connections with wider religious concepts known to the original viewers. Other babies with similar characteristics were recovered at Tlapacoya and

Tlatilco, some of them hollow like this one and others created out of solid baked clay.

This pudgy infant shares some iconographic and stylistic characteristics with sculpture from San Lorenzo, but it reportedly came from Las Bocas, in the modern state of Puebla. There a number of Olmec-style ceramic objects, including vessels and figurines, have been found. Several possible interpretations of the identities of these babies exist. For example, they could be portraits of children of important families with supernatural characteristics, or perhaps they are idealized portraits of infant deities. There is a long tradition of infant deities in Mesoamerica, which were seen as emerging and potent in their small form, and also demanding care. They could be tributes to deceased infants that left this world too early, or representative emblems of the primordial founders of whole lineages or families. Regardless of the function or intent of the artists, they made the hollow sculptures very lifelike, probably for use on ritual occasions during village life. This baby playfully gazes upward and raises a finger to its mouth, as if playing on the ground as the center of attention during a family gathering. The application of the red pigment, including hematite and cinnabar, may have marked it as a powerful effigy in both the life and death of its caretaker.

In some cases, the ceramic effigies may have served as substitutes for actual infants in a sacrificial or dedicatory rituals at important places, as there is compelling evidence of Olmec infant ceremonial burials. Mexican researchers working at the extraordinary, waterlogged site of El Manatí ("the manatee"), to the southeast of San Lorenzo, found dismembered bones of newborns, perhaps neonates, and a primary infant burial in the fetal position. These were associated with miraculously preserved wooden busts, rubber balls, and greenstone axe caches. The faces of the wooden
30 busts are evocative of similar expressions found on the ceramic babies. The sculptors of the wood figures only lightly hinted at limbs, again confirming the early metaphysical beliefs that the head was the main center of the human self, although they may have once been clothed or wrapped in other materials. Infants are also represented in later figures in greenstone and jade, and they often have feline features such as fangs and stylized eyes. Other images depict babies with cleft heads, identified as personified maize sprouts or plants, a concept that persisted into the beliefs of subsequent cultures. The preoccupation of Olmec peoples with child-rearing and the mythological connections between the life cycles of infants and agriculture transcend time and space, still relevant to any peoples today.

30 Anthropomorphic Bust, 1100–600 BCE

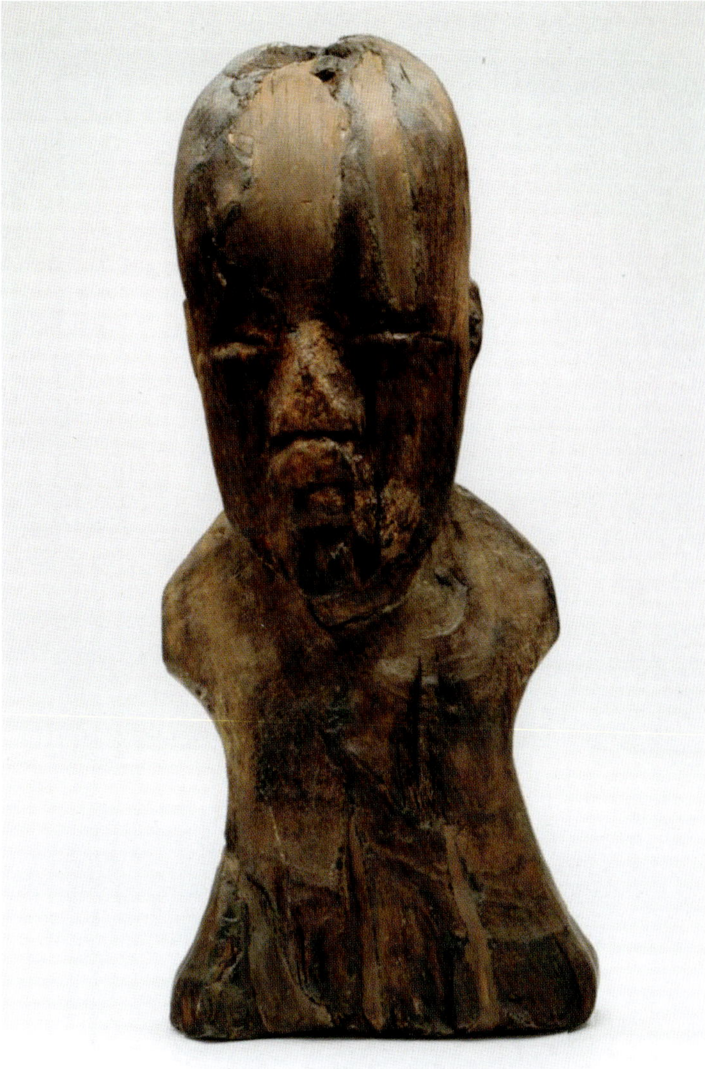

31 Highland artists also excelled in relief sculpture in early Olmec style, especially at the site of Chalcatzingo, in the modern state of Morelos. Sculptors at the site created elaborate narrative art that included supernatural felines, ruler figures, and feathered serpents. The origins of the serpent with feathers from the Olmec period is significant, as the celestial creature persisted as a subject in Mesoamerican art and even inspires artists around the world today. Another significant

foundational visual trope innovated by Olmec artists is that of a cave inside a mountain that took the form of an animate creature with a gaping maw. On Monument 9, for example, Chalcatzingo artists depicted a frontal view of a cave creature, with lozenge-shaped eyes and vegetal projections from the four corners of its quatrefoil- or cruciform-shaped mouth. This monument was looted in the 1960s and recently returned to Mexico after having spent decades in museum and private collections. The opening serves as a tangible portal, a cave entrance through which rulers, ritual practitioners, or objects could pass. It represents a mountain with water (known in the later Nahuatl language as *altepetl*, "water-mountain"), which became one of the primordial central places for Mesoamerican societies (see chapter 10).

La Venta

After about 1000 BCE, residents of San Lorenzo may have migrated to other places where they constructed massive rectangular plazas similar to those at the center. The widespread influence of artists there gradually waned as the large site was abandoned. One of the destinations where San Lorenzo

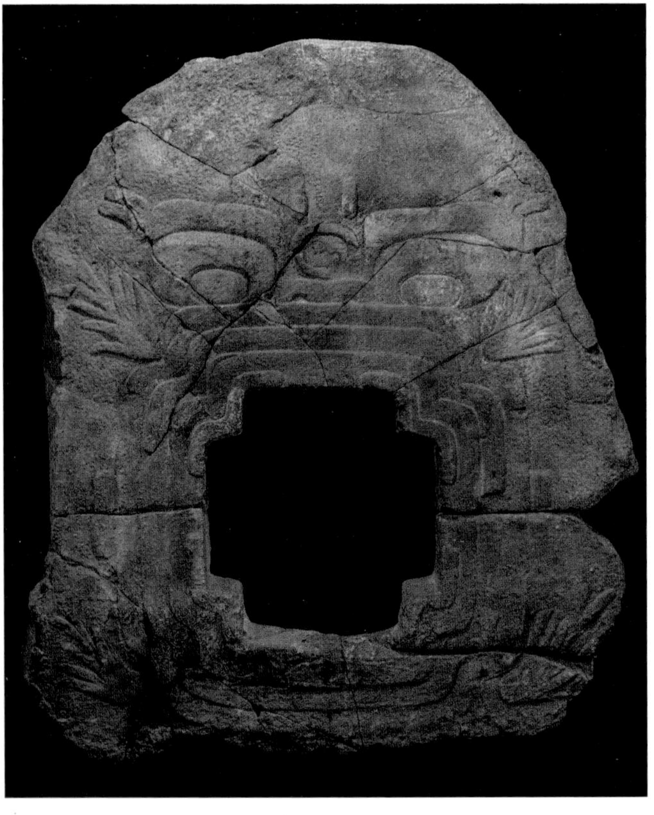

31 Zoomorphic Relief, 800–400 BCE

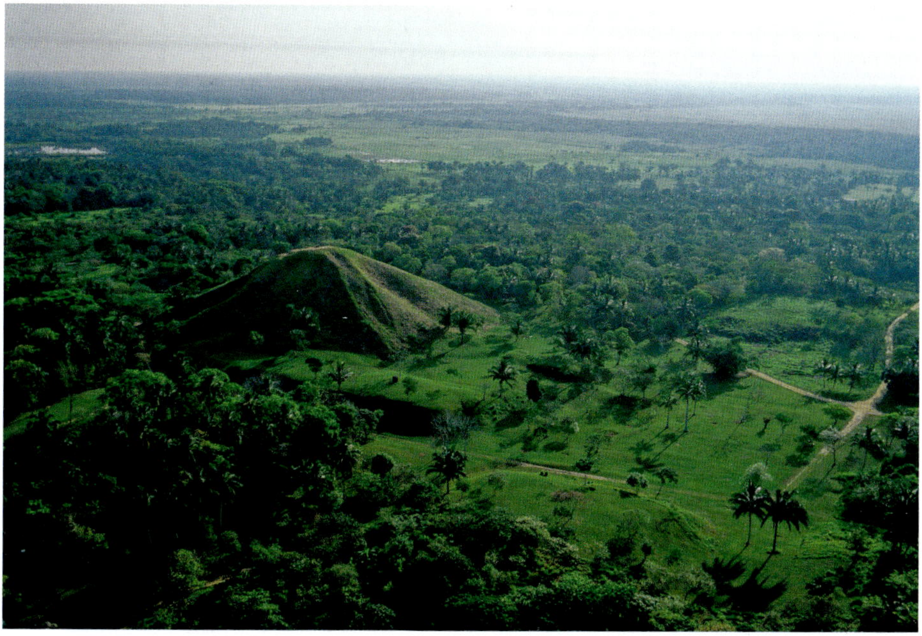

32 Aerial Image of La Venta, Mexico

residents may have gone to is the major site of La Venta, now in the state of Tabasco. The apogee of Olmec style in the mid-first millennium BCE occurs with the time of greatest cultural activity at this place, on the east side of the River Tonalá, about 5 miles (8 km) from the Gulf Coast. Marking the central ritual
32 precinct of La Venta is a pyramid more than 98 feet (30 m) tall, likely a representation of a primordial mountain. La Venta is notable for its extraordinary communities of artists, whose dexterous abilities especially focused on shaping local stone and imported greenstone in addition to baked clay.

Showcased at both the Museo Nacional de Antropología in Mexico City and the Parque-Museo La Venta in Villahermosa, Tabasco, are some of the most impressive and enigmatic sculptures in the ancient world. Notably, giant mosaics composed of rectangular blocks of serpentine, a greenstone that was frequently used by ancient Mesoamericans, are laid out in Villahermosa. This yellow-green mosaic pavement was not for walking on, however. This pavement and several others were interred after they were assembled as massive offerings. Buried deep within platforms at the Olmec center of La Venta, they would have played an invisible but salient role in the minds of their creators and admirers. Laden with abstract

symbolism, they perhaps were dedicatory for the spaces above
them or a way to honor a long-lost deity or natural force. Recent
interpretations of these sculptures have also emphasized the
importance of the process itself, that is, the assembling of the
stones was rife with social meaning.

Archaeologists also recovered one of the earliest and richest
series of tombs from Mesoamerica at La Venta. In the burial
known as Tomb A, for example, residents placed mortuary
bundles within walls and a roof constructed out of thirty-eight
natural basalt columns. Within this massive offering was an
33 exquisite small-scale depiction of a female figure, giving key
insights into Olmec aesthetic and material values at the time.
The diminutive figure, perhaps created from rare green jadeite
imported from farther south, shows a woman sitting cross-
legged wearing a knee-length skirt or wrap dress. She holds her
arms in front of her torso in a gesture seen in other sculptures
of deities holding ritual objects, or perhaps the pose itself had
a courtly meaning. The woman's hair is delicately rendered
to frame her face and ears; perhaps small attachments once
dangled from her pierced lobes. It may be that the carver
followed Olmec conventions of representing divine beings
with slightly enlarged eyes and a downturned mouth, but this
woman may also be a human being similar to those featured in
27, 28 the colossal heads. An oval mirror pendant, represented here
by an inlay of specular hematite, would have been a powerful
part of Olmec ritual regalia; a full-sized magnetite plaque
was found in the tomb with this figure. As a final part of the
creation and deposition of the sculpture, she was painted with
cinnabar along with other contents of the tomb, enlivening
the composition and underscoring La Venta's ruling families'
access to such imported minerals.

Other dedicatory offerings of human or supernatural figures,
34 such as the renowned group of figures known as Offering 4,
hint at both a structured ritual life of La Venta leaders and a
broader play with transposing scale in Olmec thought. The
original offering, presumably placed around 800 BCE to 700
BCE, consisted of sixteen standing figures facing inward
and framed by six vertically arranged axe forms, giving the
impression of small-scale standing monuments. Just as these
celts could be stelae, perhaps the large stelae were considered
monumental celts. Several of the figures may have been
older sculptures, including one with a broken arm, and were
carved from imported serpentines or jadeites rather than local
stones. The celts included pieces reworked from another object
made of a paler stone. Evidence from excavation suggests
that approximately a century after the original deposition

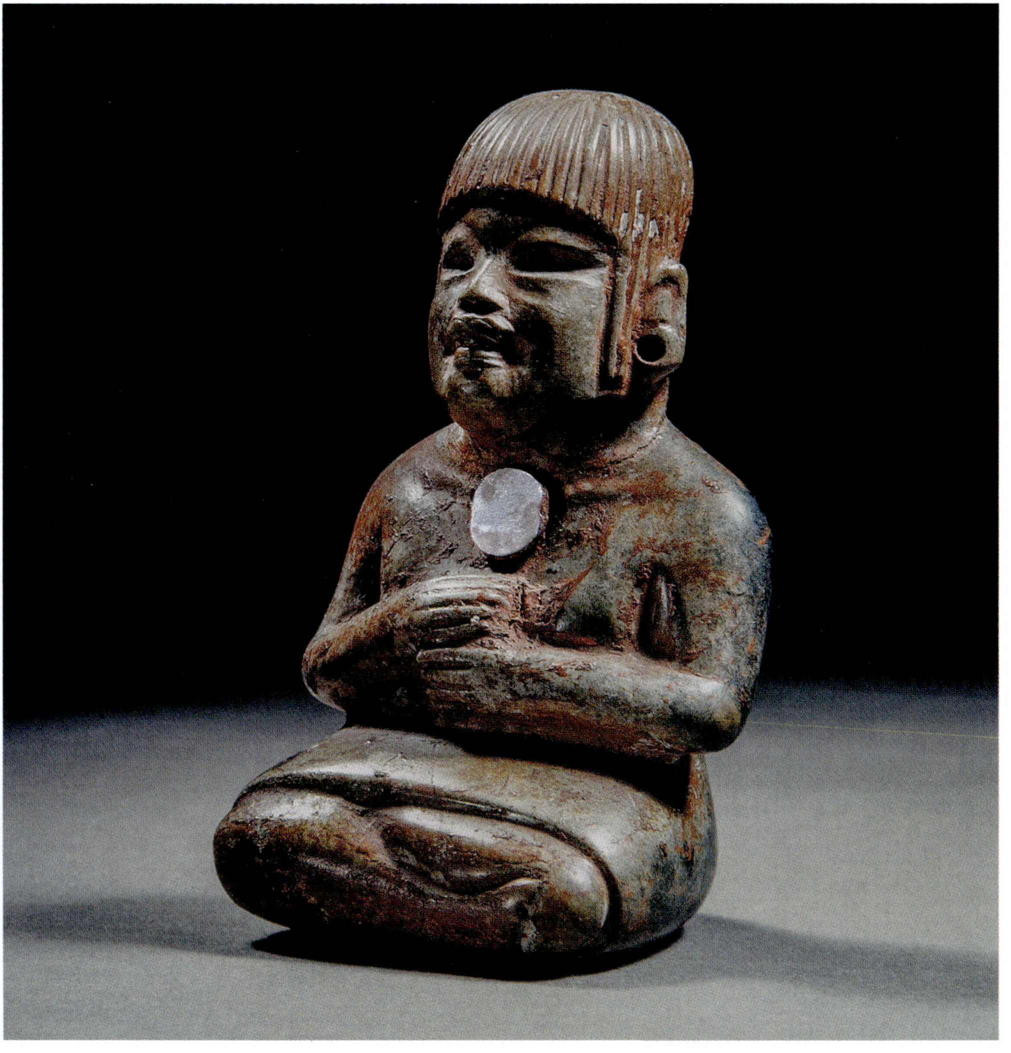

33 Seated Female Figure, 900–600 BCE

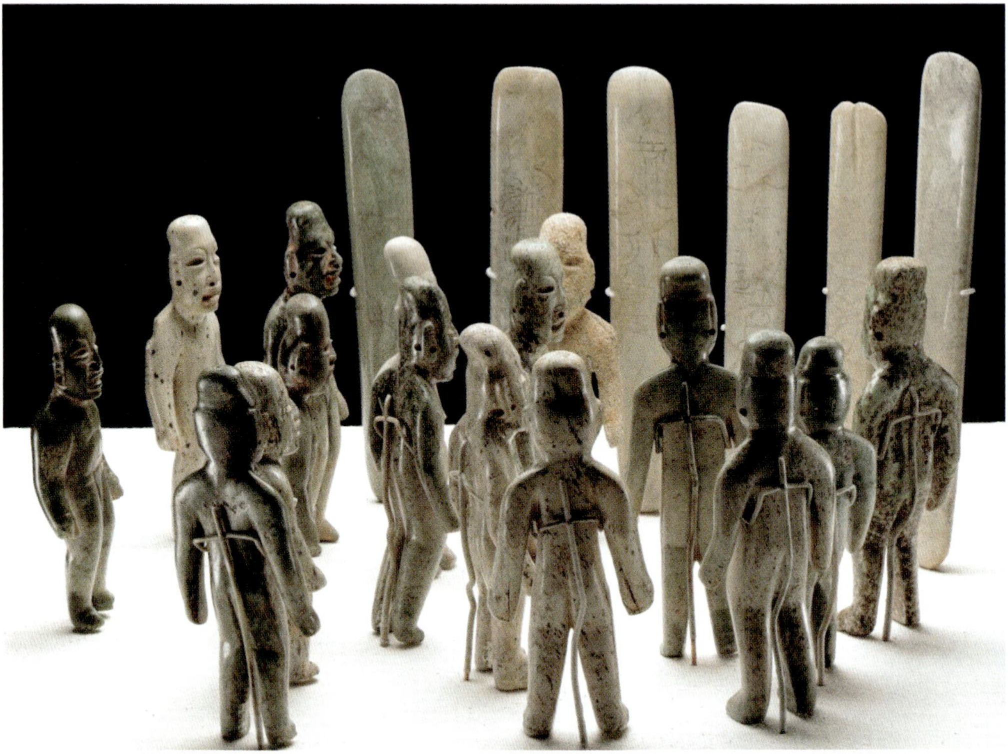

34 Offering 4, 800–700 BCE

of this tableau, a precise excavation revealed the offering for descendants, who promptly reburied it. The scene represented by the jade figures was so important that the community of La Venta held its location in memory, consulting or commemorating it years after its initial burial, similar to later
95 documented practices of opening ancestral tombs.

Monumental sculptures from La Venta demonstrate how local sculptor communities excelled at both low-relief sculpture and carving figures in the round. A series of large monuments, known as altars but perhaps originally functioning as thrones, exemplifies such creativity in playing between two and three
35 dimensions. For example, La Venta Altar 4 depicts a ruler emerging from a cave, grasping a coiled rope that runs around the base of the sculpture. The naturalistically rendered muscular figure, wearing a headdress, loincloth, and large collar with pectoral assemblage, leans forward in an active pose. The frame of the cave around him recalls Chalcatzingo Monument 9, as the four corners of the cave are marked with

sprouting plants, so the altar could be a symbolic mountain. Above the ruler in a surface projecting over the cave, the artist has sculpted in low relief a mythological creature in frontal view, with a gaping mouth marked by crossed bands and fangs. Although the layered meanings of this complex scene are not immediately accessible to modern viewers, the sculptor memorialized this individual in a moment fusing the real and historical with the sacred, a hallmark of aesthetic approaches in subsequent Mesoamerican traditions.

Sculptural techniques, perhaps perfected for the working of harder stones like jade, allowed Olmec artists to shape the softer volcanic stone basalt in astonishing ways. This ability shines in the sculpture known as *The Wrestler* discovered in the 1930s in Veracruz and purchased for the Museo Nacional de Antropología. Similar to the individual on the altar from La Venta, this figure wears a loincloth and leans forward in an active pose with both arms raised to chest height. The artist's skill is visible in the subtle curves of the musculature, the articulation of the fingers and toes, and the soft fleshiness of the figure's torso where the loincloth meets the midsection. The figure stands out from other Olmec works with a delicately defined mustache and beard framing the stoic gaze of the

35 Altar 4, 800–400 BCE

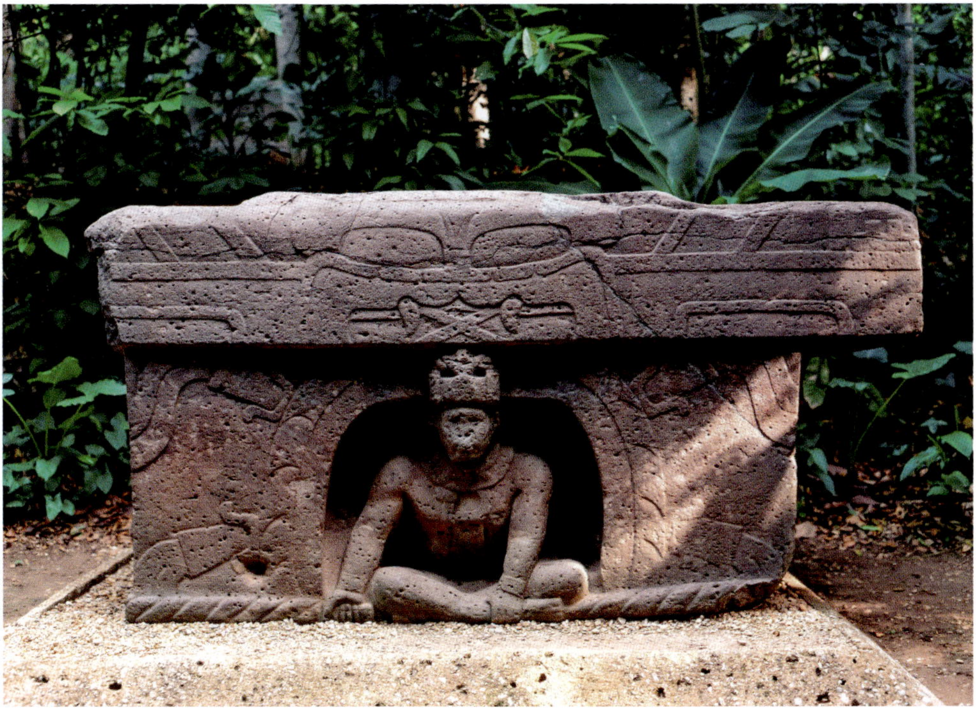

figure. Although the figure's hair is not defined with carving, the sculpture may have once been adorned with a perishable headdress, and earrings may have once dangled from the pierced holes in the figure's lobes. Perhaps an ancestor immortalized in this enduring stone medium, *The Wrestler* still captivates viewers as it once did in its original context.

Though Olmec buildings and wooden structures may have been carved and brightly painted, very little evidence of the painterly traditions from this time survives. One important
37 example comes from the cave paintings of Oxtotitlán, Guerrero, with large passages painted in the Olmec style. The location of this site far to the west of the Olmec heartland and to the south of the Basin of Mexico underscores the widespread distribution of the style. In a mural known as C-1, a brightly painted central figure sits atop a large, fanged creature with eyes marked with cross-banded pupils, similar to the one carved on the La Venta throne above. The figure sits with

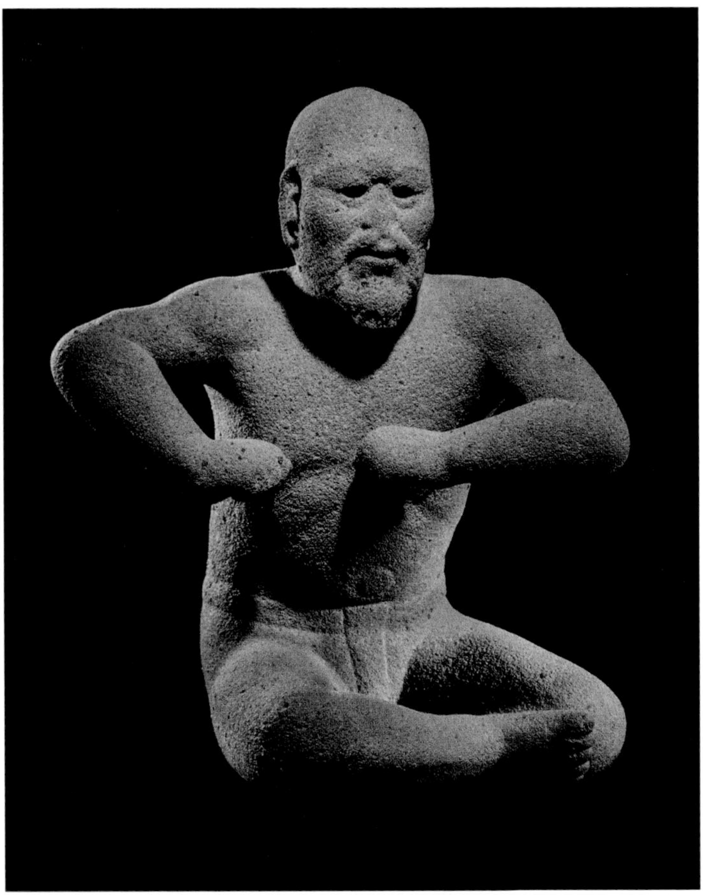

36 Anthropomorphic Sculpture, 1300–600 BCE

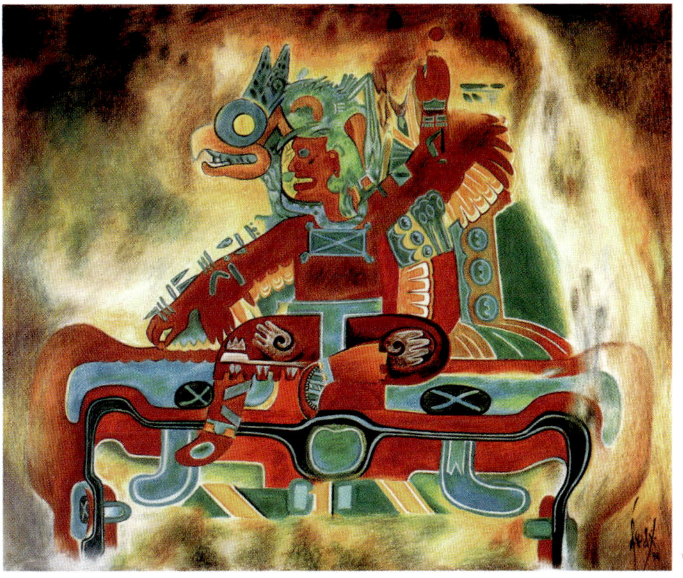

37 Ayax Moreno, Reproduction of the Oxtotitlán Cave Mural C-1. Olmec, Mexico

one leg crossed, while raising his left arm above his head and extending the right arm in front of his gaze, grasping a small round object with his thumb and forefinger. His elaborate regalia consists of footwear, a red loincloth and skirt garment decorated with handprint designs, and a large bird headdress and feathered cape resembling wings. The green bird with orange beak may reference a raptor, or perhaps the resplendent quetzal (*Pharomachrus mocinno*), the green feathers of which were prized for their luminous blue-green shimmer that related them to jade. Most notably, the artist made clear that this is a scene of a human impersonating an avian character; the bird headdress is depicted in an "X-ray" fashion so the profile of the wearer, also adorned with a jade nose ornament, is clearly visible.

Legacies (400 BCE–250 CE)

The artistic fluorescence at La Venta between about 800 BCE and 400 BCE is now seen by scholars as one of many contemporaneous movements in Mesoamerican sculpture. It is clear that by the early first millennium BCE artists had developed an aesthetic universe and geometric scheme to express complex mythological themes populated by specific characters represented with particular conventions. They were able to create novel forms and images that look back to primordial ideas of origin. The widespread influence of the Olmec style is seen all across Mesoamerican art, especially in

the aesthetic expressions of natural phenomena: mountains,
the sun, rain, and maize. Other communities throughout
Mesoamerica began to shape jade figures, pectorals, and beads,
such as the peoples in what is now Guatemala or others in
Oaxaca; even as far east as Honduras or south as Costa Rica,
residents were importing Olmec-style jades and depositing
them in large numbers at the center of their communities.
Such features of Olmec art seem to have guided later artists,
who departed from known ways of representation to create
new visual cultures, such as those known from the Maya area,
Teotihuacán, Oaxaca, Veracruz, and the great Mexica Empire,
to be described in subsequent chapters. The same mountains
and caves that inspired Olmec masterworks such as the
Chalcatzingo and La Venta monuments affected artists and
their patrons until the invasion of Europeans in the sixteenth
century and beyond.

Another important innovation that occurred during the
Olmec period is the use of written script to represent speech,
marking Mesoamerica as only one of three areas in the world
that independently formed a writing system. By the later
periods of San Lorenzo's occupation, there is evidence that
symbols were employed to record linguistic information in a
38 codified way, such as on the object known as the Cascajal Block
from approximately 900 BCE. Although not deciphered yet,
the general consensus is that the incised text that appears on
the block is consistent with Olmec iconography and displays
a syntax conforming to the expectation of early writing. Later
monuments in the region, such as some from the site of
Cerro de las Mesas, Veracruz, confirm that mathematics, the
calendar, and related scripts developed independently in the
Isthmus of Tehuantepec, perhaps from precursors like those
represented in the Cascajal text, though, notably, it does not
contain overt numerals.

In the Olmec heartland toward the end of the first
millennium BCE, scribes began carving monuments with
a script known as Isthmian (or Epi-Olmec), which features
dates recorded in the same notation as later Mesoamerican
calendars. The textual content remains largely undeciphered,
however, despite attempts to compare the script to later
39 languages. One work known as the Tuxtla Statuette, bearing
Isthmian script, provides crucial information about sacred
beings and ritual performance. The rounded greenstone
carving depicts either a human impersonating an avian
character or a supernatural being, complete with a large duck-
37 or heron-billed mask and a winged cape. Similar to the cave
painting above, the carver went to extra effort to emphasize

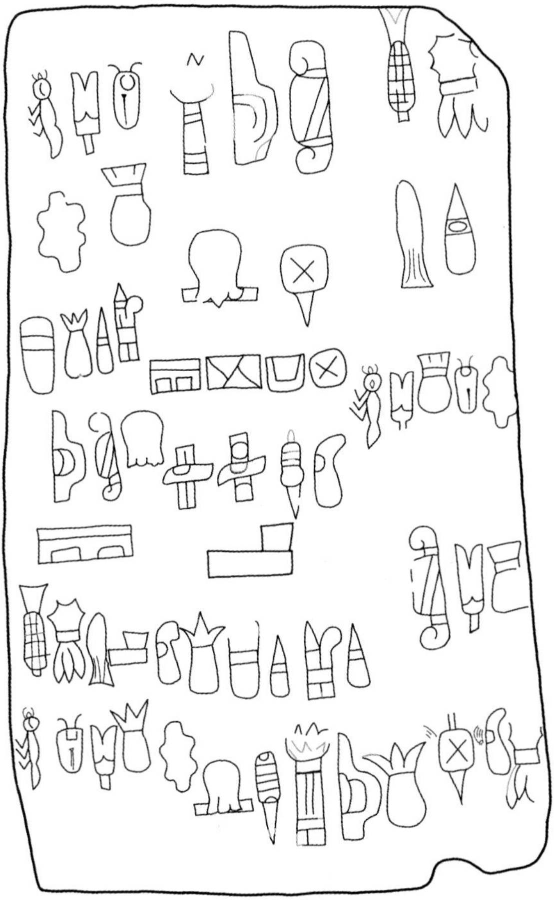

38 Michael D. Carrasco, Drawing of the Cascajal Block

the humanness of the subject here, even though birdlike legs poke out from under the wings. The human's ears are adorned with earflares, and otherwise, no other limbs are visible. Lightly incised all over the body and wings of the figure are columns of the Isthmian script, including a calendar date of 162 CE, centuries after the heyday of the Olmec centers of San Lorenzo and La Venta, signaling shifts in visual and scribal cultures. This is one of the earliest known dates in the count of linear time used by the later Maya peoples (see chapter 4). The scribe also included hieroglyphs of nobles or deities in profile, which could be proper names referring to the individual or god depicted in three dimensions.

Though removed in time and space by great distances, subsequent artists in Mesoamerica and even beyond clearly

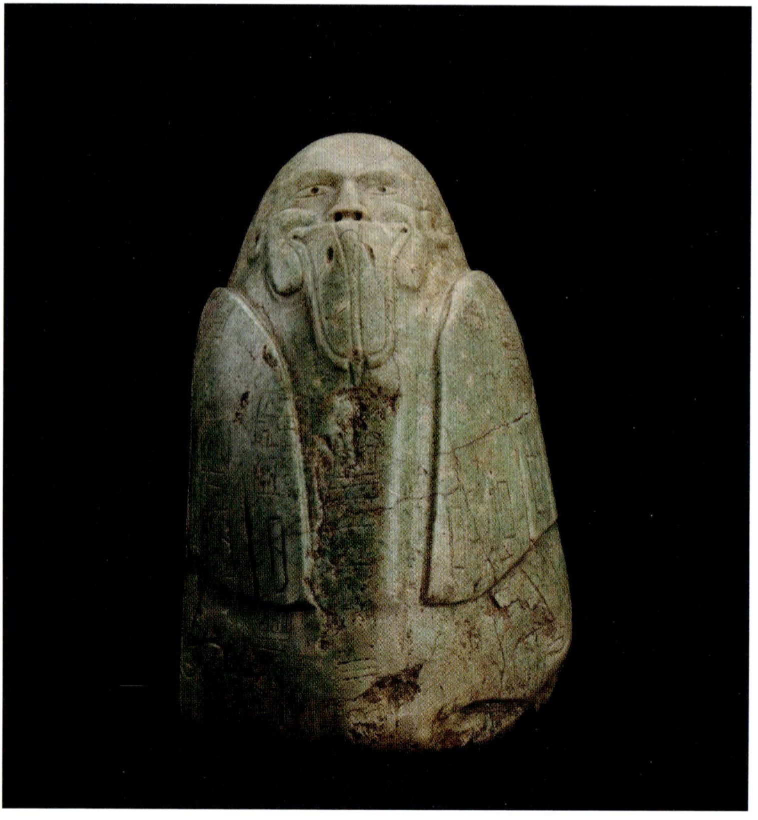

39 LEFT Anthropomorphic Figure, 162 CE
40 BELOW Winged Pectoral, 900–400 BCE (carved)

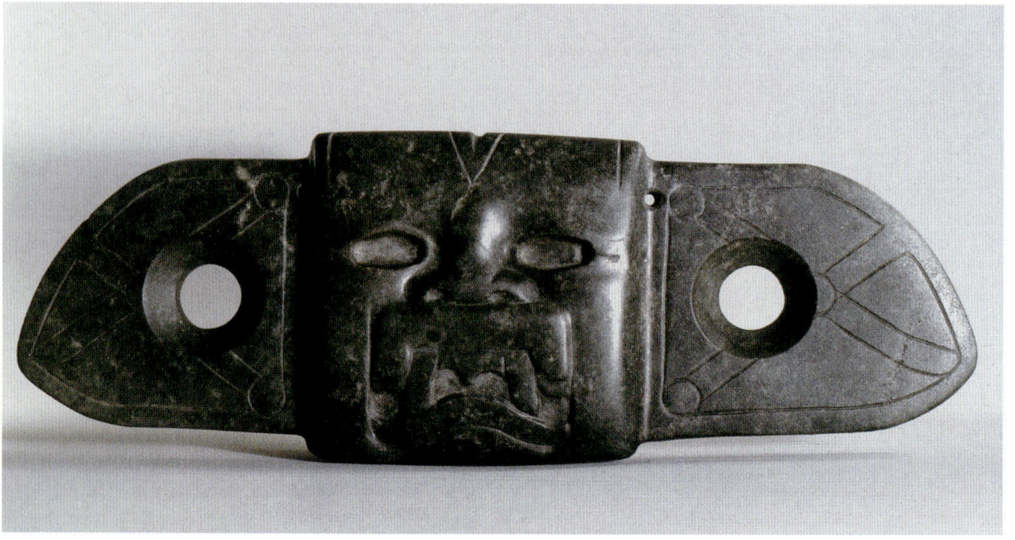

appreciated the antiquity and quality of Olmec works as heirlooms. Often artists in the Maya region seem to have obtained Olmec jade and greenstone creations and reworked them with their own imagery and texts. A winged pectoral made of quartzite or serpentinite is one such object with a complex biography. Probably first made in the Olmec style in western Mexico, the central face of the pectoral is that interpreted as a maize deity, with almond-shaped eyes, a downturned fanged mouth, and clear V-shaped cleft in the forehead. Centuries later, an early king in the Maya area obtained the heavy ornament, commissioning a scribe to incise his portrait and a text proclaiming his accession to the throne on the reverse. The king, shown as a youthful man, sits cross-legged in profile, wearing an elaborate headdress, facing two columns of paired hieroglyphic signs. Although the text bears resemblance to later Maya texts, it remains only partially deciphered, underscoring the exciting research in the field of early arts of Mesoamerica in years to come.

Part II
Royal Patrons and Their Artists

By the early centuries CE, a distinct shift in the arts of the Americas is perceptible in the material culture. This time period is characterized by the spread of city-state forms of political organization that centered around powerful, elite families or individuals. These same patrons dominated the rising long-distance trade of materials and concepts and exerted control over artistic production. They cultivated communities of practice that allowed talented individuals and workshops to perfect their skills in weaving, metalworking, and carving over generations. These creative individuals brought foundational origins stories and divine characters to life through architecture, objects, and personal regalia. Art, a vital tool for leaders to lay claims to landscape and subjects, became even more important to political strategies than in previous time periods. Newfound political competition between different groups also laid the groundwork for artistic freedom for neighboring makers, as they seemingly sought to outdo one another with their work.

Visual art thus formed an important basis of a distinct form of rulership that developed in the Americas. In certain cases, it furthered agendas of royalty and supported dynastic sovereignty. Royal individuals were self-proclaimed supreme authorities over land and subjects, bolstering their narratives by accumulating wealth and influence over the production of both luxury and subsistence goods. They practiced dynastic succession, in that the accumulated authority and material wealth were passed down through inheritance to the next generation. In many instances, these dynasties used art to connect themselves to divine forces, either as the protagonists of sacred narratives or through embodiment as they donned regalia imbued with god images.

Royal Patrons and Their Artists

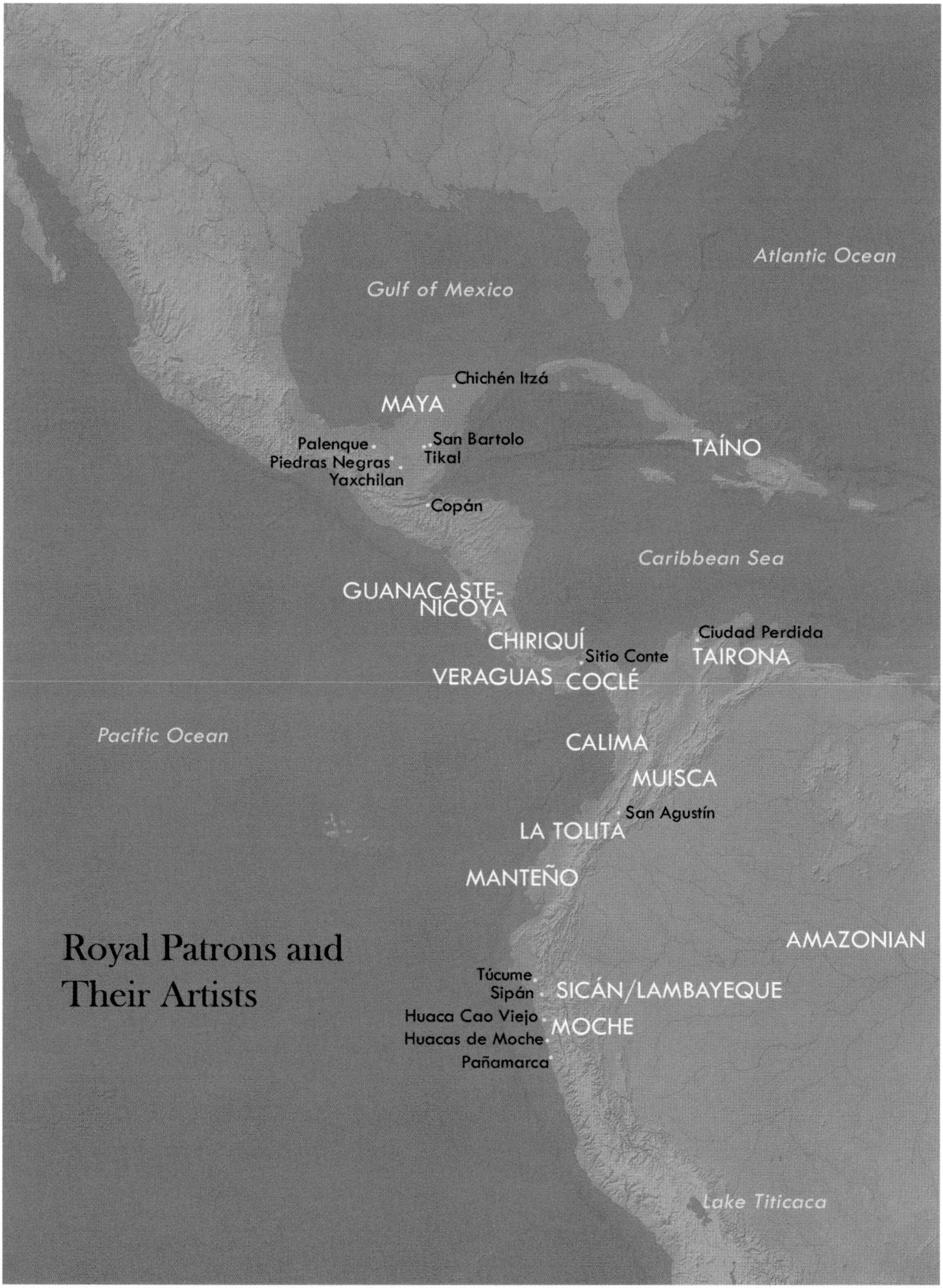

The next three chapters focus on key case studies in art and royal politics from the north coast of Peru, the Maya lowlands, the lands and islands that span the Isthmian and Caribbean zones between southern Central America and the northern Andes, and the vast Amazonian region. A variety of historical factors—relative lack of archaeological attention, devastation at the hands of European invaders, and modern political struggles, to name a few—have contributed to the marginalization of art from the Caribbean region, Central America, the northern Andes, and the Amazon Basin. One distinct cultural practice stands out: the builders in these regions tended to create superstructures out of wood, rather than stone or mudbrick, so nothing architectural survives in archaeological contexts apart from basal platforms. Recent advances in the study of objects representing visual cultures from these regions, however, allow them to be in conversation with their peers from the Maya region and the Moche homeland on the north coast of Peru. A reevaluation of the evidence underscores the deep connections shared throughout the region in objects, imagery, and elements of political systems such as rulers' claims to divinity through materials and iconography.

Chapter 3
Mountains of Mud Brick: Moche (300–800 CE) and Their Successors

The small mountain known as Cerro Blanco (not to be confused with the sand dune in southern Peru of the same name) is a striking stone peak overlooking the Pacific Ocean outside of Trujillo, Peru. Its variegated colors and symmetric cone make it stand out from the desert landscape. The Moche River passes this final peak on its way westward to the Pacific, irrigating the valley below. Approaching Cerro Blanco by vehicle today it becomes clear that the beautiful face of this mountain has been altered in some way. Growing from the foot of the mountain, where stone meets sand, are rectilinear walls made of mud brick. As if sprouting from the very cracks of the mountain's face, the massive archaeological complex of Huaca de la Luna faces across the remains of a city toward the Huaca del Sol, a mega-scale series of superimposed platforms. The builders who constructed the Huaca de la Luna integrated the natural rock at Cerro Blanco into the complex of plazas, patios, platforms, and walls, the silvery sedimentary rock contrasting with the dusty
41 brown bricks. Closer inspection reveals that both the exterior and interior walls are covered with colorful friezes containing mythological imagery.

This detail of the frieze exemplifies the exuberant energies expended by artists of societies known as Moche that dominated northern Peru in the mid- to late first millennium CE. In this diamond pattern, which seems to quote a woven textile at monumental scale, a central face peers out, modeled in three dimensions as if emerging from the building. The fanged jaws and enlarged eyes draw the viewer's attention in its threatening stare. The hybrid being shows elements of sea creatures, as dark-colored tentacles seem to radiate outward. It is surrounded by another diamond of stylized beings that are yellow with red-and-white eyes on an almost pixelated,

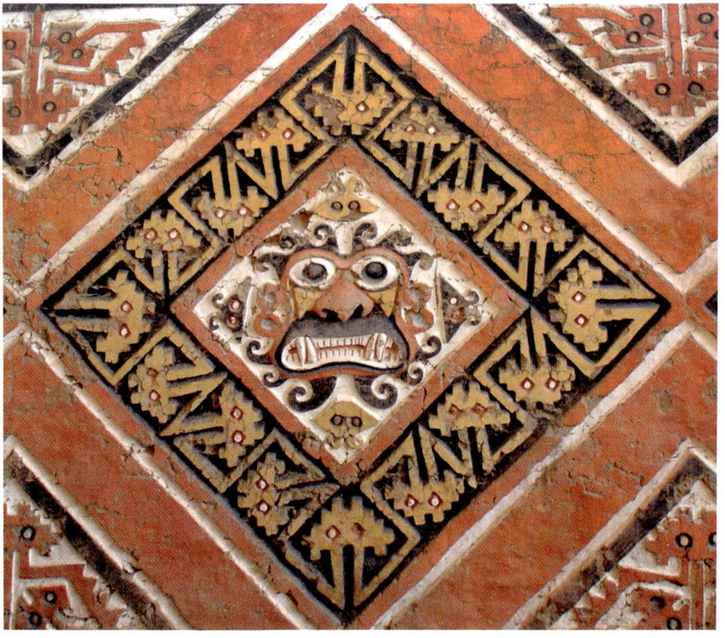

41 Frieze, 300–600

triangular head. These fishy creatures, possibly rays, look like they belong in an early video game and are all connected with a series of angular lines raised from the dark ground. Were the sculptors here representing a supreme deity, or simply one of many supernaturals seen to be observing the human activities on the plazas below?

These monumental compositions of stylized supernatural creatures complement realistic Moche depictions of people, animals, and plants. In fact, a hallmark of the Moche tradition
42 is the naturalistic rendering of humanlike faces across media. This life-sized gilded-copper mask inlaid with shell and stone and decorated with red pigment shows perhaps a male individual wearing face paint. Holes in the hairline and earlobes suggest that this mask was part of a larger assemblage that might have formed a dedicatory or funerary offering. The formation of the lips, slight curvature of the cheekbones and brows, and tapering into the neck all add remarkable lifelikeness. Although the metalworker sculpted and gilded a symmetrical and well-proportioned head of this individual, the painted motif around the chin adds a symbolic element, depicting what might be a representation of tattoos or body paint in the form of small mollusks in a line around the mandible.

Moche metalworkers also achieved extraordinary technological prowess; the surface of this mask was gilded by electrochemical replacement plating, a technique not perfected in Europe until centuries later. Earlier metalwork (see chapter 1) was largely composed of native metals, as opposed to alloys, that would have been collected in small nuggets and transformed through hammering. By the time that Moche societies developed, artists in the region had adopted or perfected metallurgy, which involves the extraction of metals from compound ores using smelting or the application of high temperatures. Moche patrons procured copper ores at a grand scale during the fourth through tenth centuries CE, reflected in the large quantity of copper objects recovered archaeologically. Clever metallurgists also perfected techniques of surface manipulation, such as gilding or silvering, which gave ornaments the appearance of one or more metals, even when the alloy was mostly copper. Gold in its natural state is much more flexible and malleable than copper, so gilding achieved the aesthetic goals of luminosity while maintaining structural integrity of such objects like the mask below.

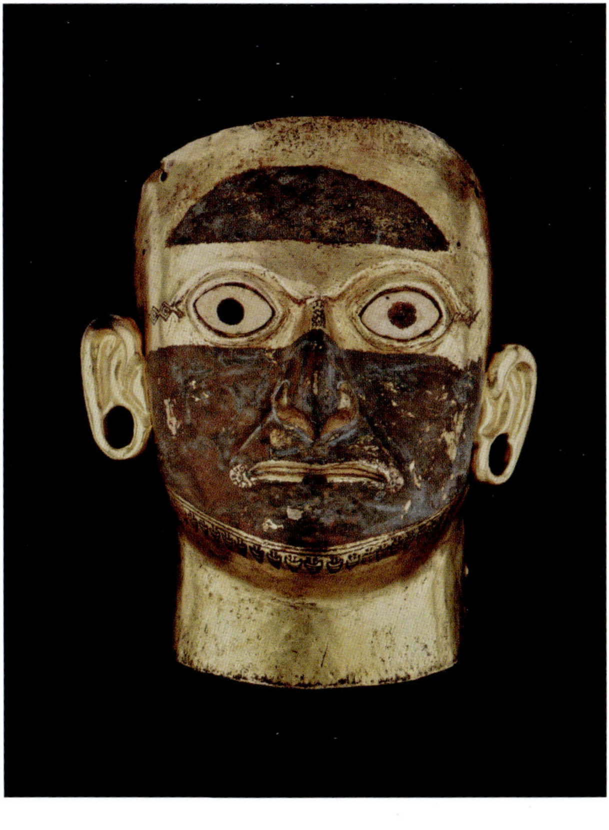

42 Mask, 300–400

Directly across a sediment-covered floodplain from the Huaca de la Luna, once occupied by an urban center, lies a massive adobe platform—the Huaca del Sol. The largest constructions of the Moche had been long abandoned and were in ruins by the time that the Spanish arrived. The invaders quickly recognized the richness that lay within the constructions, however, and they diverted the Moche River to wash away the mud bricks of the Huaca del Sol and reveal its long-hidden wealth. Many of the thousands of bricks composing the Huaca del Sol carried designs that have been interpreted as makers' marks, hinting at complex civic organization. Perhaps the surrounding communities paid tribute to the ruling family in the form of architectural bricks. The Huaca de la Luna and Sol building complex (collectively known as the Huacas de Moche), however, seems to be less of a sort of imperial capital and more of a first among equals of Moche royal courts, at the heart of what was a network of independent city-states in neighboring coastal valleys.

A succession of major tombs has been discovered at a string of such adobe platform complexes all along the coast of Peru, from Piura in the north to the Casma Valley in the south. Wealth and power seem to have been concentrated in several river valleys: the Lambayeque Valley (Sipán-Huaca Rajada), the Jequetepeque Valley (Huaca Dos Cabezas; San José de Moro; La Mina); the Chicama Valley (Huaca Cao Viejo); the Nepeña Valley (Pañamarca), and the Piura Valley (Loma Negra). From available evidence, there seems to have been an organization in which individual dynasties controlled courtly capitals, perhaps functioning as separate city-states united by language and cultural practices, rather than one group exercising overlordship, imperialism, or other collective political strategies.

Moche artists built upon prior visual cultures and experimented with new architectural geometries, an expanded color palette showcasing newly discovered pigments and techniques, and new subjects. A rich belief system and philosophy of nature are highlighted from the archaeological and art-historical evidence from the Moche. Certain important families, represented by large, multi-generational funerary chambers, claimed access to divine forces and supernatural identities, though no written record exists of their names or their religious beliefs. Consistent visual elements, such as fanged deities, feline beings, and predatory raptors, were continuous from the previous visual cultures on the coast (see chapter 1). Moche artists recombined them and infused new characters with ancestral features to serve their patrons' agendas. The astonishing preservation of the desert climate has allowed

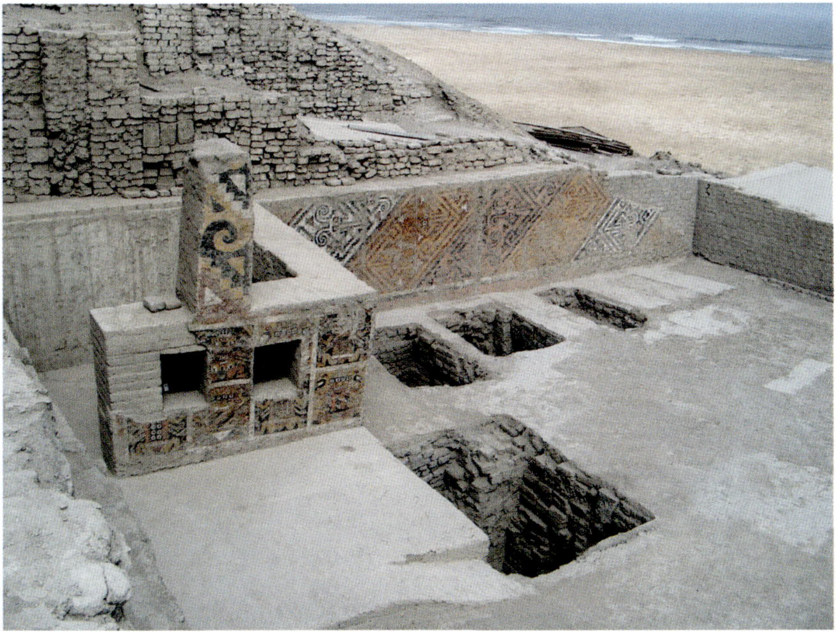

43 Huaca Cao Viejo, Peru

scientific research on organic remains, including human bodies, plant fibers, and animal tissues, that give a fuller sense of the material and symbolic world of the Moche. The subsequent case studies home in on important rulers and the products of their artists, who were some of the most accomplished makers in the ancient world.

When the team excavating at Huaca Cao Viejo, in the Chicama River Valley, began to peel back the melted mud-brick deposits from the side of the pyramid, they encountered a familiar scene like the one discovered at Huaca de la Luna. As if almost a smaller-
43 scale version of the great architecture to the south, the friezes at Huaca Cao Viejo repeated some of the same themes as had been seen at Huaca de la Luna. Diagonal bands in complementary colors contained similar stylized creatures. Images of new characters that may be deities were framed by Andean condors, guarding an interior room that may have admitted only a chosen few. Standing out in high relief on the exterior of the temple are repeated images of captives, bound by ropes and seemingly in eternal procession. These could be vanquished enemies from rival royal courts, captured in a battle or a raid; the taking of captives and its memorialization increased during this time. In perhaps a gruesome nod to the actual living captives, femurs were inserted

perpendicularly into the walls and covered with adobe before being painted to give depth and dimension to the sculpted facade. The human remains of conquests literally built up the stage for celebrating the prowess of their captors, underscoring the threat of violence as a part of rulership.

Archaeologists soon uncovered spectacularly preserved ritual spaces on the interior, also painted with geometric abstract designs. Near these spaces, giant shaft chambers in the pyramid's floor were originally cut out to serve as the final resting place for a very important leader of the polity at Cao. Careful excavation combined with comparative analysis of other elite tombs and narrative burial scenes on painted ceramics identified the primary tomb of a ruler and tombs of other important individuals. Accompanied by rich offerings and a sacrificed male attendant, as was the custom for peer rulers at other places, the ruler of the polity centered at Cao was carefully wrapped in a large funerary bundle with a possible sacrificed retainer and hundreds of luxury objects. This included war clubs, spear throwers with darts, and other objects typically depicted with male rulers on painted pottery. The tomb's primary occupant, however, was a twentysomething woman.

The Señora de Cao, as she became known, lay at the center of the bundle, so well preserved that the queen's braids were intact and her tattooed skin was visible. Archaeologists revealed her extraordinary riches as they carefully unwrapped the bundle. As an example of her control over resources and her patronage
44 of Moche artists, the Señora de Cao had at least forty-four nose ornaments made: delicate, bimetallic creations of gold and silver that depicted marine and mythological beings. Distinct from others known in the corpus of Moche art, the nose ornaments, possibly inherited or traded, were undeniably and inextricably linked to her and not bequeathed to her successor. Silver and gold symbolized the duality between the sun and the moon and male and female, and Moche metalworkers were experts at combining the two and treating the surface to emphasize this contrast. They divided the compositions in inventive ways: bilaterally mirrored, vertically repetitive, concentrically squared, or even diagonally opposite. Some ornaments emphasized specific marine creatures, such as shrimp, in silver, while crabs and other serpent-like creatures shone in gold. The pyramid overlooked the Pacific Ocean, so the ruler there coopted its life forces to project authority to her subjects.

The preservation in her tomb was notable, and evidence suggests she died in complications from childbirth or shortly thereafter, around 500 CE. A ceramic vessel that accompanied the burial depicted a female healer with a mother and female

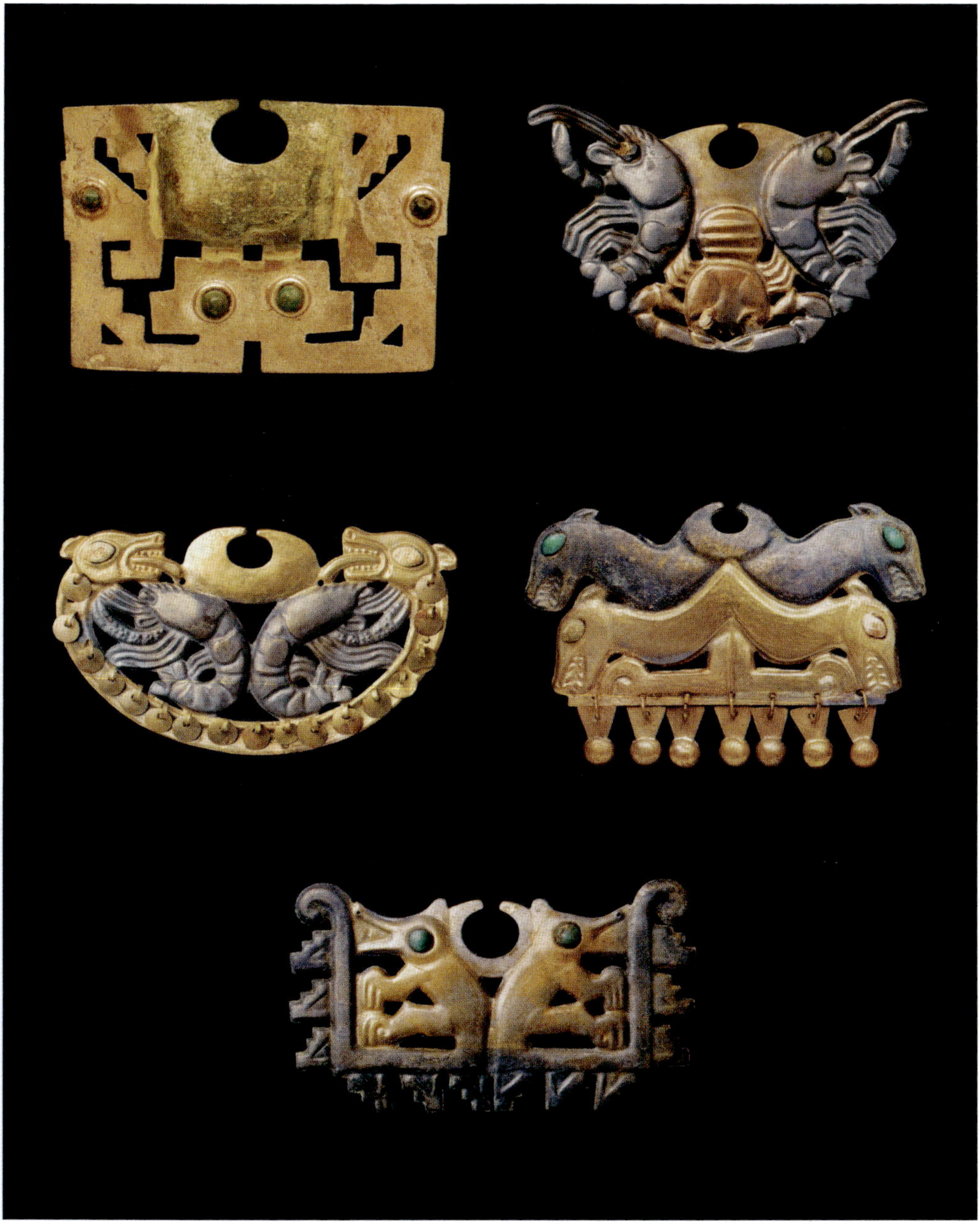

44 Bimetallic Nose Ornaments, c. 500

child, perhaps alluding to the events leading up to her untimely demise. One of the garments buried in the nearby tomb of a
45 male occupant depicted a humanlike figure composed of textiles and gilded copper ornaments, which has aided interpretations of similar assemblages that are not as well preserved or have been decontextualized in museum collections. The stylized face depicted on this garment has inlaid eyes and an aggressive, mid-grimace fanged mouth. The raised clenched fists and splayed feet give the impression that the figure is jumping at the beholder, so perhaps this composite garment played an imposing role in the martial regalia of the Señora de Cao's close associates.

A slightly later ruler in the Lambayeque Valley farther to the north was interred in perhaps the richest unlooted tomb in the Americas, excavated at the site of Sipán. Now known as the Lord of Sipán, the male occupant of the tomb, at the age of 35–45 between about 640 and 680 CE, was laid out with luxury objects made of gold, turquoise, shell, copper, textiles, and ceramics, along with several sacrificed humans and animals. The regalia found within the tomb, including earspools, headdresses, belt rattles, and shell collars, confirmed to archaeologists that the elaborate characters populating scenes of Moche art, such as painted vessels described below, may have been depictions of actual historical characters embodying divine beings and playing out ritual roles. Alternatively, the rulers could have coopted the personas of the mythical beings, becoming avatars of them in ceremonies. The sacrificed attendants, including two adult males, three younger women, and an adolescent, may have been family members of the deceased.

46 One impressive ear ornament exemplifies the high caliber of artistic talent at the court of Sipán. The earspool, one of two expertly pieced together from hammered gold and turquoise mosaic, depicts a reduced-scale warrior in three dimensions, flanked by two smaller attendants in profile. The earspool's warrior wears regalia that mirrors the full-sized set interred with its wearer: a crescent-shaped headdress and nose ornament, earspools, collars, belt rattles, and a war club. The attendants wear battle regalia composed of tiny tesserae of turquoise set into a wood backing; in fact, two adult males buried with
107 the Lord of Sipán might be the ones depicted here. The use of precious stones to create mosaic designs is a Moche innovation that builds on previous inlay techniques. In a great feat of metalworking, the tiny owl-head necklace worn by the warrior is strung with two gold wires through near microscopic holes in each tiny bead. More than a dozen tombs have been excavated at Sipán, and the intergenerational wealth deposited there

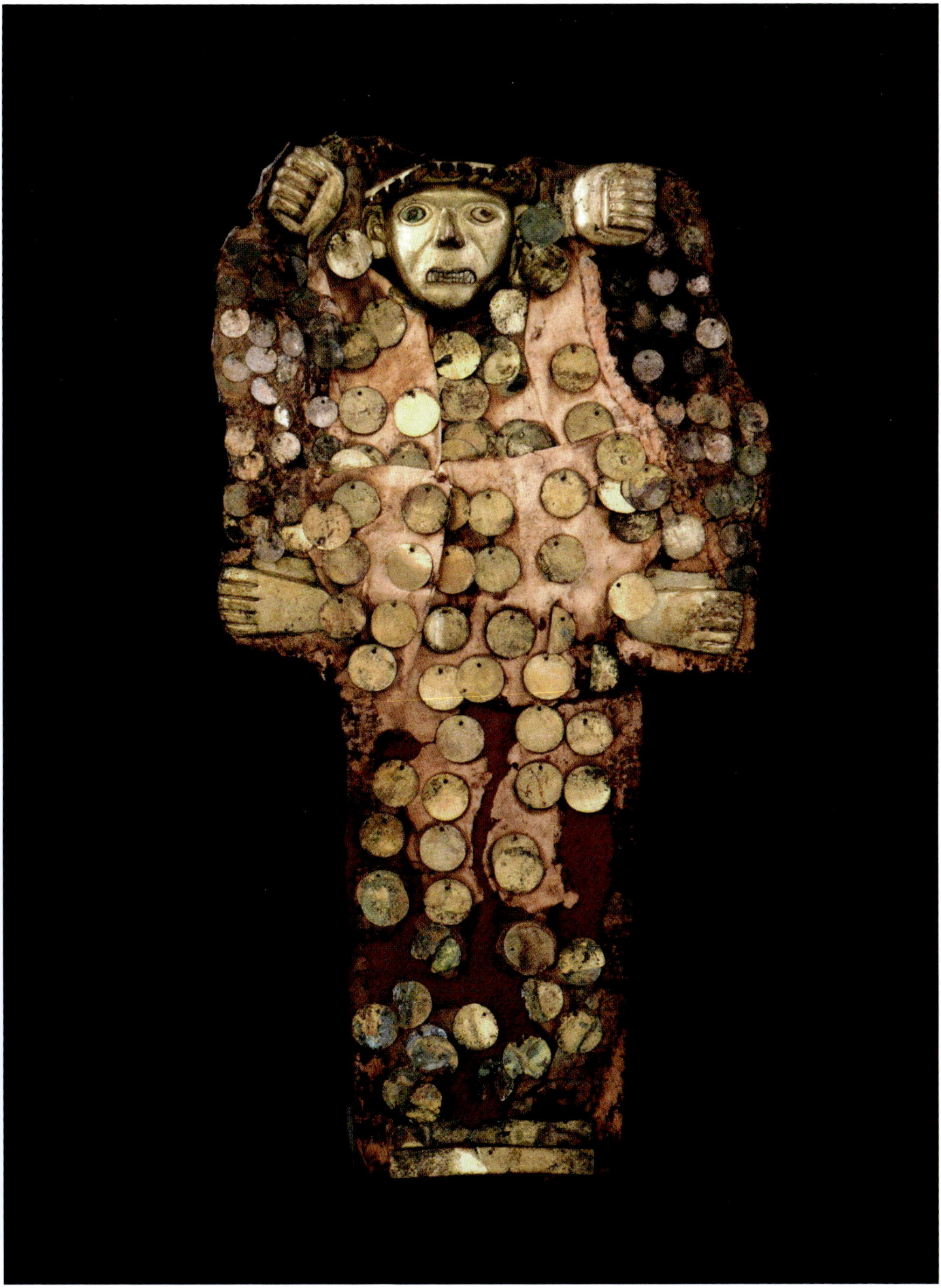

45 Ritual Garment, c. 500

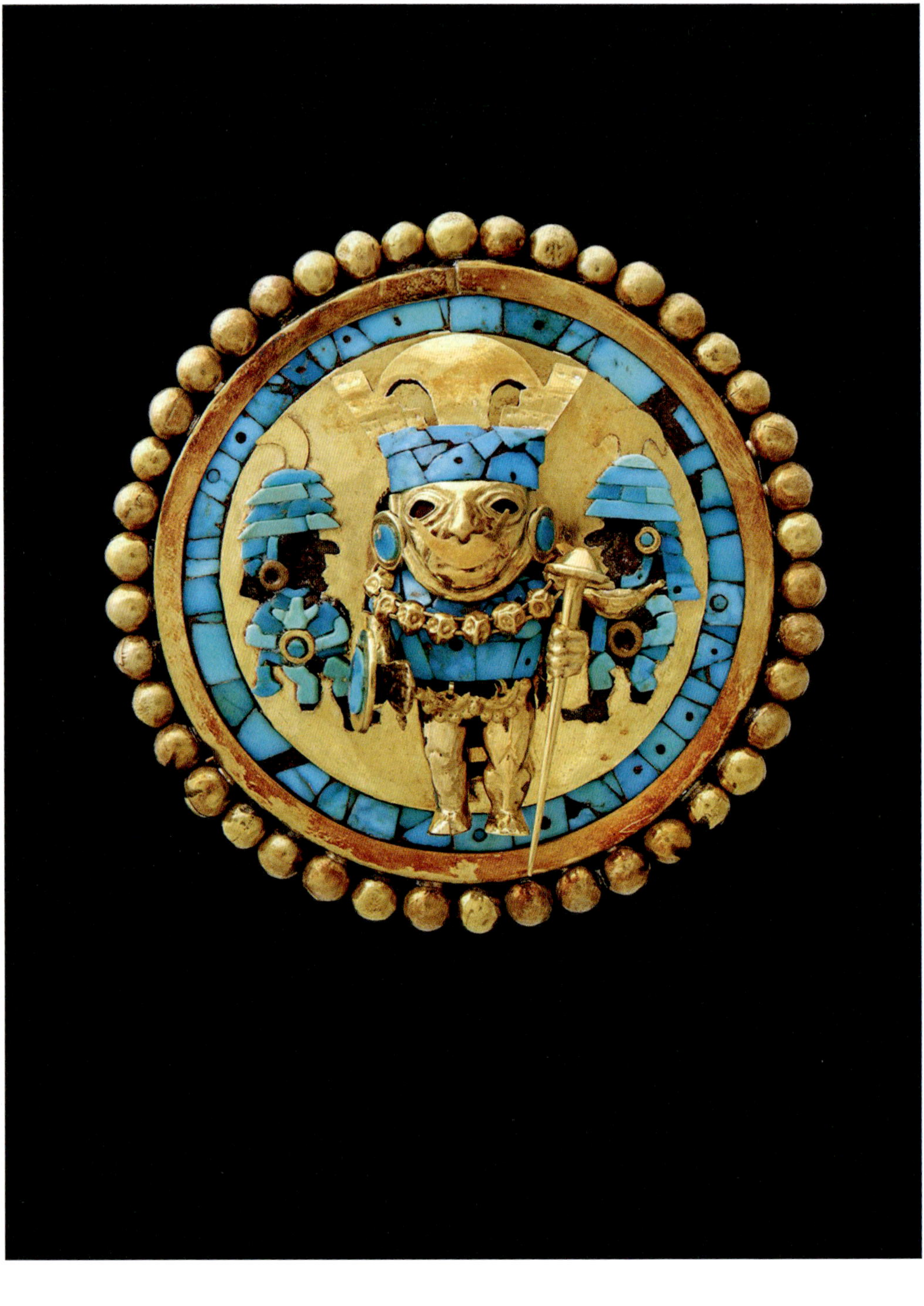

46 Ear Ornament, 640–680

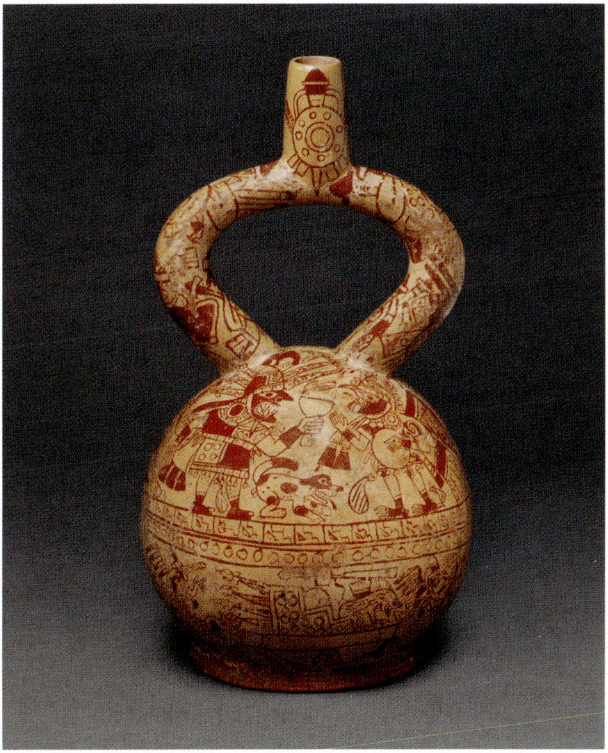

47 Stirrup-spout Bottle, 500–700

illustrates the political power that these Moche rulers wielded, both in access to imported resources and in the artists serving the competing royal courts.

Moche potters and ceramic painters also achieved a high level of sophistication throughout the north coast in both rendering elaborate painted scenes and naturalistic modeling in three dimensions. They also pioneered the large-scale use of molds to replicate iconographic styles. In a style known as fine-line painting, characterized by cream-colored stirrup-spout bottles painted with red, brown, or black slip, Moche painters
21 excelled at fusing the real and the mythical. The stirrup-spout form is a descendant of Chavín pottery. Narrative scenes
47 abound, including one known to specialists as the Sacrifice Ceremony. The globular body of the bottle, divided into two registers, contains the main scene, and the spout-handle contains further imagery. Four main characters address each other in the upper register with a spotted dog between them: a richly adorned warrior-like figure holds a goblet up to another individual dressed like an owl and holding a shield. Behind

the bird figure are two other individuals wearing similar regalia and participating in the scene. Below this interaction is a litter, framed on the reverse of the bottle by a scene of sacrifice in which two warriors collect the blood of two bound captives.

Prior to the excavations at places like Sipán and Huaca Cao Viejo, scholars interpreted such scenes on unprovenanced vessels, without secure find spots, as primarily supernatural in content. After comparing the rich attire of the painted characters with the actual regalia recovered in royal tombs, scholars now agree that the ceremonies represented in paintings might rather be seen as real events with humans impersonating specific divine roles. In the absence of written texts, it is difficult to interpret the nature of reciprocity represented in the spilling and consumption of human blood, as represented on the vessel above. The contents of the royal tombs of the Moche, which included multiple weapons such as clubs, blades, and spearthrowers, do suggest that violence and sacrifice—or at least the rhetoric and depictions of such acts—formed a foundational part of rulership in the region.

Potters in the workshops headquartered at the royal courts
48, 49 of Moche kings and queens also excelled at naturalistic portrait

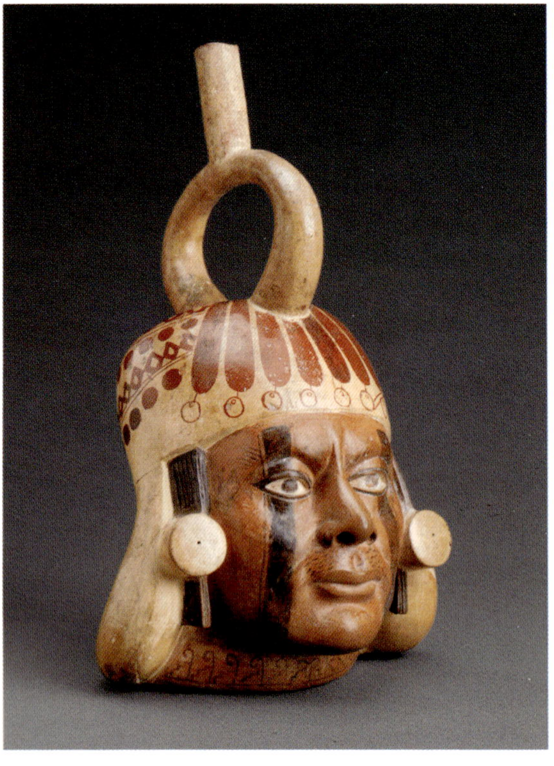

48 Stirrup-spout Bottle, 400–650

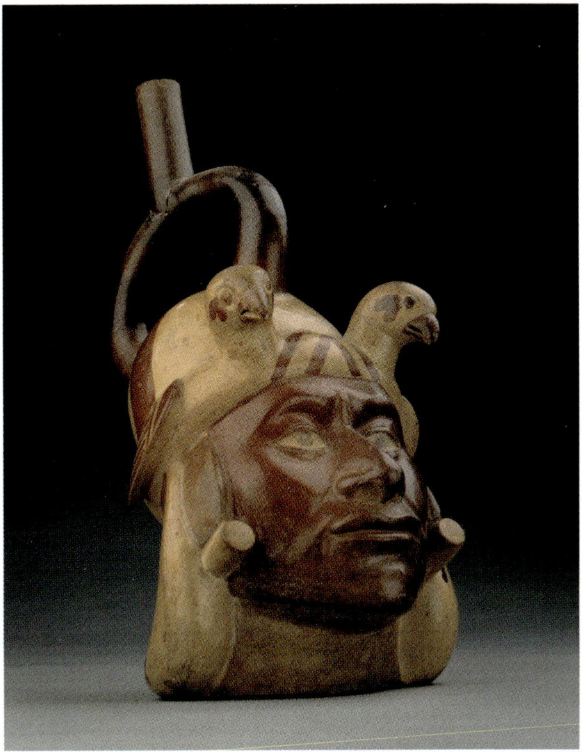

49 Stirrup-spout Bottle, 400–650

vessels, which seem to reference specific human individuals rather than idealized characters. These two stirrup-spout examples illustrate the range of forms, colors, and surface treatment of portrait vessels. One example shows a male with large black vertical stripes painted over each eye, large ear ornaments, and a headdress with geometric designs and representations of what were likely metal danglers. The painter also indicated a stubbly mustache, possibly giving a clue to the unique identity of the subject. The other example depicts a robust individual wearing ear cylinders and a headdress composed of two birds. Portrait vessels were deposited in tombs of the highest-status Moche individuals, and they were even depicted in painted scenes of courtly interaction. They sometimes even form the heads of animals. The precise meaning of the vessels is elusive; they could be portraits of important captives, disembodied heads of vanquished enemies, or the faces of important ancestors or mythic heroes.

The naturalism of Moche potters extended to a class of
50 vessels that is unique in the Americas, known as erotic pottery.

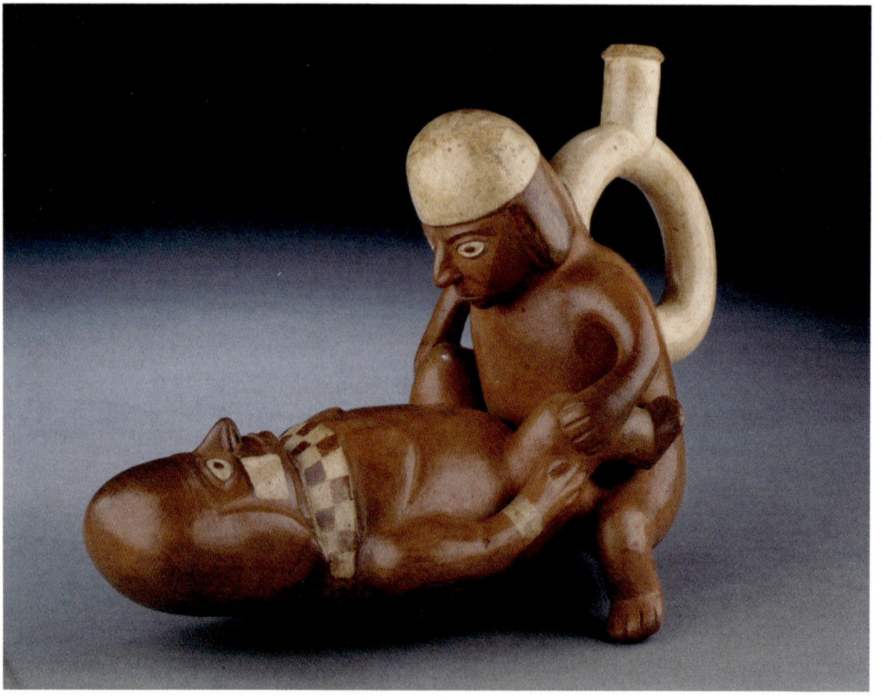

50 Stirrup-spout Bottle, 200–600

In general, artists of the ancient Americas did not depict human sex acts, or even sexualized bodies or interactions, in significant quantities. This is why the hundreds of Moche pots that show disembodied genitalia, or humans and supernaturals engaging in both procreative and non-procreative sex acts, stand out. The example here depicts two individuals with somewhat stoic expressions engaged in what might be described as coitus in the missionary position, with the figure being penetrated larger and more ornamented than its counterpart. Other examples show characters with enlarged genitalia or sexually explicit narrative scenes with multiple individuals. The potter here emphasized the collar and face paint of the supine individual and the headdress of the upright person in the reddish-brown and cream palette. There is a high degree of imagination with some vessels depicting groups of non-humans in erotic scenes, such as those with skeletons, which are by nature fleshless beings, though depicted with penises as if having an influence over fertility. These curious objects capture the different ways that Moche peoples imagined sex acts. To them, these modeled vignettes might not even have been erotic images at all in the contemporary sense, but rather, something more spiritual altogether.

In addition to painting pottery, new excavations have brought to light exciting discoveries in the world of Moche mural painting. In the Ancash region of Peru, considerably further south from the Moche Valley, archaeologists have uncovered
51 a series of paintings from about 550 to 800 CE at the complex known as Pañamarca. The artists there shared certain themes with neighboring peers, such as the Sacrifice Ceremony and a focus on female rulership, but experimented with new images like the example of double-faced individuals carrying ritual implements in this detail. The upper individual wears a plumed headdress and elaborate tunic with belt assemblage and holds up a bundle of feathers or textiles in one hand and what appears to be a ritual object composed of gold and silver in the other. The object depicts four birds, perhaps hummingbirds, diving or drinking from a flower. The individual in the lower register wears a different set of regalia and also holds similar objects while processing in the same direction as the upper character. In 2024 archaeologists uncovered more murals lining a throne room, interpreted to be for a powerful queen based on the multiple depictions of royal women. The location of the site on the southern boundary of the Moche culture area may indicate that the artistic program was meant to reach the multicultural audience of peoples interacting in this rich coastal setting. These scenes may be memorializing performances that occurred there, just as the fine-line paintings did for the neighboring kingdoms to the north.

Moche archaeology and art history have now become major fields of inquiry in the ancient Americas and many questions remain to be answered. Further investigation can address the origins of the unique visual culture, which builds on precedents in Chavín and Cupisnique objects, as well as the development of artisanal skill in working with new materials such as copper. Moche artists also give agency to non-human beings—even humanmade objects or vegetables. What are the implications for Moche thoughts on the nature of things and personhood for the global history of art? Further readings of this crucial body of material can provide new perspectives on ancient politics in the Americas and beyond.

Sicán/Lambayeque

The political systems that united Moche courts throughout the coast of Peru transformed around the ninth century. New royal courts known as Sicán or Lambayeque culture sprouted up not far from the Moche heartlands around modern-day Chiclayo,

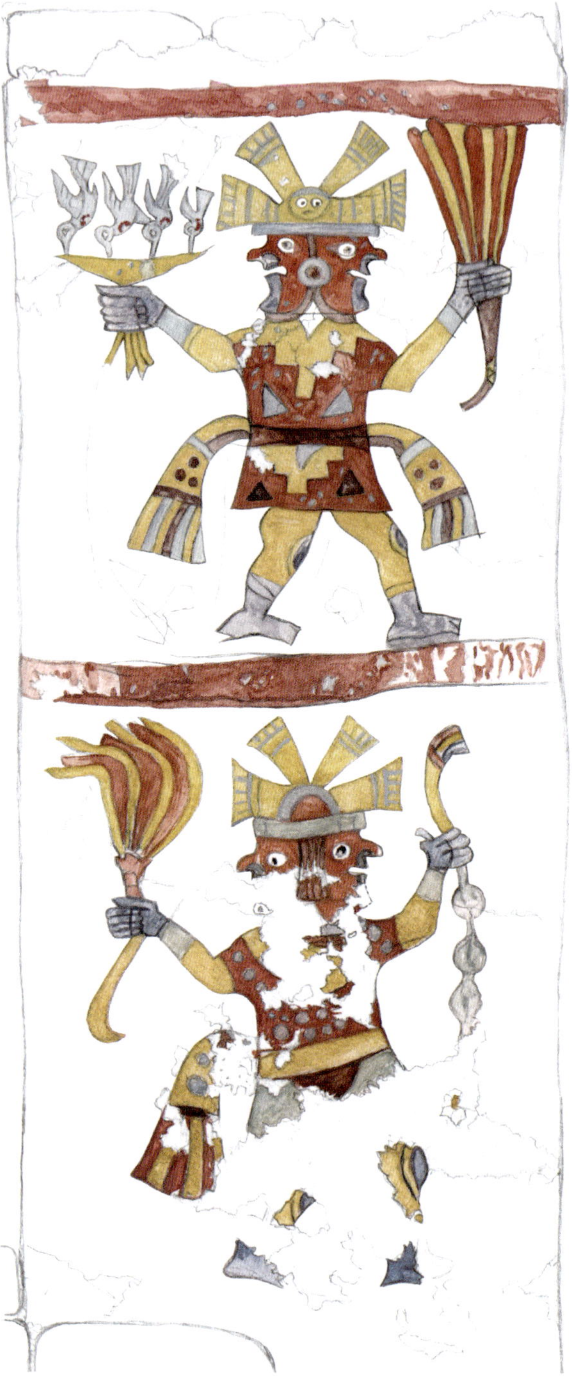

51 Pedro Neciosup Gómez, Illustration of Mural

Peru, and this shift in settlement and governance is reflected in the new art styles. New works seem to have emphasized stylized supernatural beings over the naturalistic and narrative representation created by previous communities of practice. The quantity of funerary goods, including mold-made ceramics in large numbers, seemed to reign over quality as artists focused on repeated, simpler depictions of supernatural beings rather than intricate renderings of human rulers. Ceramic artists used firing techniques to produce brown or black wares that borrowed from Moche forms and subjects but are markedly distinct in their simplicity and repetitiveness. Monumental scale of mud-brick buildings continued to be a priority, and
52 many of these later pyramids, now having a melted appearance due to centuries of the rare coastal rains that appear during El Niño, still tower over the north coastal landscape.

The accumulation of wealth in the form of gold and other metals, shell, textiles, and feathers reached new heights during this period. Stacks of gold and copper vessels accompanied rulers in their tombs, as if to prepare them to host an ostentatious feast in the afterlife. Descendants also buried rulers
53 with multiple sets of regalia, such as larger-than-life masks portraying the stylized Sicán deity. This example, composed of hammered gold alloy sheet and adorned with silvered copper plaques, cinnabar paint, and gold danglers, eventually wrapped in textiles, epitomizes the regimes of value of different luxury materials for Sicán or Lambayeque kings or queens. In fact, another mask excavated from a queen's tomb at the site of Chornancap was composed of silver instead of gold, connecting the female ruler to the material symbolizing the moon.

The metalworker of the gold mask created a symmetrical composition with squared ears terminating in earspools, a large nose that projects outward almost naturalistically, and teardrop-shaped eyes with hemispherical pupils. From the pupils emerge needle-like projections, which may be the artists' expression of the deity's omnipotent vision or supernatural surveillance. The twenty dangling plaques would have been activated in motion, creating a shimmering effect with musical rhythm when worn in life or processed in funerary rites. The face paint and ornaments worn by the deity here also speak to the regalia worn by human rulers. The mask would have been part of the rich funerary assemblage in the tomb of its owner; impressions of the textile that once wrapped this mask remain in the surface of the paint.

Ceremonial knives, known later as *tumi* in Quechua, were also very important to Sicán/Lambayeque kings and queens. Artists created luxury versions of crescent-shaped blades out of gold and silver, and they are often depicted in use for decapitation. Many

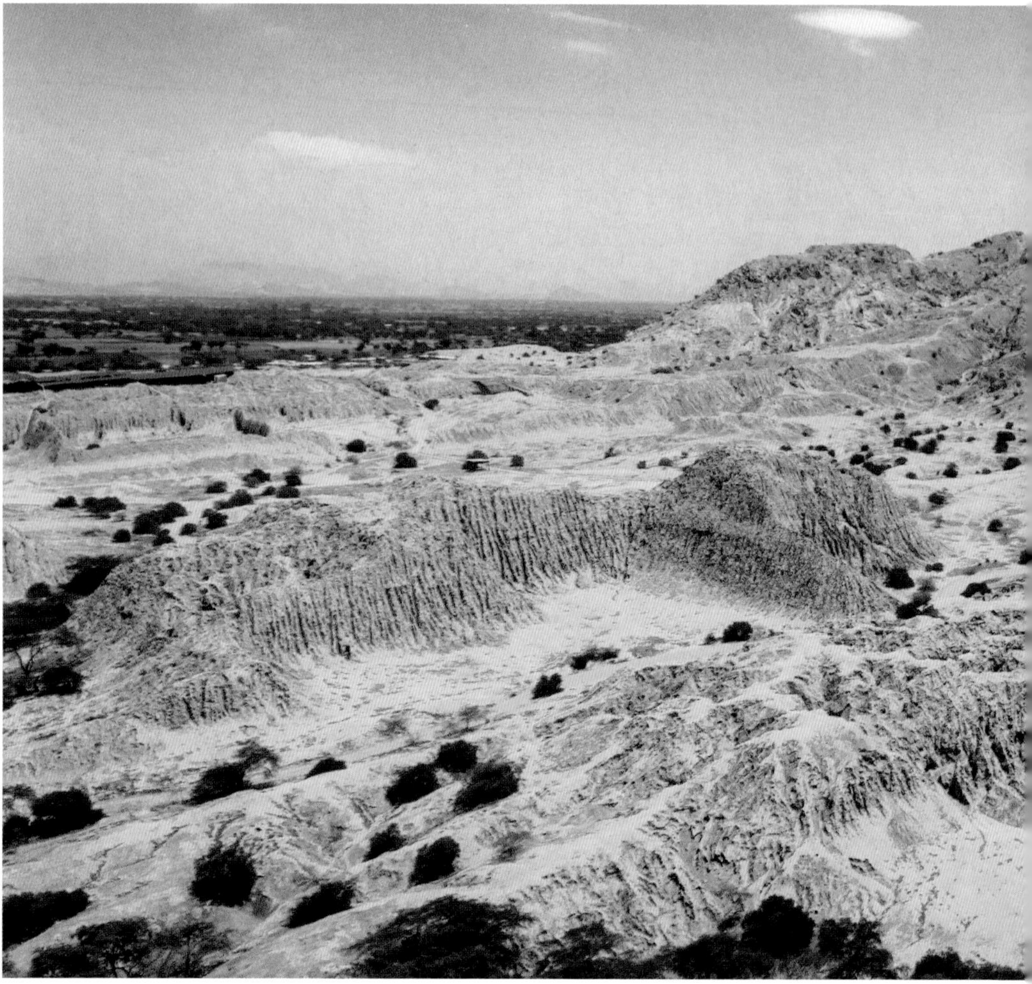

52 Túcume, Peru

54 recovered *tumi* knives feature the same deity depicted on masks on their handles. The lower part of the blade is composed of a rectangular shoulder and a semicircular cutting edge, although the malleability of the gold would probably not have allowed this *tumi* to be used for anything but a scepter. The handle of the blade takes the form of a standing deity figure wearing a large crescent-shaped headdress, similar to the large-scale ones that adorned Moche rulers in the past. The goldworker emphasized the head of the individual, who shares the same characteristics of the deity portrayed in the mask above. Turquoise inlays

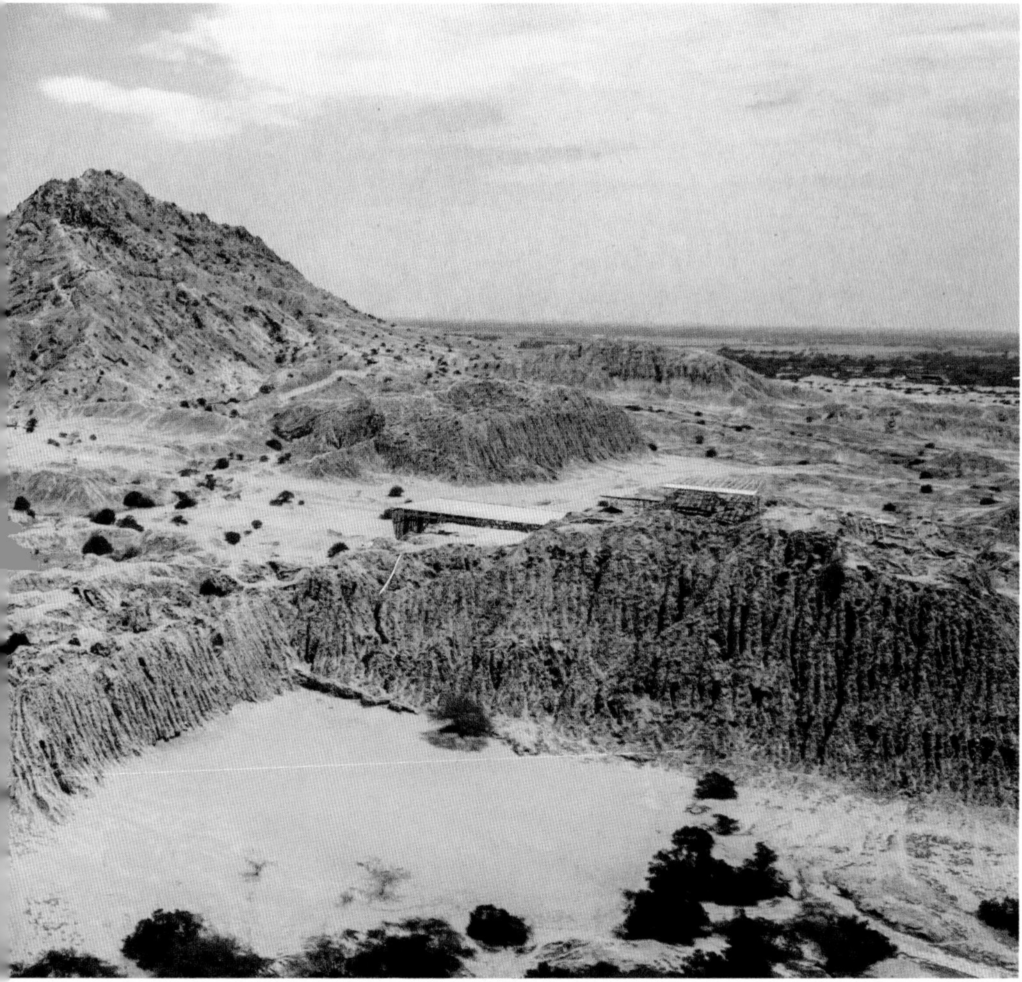

emphasize the ear spools as well as the visor or cap element of the crested headdress, which fans out with zigzag and spiraled openwork designs. The deity wears a tunic or tabard, and winglike elements protrude from behind his arms, which are bent so the hands are touching the torso. This beautiful knife captures both the divinity that rulers were claiming as well as the sacrificial rites needed to maintain order through reciprocal offerings.

After about the twelfth century, the political power of the Sicán lords eventually waned, and powerful rulers in the Moche

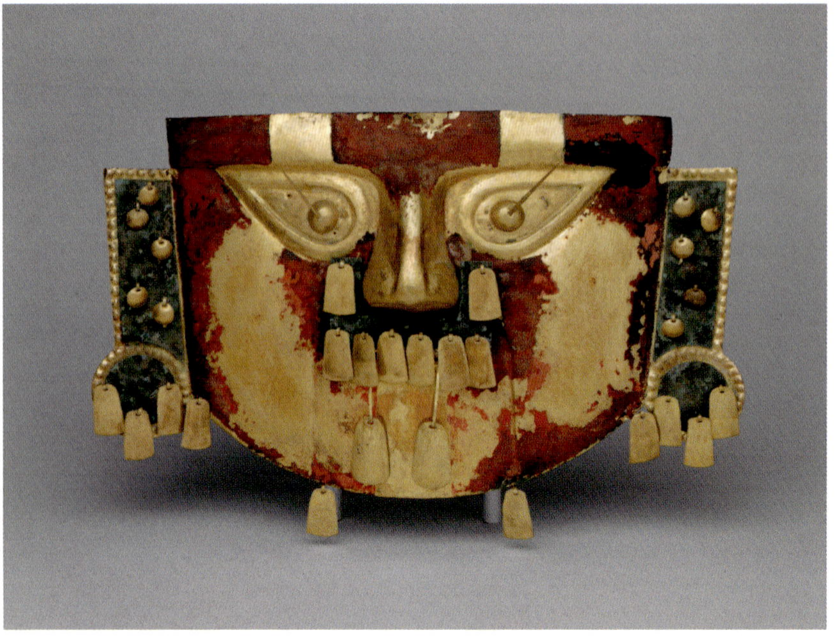

53 Funerary Mask, 900–1100

Valley to the south consolidated control at the imperial mega-palace compound of Chan Chan near what is now Trujillo, to be discussed in chapter 9. Although subsequent artists shaped some of the same materials as the Moche and Sicán/Lambayeque artists, and continued to use some of the religious symbolism, the traditions described in this chapter stand out as some of the most exciting artistic innovations of the ancient Americas, and, indeed, the global past. These innovators of mud-brick monumentality and masterful metalwork brought deities to life through representations and regalia used by their patrons in ceremonies of divine embodiment. This region also draws into sharp focus the presence of powerful female rulers as a defining aspect of politics in the Americas, such as those known from the contemporaries to the Moche kings and queens, the Maya.

54 *Tumi* (Knife), 900–1100

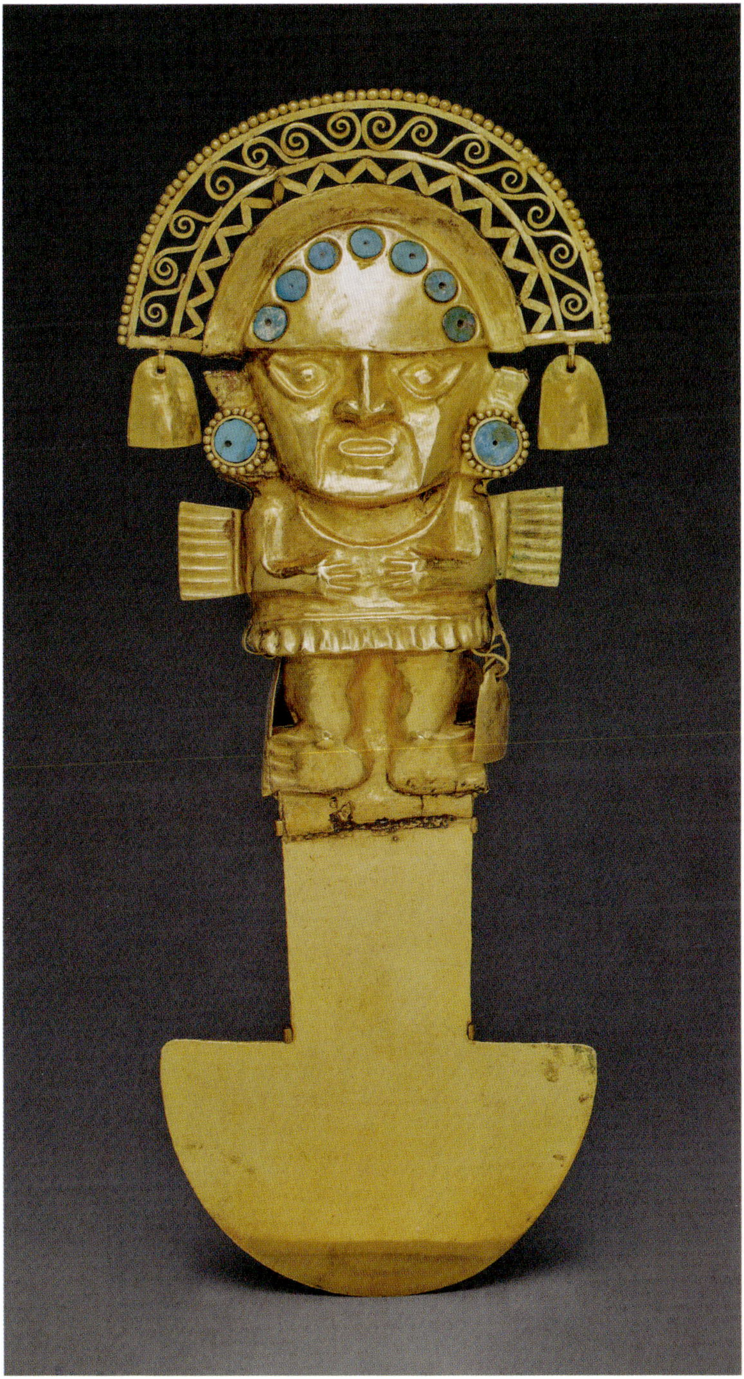

Chapter 4
Mountain Pyramids: The Ancestral Maya (100 BCE–1300 CE)

In the first millennium BCE, peoples in the region of the
Yucatán Peninsula who spoke related Mayan languages
began to create communities centered on large plazas and
monumental buildings. These gathering spaces became the
stages for elaborate ceremonies and the seats of political
power for elite families who yielded dynastic rulers for many
centuries. These royal courts also produced some of the most
important sculptural and painterly workshops in the ancient
world. Only the ancient Maya have a deciphered script (though
progress is being made on later Nahuatl texts, see chapter 10),
so the names of individual artists who signed their names at
38, 39 certain times and certain places are now known. The corpus
of texts interpreted as historic records was associated with
a calendar recording both an absolute count of linear time
adopted from prior traditions and innovative cycles of years
and months. This allows an unparalleled level of detail to be
recovered about the lives of these artists and their patrons and
compared with other global moments in the first millennium.
Narrative art depicts the birth of gods from mountains; the
trials of the deities of sun, rain, and maize; and rich historical
scenes with self-proclaimed divine kings and queens.

The origins of Maya art lie deep within Mesoamerican
traditions, and certain elements of Olmec style appear in
55 early compositions, such as the murals dating to about 100
BCE or before discovered at the site of San Bartolo in northern
Guatemala. In this section of the North Wall, the composition
is divided into two different passages by a colorful and
exuberant depiction of an animate mountain. On the viewer's
left, a unique scene unfolds in which a double-chambered
gourd seems to explode. From a V-shaped cleft emerges an
infant wearing a headdress along with streams of blood.

Arranged around this central point, forming a quincunx of babies, are four other infants that have distinctive features. All show umbilical cords; the two babies on the left are solid red while on the right they are red-and-white striped. Observing this whole scene is a standing supernatural figure with a downturned mouth consistent with earlier deity depictions, wearing an elaborate headdress and feathered shoulder ornaments. The quincunx geometry; the winged deity depiction; and even the color scheme of reds, yellows, blacks, and whites are consistent with earlier Olmec mural paintings.

The other side of the North Wall mural, to the viewer's right, shows a procession of characters leading toward the central mountain, inside which are kneeling two figures bearing a basket of tamales and another gourd, either full of water or perhaps related to the enlarged gourd mentioned above. The mountain itself received the most detailed treatment, underscoring its primacy as a protagonist of the scene. It has an elliptical eye marked with a quincunx and its giant maw opens to the right, with a curvilinear stalactite tooth and red volutes emanating from its throat. The artist made sure to mark this as a wild place: animals and plants sprout from its upper surface and interact with each other. This contrasts with the planar and horizontal setting of the procession scene extending to the viewer's right.

Receiving the gifts of food coming from this mountain cave is the red-painted maize deity. He is followed by three women, two kneeling and stacked vertically, and one standing with elaborate regalia, perhaps the divine counterpart to the male deity. Two final figures are painted black and red and they carry bundles on their heads. The painters emphasized idealized proportions and sinuous lines of the bodies, a hallmark of early Maya painting and sculpture. All of this action takes place atop an enormous feathered serpent whose head faces skyward and whose body is marked with black footprints, a reference to travel or pilgrimage. The sophistication and mythological content of these murals hint at a very complex religious world in the late first millennium BCE and suggest that many more such iconic paintings lay undisturbed in other ancient ruins. The function of such murals may have been to commemorate a special occasion, such as the accession of a new ruler, or to serve as a venerated place of instruction on sacred themes for the elite families of San Bartolo. Similar imagery to these lowland paintings also occurred around the same time in the highlands of Guatemala and the Pacific coast of Chiapas, Mexico.

In the first centuries CE, architects and engineers created tangible mountains as funerary monuments and large plazas

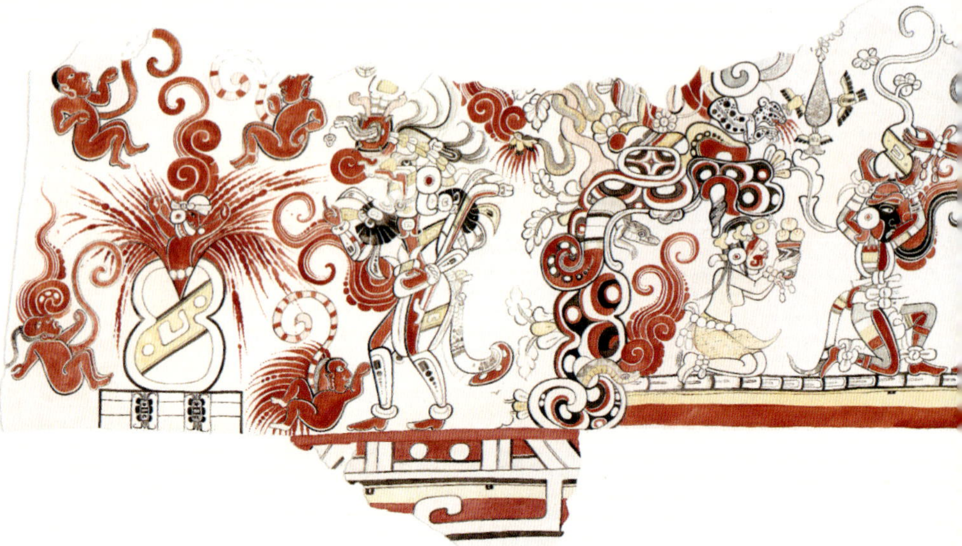

55 Heather Hurst, *North Wall Mural Illustration*

as stage sets for periodic ceremonies. The great plaza and large
56 pyramids at Tikal, Guatemala, are perhaps some of the most emblematic complexes of buildings in the Maya region, not least of which for its use as a setting in the film *Star Wars Episode IV: A New Hope* (1977). Builders created the two steep, stepped pyramids, known as Temple I and Temple II, in the late seventh or early eighth century to immortalize a royal couple at Tikal. Each pyramid is crowned with a series of rooms composed of cut and sculpted stone blocks that support a lofty roofcomb, a decorative vertical projection that extends the height of the building. The orientation of Maya buildings and plazas generally follows the cardinal directions and solar alignments, as builders infused these spaces and structures with celestial meaning. The open plaza space at Tikal is dotted with standing vertical monuments known as stelae and rounded monuments known as altars, which lie horizontally on the plaza floor. These stone works record portraits of rulers and hieroglyphic texts recounting historical events in the lives of the Tikal dynasty.

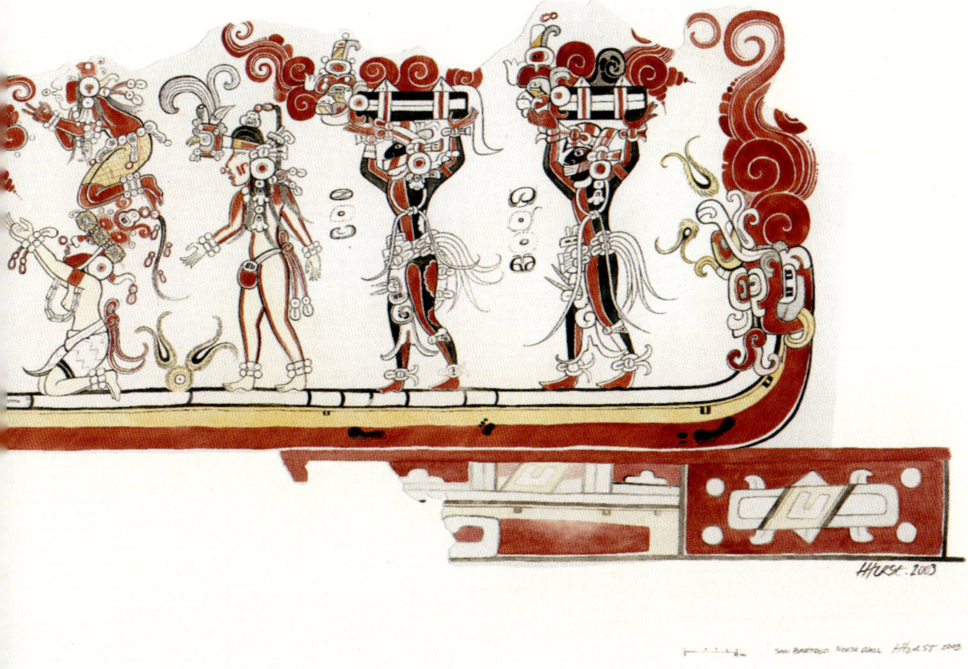

This is what distinguishes Maya art from other traditions: the rich historic information that the decipherment of the hieroglyphic script has brought to life. Beginning most likely with the bar-and-dot numeration and the graphic depiction of calendric time periods and astronomical cycles, Maya writing grew into a complex logosyllabic system. This means it was composed of both word signs (logograms) and signs that represented syllables (syllabograms), rather than an alphabet like English. For example, the word *witz*, which means "mountain" and also refers to a man-made pyramid, could be written with one sign for WITZ or spelled out with syllables *wi-tz(i)*. Buildings could have the faces of *witz* creatures built into their facades, marking them as primordial creation places, so that the rulers could place themselves at the center of cosmic narratives. Maya hieroglyphic writing changed over time, and variations between sites testify to the creativity bursting from different scribal communities in different kingdoms. The script, like most narrative scenes in Maya art, is read from left to right

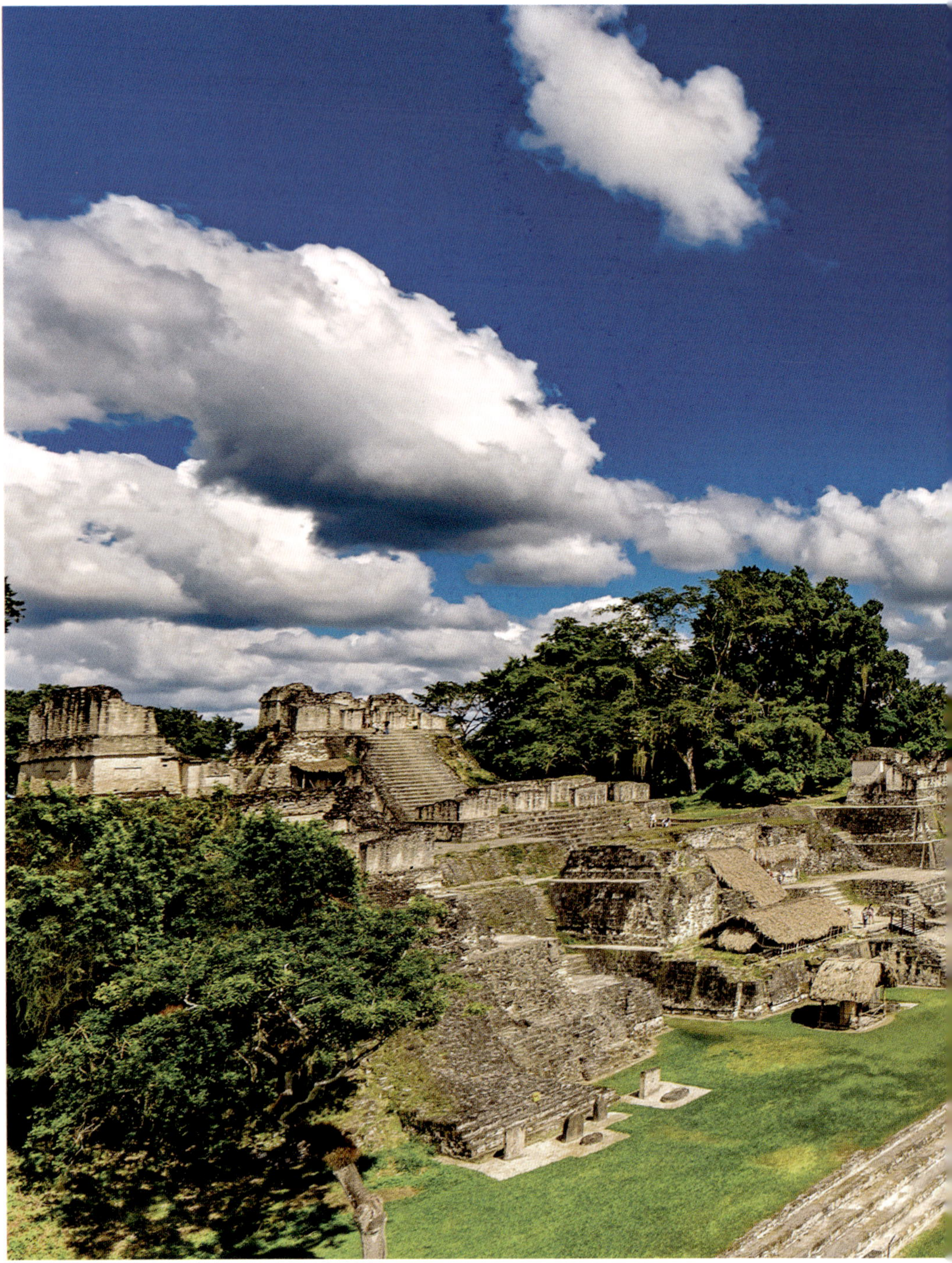

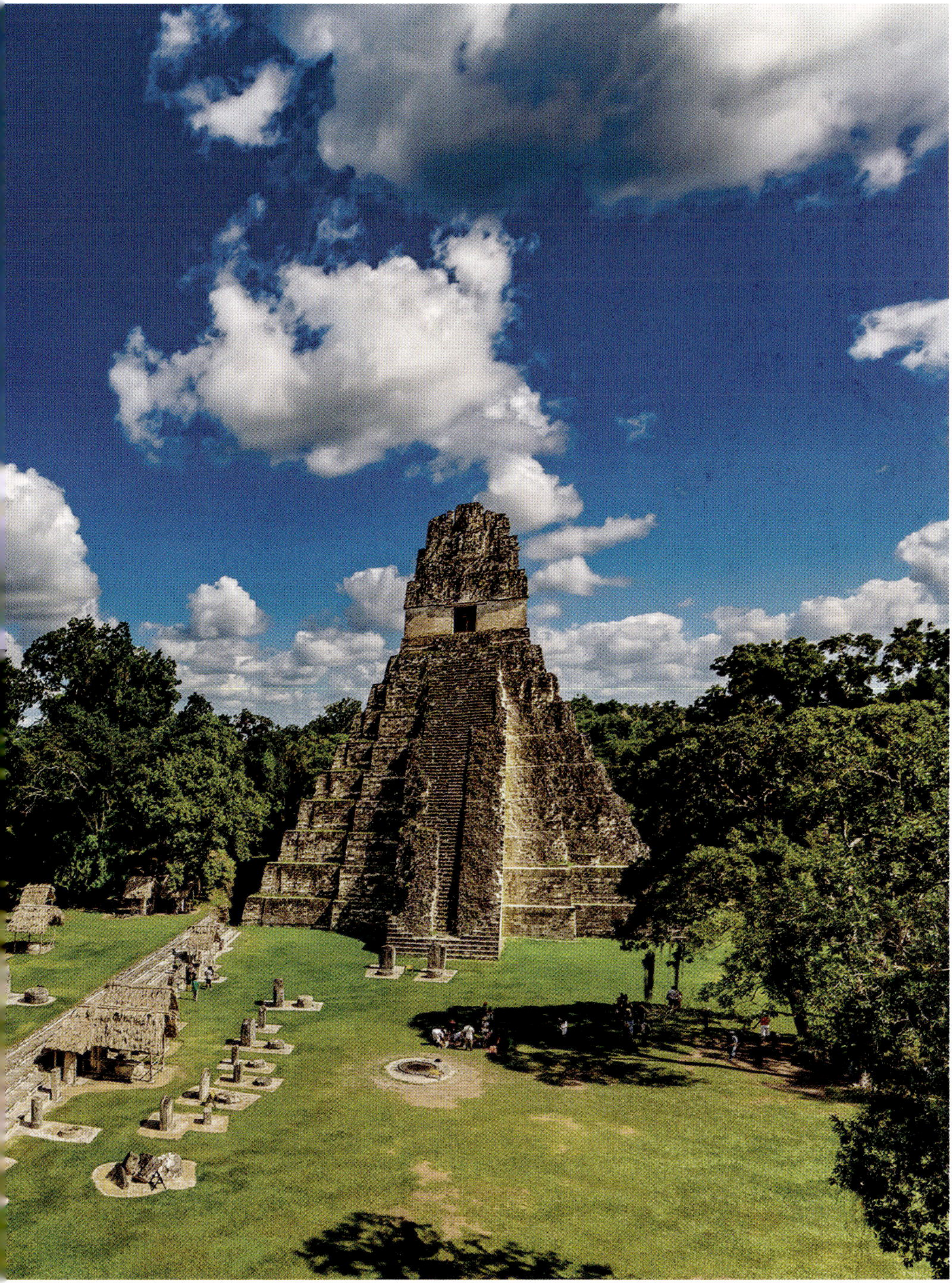

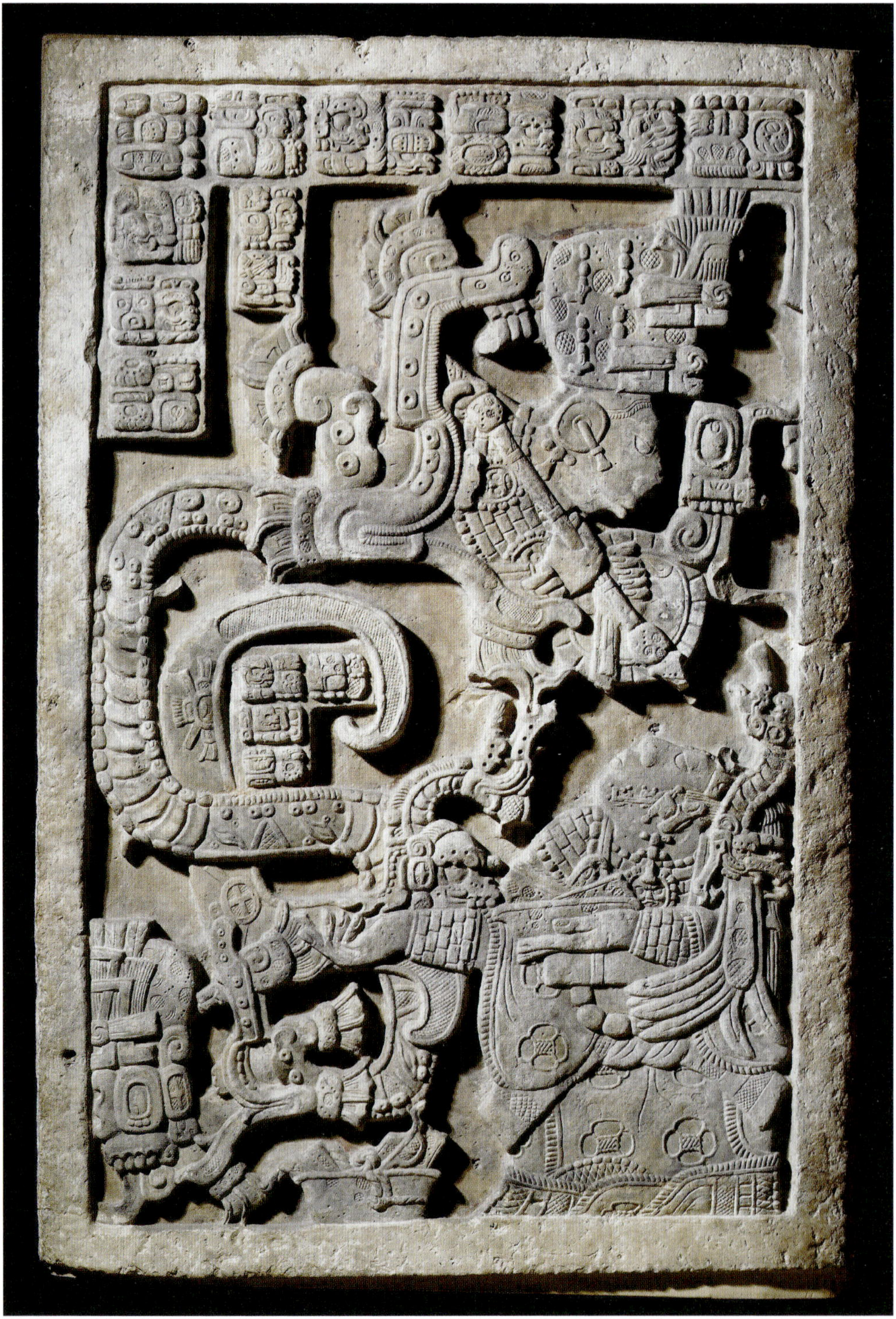

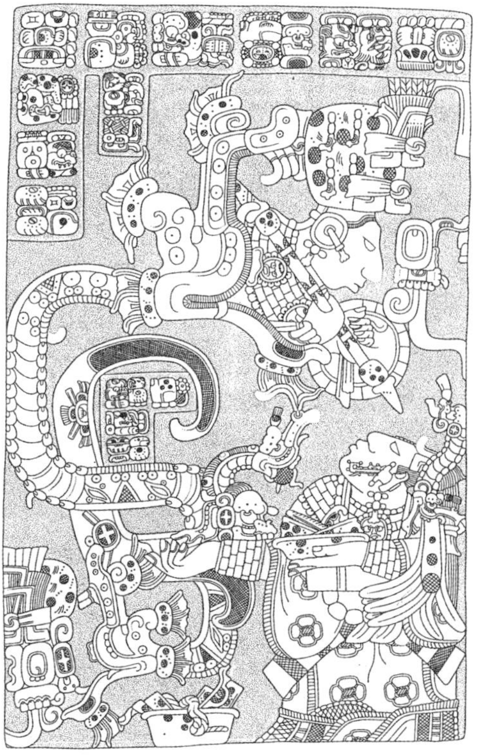

57 OPPOSITE Lintel (Yaxchilan Lintel 25), 723
58 RIGHT Ian Graham, Drawing of Yaxchilan Lintel 25, underside

and top to bottom, generally in paired columns or single-glyph rows or L-shapes.

57, 58 One monument dedicated in 723 CE from the site of Yaxchilan, located on the Mexican side of the border with Guatemala delineated by the Usumacinta River, captures the vitality of Maya art and writing. The complex image centers around the primary subject, a richly dressed woman in the lower right corner of the frame. She is kneeling as her elaborate embroidered gown drapes over her arms and legs. The fabric contains flowerlike motifs and fringed seams. She also wears two beaded arm cuffs and a wide beaded collar, presumably representing jade. She faces upward and her headdress extends downward over her shoulder. The headband is in the form of a double-headed serpent, one facing upward, and the downward-facing serpent opens its jaws to emit a splay of feathers. An elaborate ear ornament contains a spool and a beaded backing, also probably jade. She is one of the best known Maya queens, named Lady K'abal Xook (mid-seventh century–749 CE). Her portrait underscores the Maya sculptors' approach to realism characterized by a consistently stylized human form, the tension between real objects and imagined supernaturals depicted in the same frame, and the interdependence of subject and caption.

She holds up both hands in front of her. Her right hand seems relaxed as it reaches to the viewer's left holding a ceremonial headband similar to the one she's wearing, and the left hand tightly supports a flaring bowl in front of her chest. The bowl contains ritual implements, including strips of paper that are dotted with what has been interpreted as her own sacrificial blood. On a different lintel in the same building, she is shown drawing a thorn-studded cord through her tongue to produce blood, the royal substance. A similar bowl is placed in front of her on the ground, also filled with ritual implements and bloodied paper. The rest of the baroque carving would be difficult to interpret, if the scribe had not included hieroglyphic text framing the scene as well as an L-shaped glyphic passage in front of the queen. The text allows a closer reading of the scene.

In October of the year 681, Lady K'abal Xook, the wife of king Itzam Kokaaj Bahlam III (mid-seventh century–749 CE), summoned a patron deity, a locally revered god named Aj K'ahk' O'Chahk. Two glyphic metaphors are important to this statement. A hand grasping a fish is translated to *tzak*, summon, giving the deity slippery and shimmering qualities that make it similarly hard to capture. Specifically, she summoned the "flint [knife and] shield" of the deity, which is taken to mean military might symbolized by the paired weapons. She is also said to be impersonating (*ubaahil aan*) another lady, maybe an ancestor or deity, embodying this force as she summons the patron god. This layering of the contemporary, the historical, and the supernatural is a hallmark of Maya sculpture from what is known as the Classic period, defined by the use of monumental inscriptions between roughly 250–900 CE.

The virtuoso sculptor (or sculptors) chose to represent the act of summoning in conjunction with the king's accession in 681 CE as the emergence of a double-headed bony serpent, perhaps a reference to a centipede, hovering over the offering bowl in the center of the scene. From the lower jaw, in the lower left corner, comes a ceremonial mask that includes a round goggle-like element atop a skeletal maxilla, from which pours out volutes of fluid. From the upper, larger mouth of the serpent emerges the bust of a human figure, perhaps the husband of the protagonist, who wears the guise of the patron deity: the same goggle mask with skeletal jaw. The artists here, however, suggest that this is a human wearing a mask; it is represented in "X-ray" technique so the viewer can see the figure's entire profile. He holds a spear and a shield, a visual reference to the martial power. While

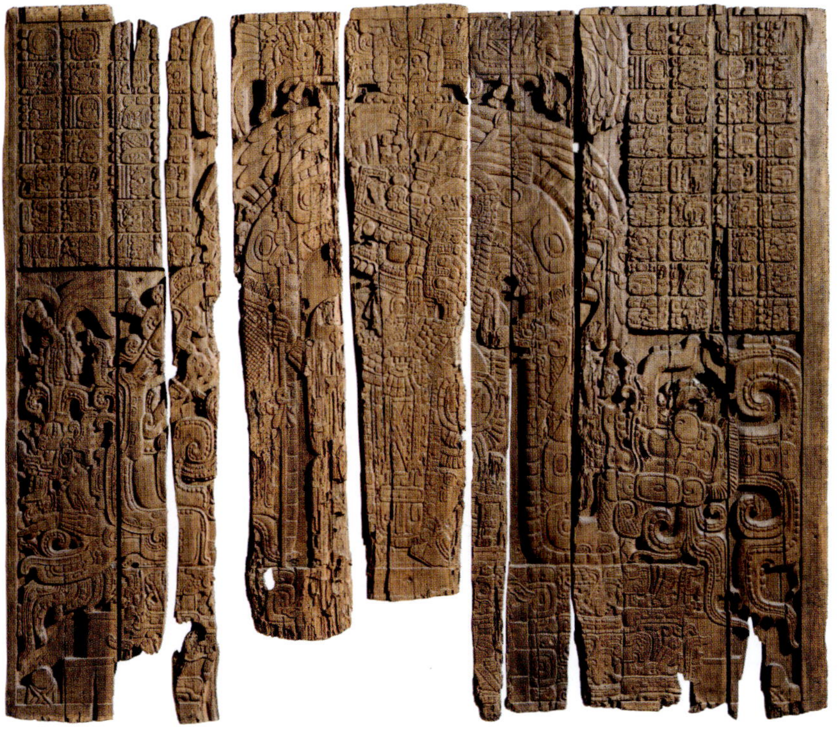

59 Lintel (Temple IV Lintel 3), 746–47

the king is said to summon this deity, Lady K'abal Xook is an important protagonist here, underscoring the important role of Maya women as rulers in their own right, and as wives, mothers, and grandmothers. The scene on a doorway lintel would have originally faced downward, greeting visitors with this imposing mythic-historical moment as they entered the inner sanctum.

59 A different doorway lintel from Tikal, this time carved out of the hard wood of the chicozapote tree (*Manilkara zapota*), shows a similarly complex scene starring a victorious lord atop his vanquished enemy's captured palanquin. The event depicted took place in the mid-eighth century after the ruler of Tikal, known as Yik'in Chan K'awiil (late seventh century–after 746 CE), defeated his rival of the royal court of El Perú-Wak'a, located to the west of Tikal in Guatemala, in a decisive battle described in the text. The ruler, embodying a deity, sits atop a throne on the palanquin in the center of the lintel. The sculptors show him confidently armed with a spear and shield at the center of the busy image. The lower right and left corners show the lashed poles of the vehicle, suggesting that this patron

deity object may have been physically borne to Tikal, where the artists presumably saw this reenactment after the battle victory. Arching over the king is the feathered serpentlike patron deity of his defeated enemy, and this act of procession must have been interpreted by beholders as one of dominance and complete humiliation of the competing dynasty. The monument also speaks to the dexterity of Maya sculpting in wood, which only survives in very rare examples to this day because of the elements in the harsh tropical climate.

The dynasty based at Tikal at this time cultivated exceptional artistic talent. The ruler depicted on the wooden lintel was
60 also delicately rendered by a jade carver as a small-scale mosaic portrait on the lid of a cylindrical vessel, mirroring one that portrays his father. The Tikal jade worker here obtained fragments of the highest quality bright green jadeite. Then, dozens of square and trapezoidal plaques were shaped around a wooden vessel to create a cup with a sloped lid. Atop the lid, the jade carvers created a naturalistic depiction of Yik'in Chan K'awiil, including fleshy eyes, a prominent nose, and mouth slightly open, as if the shiny stone visage were in the midst of speaking. The king sports a layered hairstyle and ear ornaments with tiny dangling beads, suggesting that he might be in the guise of a maize deity. A large beaded necklace also adorned the neck of the jade effigy, just as one would have adorned the king himself. This small-scale embodiment of the ruler as a jade figure was recovered in what was likely his final resting place.

Jade as a material symbolized water, vegetation, and agricultural fertility in crystallized form to the ancient Maya. In the glyphs it is known as *yax tuun*, which is the blue-green and first or primordial (*yax*) stone (*tuun*). This deep-rooted value placed on the hard green mineral appears to have emerged in the Maya area roughly contemporaneously with peer societies such as Olmec La Venta (see chapter 2). Recent archaeological finds include Olmec-style jades recovered in early Maya tombs and dedicatory offerings, suggesting a rich early trade in jade from the Motagua River region in southern Guatemala near the border with Honduras. By the seventh and eighth centuries CE, the color of jadeite that was most prized was the bright apple-green color, sometimes known as imperial jade, which mimicked the verdant shades of emerging corn plants.

Jade and other greenstones were also used for the mosaic funerary masks of deceased rulers as they were envisioned
61 to undergo apotheosis into maize deities. Such masks made human flesh godly using incorruptible materials like polished stone, seen to be eternal. The elaborate tomb of K'inich Janaab

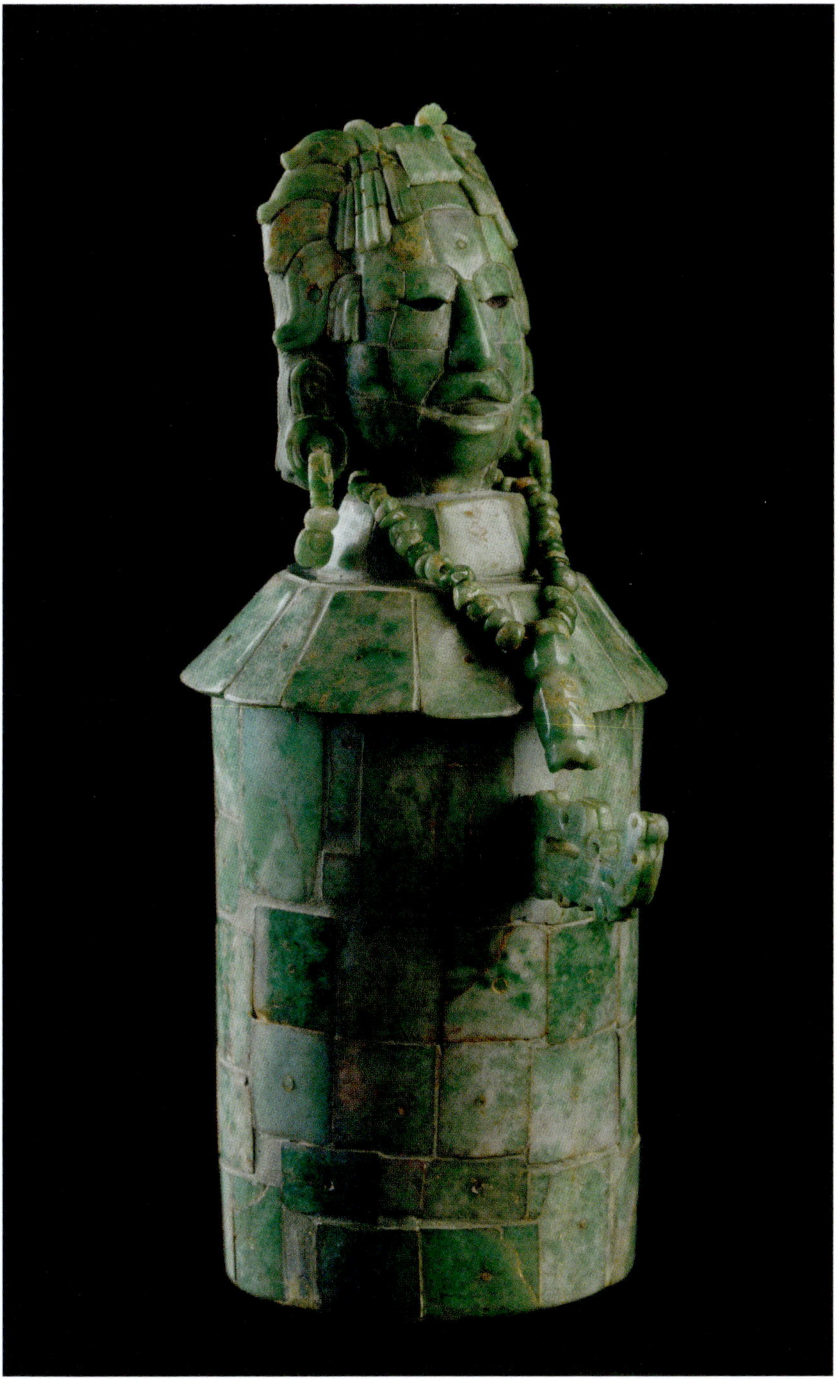

60 Mosaic Vessel, 700–50

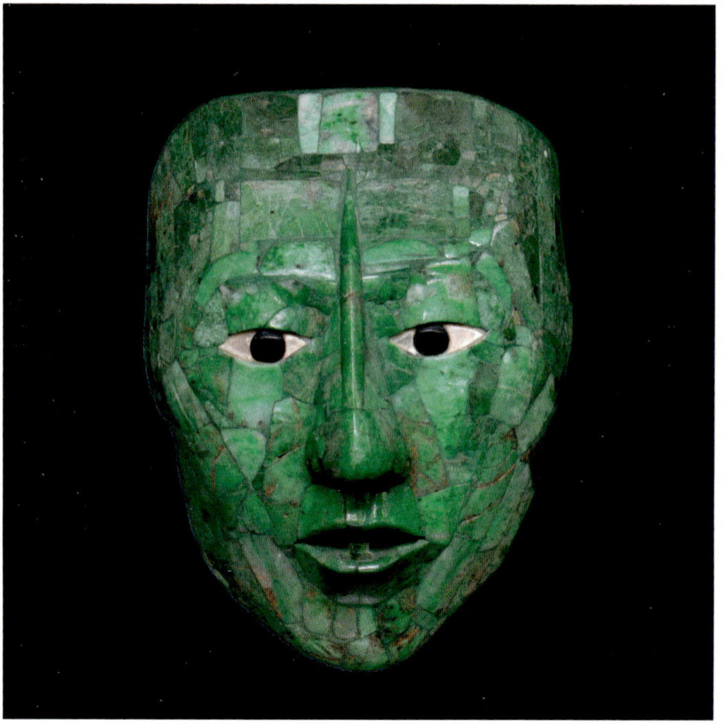

61 Mosaic Funerary Mask, 683

Pakal I (603–83 CE) at the site of Palenque, now in Chiapas, Mexico, is legendary for its complex deposits and rich artistic program, including the elaborate sarcophagus lid. It was discovered in 1952 at the bottom of a buried staircase inside the pyramid known as the Temple of the Inscriptions, so named for the extensive hieroglyphic wall panels in the main chamber detailing events in the life of Pakal, as he is known. The corbel-vaulted tomb chamber below contained a solid stone sarcophagus with the king's remains, covered with red cinnabar. The surface of the sarcophagus lid shows a youthful Pakal reborn from the jaws of a cenote, from which also grows a resplendent tree. The ancestors of Pakal are also depicted as emerging trees along the sides of the sarcophagus lid. Thus, from this mountain, the temple itself, the Palenque dynasty would be reborn after the patriarch was planted in his rich tomb, symbolic of a cave.

The mask itself is an impressive feat of mosaic portraiture composed of more than three hundred tesserae of jadeite forming the face and shell irises with obsidian pupils as the engaging eyes. In fact, there were some pieces of jade that were reworked from other objects which might have been heirlooms in the Palenque dynasty. The tonality of the jades was subtly arranged by the artist to give extraordinarily lifelike qualities to the cheeks and brows. The skillfully shaped lips part, revealing front incisors carved into a T-shape; this dental modification was symbolic of the word *ik*, wind or breath, and represented by the T-shaped hieroglyph. This act gave the mask itself sacred breath, exhaling outward for eternity as it adorned the face of the deceased ruler. A similar mask, though composed of a local malachite greenstone, adorned the body of the queen known as Lady Tz'akbu Ajaw (early seventh century–672 CE), the wife of K'inich Janaab Pakal I; she was also coated with cinnabar in her nearby funerary chamber.

Palenque was one of the world's great artistic centers. In the eighth century, Pakal's descendant, K'inich Ahkal Mo' Nahb
62 (678–730s CE), cultivated some of the most accomplished low-relief sculptors to have ever picked up a stone chisel. These scenes fused the religious and historical, placing the rulers of Palenque as key protagonists in the centuries-long dramas of patron deities and celestial happenings. In this passage, we see a kneeling figure who reaches up with his right hand to grasp the left hand of the standing king. The sculptor conveyed subtle emotions of devotion of the figure with delicate curves in the slightly upturned face. The woven garments worn by the attendant are striking in their elaborate fringed details. His large collar contains three halves of a thorny oyster bivalve, likely *Spondylus*, and jade beads also adorn the necklace and wristlets. An earflare also supports an obsidian element that dangles to the side of the cheek. The resplendent hair is bound by a royal headband, complete with small deity heads with upturned noses. He holds a cloth bag that likely would have contained ritual incense for the king's use in ceremony. This panel, which would have been inserted into the wall of a building, shows the ability of Maya sculptors to achieve what could be considered true portraiture, in which they sought to capture a naturalistic likeness of even a secondary figure in this detail.

The religious nature of Maya art is inseparable from the historical and political, but many painters and sculptors focused solely on supernatural narratives or origins stories as their subjects. One of the finest examples comes from fine-
63 line ceramic art, such as a cylindrical drinking cup painted in what is known as "codex style" for its resemblance to the way in which later manuscript painters created screenfold books. Here a youthful rain god, named Chahk in the hieroglyphs, dances while wearing a loincloth knotted at the waist. He wears a pectoral and shell ear ornaments as he grasps the

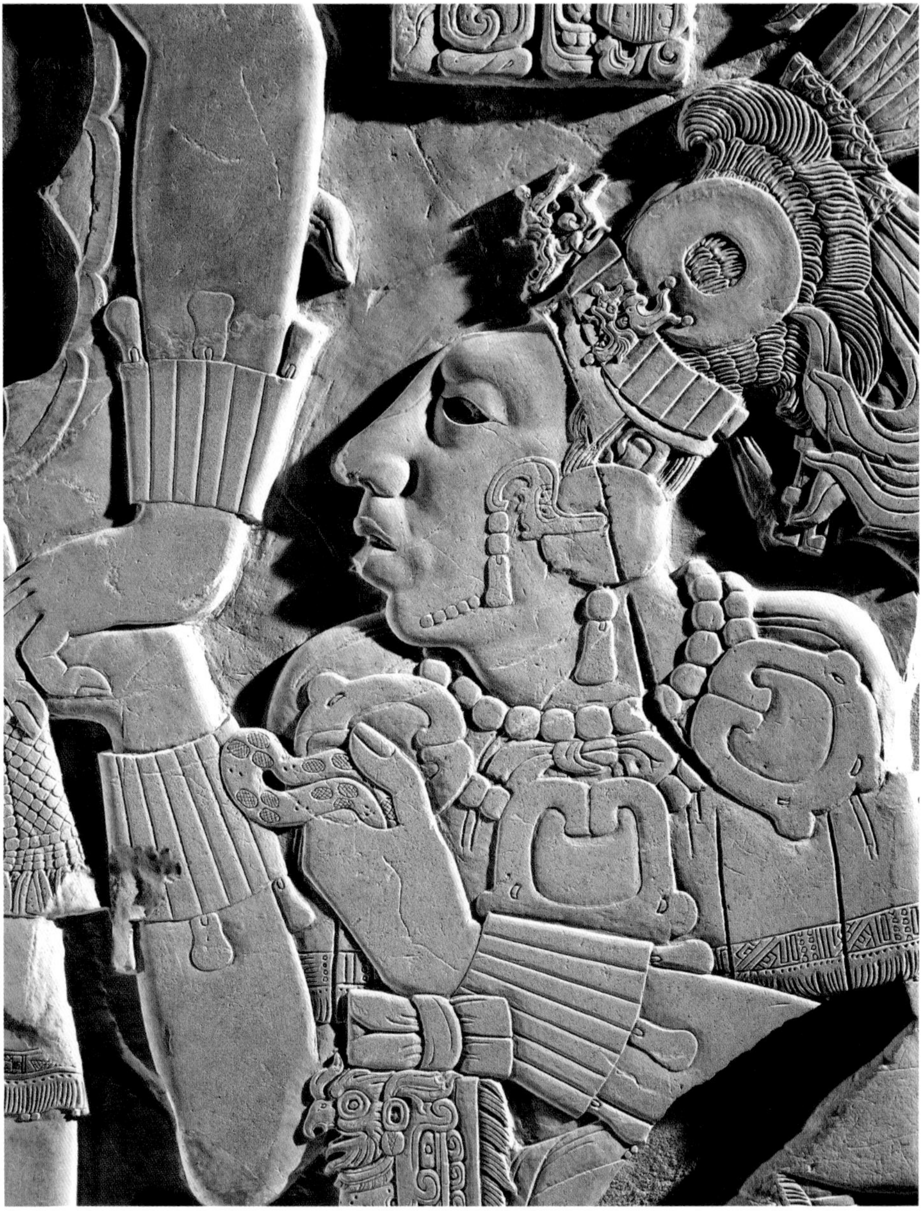

62 Relief Panel, 700–800

wooden handle of a shining stone axe in his right hand, and his left hand holds a circular stone. His humanlike quality is emphasized by the artists' brush strokes in the distinguished profile of the face, the point of the elbow, the ankle joints, and finger- and toenails. The underside of each leg, however, is marked with a scale pattern, evoking a shimmering and wet aquatic creature.

Similar to the mural scene above, the setting is an animate mountain, represented by the large jawless creature in front of the rain god, upon which is reclining a supernatural baby jaguar. On the right of the baby is a frightening creature of the night, with a skeletal head marked with bone sutures and two extruded eyeballs, insect-like carapace, distended belly of a corpse, and spindly legs with knobby knees. This is likely a

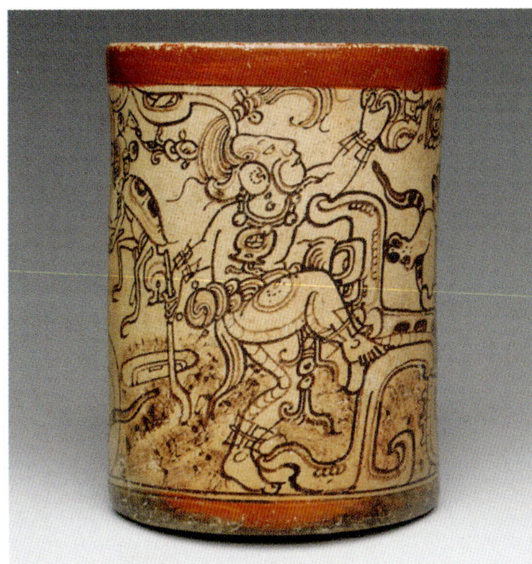

63 RIGHT AND BELOW Cylinder Vessel and Illustration of Cylinder Vessel, 700–800

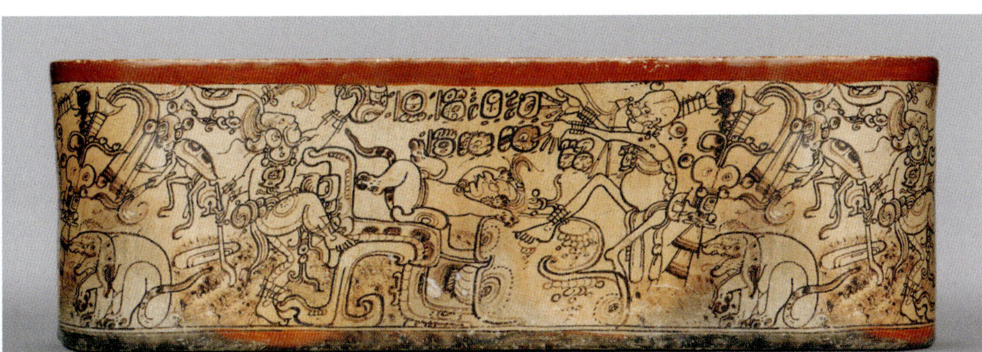

death god, a denizen of the Maya underworld who plays a role in this origin story of the birth of the baby jaguar. He dances too, mirroring the opposing deity's motions while accompanied by a firefly and a dog with spotted tail and ears. The text does not contain much information as to the specific scene, but names the owner of the vessel as an individual holding the title of *k'uhul chatan winik*, holy person from the Chatan place, a yet-to-be-identified kingdom. The word *k'uh*, which forms part of the ruler's title, is very important in understanding Maya religious art. *K'uh* plays a conceptual role as "god" or "sacred thing," similar to the Caribbean zemí (see chapter 5), Andean wak'a or *camay* (see chapter 9) and Mexica *teotl* (see chapter 10). Thus, rulers were marked as *k'uhul*, having a divine or godly quality.

Maya ceramics did more than hold things to eat and drink, such as tamales or chocolate. For kings and queens, they also served as markers of their wealth and as diplomatic gifts to cement loyalty with rivals or regional allies. They were also meant to be performative, perhaps serving as guides for song or poetry during ceremonies. As mentioned, the calligraphic style of some ceramic painters suggests they also painted books; although no books survive from the first millennium CE, some ceramics depict scenes of people writing. The painting is often so detailed that it must be appreciated at close viewing; the beholder is invited to turn the cylindrical vessel around to make different parts of the scene appear. The portability of ceramics, unfortunately, has made them targets for looting and trafficking to international markets in modern times.

One aspect of Maya religion, the ephemeral sounds and sensorial experience of activating ritual substances using sculptures, is only partially available to scholars today. It is only found in traces of perishable materials such as incense or inferred from the structure of archaeologically recovered instruments such as drums, flutes, or trumpets. Skilled potters
64 created incense burner stands in the forms of gods, such as this example also from Palenque. The central figure is seated atop a horizontal surface, from which emerges a smaller-scale individual. The rendering of the torso and legs of the figure is remarkably realistic, similar to the serene pose of a human ruler. The large, beaded collar and bracelets are also similar to depictions of royal regalia. The hands of the figure, however, morph into jaguar paws, and the head of the figure is that of a deity known as the Jaguar God of the Underworld, an embodiment of the sun as it traverses the underside of the world at night. This deity is recognized by the undereye loops that combine on the bridge of the nose into a twisted, cruller-like element, and jaguar ears also emerge

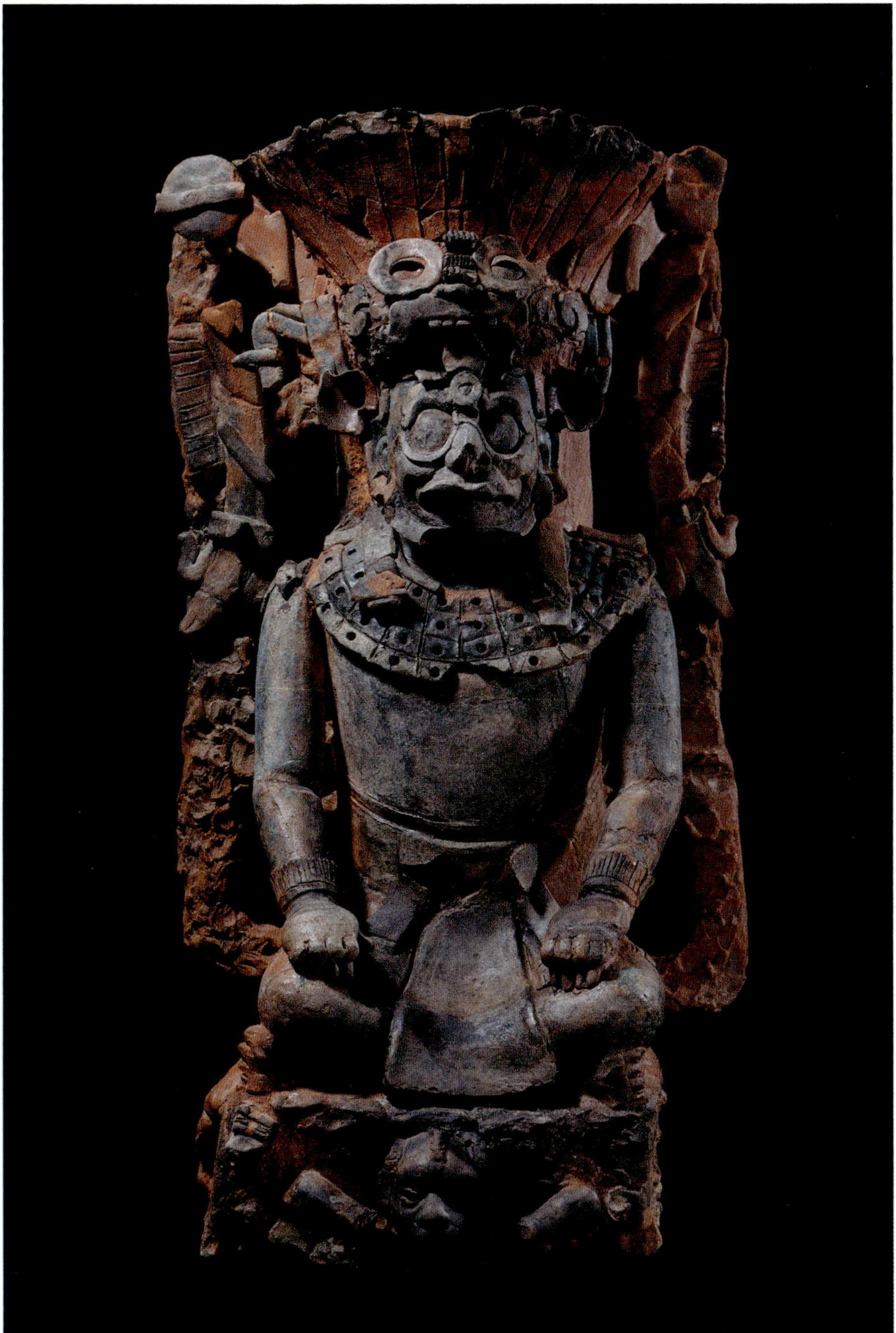

64 Incense Burner, 600–800

from the sides of the head. This particular deity even wears
145 the headdress representing another deity, symbolized by the disk-like goggles and U-shaped mouth framing the figure's forehead. As one would burn incense in the sculpture, a strand of communication symbolized by the smoke would have been opened between the mortal plane and the divine realm.

Other modeled clay objects that feature prominently in Maya art are figurines and musical instruments, also part of the rich
65 ritual lives of Maya royal courts. Figurines depict high status men and women, deities, and animals, and often a combination of the above. One delicate whistle from the seventh through ninth centuries depicts a young maize deity emerging from a plant. The artists modeled the god to have a serene pose, facing forward with lips slightly parted, arms folded across his torso. The elaborate jewelry and hairstyle are accented with a pigment known as Maya blue, an infixation of natural indigo dyes into local clays that is remarkably persistent on archaeological objects. Figurines vary widely in facture and function; one of the queens of the site of El Perú-Wak'a, for example, was buried with a full coterie of figurines representing herself, her royal husband, and courtiers such as ladies-in-waiting, scribes, and even what appear to be boxers or entertainers. The island of Jaina, off the western coast of the Yucatán Peninsula in the modern Mexican state of Campeche, functioned as a necropolis for important families of the northern lowlands. There they were buried with multiple figurines that were often made in molds and could double as rattles or whistles.

In contrast to the intimate nature of Maya ceramic arts, stone sculpture depicting deities was often meant to be seen by larger audiences and from longer distances. One of the most important sculptural workshops in the ancient world was founded by the stone carvers at the site of Copán, Honduras. There, over the course of centuries, artists shaped volcanic tuff and other stones to create an extraordinary sacred and historic landscape populated by monuments to divine beings and kings and queens. One such structure at Copán, now known as Temple 22, was dedicated in 715 CE by the ruler Waxaklajuun Ubaah K'awiil (mid- to late-seventh century–738 CE). This ruler placed particular emphasis on his connections to the divine; he is shown on multiple stelae impersonating patron deities of the Copán dynasty.

He commissioned a paradisical sculptural program
66 depicting maize deities dancing on corn mountains. The living mountains marked the pyramid itself as a re-creation of a primordial place, and the multiple versions of the dancing maize gods acted out the legendary scene. This well-preserved

65 Whistle with Anthropomorphic Figure, 600–900

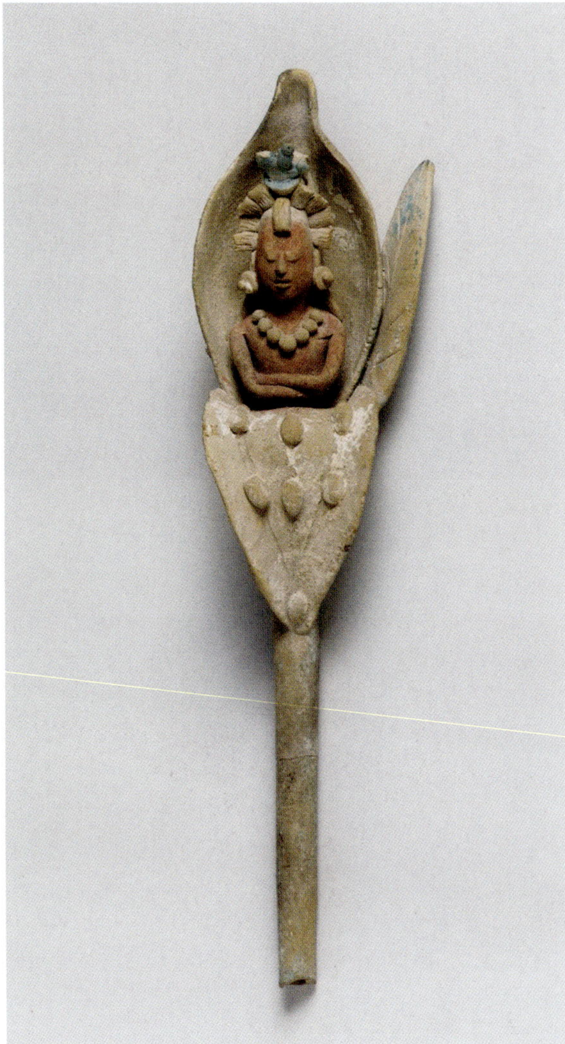

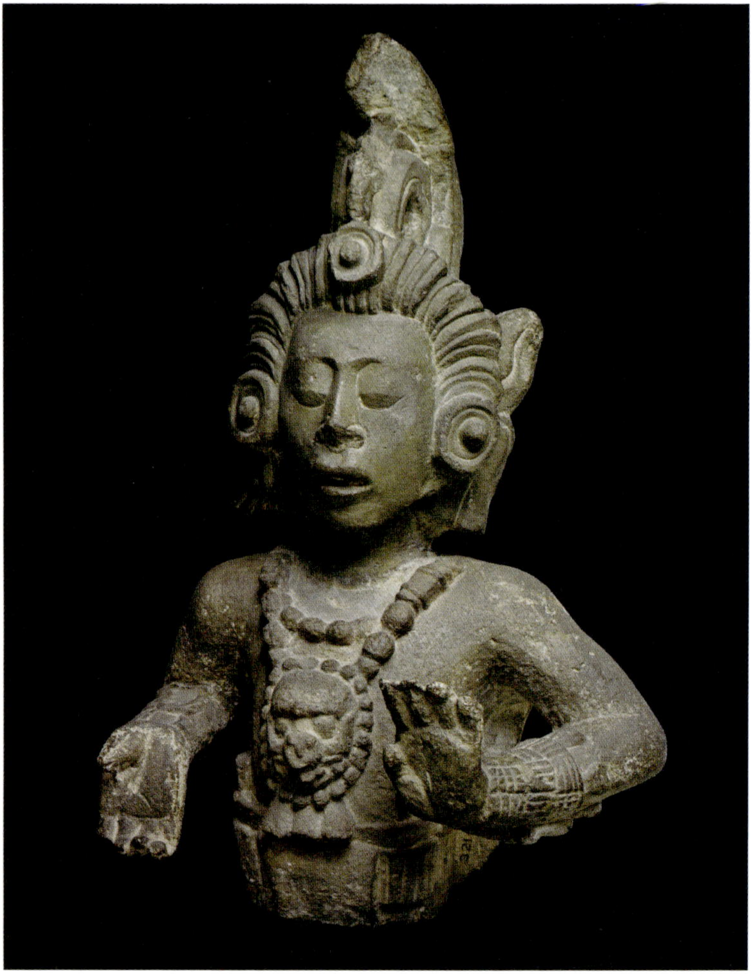

66
Anthropomorphic Sculpture, 715

example of one of the maize gods includes the head and torso of the corn deity in a serene pose of dance. This resplendent adult deity would have been seen as a personification of corn swaying in the breeze at the height of its growth season. He raises both arms, with the right arm palm up and the left arm palm down, and gazes forward, mouth slightly open. He wears bracelets, a belt assemblage, and a large pectoral featuring the face of a different deity. From the back of his head emerges corn vegetation, equating his swept back hair with the silk of the corn plant. The maize god's hair is also bedecked with jade jewels, embodying agricultural fertility and abundance.

Jade, in fact, may have played an outsized role in the political jostling of Copán and its neighbors, especially the dynasty centered at the site of Quiriguá, Guatemala. These two royal courts were strategically located near the geological fault that produced raw jadeite boulders. Rulers of these places likely sought to control or oversee trade routes for the commodity
90 over centuries as peoples throughout Mesoamerica desired jade. The decipherment of texts from both sites has illuminated one of the most dramatic political conflicts known from the Americas between these two dynasties. The ruler who created Temple 22's impressive sculptural program had a loyal vassal at Quiriguá who eventually turned on his overlord, capturing and beheading him in 738 CE. At Quiriguá, the ruler, known as K'ahk' Tiliw Chan Yopaat (*c.* late seventh century–785 CE), used his newfound fortune to sponsor some of the tallest stelae ever carved, with one monument reaching 25 feet in height (7.62 m) and weighing 30 tons. After this major upheaval, the dynasty at Copán continued to sponsor talented communities of artists, but by the late eighth century, the sculptural output was greatly reduced from its peak decades earlier.

Unfortunately, none of the names of any sculptors from places like Tikal, Palenque, or Copán survive in the epigraphic record. Other Maya sites provide a great deal about artists' identities and the organization of sculptural ateliers, where authorship was celebrated and allowed to be recorded in the form of scribal signatures. The royal court at the site known as Piedras Negras, in Guatemala on the Usumacinta River, sponsored a vibrant sculptural community with many individuals working throughout the reigns of several successive kings. In fact, the patterns of inscriptions at Piedras Negras were part of the evidence that allowed the historic content of the hieroglyphs to be identified in the first place. Several monuments there show a clear hierarchy of a head sculptor working with numerous other sculptors. Some sculptors even worked on monuments known to be from subsidiary sites ruled by leaders loyal to the kings of Piedras Negras. The sculptors were thus active agents in the political agenda of the rulers, not just at their home base, but they could be sent out to decorate allies' buildings in service of political claims.

The extraordinary products of sculptural workshops at the site of Piedras Negras in the late eighth century underscore the role of art in times of political turmoil. Produced by two sculptors, one by the name of Wajaat Na Chahk (active *c.* 782–95 CE), a masterfully detailed panel commissioned around 795 CE by ruler K'inich Yat Ahk III (750–*c.* 808 CE) shows the height of
67 relief sculpture at the site. It shows a retrospective scene taking

place in the time of his ancestor, Itzam K'an Ahk IV (b. 701 CE), who ruled from 729 to 757. The former king sits in pride of place at the center of a feasting scene in which local officials and loyal subjects gather with the courtly attendants. The scene, looking back at the glory days of this ruler, commemorates a great meeting and celebration, supervised by the dynasty's patron deities. The sculptors worked at a remarkably small scale but were able to depict realistic details, from the elaborate throne that the king adorned with textiles and a jaguar pillow, to the ruler's delicate knuckles as his hand rests on the throne's edge while he leans forward to address his visitors. In a rare instance, the hieroglyphic text records first- and second-person speech from the king as he presides over the celebration. This investment in dynastic reverence can be seen as a last-

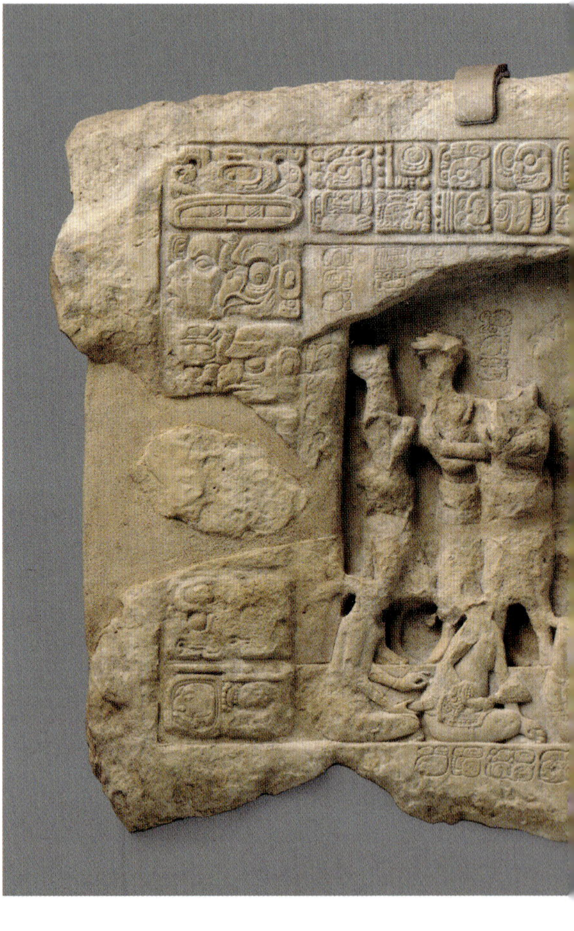

67 Wajaat Na Chahk and collaborator, *Relief Panel (Panel 3)*, c. 782–95

ditch effort to proclaim legitimacy in the region. The king who commissioned the panel was killed by a rival ruler from Yaxchilan a few years later, and monumental carving ceased at Piedras Negras soon thereafter.

Art and architecture of the ancient Maya have long been recognized as part of the world's great visual traditions. The recent decipherments of historical accounts and origins stories have only enriched the modern understanding of this Indigenous way of thinking, writing, and building. In the global context, the Maya case study underscores the seemingly universal impulse of those with political power, such as the great kings and queens of Tikal, Yaxchilan, and Piedras Negras, to employ artists as part of their strategies of control and legitimation. Sculptors and painters created public visual

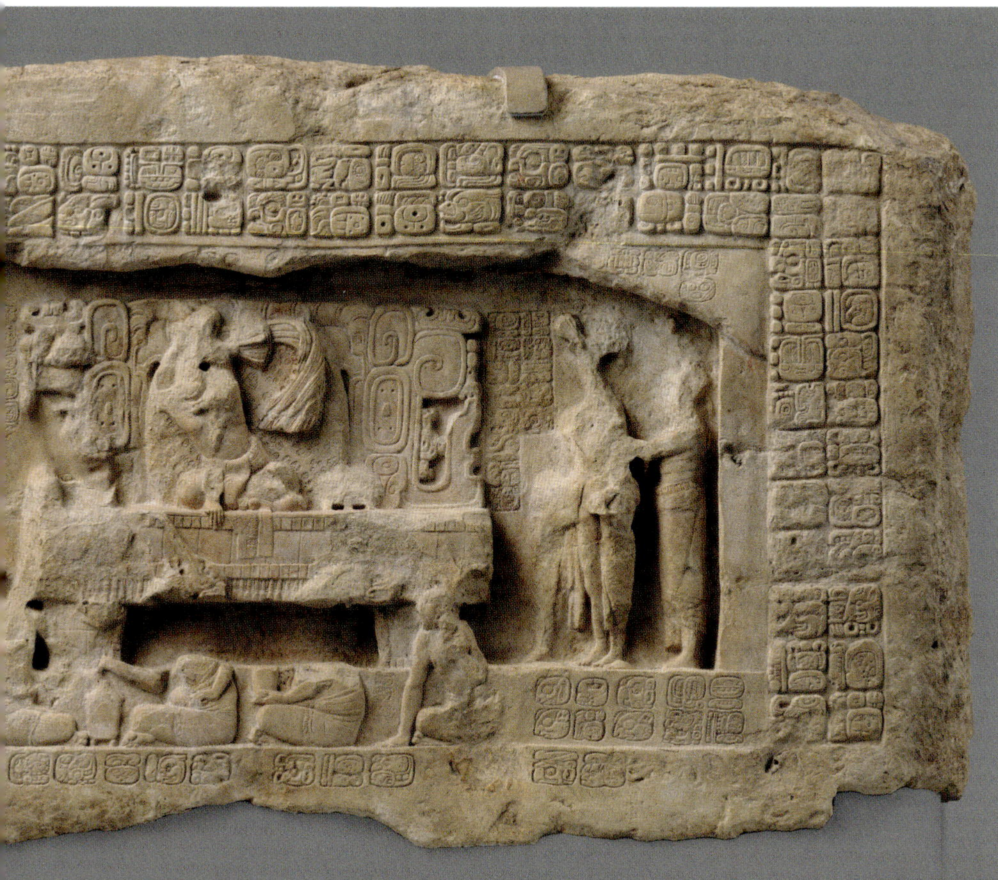

narratives reminding the beholders of the great deeds of their sovereigns. The political competition between these Maya royal courts, connected by trade routes for preciosities like jade and a shared written language, spurred on artistic innovation at places like Copán and Quiriguá. As with the Moche case described in chapter 3, these bursts of creativity led to the iconic monuments and delicate painted scenes that continue to inspire awe in viewers today.

Later Maya Art

After the ninth century, people migrated away from the major
68 centers in the southern lowlands and cities such as Chichén Itzá became focal points of artistic practice. Remarkably different from its contemporaries in the southern lowlands, Chichén Itzá, in the northern part of the Yucatán Peninsula, is noted for its square stepped pyramid, called the Castillo; the Temple of the Warriors pyramid that emerges from the long hall of columns known as the Northwest Colonnade; and the Great Ballcourt, the largest ever created in Mesoamerica. The architecture that is visible today has a clear connection with traditions in Central Mexico, most notably the Toltec site of Tula, in Hidalgo (see chapter 10). While the political nature of the relationship between Chichén Itzá and the faraway sites remains unknown, what is clear is that artists practicing there were familiar with both Central Mexican and Maya visual cultures. The sculptural program at Chichén Itzá then presents itself as multicultural, signifying long-distance contacts and migration of peoples in the region. The artists there excelled at what can be considered visual code-switching, employing different images and iconography in the same city in different contexts. Builders there also experimented with different geometries, such as the Caracol, a building featuring vaults arranged in concentric rings and a conch-shell spiraled staircase, but still adhered to Maya ideas of space divided by the cardinal directions and buildings oriented to astronomical movements.

Chichén Itzá was also clearly a pilgrimage center, with people visiting the city over centuries to participate in ceremonies such as the ball game. An important component of Mesoamerican societies in general, and Maya cities especially, a game played on a rectangular court with a rubber ball was more than mere sport, having religious and political dimensions in its various iterations across time and space (see chapter 6). Builders at Chichén Itzá constructed their enormous ballcourt and artists decorated the surrounding structures with low-relief friezes and murals. Visitors to Chichén Itzá in the past also came to make offerings to the great water-filled sinkhole known as the Sacred Cenote. A place resembling a collapsed cave where the limestone shelf of the Yucatán was ruptured, the cenote was thought of as a portal between the human realm and the watery underworld. Dredging in the early twentieth century revealed an astonishing quantity of luxury goods, such as gold, jade, shell, incense, and other materials, presumably left by visitors over many centuries. Jade objects that once belonged to rulers at places like Palenque and Piedras Negras were carried there and tossed into the water. Even objects created in faraway kingdoms in Costa Rica and Panama, such as gold bells or disks, were offered to the cenote during this time of increased long-distance trade (see chapter 5). Maya artists even reworked disks from Panama, hammering them into foil-thin pectorals and embossing scenes of local deities and rulers.

Artists in the northern Yucatán Peninsula from the period after 1000 CE until the Spanish invasion in the sixteenth century created fewer monumental representations of rulers and deities but still excelled at mural programs and small-scale paintings in screenfold books known as codices. One example from about the thirteenth through fifteenth centuries, known
69 as the Dresden Codex (after its modern repository), enshrines gods and humans in an almanac-style narrative that includes tables of calendar days and astronomical observations. Over seventy pages are divided into different registers that combine hieroglyphic text and depictions of deities and supernatural events. Scribes produced bright colors with mineral pigments as well as the unique recipe for Maya blue. The depiction of pre-colonial books, though they tend to be in supernatural contexts being read or written by deities, indicates that the codex tradition was foundational to the maintenance of royal courts. This is precisely why the Spanish religious authorities sought them out as idolatrous in the sixteenth century.

Although communities of Maya artists in the post-invasion world were vastly transformed by disease and orchestrated campaigns of violence, creativity lived on during the Spanish viceregal period and into the incipient republican governments of the nineteenth century. When scientific archaeology began in earnest in the Maya region, it was the engagement with Maya descendants in Mexico and Guatemala with ethnographic and linguistic research that unlocked the rich content of the art and texts. One account in particular from the K'iche Maya groups in highland Guatemala recorded around 1700, but perhaps originally put on paper in the sixteenth century, is known as the Popol Wuj. The Popol Wuj tells the origin stories of the K'iche people and actions of the gods on their sacred landscape. Many

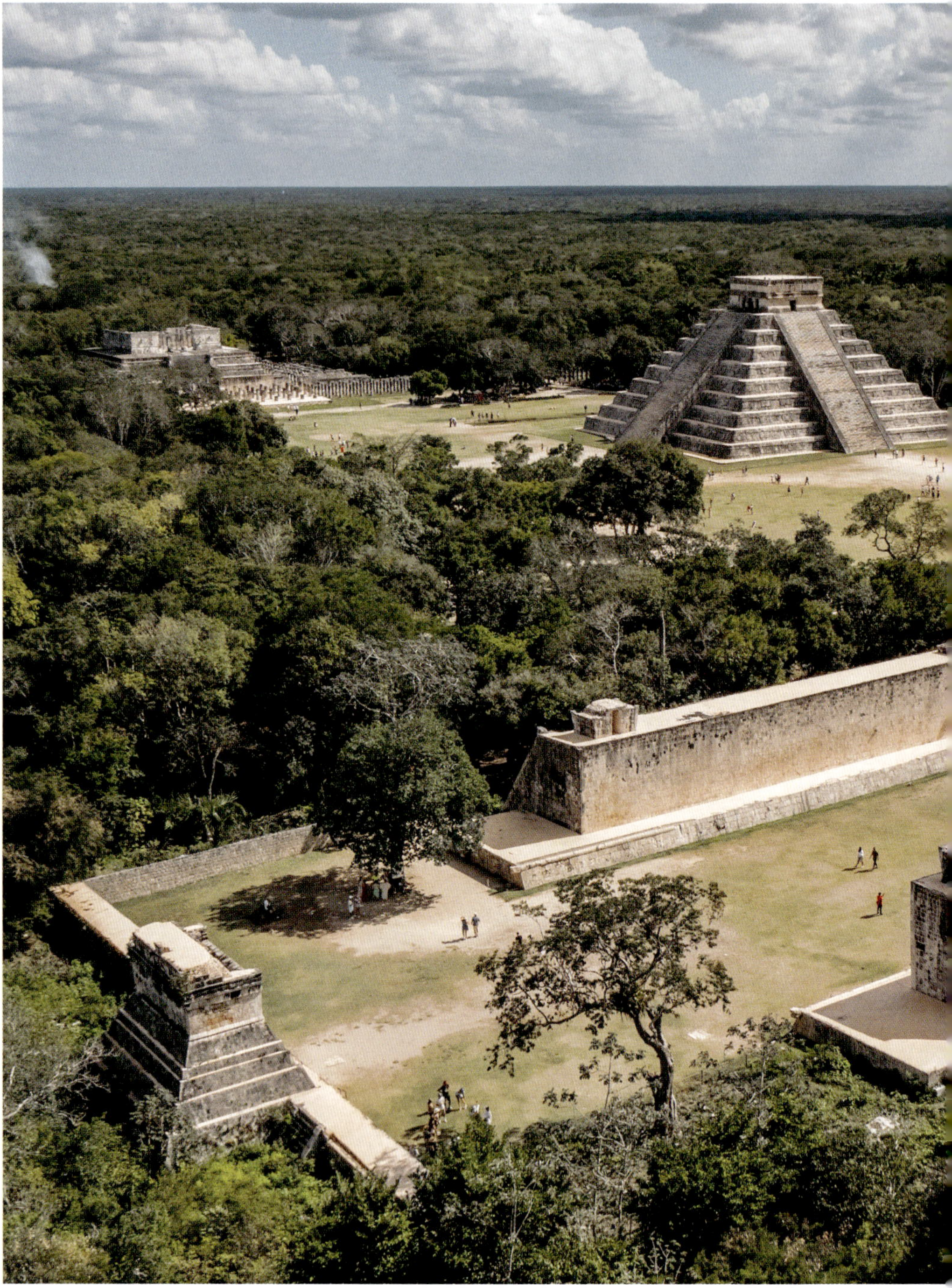

 Chichén Itzá, Mexico

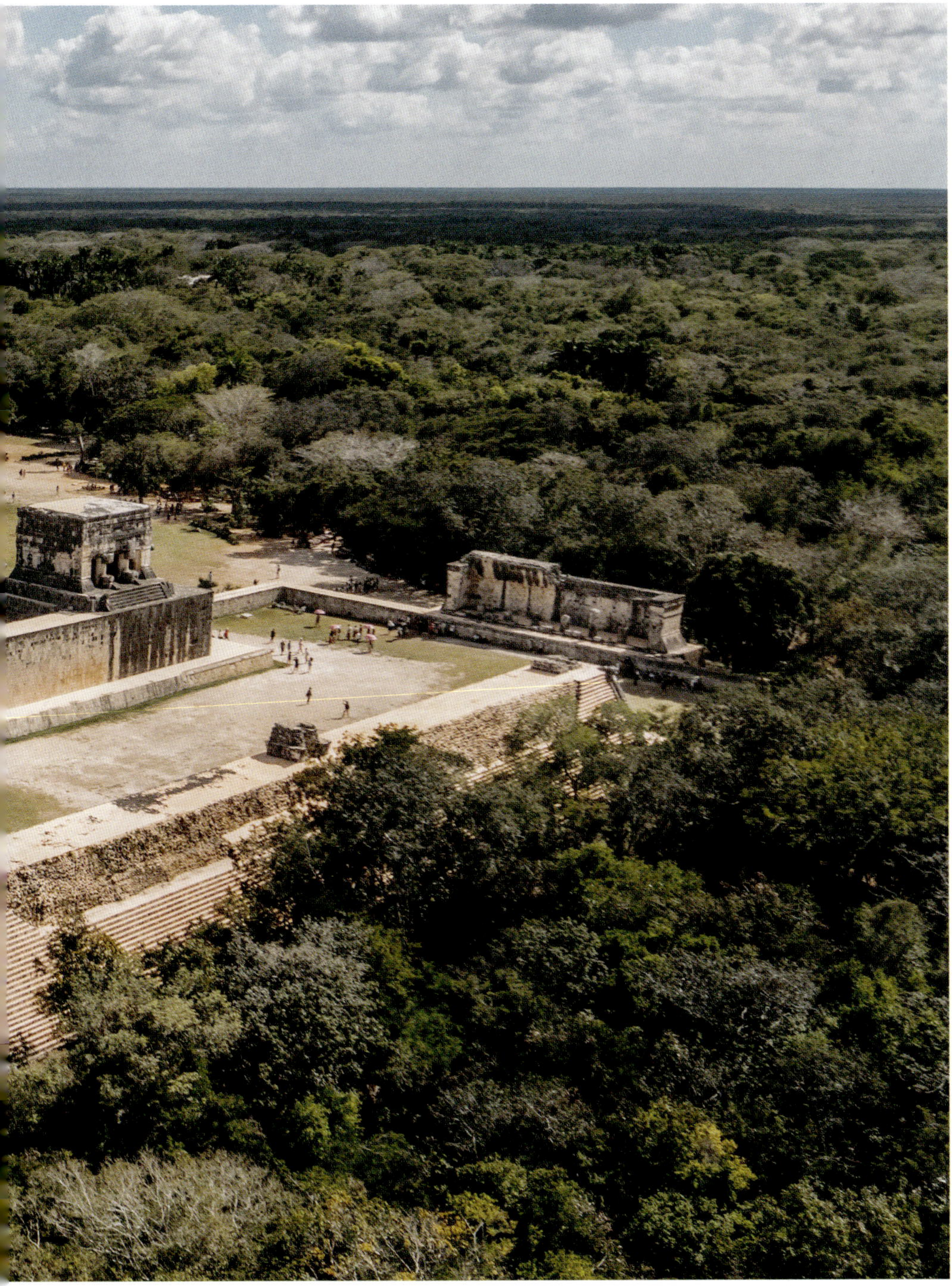

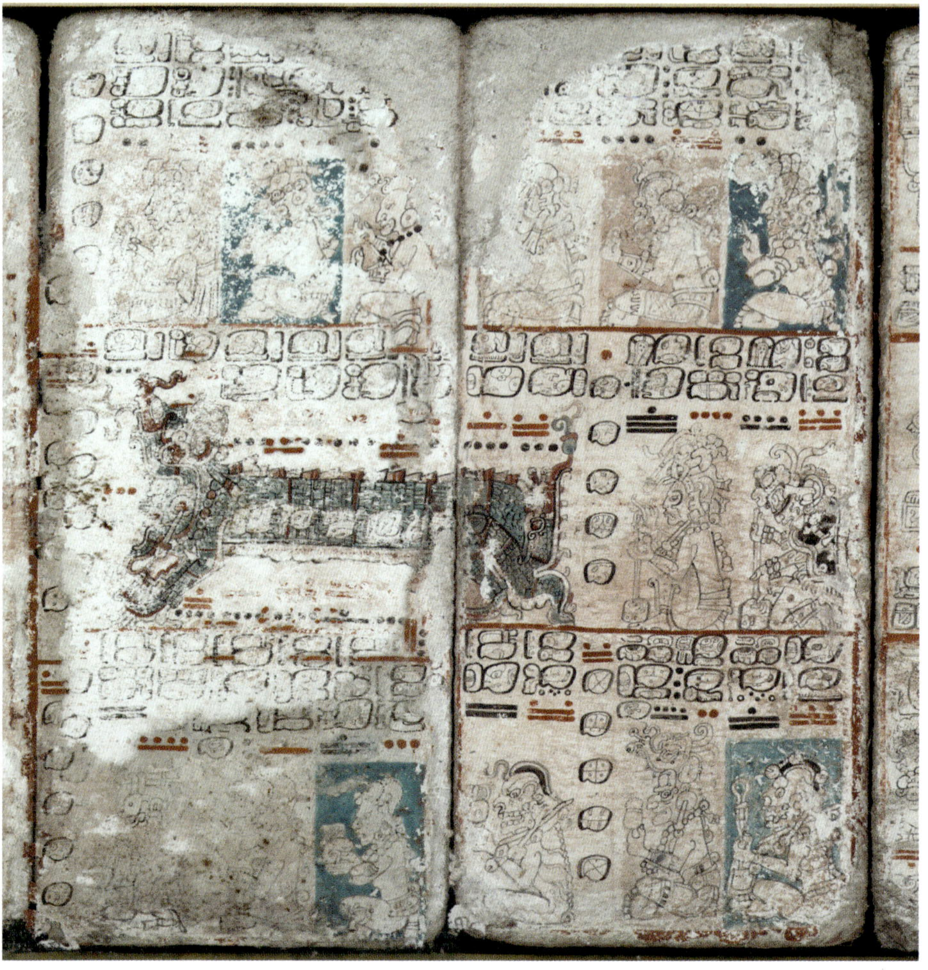

69 Pages from Dresden Codex, 1250–1524

of the stories from this epic describe characters very similar to those depicted in art from many centuries before. It testifies to the rich oral traditions that were passed down through the centuries and that still survive today in communities in the region and in diaspora.

Chapter 5
Extracting Brilliance: The Northern Andes, Central America, the Amazon, and the Antilles (100 BCE–1500 CE)

Ecuador

Representing one of the most important ecosystems in the world, the modern country of Ecuador embodies coastal bounty, mountainous richness, and abundance from the diverse equatorial forest. As mentioned in the introduction, this confluence of natural factors provided a rich social foundation for artists who skillfully manipulated clay and carved stone as early as the third millennium BCE. The rich ocean currents of Ecuador allowed for societies in coastal regions to flourish and inculcate creative aesthetic traditions. Highland and Amazonian regions were also home to complex societies who created large settlements and unique visual cultures expressed in sculpture and personal adornments. Rulers in the diverse groups on the western coast of Ecuador collectively known
70 as Manteño, for example, commissioned elaborate thrones, which may date to between 500 and 1500 CE; these provided a privileged vantage point from which to oversee community functions in the centuries before the Spanish invasion. Some of these thrones contain imagery of what could be ancestors, richly ornamented in their stone portraits, and literally supporting the ruler currently sitting on the throne.

The example here from the site of Cerro Jaboncillo, Manabí Province, was carved from a solid boulder into a U-shaped throne seat supported by a humanlike figure. The person on the lower portion, perhaps a male, is richly adorned in a flaring headdress, elaborate ear ornaments that could be depicting gold or shell mosaic, and a wide beaded collar

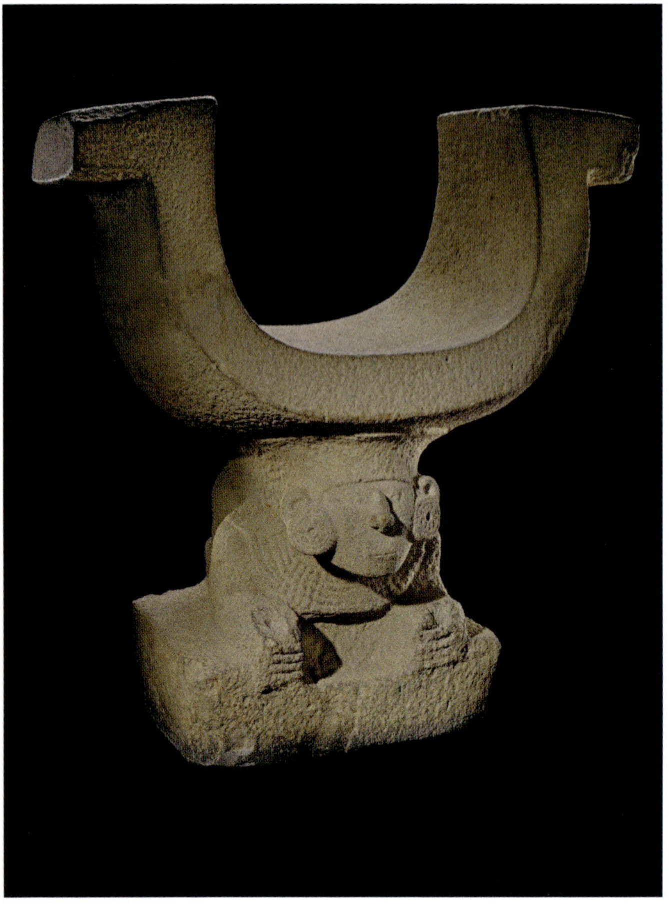

70 LEFT Throne, 500–1500
71 OPPOSITE Anthropomorphic Figure, 350 BCE–350 CE

that drapes over his torso. The sculptor depicted a stoic face with little individualized detail, which could indicate that the figure represents an ancestral or divine figure; ceramic incense burners from the same time period also depict similar individuals with regalia seated on benches. The hunched over or forward-leaning person carries the large stirrup-shaped throne seat on his head, so that the living ruler seated above was intimately associated with the throne figure, coopting its ancestral power. Evidence from surrounding sites suggests that there may have been groups of seats placed in large gathering halls. Another possibility is that instead of living rulers seated in the U-shaped thrones, they once held the funerary bundles of ancestral figures, allowing the previous generations to be present in the community life of their descendants.

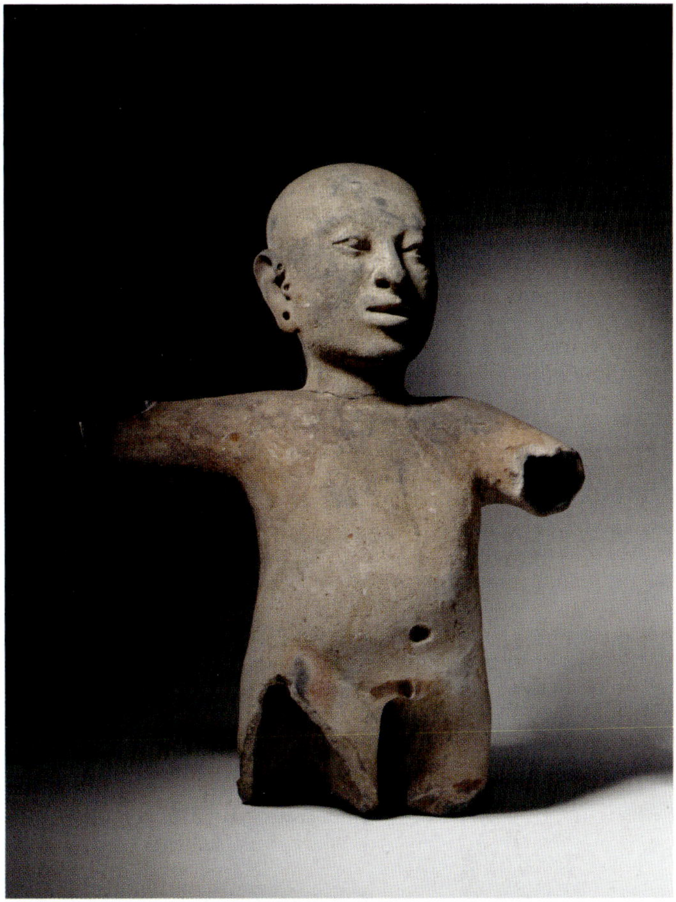

Potters in several regions of ancient Ecuador reached new heights in modeling human figures and supernatural beings in large-scale ceramic effigies when compared with earlier traditions in the region and contemporaneous styles from other parts of the ancient Americas. Often they were painted with bright colors, some with a blue that is similar to Maya
71 blue. One fragmentary example of a large hollow sculpture from the cultures known as La Tolita, from the northern coast of Ecuador and southwestern Colombia, exemplifies the skill of artists in capturing human emotion and movement in fired clay. Although the figure is nude with a visible navel, it perhaps would have been adorned with mold-made ceramic garments or metal regalia through the piercing holes created in the ears and nose, as seen on other examples. The right arm of the

figure, though missing, is raised as if to display something or throw a weapon such as a spear. The open eyes and slightly parted lips would have greeted the beholders in this aggressive posture, as if to warn them or proclaim authority. Although silent now, this snapshot, perhaps of an important historical figure, speaks to contemporary audiences through its moving gaze. The profusion of such realistic depictions among the La Tolita assemblages is noteworthy, as they depart significantly from both previous and later traditions in the region. The arts of ancient Ecuador as a result constitute one of the exciting opportunities for new investigations in the coming years.

Colombia

Contiguous with Ecuador, the rich biodiverse hotspot of Colombia in the northern Andes has been home to a succession of important societies that resisted the Spanish invasion and survive in several Indigenous groups today. The fertile valleys and rich coastal waters off both the Pacific and Caribbean coasts nurtured communities of artistic practice that created complex works in stone, ceramic, and, especially, metal. The goldworkers in what is now Colombia achieved some of the

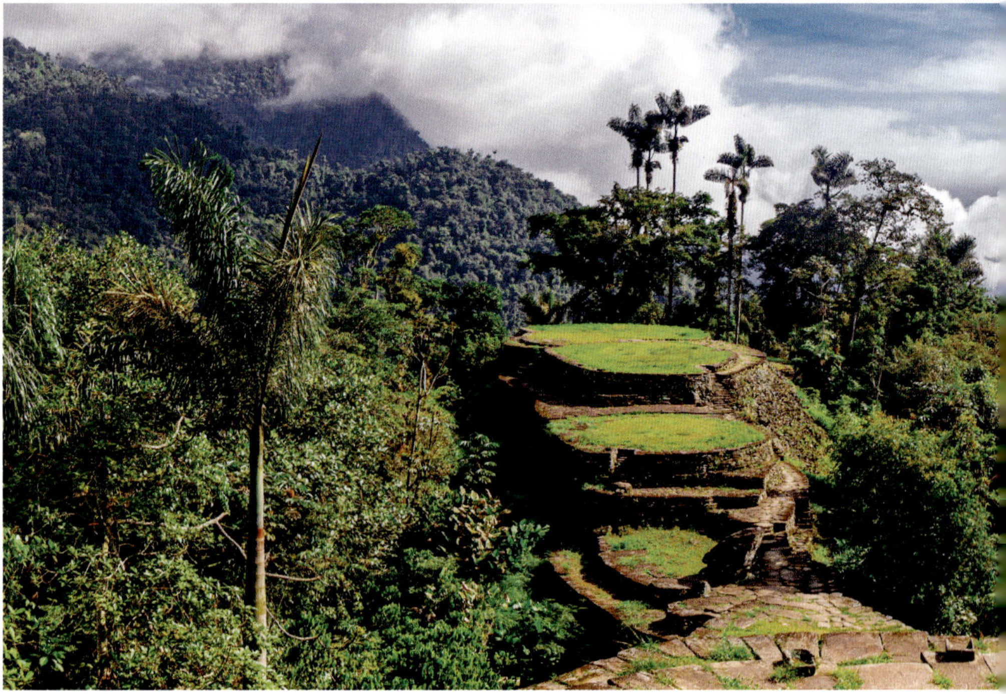

72 Ciudad Perdida, Colombia

most impressive feats of casting and hammering in the ancient world, adorning their patrons with extraordinary regalia unlike that seen in other parts of the Americas. Architects in the northern Andes engineered impressive cities in the coastal mountains, such as the famed Ciudad Perdida or "Lost
72 City" in the region of the Sierra Nevada de Santa Marta. Such places were built by the ancestral peoples known as Taironas, antecedents of the Kogis and the Arhuacos who live in the region today, likely for both strategic reasons as defensible locations and symbolic reasons connected to concepts of a sacred landscape. Widespread themes permeate the ancestral visual cultures of the region, such as a clear artistic focus on conferring onto rulers the powerful properties of raptors, jaguars, and other predators or marine creatures.

In the early 1990s a hitherto unknown archaeological culture came to light after an unfortunate event of mass looting at the Hacienda Malagana, in the Cauca River Valley. The society, dubbed Calima-Malagana, flourished in the late first millennium BCE and early centuries CE. Although
73 the tombs were not excavated scientifically, the documented objects in museum collections that contain emeralds and

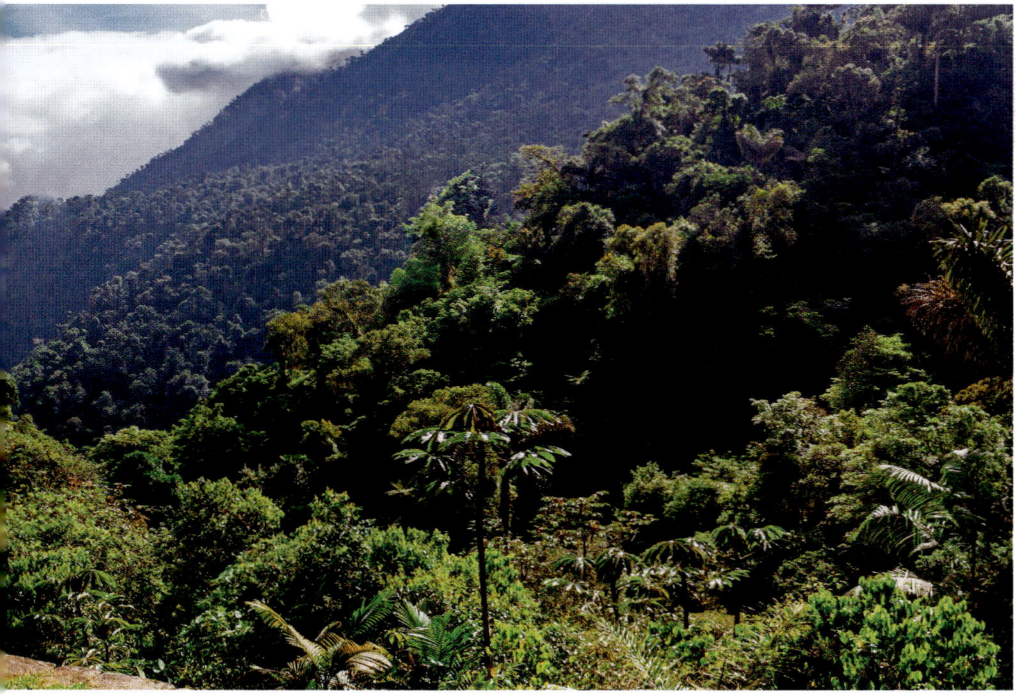

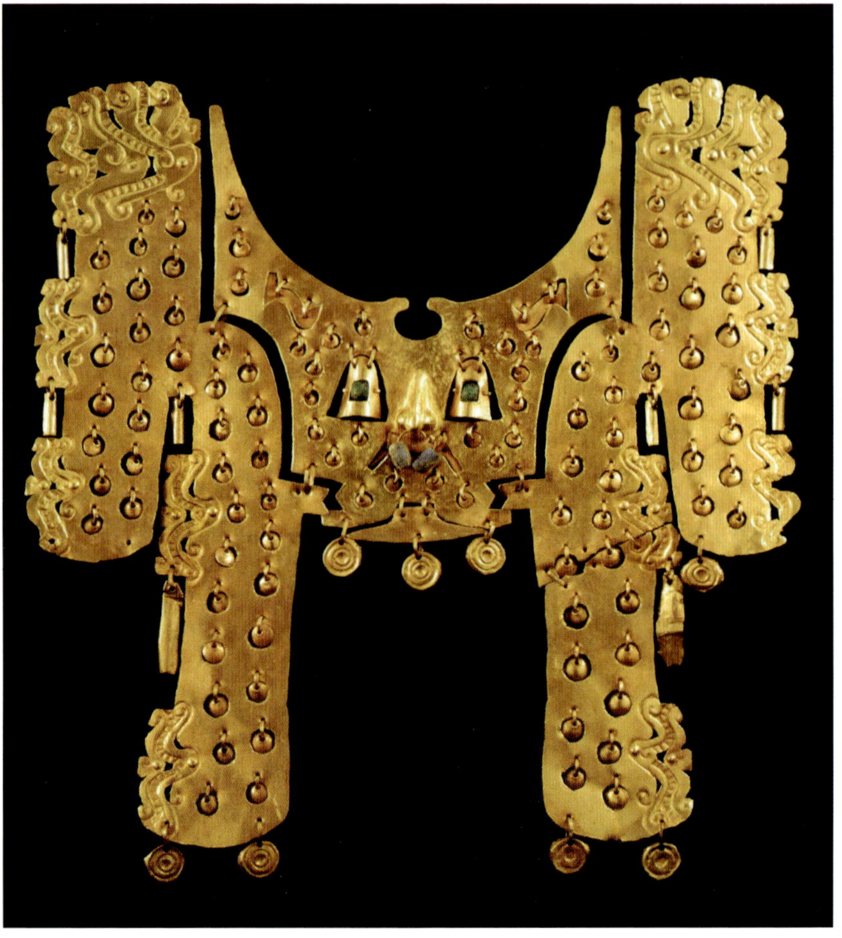

73 Mouth Mask, 100 BCE–300 CE

other precious stones coming from other regions testify to the long-distance trade networks of Malagana rulers and the skill of the goldworkers from whom they commissioned elaborate regalia. The fineness and pristine condition of Malagana gold ornaments suggest that they were rarely, if ever, worn in life, and may have been commissioned only as funerary
20, 44 assemblages. This particular nose ornament, made to clip into the wearer's septum and hang over the lower portion of the face, illustrates the imaginative world of artists in this area.

The mouth mask unites four pieces of hammered gold sheet in a fantastical composition that plays with two and three dimensions. The central element is a humanlike face, composed of gumdrop-shaped eyes that are highlighted by greenstone inlays, a naturalistic nose adorned with a ring and bluestone ornaments, and an articulated chin with three sequins with concentric circles. The stepped sheets suspended from either side of the face take the undulating form of four limbs. The frontal view allows for the simultaneous interpretation of the feline body as crouching down or leaping up; the claws are represented as reptilian profile jaws opening up toward the outside of the wearers face. Dozens of cutouts have been filled with rounded sequins attached with thin gold wires. The dazzling effect of all these dangling parts when worn would have created the image of a supernatural jaguar in motion.

Diverse societies in Colombia adorned the bodies of their rulers with similar gold and precious stones and also depicted rulers wearing such regalia in metal and ceramic arts. Some of the finest works of gold come from the societies known as Calima-Yotoco, centered in the region around the Cauca Valley, near the modern-day city of Cali, Colombia. One
74 particular object, a lime container in the shape of a feline, underscores the fine skills of working metal developed in this part of the Andes. The goldworker shaped sheets of gold and folded or wired them together in the form of a crouching feline, perhaps a jaguar ready to pounce, with its tail arched over its back. With diamond-shaped eyes and fangs, the jaguar serves as a container for powdered lime with a small gold dipper that would be inserted in the shoulders of the figure

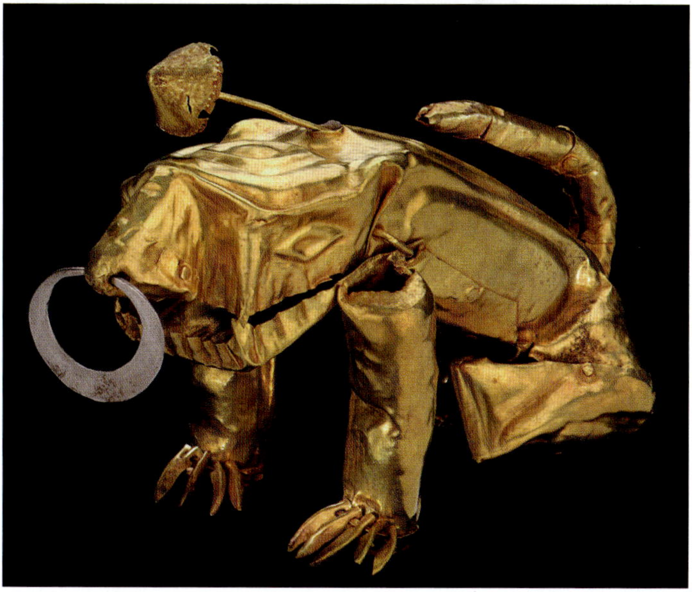

74 Zoomorphic Lime Container, 100 BCE–800 CE

to retrieve the substance. When chewed with coca leaves in spiritual ceremonies, the lime activates the alkaloids to create a powerful stimulant. Notably, the jaguar's snout is pierced, and from it hangs a semi-lunar ornament of a different color. Research in Colombia shows that this metal is platinum, probably mined with gold in the region. This is the only tradition in the ancient Americas in which metalworkers were able to isolate platinum due to its very high melting point.

Farther south, artists in the cultures known as San Agustín perfected large-scale sculptural techniques to create iconic monuments that memorialize rulers and divine fanged beings in stone. The standing rulers are often shown as warriors,
75 such as one example in which the subject, wearing a geometric loincloth, grasps an axe and a shield. The figure has exaggerated facial proportions, including prominent canine teeth, but wears what might be a headdress made of gold or other precious materials such as feathers. These supernatural figures, which once would have been brightly painted, were arranged in megalithic tomb constructions as powerful guardians over the ancestors who were laid to rest within these complexes. Such megalithic tombs can be compared to others, such as the earlier ones at La Venta (see chapter 2) or at Wari (see chapter 7).

The sixteenth-century Spanish colonization of Colombia was fueled by tales of rulers and cities covered in gold, known as El Dorado, or "the golden one." This myth may have originated from the Muisca societies of the eastern Andes in Colombia, near the modern-day capital of Bogotá. There, metalworkers created elaborate gold works for regalia and dedicatory offerings beginning around 600 CE and continuing until the European invasion. The assemblages of sacred materials offered in caves, lakes, or other important points on the landscape consisted of votive figures made of precious metals, as well as ceramics, emeralds, textiles, or plant products such as food, coca, or tobacco. Important research in Colombia has shed light on the meanings behind Muisca metal figures as well as the metallurgical technology employed to create the gold or gold-alloy objects. The goldworkers used exceptional skill in lost-wax casting, using wax models to create molds into which the metal is poured, combined with a symbolic vocabulary and local concepts of scale to imbue offerings with important social meanings.

76 For example, a goldworker captured a snapshot of an important ceremony that took place aboard a large raft. Cast from one wax model of sheets and small tubes, this raft contains a larger figure at center, seated on a curved, portable throne, attended by eight smaller characters. The others in the

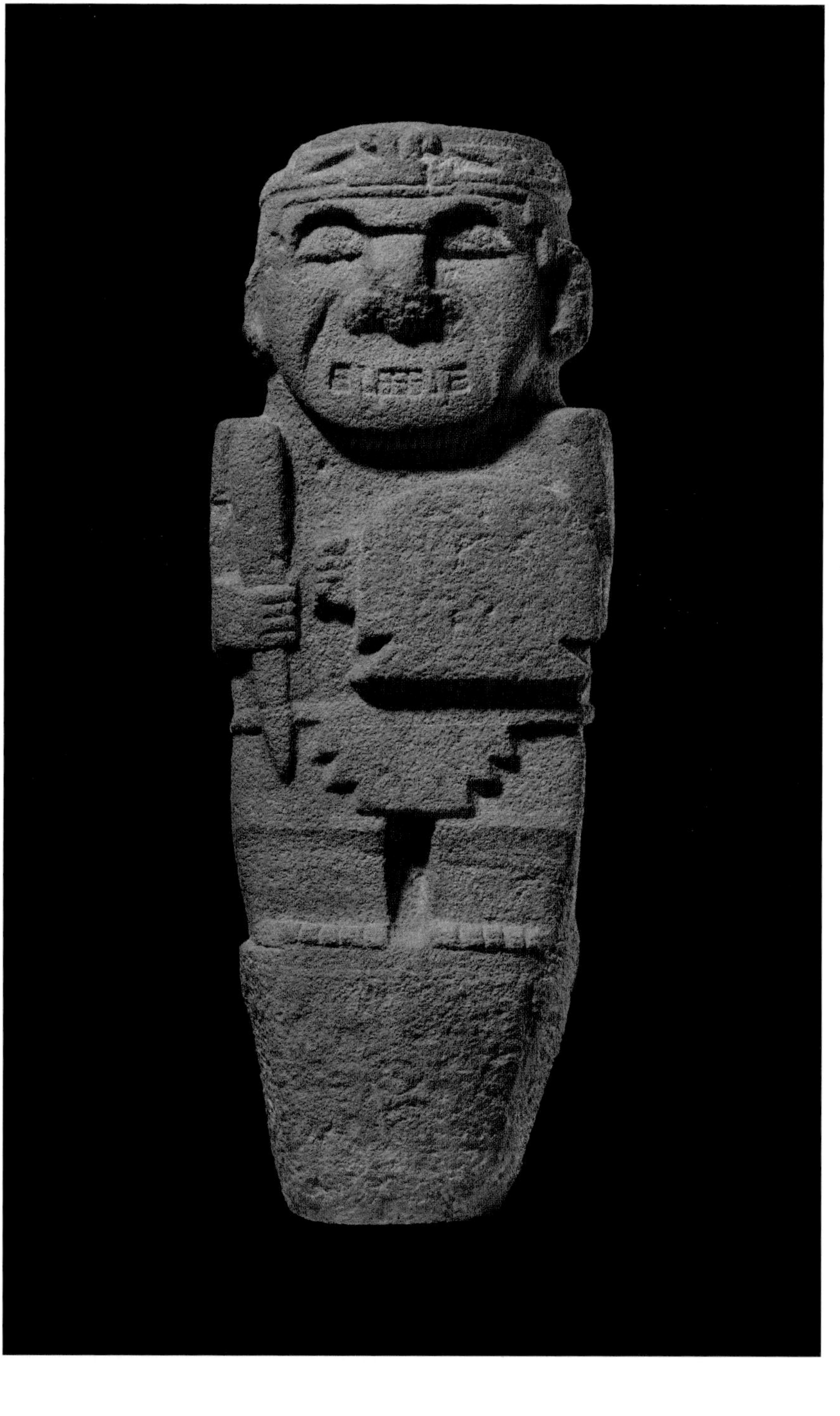

75 Anthropomorphic Sculpture, 1–900

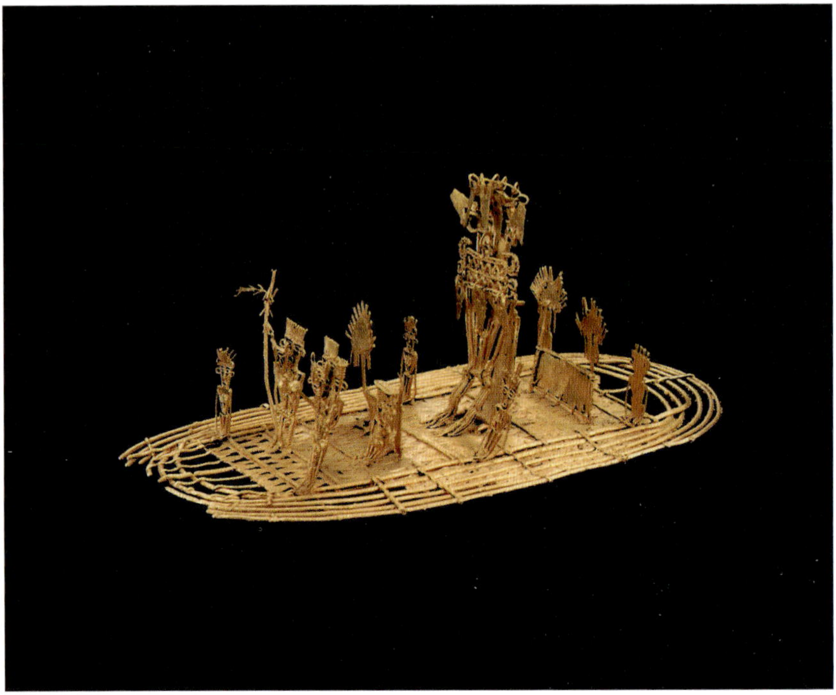

76 Votive Figure, 600–1600

scene, possibly attendants like courtiers or ritual specialists, face away from the ruler, a practice documented in the Isthmo-Colombian area in which engaging in a direct gaze toward powerful leaders was prohibited. There are fans on staffs that may represent feathered standards or heraldic symbols. The principal figure wears a large nose ornament, headdress, and earrings, all with trapezoidal danglers that would have moved, catching the light as full-scale versions would have on similar regalia. Similar small-scale scenes in metal depict rulers on litters or in enclosed residential structures that represent the seats of Muisca political power. Close examination of Muisca votive figures shows that the artists chose not to remove or correct imperfections, even leaving most of these figures unpolished, suggesting that there was great symbolic meaning in the act of casting itself that was necessary to preserve in the finished works.

Costa Rica and Panama

During the first millennium, artists in what are now the countries of Costa Rica, southern Nicaragua, and western

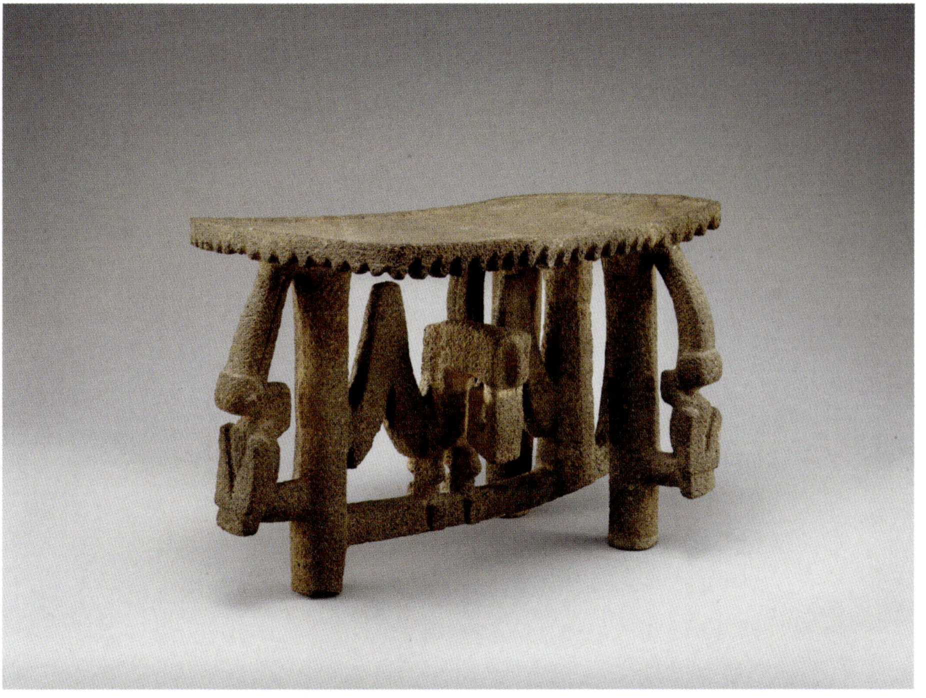

77 Metate, 100–500

Panama developed unique art styles in large sculptures and luxury regalia. Especially notable from this region are large-scale works in volcanic rock, ranging from architectural platforms made from river-smoothed boulders, perfectly shaped stone spheres that marked the residences of important local rulers, and incredible feats of subtractive sculpture in the form of tools known as metates, the Spanish word originating from a Nahuatl term for grinding stone. Metates are, in fact, multivalent objects that function as both a grinding surface for foodstuffs and possibly a seat upon which important leaders presided, as depicted in ceramic figurines. The stone metates also served as surfaces upon which the deceased rulers were sometimes laid to rest along with their prized possessions.

Sculptors infused these metates with imagery of powerful
77 creatures such as felines, crocodilians, and birds. This example, used as a grinding stone or ceremonial seat, shows the concave upper surface decorated with crenulations, and three cylindrical legs supporting the scene. Each leg has a long-billed bird perched on it, with the bill connected to the lower surface of the seat. The central element depicts another stylized bird

carved in the round with pointed angular wings, a long neck,
and a curved bill, perched on a horizontal bar. The daring
vision of the sculptor is on exhibit here: they started with one
large, round boulder, and delicately removed all the negative
space to create the metate form.

Stone carvers in Costa Rica also excelled in transforming
harder materials into personal regalia. In the mid-first
millennium CE, long-distance trade between Costa Rica and
Mesoamerica to the north brought jade southward. These
34 objects often traveled as celts or axes, and artists reworked
them into figure pendants in the form of humanlike
78 individuals or avian creatures. One example, excavated at the
site of Talamanca de Tibás, was part of a funerary assemblage
of a young person buried atop three metates. The important
person in this tomb likely wore this pendant in life, strung
through the transverse drill holes at the bird's neck. The
stylized crests and prominent beak may suggest that the bird
is a harpy eagle, or even a human donning the visage of such a
bird of prey in performance.

After about 500 CE, rulers in Costa Rica also commissioned
works in gold, including pendants and bells created using
the lost-wax casting technique and hammered gold plaques
79 and disks. One kneeling figure vessel from the Pacific region

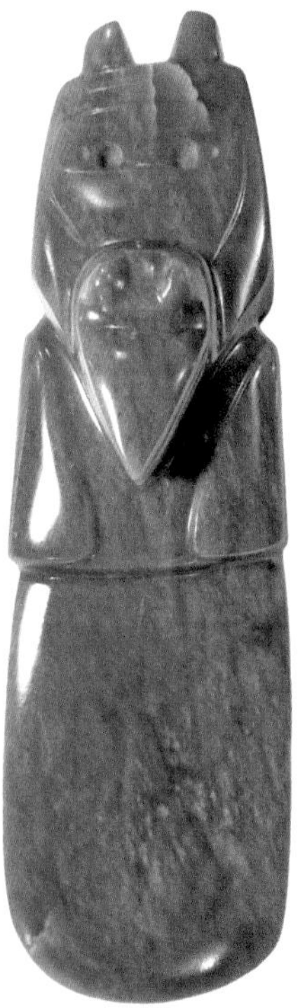

78 Zoomorphic Pendant,
300–500

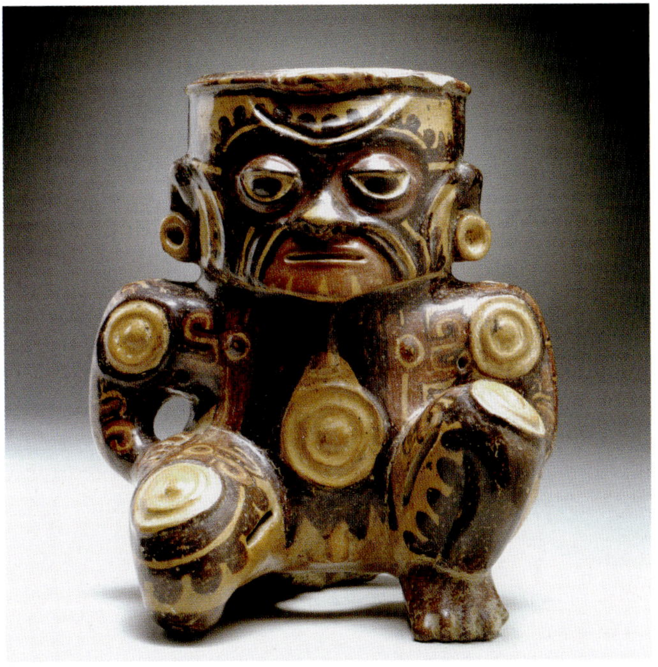

79
Anthropomorphic Vessel, 500–800

of Guanacaste-Nicoya illustrates an individual wearing such gold disks along with gold earflares. The male individual is decorated with elaborate zoomorphic designs in body paint and wears gold disks on his torso, shoulders, knees, and rear hips. The presence of both greenstone and gold in the regalia of important people in Costa Rica underscores the range of social connections present in this region that generated the flow of materials and ideas.

In ancient times as in the contemporary world, Panama was the center of the Americas, a vital landscape that served as a nexus of communication and exchange between North and South America and between the Caribbean and Pacific. Early populations settled in Panama and the rich maritime and terrestrial resources of the isthmus allowed for diverse societies to develop over time. The long-distance trade that ancient Panamanians generated is evidenced in the wide array of luxury materials recovered by archaeologists in some of the richest tombs ever found in the Americas. Over centuries in central Panama, for example, rulers of the societies known today as Gran Coclé commissioned artists to create iconic works of gold, bone, shell, greenstone, and other materials that adorned their bodies and accompanied them in their final resting places.

Although many archaeological finds in Panama came to international attention in the nineteenth century as the cross-isthmus railroad and canal were being created, scientific excavation in the region began in earnest in the early twentieth century. In the 1930s scholarly attention turned to Sitio Conte, named after the landowners where the site was located, and the Peabody Museum of Harvard University and University of Pennsylvania Museum conducted excavations on an impressive array of tombs, sometimes superimposed with later ones or cut into earlier ones. The site represents a necropolis used by wealthy royal families over the course of at least five centuries, in which the descendants reverentially buried their ancestors. Little is known about these dynasties; no residences have been located yet and no texts or narrative arts survive at present to provide more context for the Gran Coclé.

80 The gold works present at Sitio Conte, however, with their dense image programs, formed some of the most elegant sets of regalia known from the ancient world. The most complex burial excavated by the Harvard University team, known as Grave 26, contain circular gold plaques embossed with complex imagery, gold arm cuffs and greaves, golden beaded necklaces, and pendants made from agate and other precious stones. The large disk here, depicting two crocodilian creatures in mirror image facing away from each other in profile, was associated with the grave's principal figure, who presumably wore the greenstone-and-gold ear rods with floral finials as well. The burial also yielded pendants depicting supernatural creatures, perhaps insects, with abdomens made of precious gems. The examples here show polished lavender quartzite and a remarkable 112-carat uncut, polished emerald, which was likely imported from the northern Andes.

The imaginative visual culture among Gran Coclé artists is
81 also on view in the hundreds of exquisitely painted ceramic vessels recovered from Sitio Conte and related sites. One plate from the Penn Museum's excavations is covered with complex imagery of reptiles, birds, and deer that radiate outward from the vessel's central point. The interior surface depicts birds with hooked beaks interspersed with crested saurian creatures, all in mirror image in heart-shaped fields, connected by darker passages that incorporate a Y motif. The exterior shows a different scheme, in which alternating deer heads and antler finials revolve around the ring base of the plate. Recent studies of potters' fingerprints from the nearby site of El Caño have addressed the identities of potters among the Coclé, positing

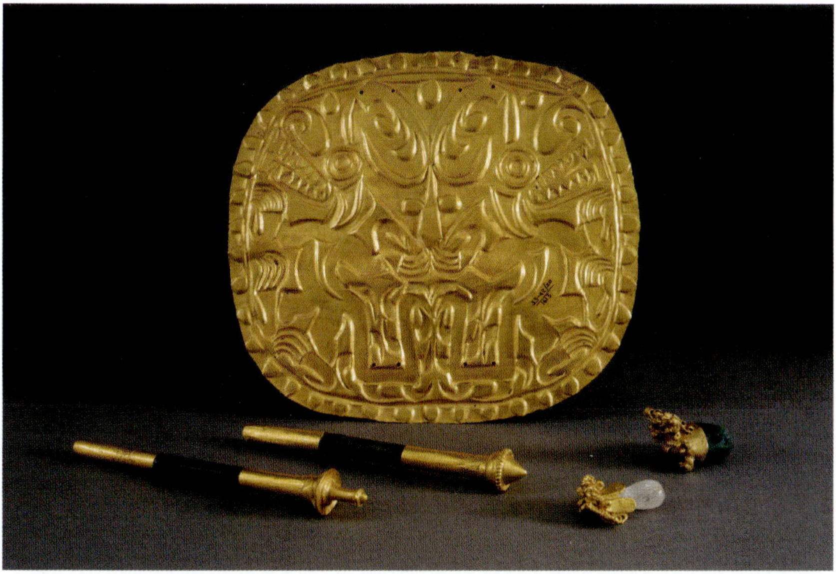

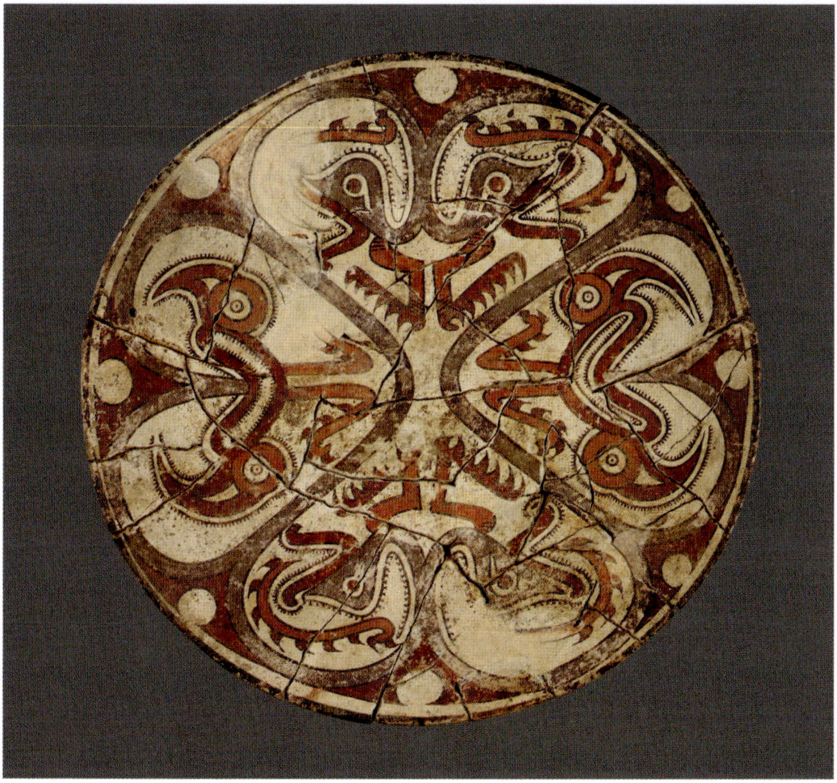

80 TOP Funerary Assemblage, 700–900
81 ABOVE Plate, 700–900

a communal method of production that involved adult males, adult females, and juveniles.

Subsequent to Gran Coclé there were several societies in the isthmus that continued gold-working traditions until the Spanish invasion. For example, artists of the Veraguas and Chiriquí cultures, named after the modern provinces, adorned their leaders with hammered gold plaques and a variety of pendants cast in gold. Some depict fanciful birds, many with exaggerated features and sonic elements such as metal clappers in their torsos. The Spanish referred to them as *águilas* or *aguilillas*, "eagles" or "little eagles," and they may indeed have been inspired by the largest raptor in the region, the harpy eagle. Such gold avian pendants were widely traded, having been recovered from the Antilles, the Yucatán Peninsula, and as far east as the Guianas.

Amazon

In many ways, one of the final frontiers in the archaeology of the Americas is one of the largest regions by land area, encompassing the Amazon River basin in South America. The vast expanses of mature rainforest proved to be a formidable barrier in developing archaeological projects in the area, as did the poor preservation of perishable materials. Recent excavations coupled with landscape surveys in the region, however, have revealed a starkly different picture of the ancient past than previously understood. Whereas Portuguese and Spanish colonizers in the sixteenth through eighteenth centuries mention large populations in the region, prior investigators assumed that ancestral Amazonia was populated by small-scale societies such as those encountered in the ethnographic present. New evidence from remote sensing and archaeological investigations now confirms large, densely populated settlements with distinct visual cultures that imply complex social organization for many centuries before European invasion. Researchers have now documented places where people lived, farmed, fished, buried their ancestors, and created elaborate works of art throughout the lands traversed by major rivers.

One such culture is known as Marajoara, after the large island of Marajó on the coast of Brazil, which flourished between 400 and 1350 CE. In this archipelago, archaeologists have recovered evidence of an elaborate funerary tradition
82 involving beautifully decorated urns. The silhouette of this vessel consists of a globular base and tall, cylindrical neck, punctuated by modeled elements on the sides of the chamber and at around the rim. The potter carved geometric,

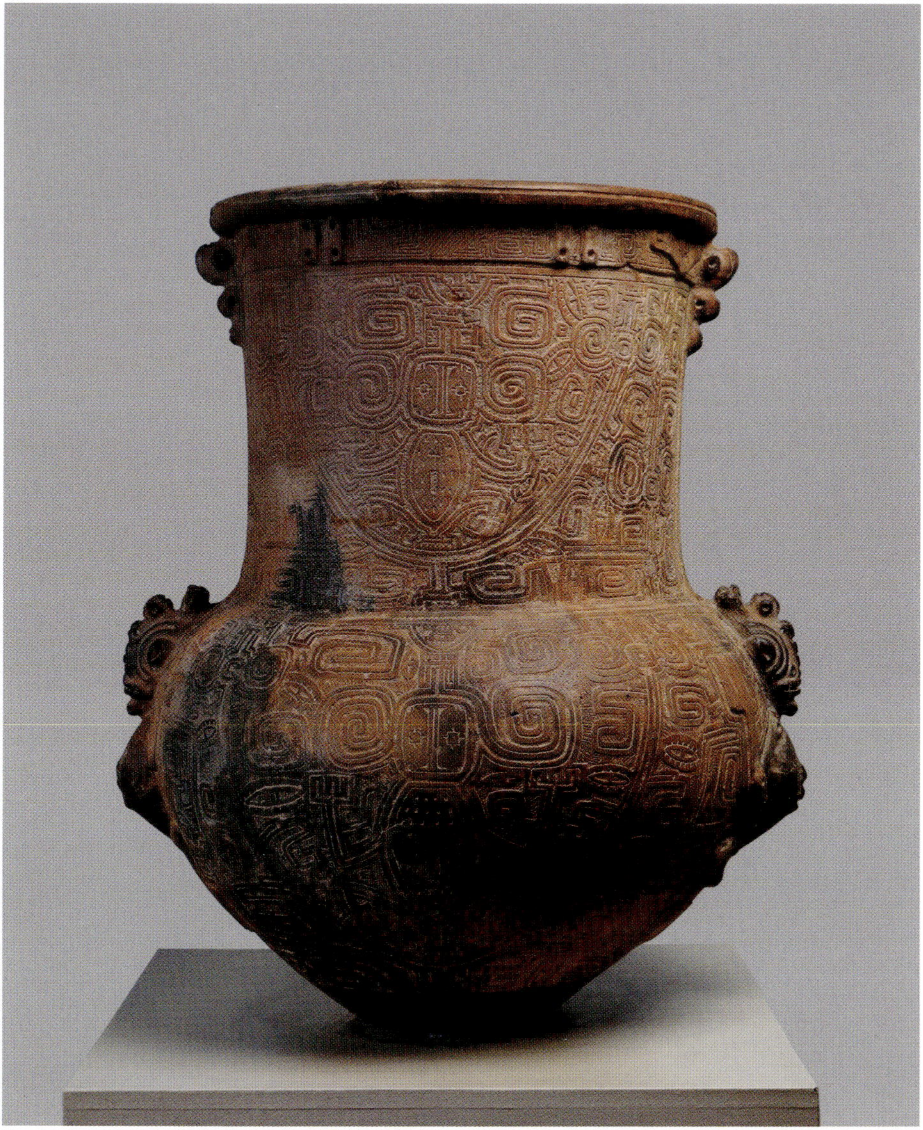

82 Funerary Urn, 400–1400

anthropomorphic, and zoomorphic forms on the entire surface of the vessel. Shifting perspectives, similar to those exhibited by Andean works (see chapter 1), also characterize ceramic arts of the region. Although any mnemonic or narrative content is inaccessible to modern viewers, the rich symbolism and repeated patterns show features of serpents such as snakeskin patterns and undulating bodies. The recurrence of serpent motifs on Marajoara works through time may indicate a now-lost origin story or mythological narrative centering on such a spiritually important, ancestral snake being. The concentric geometric motifs have been compared to contemporary Indigenous designs, such as those produced by Shipibo artists in the western Amazon, evidence of the shared aesthetic and continuity of abstraction as a defining characteristic of Amazonian visual cultures.

Several archaeological data indicate that, similar to the traditions described above, powerful individuals or families would have cultivated talented communities of artistic practice. Some of the Marajoara urns contained burials of young people accompanied by stone objects, such as axes or beaded jewelry, indicating that long-distance trade correlated with higher status of some individuals and families, and that status was inherited. The manipulation of the landscape including large earthworks in the Amazon mirrors other traditions in the Americas in which communities created elevated living and ceremonial spaces. Earthworks would have been both symbolic and practical, to manage rainfall, freshwater currents, and fish populations in the abundant seasonal wetlands created by the largest river system in the world. Peoples across the region also innovated *terra preta*, "dark earth" in Portuguese, in which farmers would enrich the sedimentary soils with ash from burned organic matter in order to increase fertility. These types of monumental projects imply either a shared vision of a large group or the direction of a singular or collective authority, or both.

Marajoara art is also notable for abundant representations of females on both funerary vessels, figurines, and ceramic-based garments known as *tangas*. Some figurines representing stylized bodies with female characteristics also share a phallic form, and often such objects doubled as musical instruments such as rattles. Potters were thus essential to the ceremonial life of Marajoara rulers and their communities; they fed them, entertained them, and sometimes even clothed them. Feasting on ceremonial occasions was an important part of Amazonian life, and the consumption of alcoholic or entheogenic beverages and tobacco played a role in knitting together the social fabric. Women as matriarchs, as food and beverage preparers, as potters, and as painters, were central.

New archaeological research is revealing that peer civilizations to those found on Marajó Island existed beyond the mouth of the Amazon, including peoples who practised polychrome ceramic traditions. Upriver, for example, at the confluence of the Tapajós and the Amazon, a culture known as Santarém developed after about 1000 CE. Peoples across this region also innovated *terra preta*. Potters from Santarém societies created beautiful vessels for eating and drinking, as well as figurines of males and females wearing elaborate regalia such as headdresses, necklaces, ear ornaments, and bracelets indicative of a special status. Artists there also shaped greenstones into such zoomorphic forms as frogs, animals that were noted for their amphibious power of navigating land, water, and even trees. Similar to other cultures at this time, such valuable stone objects were traded widely among the Amazon, the Guianas, and even the Antilles archipelago before European colonization.

The Antilles Archipelago

The Caribbean Sea connected peoples all throughout the islands and coastlines for thousands of years before the invading Spanish set foot in the region. The diverse societies mentioned above from Colombia, Panama, Costa Rica, and even the Maya peoples farther to the north traded with each other and with the groups in the Antilles archipelago, known today as the Taínos. Accomplished canoeists on the open sea, people moved from the northern reaches of Amazonia to the Antilles as early as the fifth millennium BCE. Such was the centrality of sea travel on these vessels: the term *canoe* itself is borrowed into English via Spanish from the Taíno language. People migrated in different waves from northern South America, bringing with them both agricultural and art-making traditions, and established social relations and intergroup politics. Some notable features in the islands include architecture such as rounded platforms lined with stones and topped with perishable buildings, ceramic arts that bear similarities to those recovered in what is now Venezuela, and personal adornments of metal, precious stones, or shell.

By the late first millennium CE, what we consider artistic practice was likely a collaboration among male and female political leaders known as *caciques*, their ritual specialists, and those skilled at the arts of sculpture. Late fifteenth-century accounts by Spanish religious authorities describe that sculpture began with a call from the medium itself, such

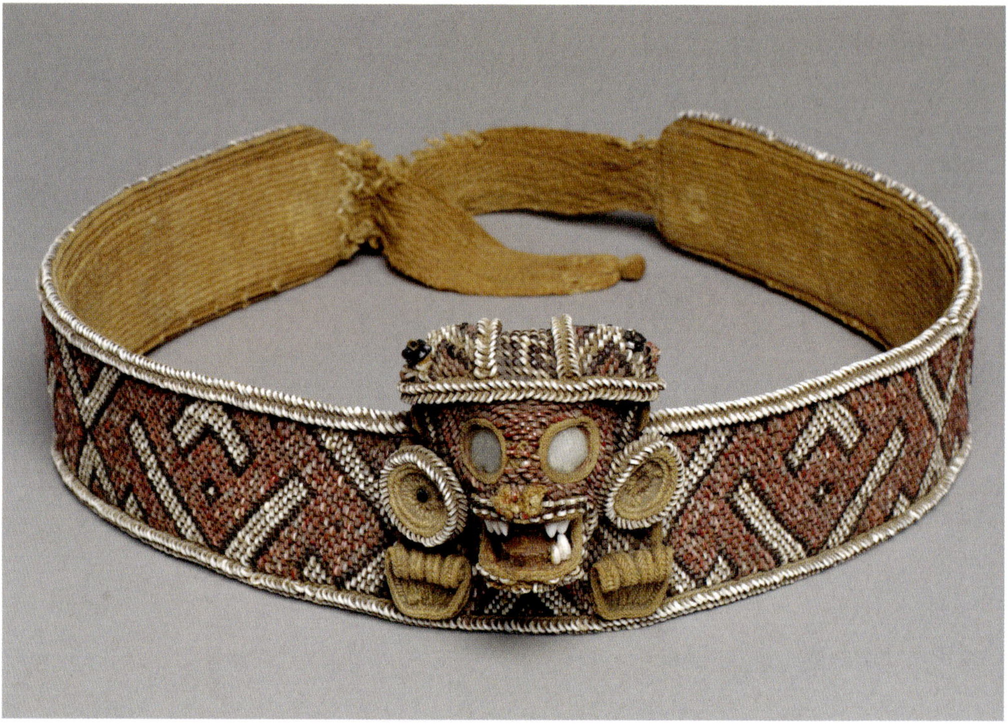

83 Belt, 1475–1635

as a tree that exhibited a special shape or material quality. The
spirit within the tree or stone, known in the Taíno language as
a zemí, would then call out to the leader and sculptor and make
its identity known. The artists would then make the identity
of the spirit manifest, investing the sculpture with the divine
power harnessed from the landscape. The political rulers or
ritual specialists would then become the caretakers of these
11 zemí figures, who had their own identities and biographies.
Zemí in the Taíno language refers not only to an object or
image but also to a spiritual and vital force pertaining to
deities and ancestors, similar to *k'uh* in the Maya area and
wak'a in the Andes.

Zemí identities, some of which were documented in the late
fifteenth century by the invading Spanish, were also built into
personal regalia and royal garments. Only one such garment,
83 a beaded cotton belt that was created in the late fifteenth
or early sixteenth century, survives today. With over 11,000
beads, the artist designed the belt with an elaborate geometric
design framing a central three-dimensional figure. The central

zemí character is a batlike being, with raised fists, wearing an elaborate headdress and large earflares. When worn, the snarling deity would have been seen as emerging from the body of the wearer, its gleaming white shell teeth ready to tear into the flesh of anyone who opposed the will of its patron. Leaders were seen as important caretakers of zemí forces. For the Taíno peoples, as in the wider Caribbean region, creative expression was inseparable from sacred concepts of zemí and the intersecting roles of political and spiritual leadership. Zemí figures, along with garments and regalia imbued with spiritual energies by the sculptors, were then activated in large gatherings, such as ceremonial feasts and performances, known as *areítos*. The Spanish authorities recognized that these songs were the equivalent of Taíno history books, with oral narratives passed down through generations.

The former stages for these gatherings were the stone-lined plazas that dot the landscape of places like Puerto Rico, which included games with a rubber ball like those seen among mainland societies in Mesoamerica. So even though the Taínos chose not to build pyramidal structures or settlements with rectilinear layouts like their peers in Mesoamerica and the Andes, evidence exists that they participated in the wider exchange networks of both materials and ideas that stretched from the Amazon to Central Mexico.

Part III
The Art of Cities

Cities or urban spaces are difficult to define in the ancient world. Even within the Americas, different regional traditions led to different scales of building, evidence of specialization in communities of practice, and bureaucratic institutions. The next three chapters address some of the most important case studies in North, Central, and South America of what we recognize as cities, settlements that grew larger than those mentioned in previous chapters such as among the Maya and Moche, and show evidence of centralized administration. Over centuries, these places either developed organically from previous traditions or were purposefully planned and built, or a combination of both. The following case studies emphasize that these traditions of urbanism are comparable to other historical traditions. Regardless of what form the cities took, though, architects and artists built important sacred concepts into the structures that spring from some of the deep-rooted traditions described in parts I and II. These places became centripetal forces for people throughout centuries as people were attracted to the cosmopolitan lives that cities could afford them. Most importantly, the aggregation of people into densely populated zones seems to have spurred some of the most iconic artistic traditions in the Americas.

City leaders from Mexico to Peru to the U.S. Southwest commissioned building programs, mural paintings, monumental sculptures, and near-industrial-level workshop production of luxury goods. The forms of leadership at these places may have been a departure from the type of royal courts seen in previous chapters. Some evidence suggests that certain place—like Teotihuacán, Tiwanaku, Wari, Cahokia, or Chaco Canyon—may have been more collectively governed than by a supreme authority like a monarch. Regardless of how their

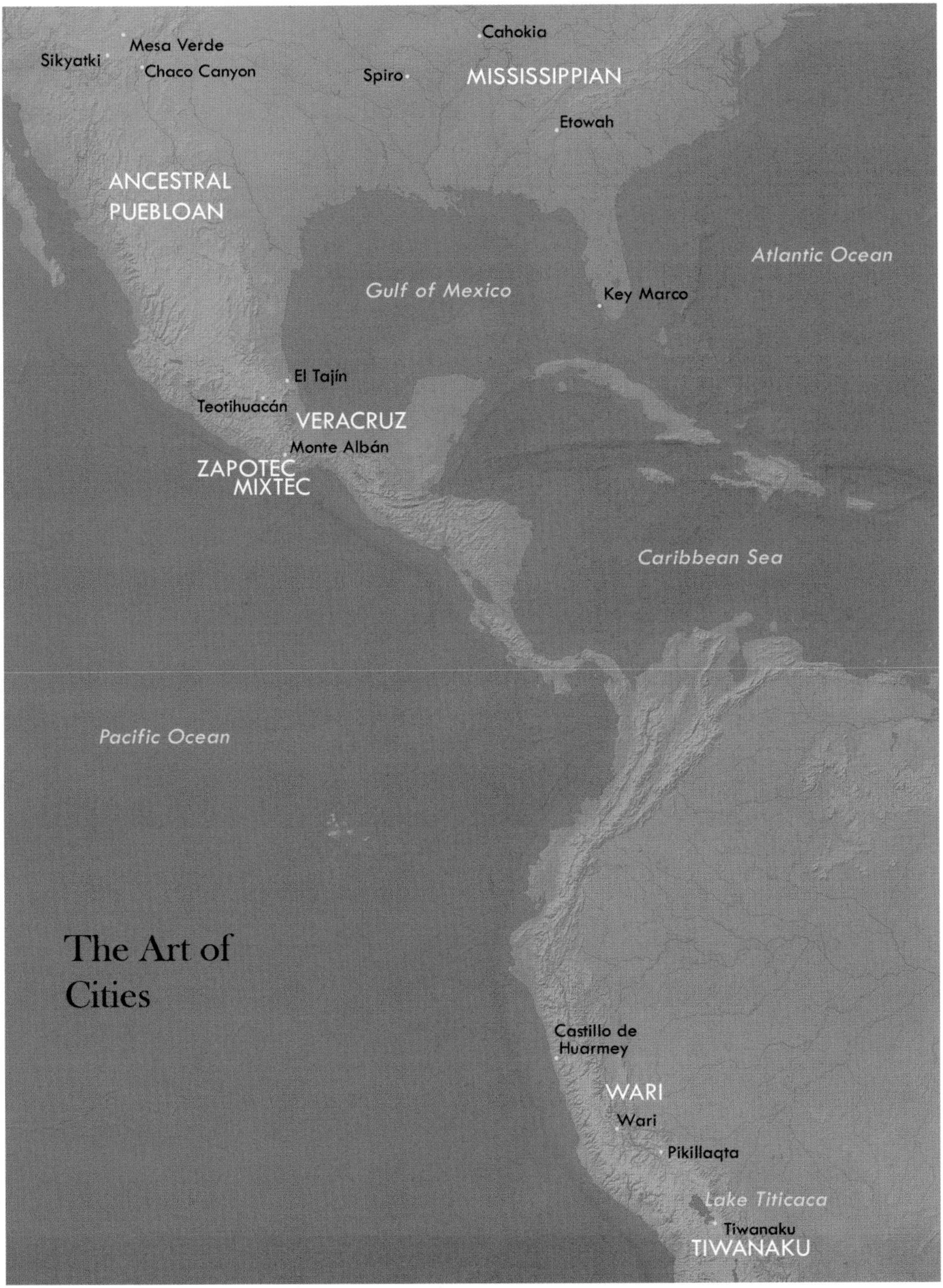

The Art of Cities

patrons organized themselves, artists were a huge part of creating that desire to live in cities. No makers are currently known by name from these places, but the ritual objects and domestic and civic sculpture they created speak for them. Their creativity amplified the message of the settlements' governors and transcended cultural differences by projecting widespread symbolic values without written texts.

Chapter 6
Volcanic Authority: Teotihuacán and its Successors (100–1500 CE)

Teotihuacán

84 When arriving at Teotihuacán, visitors are greeted with a sensory overload of sights and sounds. From a distance, the surrounding mountains appear to form part of the heart of the city itself, and only upon approaching these hulking forms on foot does it become clear that these are giant stone-faced pyramids made by human hands. These structures, known colloquially since the sixteenth century as the Pyramid of the Sun and Pyramid of the Moon, are some of the biggest pyramids by volume in the Western Hemisphere, and some of the largest ancient constructions ever built. The Pyramid of the Sun was over 200 feet in height (greater than 60 m), with a square base, each side measuring over 735 feet (225 m), making its footprint almost the size of the Great Pyramid of Giza in Egypt. They punctuate a planned urban landscape that is unique in the Americas. Wide central avenues were lined with palaces that have internal courtyards, all oriented specifically 15°28’ east of true north, and multi-family apartment compounds sprawl outward from the central axes for miles in every direction. The city covers more than 8 square miles (21 sq. km) and perhaps had over 100,000 residents at its peak. Even long after the city was largely abandoned, it loomed large in the consciousness of peoples throughout Central Mexico as a primordial origin place. The later Nahuatl term (the language of the Mexica, see chapter 10) for the place, Teotihuacán, roughly translates to “the place where humans met the gods.” Colonial chronicles reporting life in the sixteenth century for the peoples in Central Mexico, noted that Teotihuacán was the place where the gods gathered before the dawn of the current world.

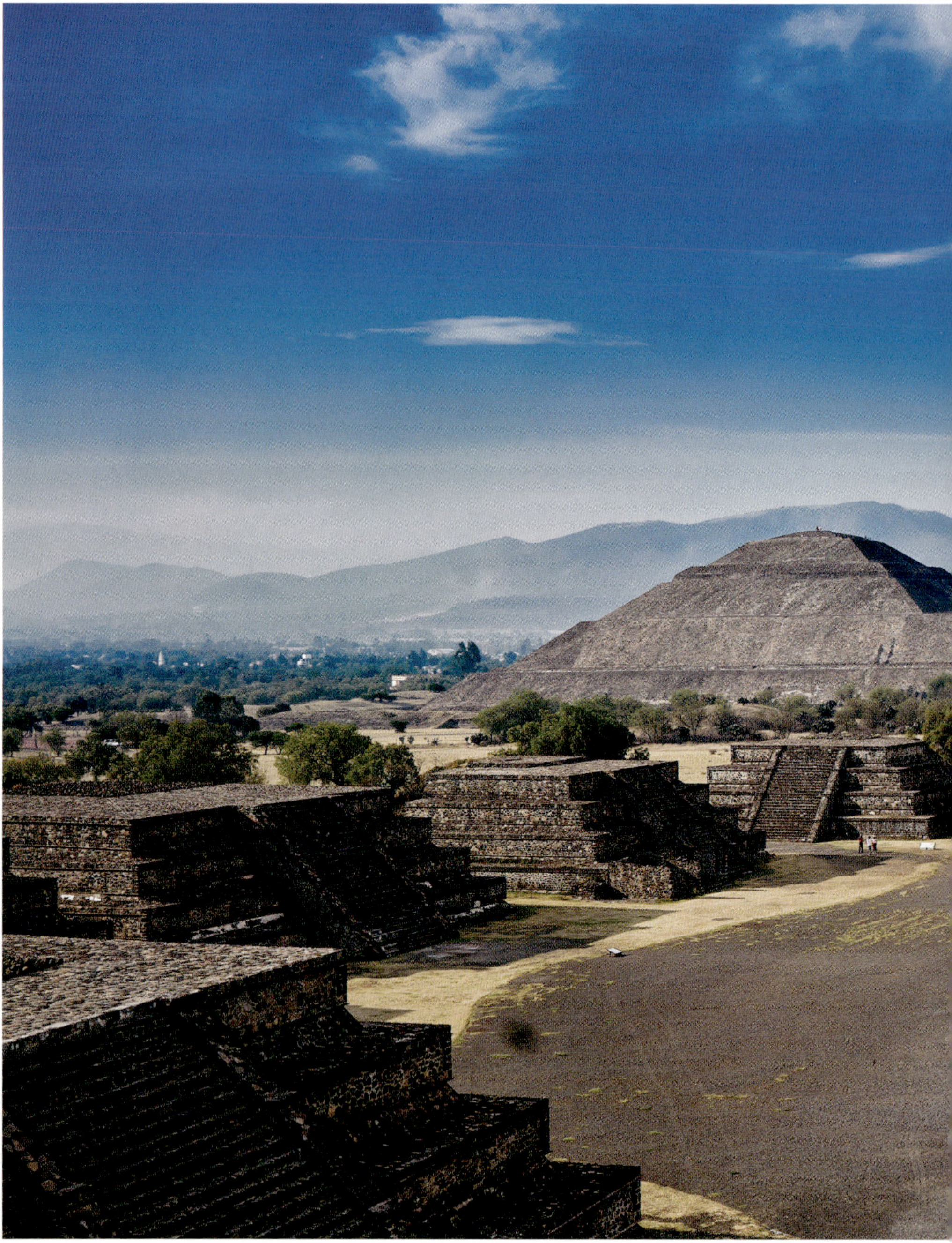

 Teotihuacán, Mexico

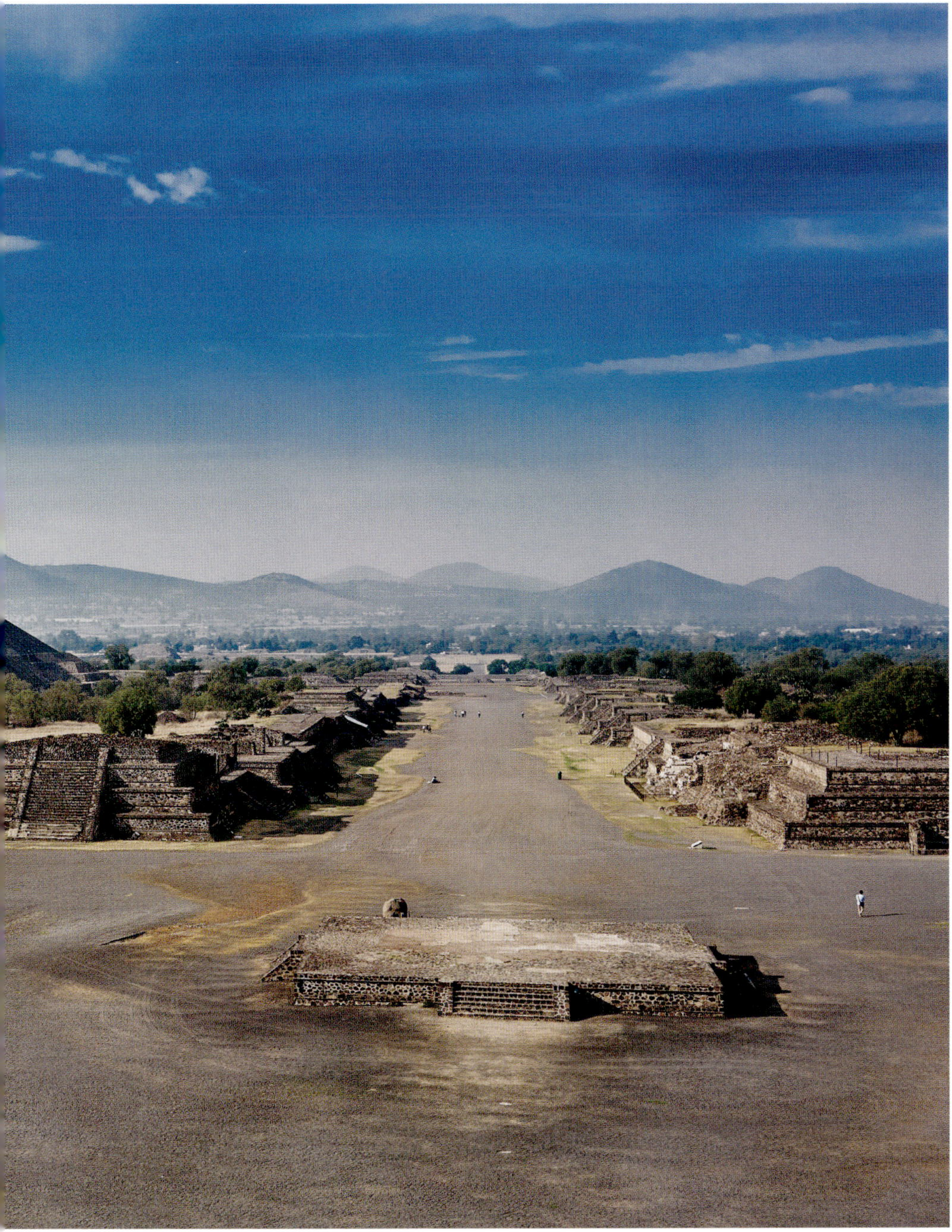

It is difficult not to use a string of superlatives to describe Teotihuacán: one of the largest and most important urban planning initiatives before European invasion; the only pre-industrial city in the Americas which multi-family, multi-story apartment compounds were the dominant mode of residence; and perhaps the earliest true hegemonic empire in the hemisphere. The one distinction that resonates with modern city dwellers is that archaeological evidence shows that Teotihuacán was truly a pluri-ethnic capital. The political and spiritual power visible at Teotihuacán clearly drew in people from far and wide, especially from the areas of Oaxaca, Veracruz, Michoacán, and the Maya region. Residents at Teotihuacán from these regions brought their own traditions of making which had developed over centuries as peer aesthetic systems.

The geology of Teotihuacán played a large role in its location and population growth. As described in chapter 2, many peoples in the area around modern Mexico City conducted long-distance trade and constructed monumental ceremonial centers. One of those settlements, known as Tetimpa, was located on the eastern slopes of the massive volcano, Popocatépetl, that is still very active to this day. Evidence suggests that at the end of the first century CE, a major Plinian eruption occurred that buried Tetimpa and related settlements under pyroclastic flow, similar to how Vesuvius buried the Roman villas at Pompeii in Italy. Unlike at Pompeii, however, Tetimpa residents seemed to have had fair warning and fled with their belongings. They did leave behind stone sculptures in central courtyard altars, which have been interpreted as volcano effigy shrines. The ritual activities that honored the nearby volcano on this domestic scale ultimately did not prevent these people from having to migrate.

The eruption of Popocatépetl may have spurred the migration of a large number of people toward the valley of Teotihuacán. There, populations in the valley began to construct large ceremonial platforms toward the end of the first millennium BCE, similar in style to the domestic platforms and courtyards in Tetimpa. Available evidence suggests that the early phase of the Pyramid of the Moon anchored the ceremonial precinct around 100 CE, with the other major landmarks, the Pyramid of the Sun and the Feathered Serpent Pyramid, constructed in later time periods. Builders constructed these two later monuments directly above caves that had been created as (or modified to be) human tunnels, marking them as primordial mountain cave places, where Mesoamerican gods were believed to have been born.

The Pyramid of the Moon, the only major monument on the central axis of the city, subsequently became a focus of ritual life at Teotihuacán. Around 250 CE builders enlarged the pyramid considerably, placing two sumptuous dedicatory offerings in the core of the building. The deposit known as Burial 2 contained a male, approximately forty to fifty years in age, interred in a seated position with his arms bound behind his back, suggesting that he was an important captive. Subsequent analysis of the skeletal isotopes and the funerary assemblage, which included greenstone jewelry, suggest that this individual was a high-status person from outside Teotihuacán. Around the person were dozens of offerings of animals such as pumas, golden eagles, a wolf, other birds, rattlesnakes, and shellfish. The pumas and wolf were buried alive in wooden cages.

Other works from contemporaneous offerings demonstrate that artists at Teotihuacán had developed a distinctive style of representing human figures. In the dedicatory chamber known as Burial 6, contemporaneous with Burial 2, archaeologists
85 recovered a unique wooden sculpture inlaid with greenstones and shell, placed atop a slate-and-pyrite disk interpreted as a mirror. Consistent with earlier local traditions, the outsized head is the focus of detail on this figure. The shield-shaped head is adorned with shell-inlaid eyes, a naturalistically modeled nose, and *Spondylus* shell mosaic lips that part to reveal shell teeth. Teotihuacán sculpture portrays human and divine individuals with very rectilinear features and only vaguely defined limbs, such as the stylized shoulders, hips, and legs here. The sculpture itself wore greenstone jewelry, including two earflares and a beaded necklace. The figure could represent an important human actor in the early history of Teotihuacán, or perhaps, a divine individual. Surrounding the principal offering of this figure were twelve sacrificed adult male captives and numerous animals that also seem to have been bound and sacrificed during this ritual dedication. Each new phase of the Pyramid of the Moon was added and dedicated with sumptuous architectural caches.

84 An imposing road known as the Avenue of the Dead formed the main north–south axis of the city. During its heyday, however, the avenue was anything but dead. Teotihuacán was one of the largest cities in the world at that time, so the avenue would have been a hive of activity. Hosts of temples and palaces lined each side of the pathway. Toward the southern end of the promenade, on the east side, residents constructed a large walled compound known as the Ciudadela (citadel), with the Feathered Serpent Pyramid at its center. It is estimated that thousands of people could have fit into the plaza of the

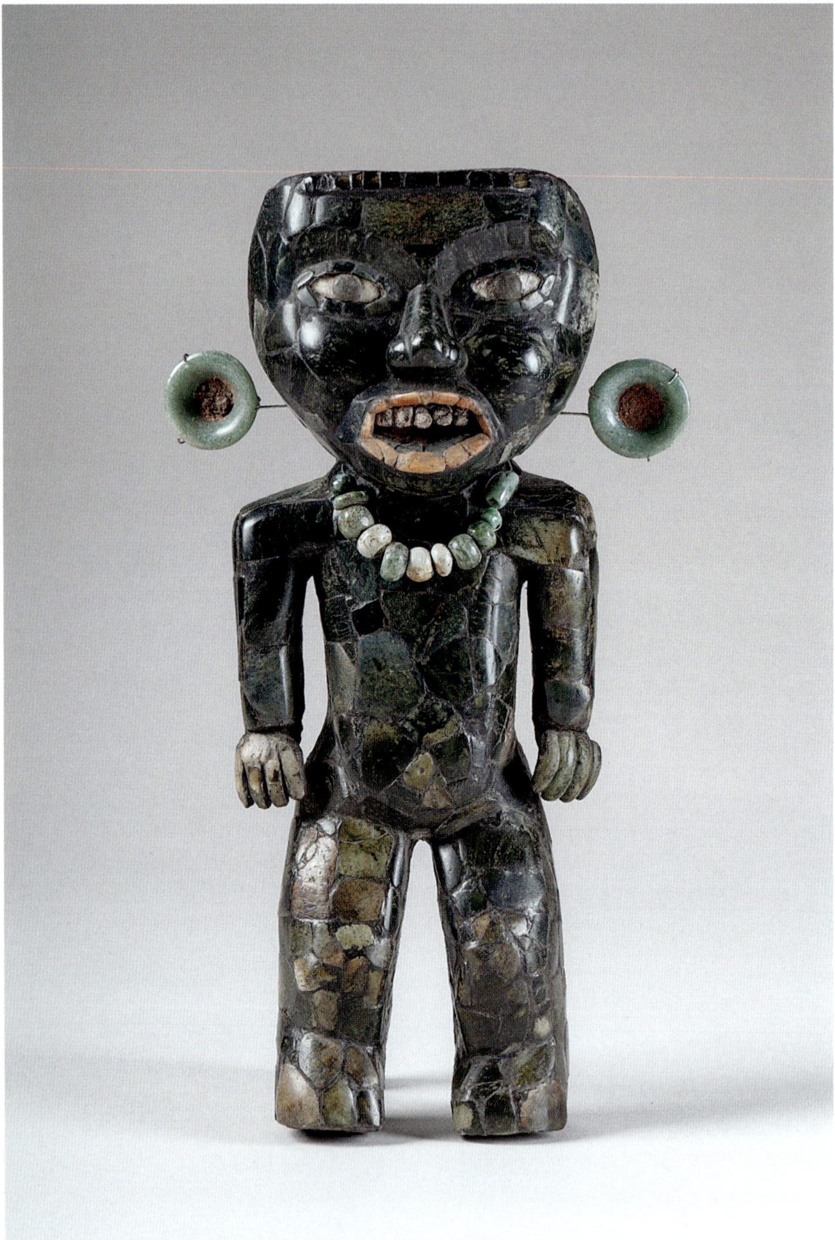

85 Mosaic Figure, 200–250

Ciudadela on ceremonial occasions, and it could have even been flooded, making the pyramidal structure in the center appear to emerge from a primordial sea.

86 The Feathered Serpent Pyramid is known for its monumental mosaic facade depicting complex images of war headdresses, serpents emerging from flowers, and marine creatures. First created around 200 CE, the pyramid features an outset stairway with balustrade and a terraced set of tiers created in a style known as *talud-tablero*, in which a sloped element supports a flat surface perpendicular to the ground line. As a large-scale dedicatory offering, more than two hundred people were sacrificed and buried under the building with various objects of shell and greenstone. Sculptors subsequently constructed the *tableros* on the Feathered Serpent Pyramid with stone blocks imported from the mountainsides outside the city, then carved the intricate iconographic program in place. These surfaces were brightly painted, making them striking visual messages of the buildings' patrons.

There are three main elements to the facade of the pyramid. First, the namesake feathered serpent emerges from a floral motif, carved in the round and tenoned into the *tablero*. The

86 Facade of the Feathered Serpent Pyramid, 200–650

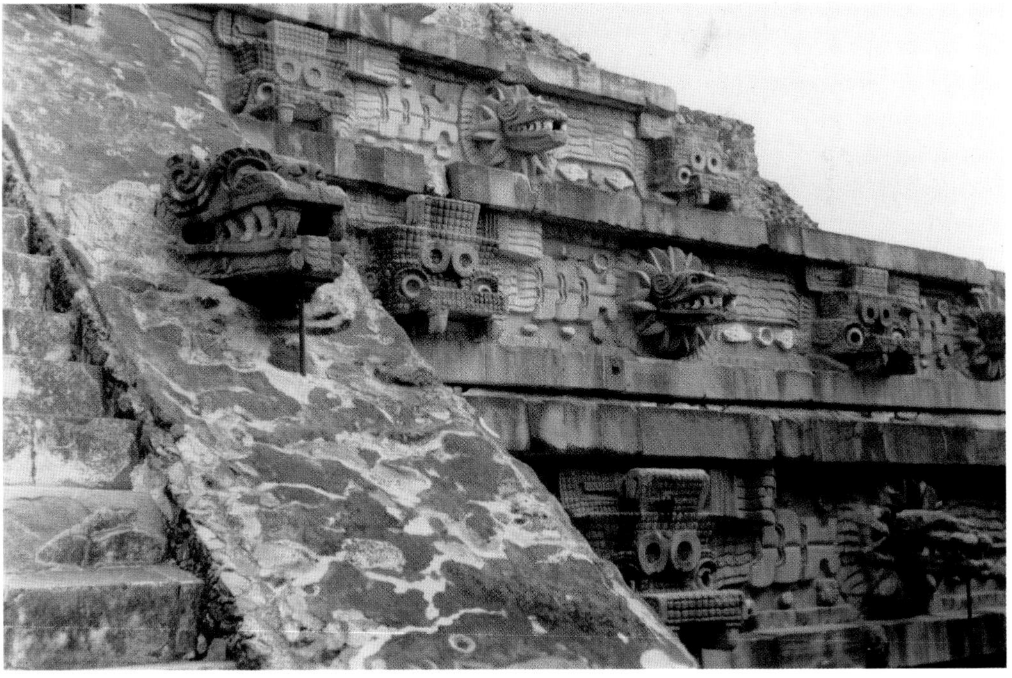

serpent head contains large rounded eyes, a scaly eyebrow that curls backward, curled nostrils, and lipped jaws that part to reveal a series of fangs. The sculptors then carved an undulating body in low relief containing overlapping feather-scales. The body terminates in a three-tiered rattle. The presence of rattlesnakes in offerings described above underscores the importance of this predatory viper to Teotihuacán mythology. The second main element to the facade is a series of floating shells in low relief surrounding the body of the feathered serpent. Through these marine creatures, the artists indicate the setting of the serpent's emergence as a watery, paradisical location, perhaps underscored by the flooding of the Ciudadela, as mentioned. Shells, which were long-distance trade goods, also symbolized preciousness and opulence.

The third element is a composite sculpture that simultaneously represents a crocodilian creature, the goggled eyes and fanged mouth mask of a local rain deity, and a mosaic headdress that served a symbol for warfare. The crocodilian creature is seen in the upturned snout and wide-set eyes depicted as concentric rings, as well as fangs lining the upper jaw. The two large rings in the forehead of the crocodilian are emblematic of a fanged rain deity seen across media at
62, 64 Teotihuacán, and, indeed, subsequently in the Maya area.
145 This god also may be a precursor to the Mexica storm god,
Tlaloc. The boxy but imposing headdress seems to be emerging from or carried by the feathered serpent, and could represent symbols of power for the builders of the Feathered Serpent Pyramid. Painted red, white, and green, these images would have had dazzling visual effects when seen from the plaza below.

Despite over a century of archaeological research at the site, a major question about Teotihuacán remains: Who was in charge? Various proposals have been put forward, from dynastic kingship to collective action, but one key component of society is generally agreed upon: a distinct emphasis on militarism. Perhaps the most compelling evidence for a model of Teotihuacán's governance as a king controlling a military comes not from the city itself, but from the Maya region over 800 miles (1300 km) away. In monuments from several different royal courts, scribes recorded a major event in the year 378 CE in which Teotihuacános marched into what is now Guatemala, presumably a martial invasion. They played a major role in reshaping the dynasty at Tikal (see chapter 4), and subsequent rulers wore insignia connecting them to the faraway city well after the decline of Teotihuacán itself. In fact, recent evidence has confirmed the likely presence of Maya-speaking peoples who traveled to Central Mexico, perhaps living in close proximity to the heart of Teotihuacán itself. Fragments of murals in the Plaza of the Columns area near the Moon Pyramid suggest that Maya artists were active there up until the fourth century.

This is perhaps what connects Teotihuacán to many other cities in the Americas: it was truly a painted city. It is estimated that tens if not hundreds of thousands of square feet of the city's walls were covered in fresco paintings. Artists developed a specific painting technique of buon fresco on an adobe support, creating a surface that remained damp longer, to which they applied brilliant pigments of red, green, yellow, black, and white. The mural painters developed different techniques for adding vibrant colors to both ceremonial and residential structures, with great emphasis on the color red. The Teotihuacán red was produced by iron-oxide pigments, and later painters relied specifically on the mineral hematite to produce the brilliant dark tone that served as a background for use with a lighter red contrasting with white. Researchers in Mexico have identified four different technical phases of mural production, suggesting that the widespread practice of painting was centrally controlled and innovation was shared among artistic communities over generations.

For centuries, the residents of Teotihuacán commissioned bright murals featuring human characters, deities, mythological narrative scenes, marine imagery, and fantastic beasts such as feathered serpents. The humanlike figures are consistent in their lack of individuality or defining characteristics, with very few exceptions. For example, some
87 compounds, such as the Tetitla Portico 11, contain repeated images of characters, perhaps god images carried in a litter, that differ very little in details. In these two images, a masked figure wears a large feathered headdress, wide collar, and draping garment, as streams descend from its outstretched arms. Those flowing elements contain marine shells, signifying preciousness and primordial fertility. The repeated figures have a glyphlike quality, as if a proper name or word came to life.

The artist could have portrayed here a human impersonating a deity or a divine figure at different moments, or related versions of the same entity at one moment. Two volutes that form a U-shaped detail extending to either side of the figure's lower torso are consistent with other depictions of offering bowls in Mesoamerican art. The truncated nature of the figure's body, in combination with this bowl-like feature, might suggest we are seeing the vision of an offering or conjuring. The owl or

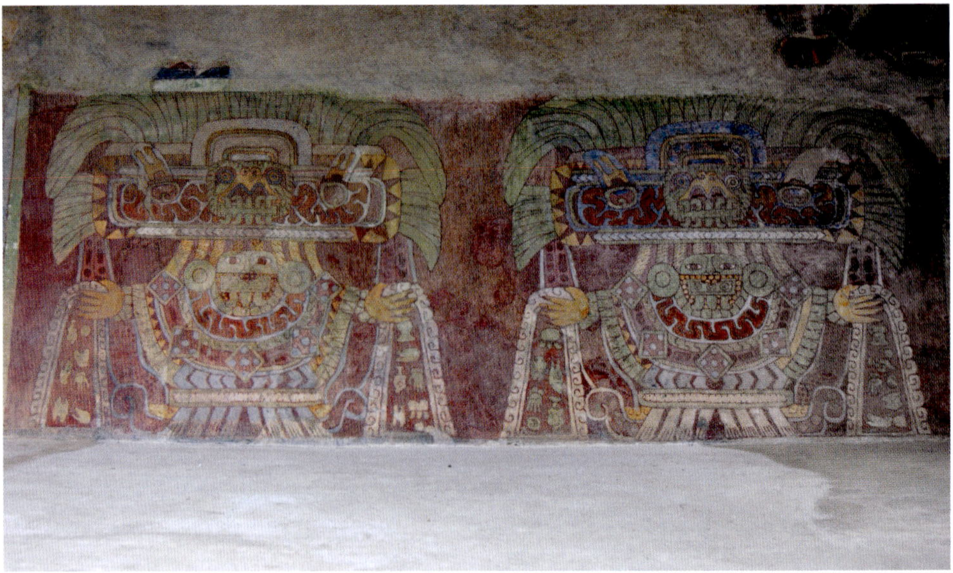

87 Mural, 200–650

eagle headdress with red crenulated star motifs also adds a skyward or celestial connotation to the scene. The nose plaque also indicates that meanings of royalty and warfare might be present here, as it bears striking similarities to those recovered
86 from the Feathered Serpent Pyramid. The eyes staring out at the viewer give this engaging scene an impactful effect.

Many other lines of evidence point to Teotihuacán being a true haven for stone sculptors. Some artists were very skilled in sculpting colossal boulders of local andesite, including the
88 largest complete monument from Teotihuacán, standing at more than 10 feet (3 m) tall. This sculpture, created between the third and sixth century, depicts a deity that has been identified as possibly a goddess associated with water. This same deity
87 may be depicted in murals, or there could have been a complex of similar but related female supernatural characters, such as the sculpted figure here. The colossal version may have been part of a group, as at least one fragmentary sculpture at the same monumental scale bears similar iconographic features. The rectilinear, prismatic nature of the sculpture recalls
85, 89 some of the smaller-scale examples in greenstone, and the architecture of the city itself. The female, identified as such by the depiction of garments such as the woven skirt and shawl or poncho (known in later Nahuatl as a *quechquemitl*), stares stoically ahead and wears a large boxy headdress crowned

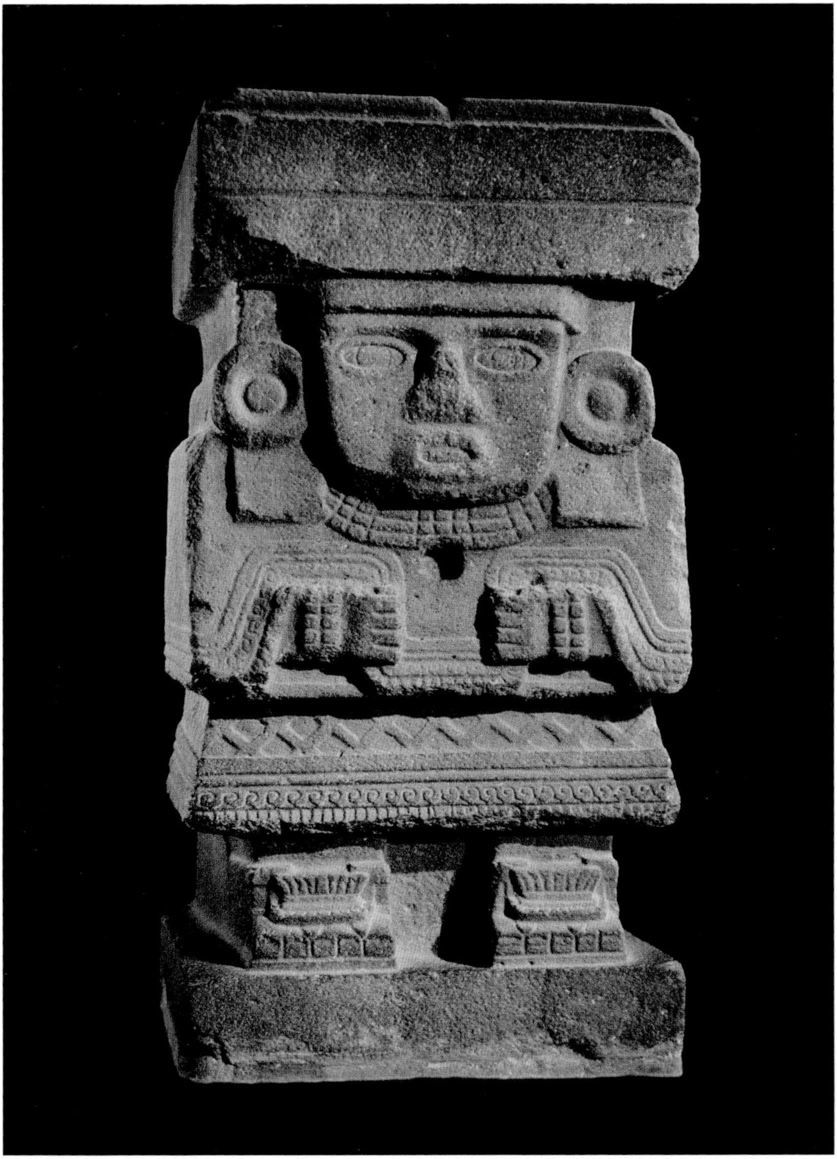

with a V-shaped cleft. She holds her arms in front of her torso, which has a large cavity in its center, which presumably once held an inlay of obsidian, shell, or precious stone. Her earflares and collar likely represent jade jewelry. This larger-than-life representation along with smaller-scale sculptures and mural paintings underscore the Teotihuacán patrons' emphasis on female imagery and watery fertility.

In addition to colossal and small-scale standing figures,
Teotihuacán artists also created greenstone objects, known
89 as “masks,” that depict stylized humanlike faces. These
disembodied heads once held inlays of pyrite or shell in the eyes and mouths or were stuccoed and painted. They may represent stylized portraits of ancestors or deities, such as a Teotihuacán version of a maize deity. They often contain drilled holes in the ears or around the interior edges, suggesting that they may have been adorned with other elements or affixed to a larger assemblage, such as a funerary bundle. These conventionalized faces stare out at modern viewers as they may have done in the buildings on the Avenue of the Dead, where only fragments were recovered, suggesting that they were subject to iconoclasm upon the abandonment of the city. In the eighth century, it seems that the central precinct of the city was burned and the neighborhoods were largely abandoned, but it is unclear on present evidence whether this was due to an environmental shock, public health crisis, external invasion, internal revolt, or some combination of these factors.

Monte Albán

The principal pre-Hispanic city in the southern Mexican state of Oaxaca is now known as Monte Albán, a capital of peoples known collectively as Zapotec. Occupied starting in the first millennium BCE, the city grew to be a large ceremonial and palatial compound situated atop a mountain. Art-historical and archaeological evidence confirms deep-rooted ties between the elite families at Monte Albán and the ruling groups of Teotihuacán. Zapotec emissaries even settled at the metropolis itself, constructing what has become known as the Oaxaca or Zapotec neighborhood at Teotihuacán. Works of art depict the interaction between the two regions, and some earlier low-relief carvings of sacrifice victims (known colloquially as *danzantes*, “dancers,” because of their contorted poses), indicate that violence between political rivals was present before the rise of Teotihuacán in Oaxaca.

Early in the history of Monte Albán, artists there created
one of the most iconic works of Mesoamerican art, in the
90 form of a mosaic belt assemblage made from jadeite and

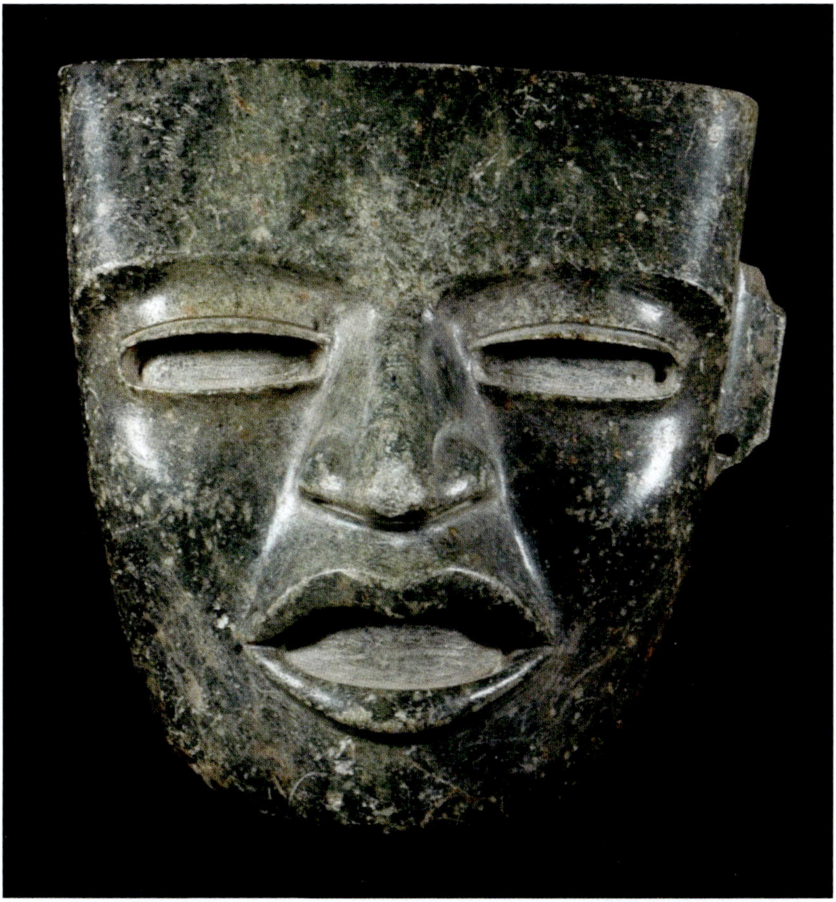

89 Anthropomorphic Mask, 200–650

other greenstones inlaid with shell. Recovered in a funerary assemblage that dates roughly between 200 BCE and 200 CE, the mask is unique in the corpus of jade works. It ingeniously combines such humanlike features as the protruding nose, feline features as the split upper lips, and batlike features in the head, including the additional upturned nose element protruding from the brow. The mouth of the mask seems to grip a T-shaped element incised with geometric designs, or it could represent the lower jaw of the composite creature. Below the mask hung three celt-shaped pendants that would have added a sonic element to the wearing of this important visage.

Monte Albán, as the city on the mountain, became an important place for the deposition of Zapotec ancestors.

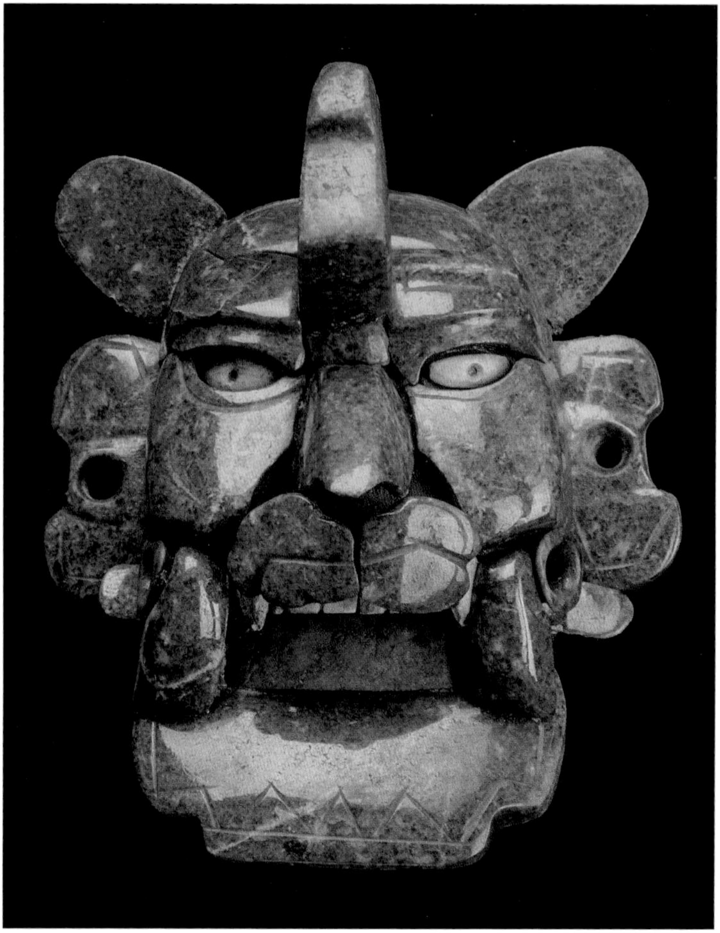

90 LEFT Zoomorphic Mask, 100 BCE–200 CE
91 OPPOSITE Funerary Urn, 200 BCE–200 CE

Potters there invented a tradition of representing deceased individuals and supernatural characters in three-dimensional
91 form as funerary urns or other containers offered in tombs. This example depicts a seated individual, perhaps a female in a wrap dress tied at the center, who crosses their arms over their chest. Wearing bracelets, a necklace, and earrings, the figure looks upward, peering out with shell-inlaid eyes as hair frames the face. The headdress dominates this composition, with a horizonal braided element terminating in cruciform plaques above the ears. Crowning the headdress is the stylized head of a monkey or other creature, with protruding snout, large fangs, outstretched tongue, and cloud-shaped eyebrows. These types of funerary urns, such as this example, were painted with

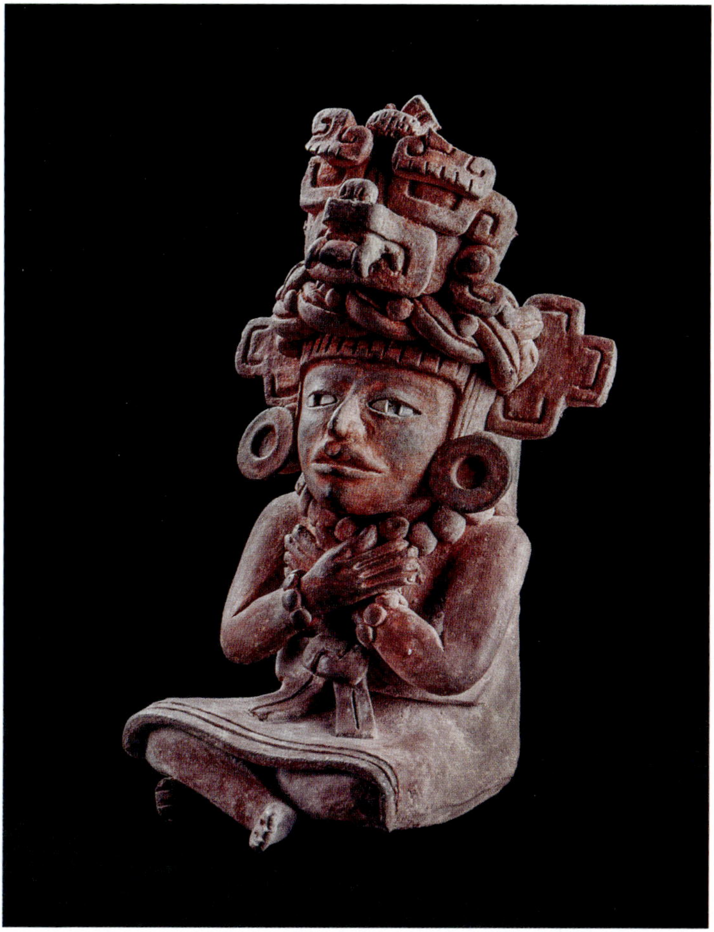

cinnabar when they were grouped together in generational tombs at Monte Albán. This urn, perhaps considered a tangible and solemn expression of grief by the person who deposited it, thus accompanied important family members into the afterlife.

Veracruz

Capturing emotion and action in the art of pottery figures and sculptures also characterized the creations in the Gulf Coast region during the first millennium CE. A particular group of hollow ceramic figurines is well known worldwide for their
92 whimsical depictions of "smiling" figures. Without texts or oral traditions, it is difficult to interpret securely the expression of this stylized standing figure here. Presumably male, the figure

wears a large skirt featuring geometric patterns and fringe, a
necklace, bracelet, earflares, and a wide headdress. Further
adornment on the body is visible in the traces of pigment on
the face and chest, perhaps representing paint or tattooing.
The front part of the headdress contains two geometric signs,
141 similar to the later Mexica hieroglyph for *olin*, "motion." The
figure's pose, grasping a rattle with his left hand and raising
his right, along with the expression of a wide-open smile
revealing altered incisors and an extended tongue, suggest a
snapshot of music, dance, or song. These figures have been
recovered buried in standing positions in large dedicatory or
funerary contexts.

Sculptors working in stone also flourished in the Gulf Coast,
creating elegant ceremonial versions of ballgame regalia.
93 Large U-shaped "yokes," so named for their resemblance to
the livestock apparatus, have been recovered by archaeologists
in funerary contexts in both Veracruz and the Maya area.
The versions from Veracruz combine motifs of frogs or toads
sculpted in the round and adorned with avian imagery, human
figures, or abstract geometric designs in low relief. Presumably,

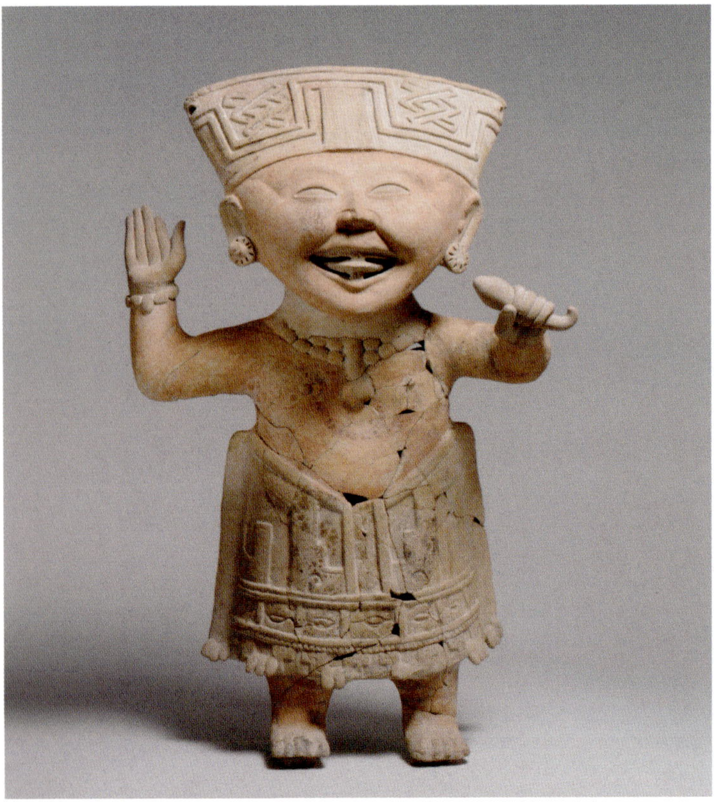

92 Anthropomorphic Figure, 600–800

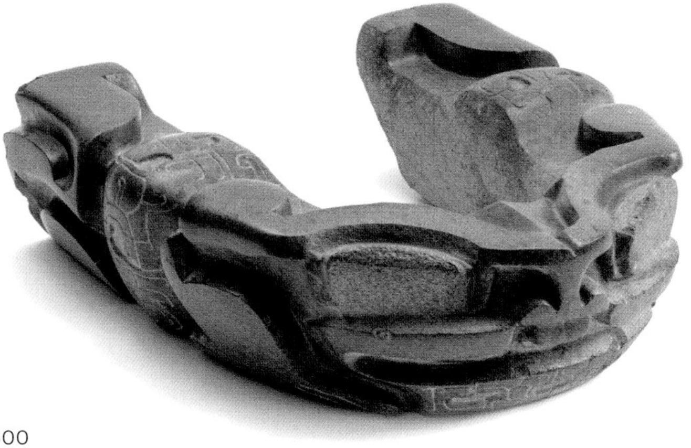

93 Zoomorphic Sculpture, 300–600

individuals from important families would have worn similarly shaped padding around the waist when engaging in the ballgame, so these enduring versions memorialize that cotton or leather regalia. Other sculptures, known as *hachas* (axes), may have been affixed at the waist or held in the hands, as seen in depictions of ballplayers.

The ball court at the site of El Tajín in Veracruz underscores the primacy of this ceremonial game in Gulf Coast life; there are no known ball courts at Teotihuacán, for example, despite murals showing people playing a kind of game. In addition to building large pyramids and sculpting freestanding sculptures,
94 artists also excelled at creating elaborate narrative scenes using mosaic stones carved in low relief. In this scene from the ballcourt, we see two individuals sacrificing a third person, above whom descends a skeletal deity from the sky. On the left, the person grasping the captive's arm wears a tiered skirt or loincloth and a large headdress with a volute projecting forward. The person on the right wears a large feathered headdress as he grasps a large stone blade that he presumably used to strike or cut the victim who lies before him. The artist(s) clearly distinguish between the three human figures and the deity. The bony hips, vertebrae, and ribcage are visible on the skeletal spirit. The way the deity's nose lightly overlaps with the captive's headdress suggests that this offering may be destined for or honoring that particular supernatural. The inclusion of a sacrificial scene in a ballcourt, with parallels in artistic programs from Maya ballcourts (see chapter 4), underscores the religious nature of the game. In some instances,

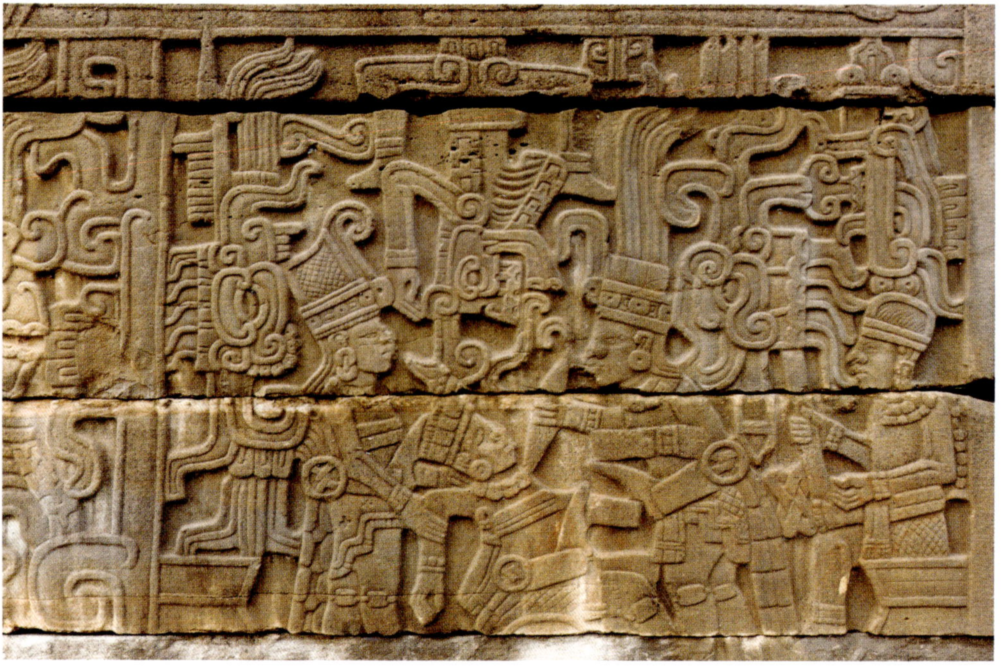

94 Frieze, 700–900

reciprocal offerings to divine forces were a part of the play and competition.

Legacies and Resonances

Even though Teotihuacán remained an ancestral place in Mesoamerican lore, its abandonment had measurable consequences on the culture history of the region toward the end of the 1st millennium. Many different visual traditions developed in the Gulf Coast region in the centuries following those described above. For example, people who spoke a Mayan language known as Huastec innovated unique artistic styles after the abandonment of Teotihuacán until the Spanish invasion. Similarly, the ancestral city of Monte Albán lived on in the consciousness of peoples in southern Mexico even until today. In the centuries before the Spanish invasion of Oaxaca, artists in the societies known as Mixtec created some of the best-known works of art from Mesoamerica, including extraordinary regalia, mural paintings, and, crucially, screenfold books.

In the 1930s the Mexican archaeologist Alfonso Caso and his team excavated one of the most spectacular tombs from the

ancient world, known as Tomb 7 from Monte Albán,
originally created in the mid-first millennium but reused
by the Mixtec in the centuries before the Spanish invasion.
The multigenerational tomb chambers included an assemblage
of luxury goods made in exotic materials such as jet, shell,
amber, bone, ceramic, and even a human skull inlaid with a
micro-mosaic of turquoise. The tomb remarkably contained
more than 100 objects made of gold and silver, including a
95 series of pectorals made using the lost-wax casting process.

This example may represent a deity known as Lord 7 Flower,
146 a Mixtec counterpart of the Mexica deity Xochipilli. The Mixtec
goldworker painstakingly composed this entire image out
of wax before casting it, depicting the bust of an individual
wearing an elaborate headdress. The central face is modeled
in three dimensions, and displays naturalistic characteristics,
including a pronounced brow and detailed eyes, a prominent
nose, and a small fringe of hair framing the forehead. The
mouth of the figure, however, seems to be either cut away or

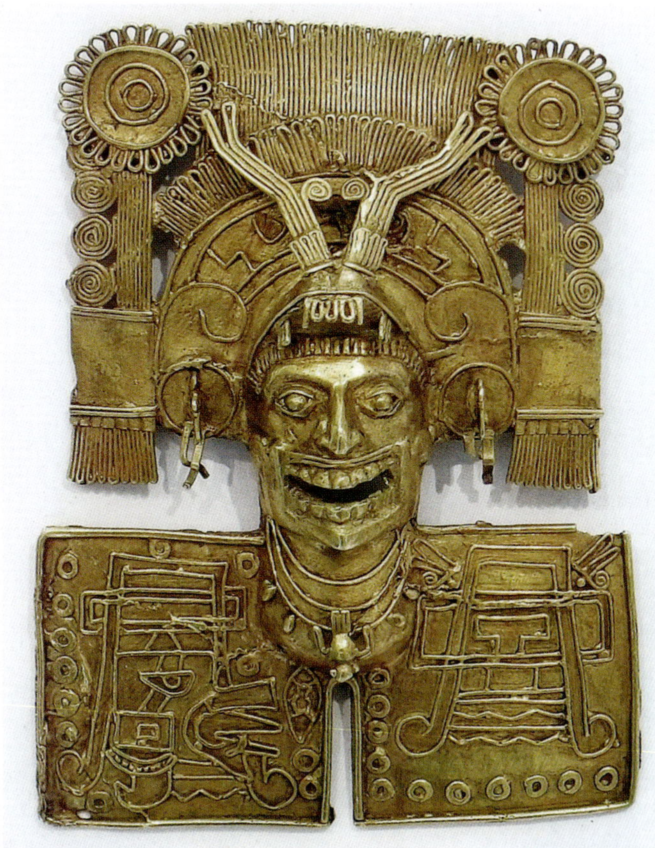

95 Pectoral,
1200–1520

covered with a mask giving it a frightful, skeletal appearance. The figure wears tiny strands of necklaces and a pendant which may represent a descending bird. The headdress is composed of an arching fan behind two main feathered or maize-tassel projections. Large floral elements are in the upper right and left corners, with textile-like features seemingly cascading down toward the shoulders.

The figure's shoulders morph into two square flanges that are reminiscent of the large flanges in earlier gold pendants produced in Costa Rica and Panama that formed the feet of frogs. Here the Mixtec artist played with two and three dimensions, marking each side with an image in false filigree on the surface of the flange. This act rendered the gold pectoral a written surface. On the viewers' left, the number 12 frames a stylized face in profile, depicting a wind deity, perhaps signifying an important day in the Mesoamerican calendar, 12-Wind. The opposite flange also contains a number 11 below a hieroglyphic representation of a year sign. These glyphs may also give clues

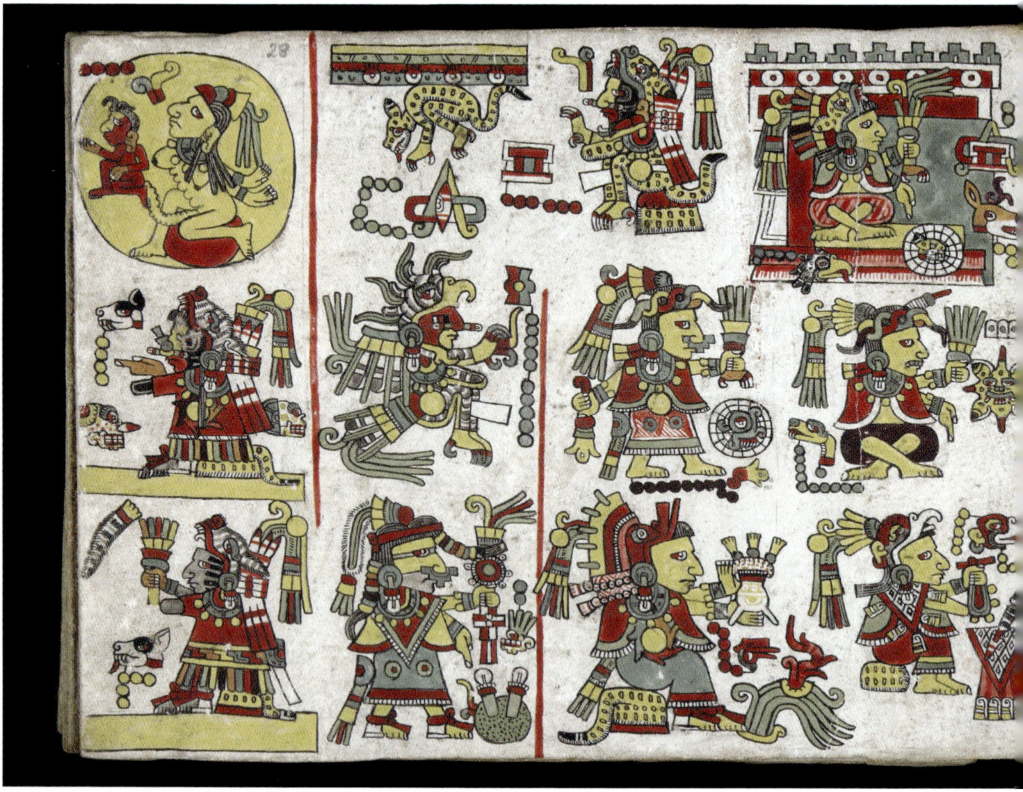

 Pages from Codex Zouche-Nuttall, 1200–1520

to the original patron of the goldworker, perhaps his or her birth date or date of accession to the throne, or perhaps even some supernatural event.

Lord 7 Flower actually makes an appearance, in fact as a walking gold pectoral, on page 82 of a Mixtec codex known today as the Codex Zouche-Nuttall. The Mixtec royal courts
96 commissioned these elaborated screenfold books to record their genealogies, histories, and religious narratives. Created on deer skin during the fourteenth and fifteenth centuries, the Codex Zouche-Nuttall records important events in the dynasties of Mixtec nobility throughout centuries. The toolkit of the codex painters included cochineal for reds, orpiment for bright yellow, and other pigments for blue-green. The narrative on these pages snakes around the red guide lines from left to right, recording the life of the eleventh-century Lord 8 Deer Jaguar Claw (1063–1115).

The codex painters mixed the real and the celestial in order to place their patrons as protagonists in sacred narratives. In

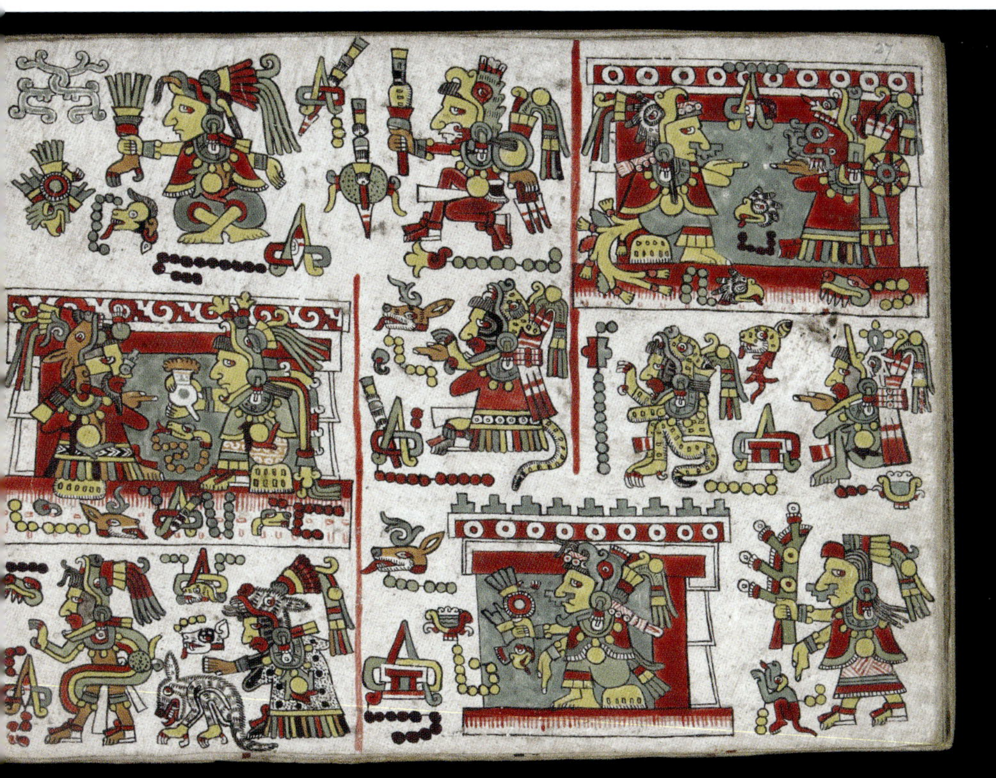

the upper-left corner of page 26, for example, the yellow disk,
perhaps a lunar or solar reference, contains a female giving
birth, perhaps an important ancestor or even a goddess related
142 to the deity the Mexica called Coyolxauhqui. A series of other
deities and important individuals featured in this generational
genealogical register hold ritual objects, including feather
bundles and tripod drinking vessels. In the center-left image
on the right page, the artists imagined the scene in which
Lord 8 Deer Jaguar Claw marries Lady 13 Serpent. They wear
regalia referencing their names and sit on thrones in a temple
decorated with a step-fret. He wears a jade nose ornament,
elaborate headdress, and skirt while pointing at her. She offers
him a chocolate vessel as part of the marriage rites. Although
the text is limited to the names and dates in this book, it
certainly would have been a powerful object during ceremonies
as orators recited these vivid histories from such illuminated
manuscripts in these ancient cities.

Chapter 7
High-Altitude States: Tiwanaku and Wari (100–1000 CE)

Tiwanaku

In the late first-millennium CE southern Andes, societies that were centered around two major ceremonial complexes dominated the visual cultures in the region. The geographic extent of similar archaeological materials, ranging from what is now the north coast of Peru to Bolivia and Chile, hints at imperial-style expansion, in which emissaries established enclaves loyal to a faraway capital. Little direct evidence remains of the political systems at the major cities now known as Wari, outside of Ayacucho, Peru; and Tiwanaku, outside of La Paz, Bolivia. With no written language, leaders at these two capitals competed for allegiance of a wide spectrum of peoples by creating striking visual cultures that did not require literacy but aesthetic legibility. This impulse for abstraction and the use of novel forms and color schemes comprise part of the legacy of brilliant architects and artists from these two capitals, which lived on throughout the later Inka Empire and even into the public consciousness today.

The dramatic landscape between the high Andes and Lake Titicaca, the highest navigable lake in the world, is at once harsh and inspiring. Peoples settled here very early on, taking advantage of favorable conditions for herding llamas and alpacas, as well as high-altitude crops such as quinoa and related grains such as *kañiwa* (*Chenopodium pallidicaule*). In the early centuries CE, residents of this region began constructing large gathering spaces and connecting them to ancestral or supernatural forces with representations in monumental sculpture. Over time, the residents created structures that became outsized in scale, including some plazas with restricted access and other platforms designed for public demonstrations

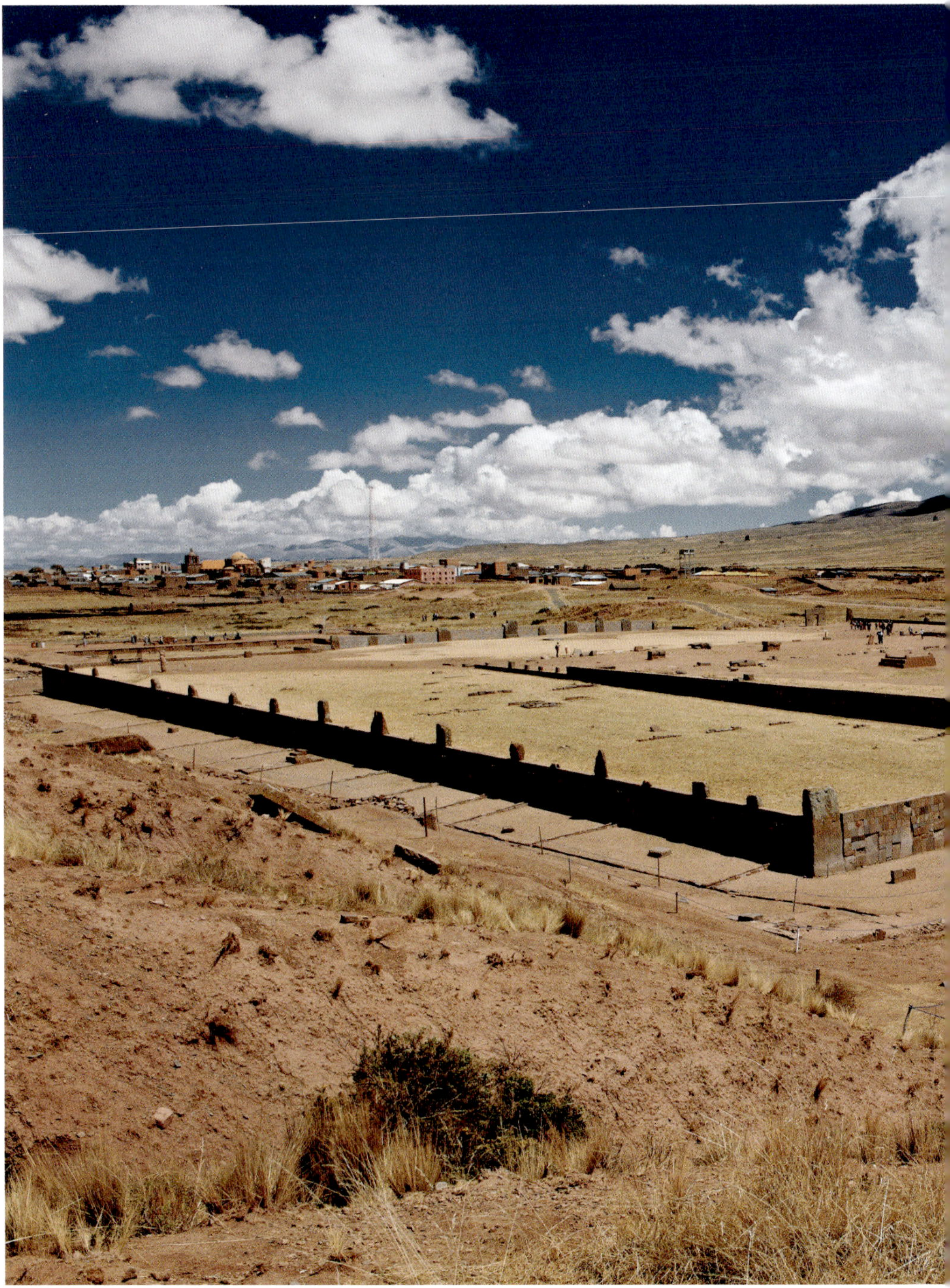

97 Tiwanaku, Bolivia

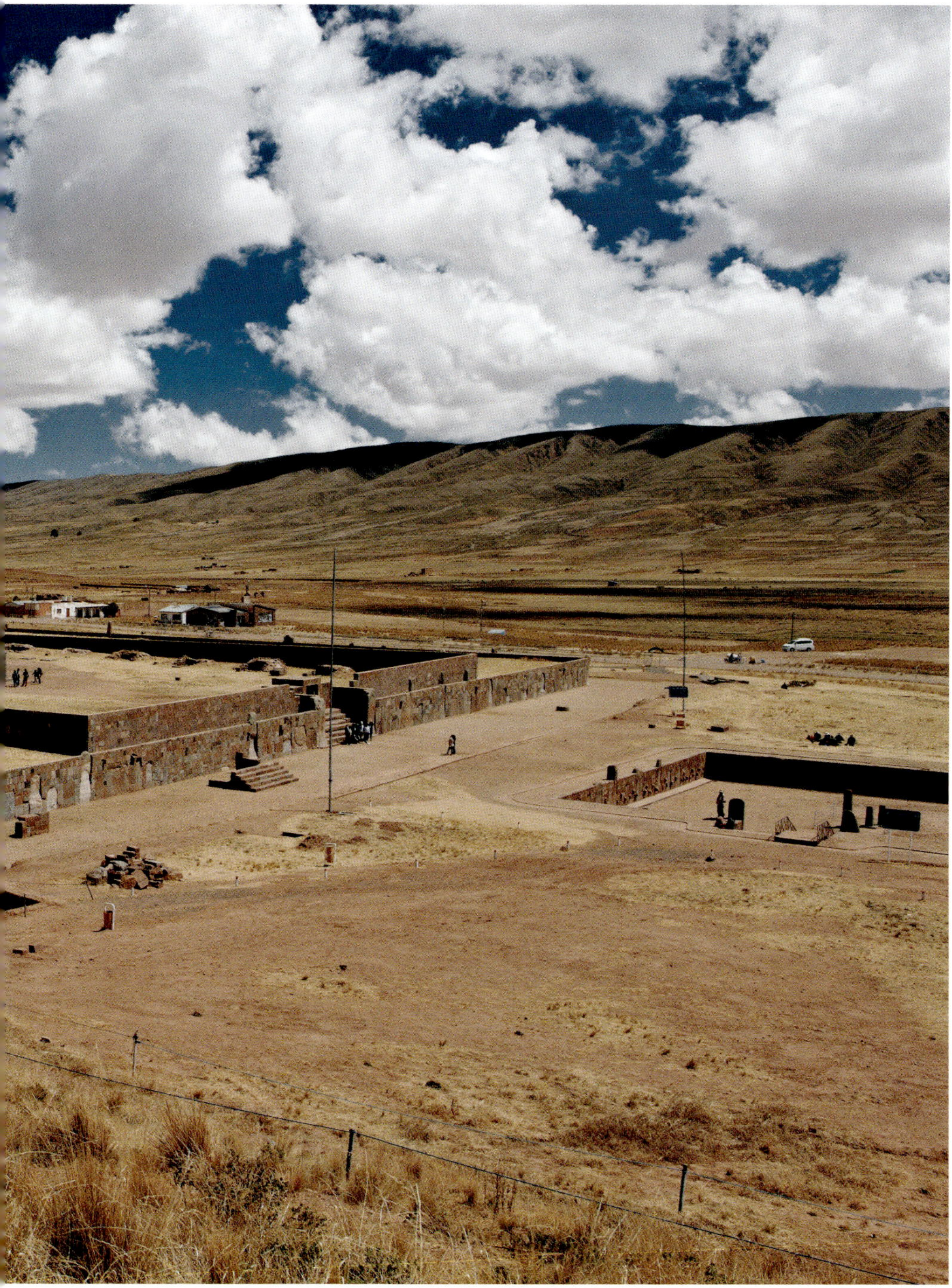

in front of thousands of people. After about 100 CE, the site
known today as Tiwanaku became a major focus of artistic
production, especially stone sculpture. Some have argued that
the ancient name for the city in the local Aymara language is
Taypikala, "Stone at the Center."

97 The alignment of the city's buildings to the movements of
the sun and stars combined with solar imagery on sculptures
and textiles hint at the celestial underpinnings of the large
plazas and ritual focus on solstices and equinoxes. One
recurring motif, known as a *chakana*, or Andean cross, is
composed of a stepped-cross shape with twenty sides that
resembles a square superimposed on the center of a cross with
four rectangular arms of equal length. This unique geometric
shape may refer to the cardinal and intercardinal directions
or the division of the mortal plane into four quarters and a
center, as what was seen in early Mesoamerica (see chapter 2).
A series of sunken plazas and enormous pyramidal platforms
based on these Andean geometries created distinct districts
presumably for different activities at the same time, or to be
used during different time periods. Figural sculptures also
15 played a role in the spaces. Similar to the tenoned heads
present at Chavín de Huántar, disembodied heads punctuated
the monumental walls in some of the major architectural
complexes. These heads display similar features as the figures
on freestanding sculptures with tall headdresses and bulging,
squared eyes (described below), although there is a diversity of
sculptural styles that could indicate that the stones are trophies
of war brought from far away. They watched attentively as
residents and visitors flocked to special gatherings. Megalithic
doorways and staircases also dictated the movement of people
throughout the center.

Sculptors at Tiwanaku transformed a single boulder of
local andesite into one of the most iconic works of sculpture
98 from the ancient world, known as the Gate of the Sun.
The lower portion of the sculpture is a perfectly flat face
surrounding a door frame with two niches to either side. The
sculptors created the frame as an inset, double-jambed door,
perhaps mimicking a wooden frame and stuccoed outer wall
from architecture of a more domestic nature. Although it is
currently detached, it might have formed the main portal into
(or out of) a major ritual space at Tiwanaku, but it was likely
moved and broken in antiquity. The arching passage of the
sculpture above the doorframe is composed of a central figure
depicted frontally in high relief and four rows of low-relief
figures and designs reminiscent of the repeated designs on
Andean tapestry-woven textiles.

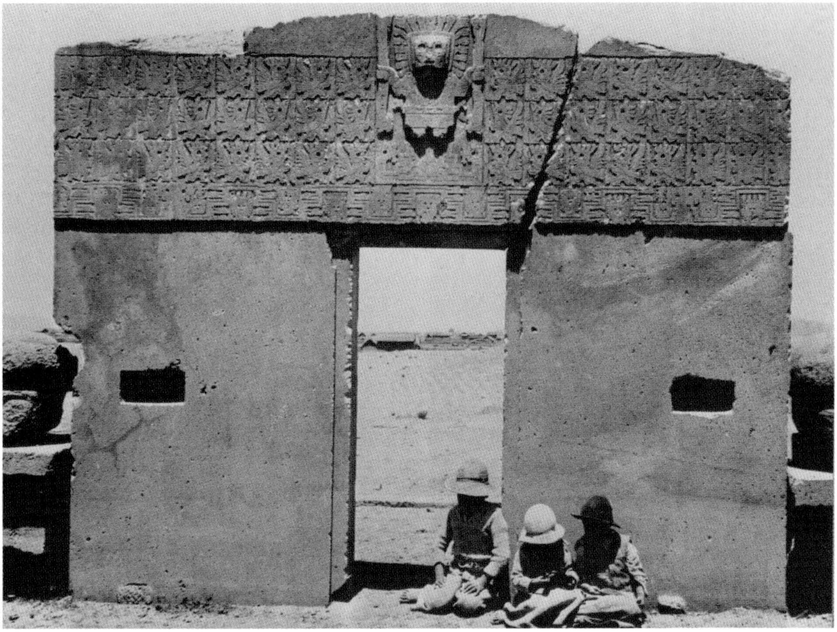

98 Gate of the Sun, Tiwanaku, Bolivia, 500–950

The lowest row contains mazelike zigzags sprouting raptor heads that frame frontal depictions of deities with feline features. Above that are forty-eight small-scale figures in profiles arranged in three rows. They all wear headdresses and capes or wings, hold staffs, spearthrowers or other weapons in front of them, and seem to be kneeling or processing while facing the central figure. At least three times the size of the attendants is the main figure, who stands atop a pyramidal structure and holds the same weapons out to the side. The individual wears a skirt and headdress, while stylized low-relief carving indicates other adornment on the body and encircling the eyes. The pyramidal structure here has been interpreted as both a reference to the nearby sacred mountain known as Illimani and part of Tiwanaku's architectural complex, thus making the large figure a leader embodying a divine figure or important supernatural patron of the city itself.

The deity has been called the Staff God by specialists, and the deity stands in a pose similar to the figures grabbing ritual
18, 51 objects or weapons in previous depictions in Moche or Chavín iconography. Large freestanding monuments at Tiwanaku, sculpted between about 500 and 1000 CE, also depict leaders or ritual specialists in rich regalia and holding ceremonial objects

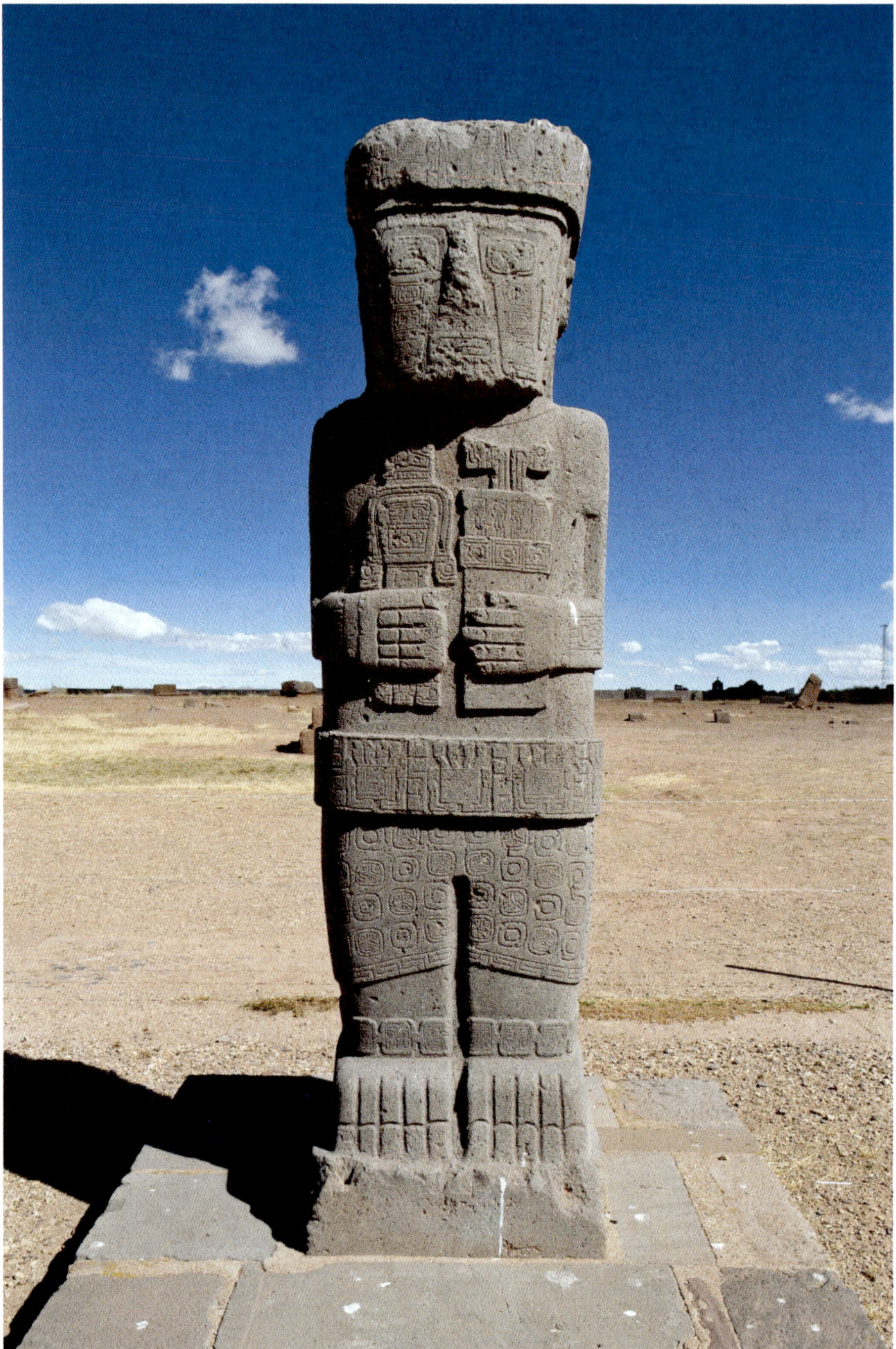

99 such as drinking vessels or snuff trays. This stela, known as the Ponce Stela, depicts a stylized person standing rigidly atop a pyramidal form. The individual wears a belt and loincloth or skirt, depicted as having elaborate woven, dyed, or embroidered designs, as well as anklets. Remarkably, the sculptor took extra measures to show that the right hand, grasping a scepter or other object, is rotated at the wrist; perhaps this action of grasping or gesturing with the right hand carried meaning to the viewers. Other marks of divinity are present in the squared, bulging eyes and low-relief carving that covers large parts of the surface, such as the tears that morph into the heads of animals streaming down its face, perhaps a depiction of face paint.

The amount of labor focused on incising the textiles on the stela figures underscores how spinning, dying, and weaving took on new dimensions in the fiber arts of Tiwanaku, as seen in surviving basketry vessels and tapestry woven textiles. One spectacular example from the third through fifth centuries
100 survives in which the weaver or weavers constructed an image similar to that on the Gate of the Sun. This version, composed of camelid fibers dyed with indigo and other natural dyes, is probably a panel from a tunic or tabard, which is open at the sides. A similar pyramidal dais appears in the lower center, but the central figure takes on a much more supernatural, solar

99 OPPOSITE Anthropomorphic Sculpture (Ponce Stela), 600–1000
100 BELOW Textile, 250–450

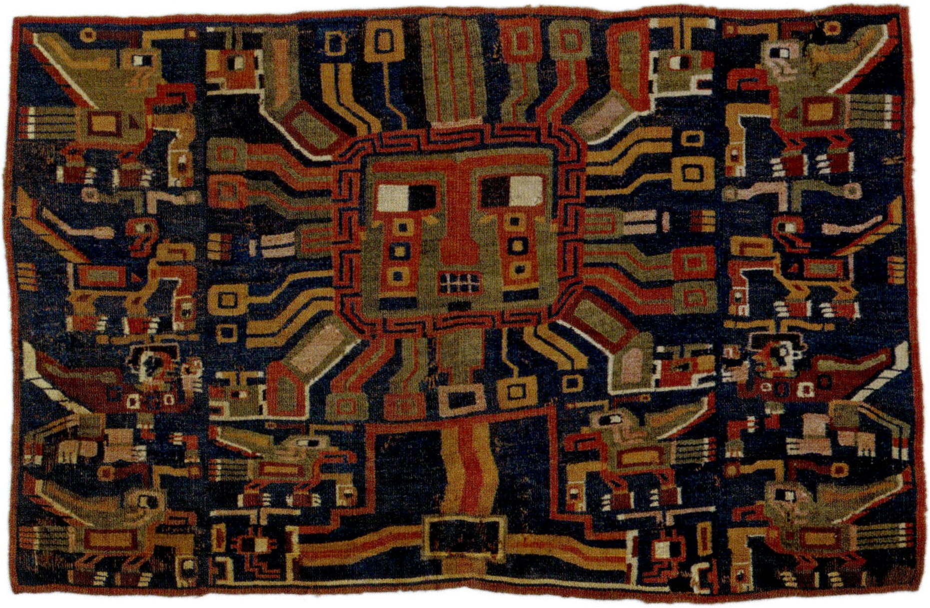

form, as geometric fields radiate outward from the squared face. Winged figures on either side face the central figure, and only two seem to follow the stone carving convention of kneeling or processing, with the rest bearing avian heads. By wearing this garment, an important person at Tiwanaku, or at a place connected with the center, would have been connecting his or her human body to the spiritual body represented on the Gate of the Sun itself.

The large sunken plazas of Tiwanaku suggest large gatherings of people, and archaeological evidence indicates the importance of communal feasting and drinking in political and religious festivals. As further evidence of the ceremonial life of the city, drinking cups and offering vessels dominate the excavated assemblages at Tiwanaku. Drinking was central to Tiwanaku ritual, so potters and woodcarvers created a particular type of vessel with a round base and flaring sides,
101 known as *kero* in the later Quechua language. This rare wooden example, from the late seventh to the early ninth century, takes the form of a disembodied head. The skilled woodcarver fused human and feline characteristics to give the face an aggressive

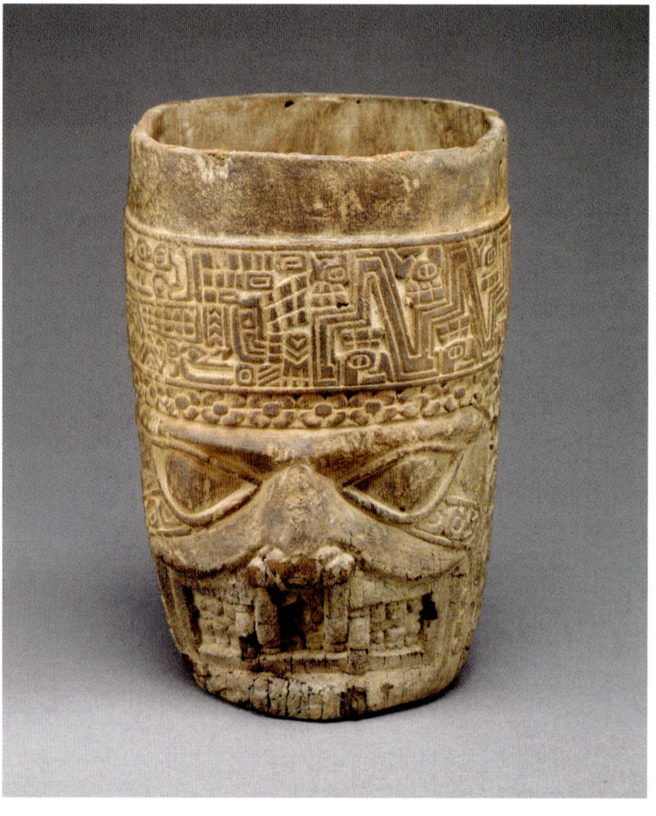

101 *Kero* (Vessel), 656–822

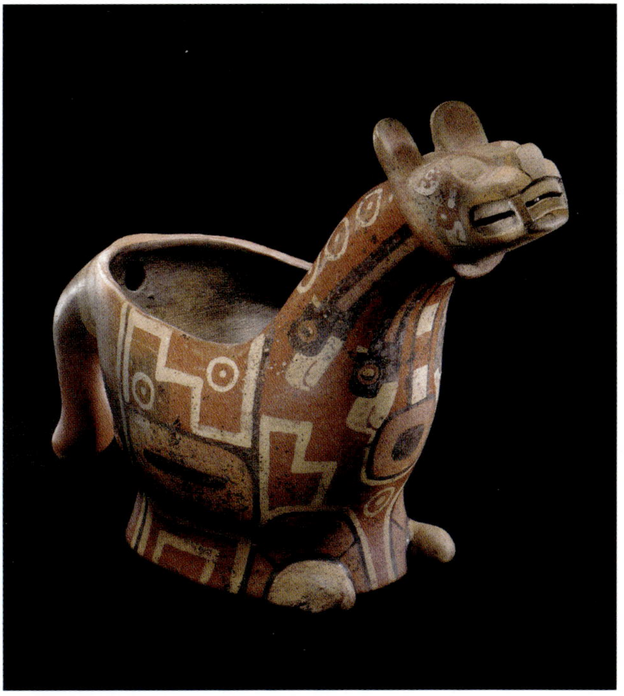

102 Zoomorphic Incense Burner, 500–1000

snarl. Framing the face is a floral motif. The figure's headdress is composed of a band around the vessel's rim, with a flying figure on the headdress along with a stepped motif terminating in avian heads. Similar to the stone figures above, the woodcarver included facial painting representing zoomorphic tears streaming away from the enlarged eyes. The fanged mouth as a supernatural motif, present in very early Andean art, persists here.

102 Tiwanaku artists also depicted important animals, including camelids or such apex predators as pumas, on vessels used for offerings of liquids or as incense burners. This feline vessel from between 500 and 1000 was likely for incense offerings; sometimes these vessels' interiors are blackened from burning. If a material such as incense were burned in this vessel, the smoke would have emerged from the open mouth of the animal's head, which features fangs and rounded ears. As illustrated here, Tiwanaku painters mastered a distinctive palette of earth tones. They also excelled at playing with two-dimensional proportions and abstracted features of stylized beings as they stretched the painted passages around the modeled clay. On each side of the vessel are white step-

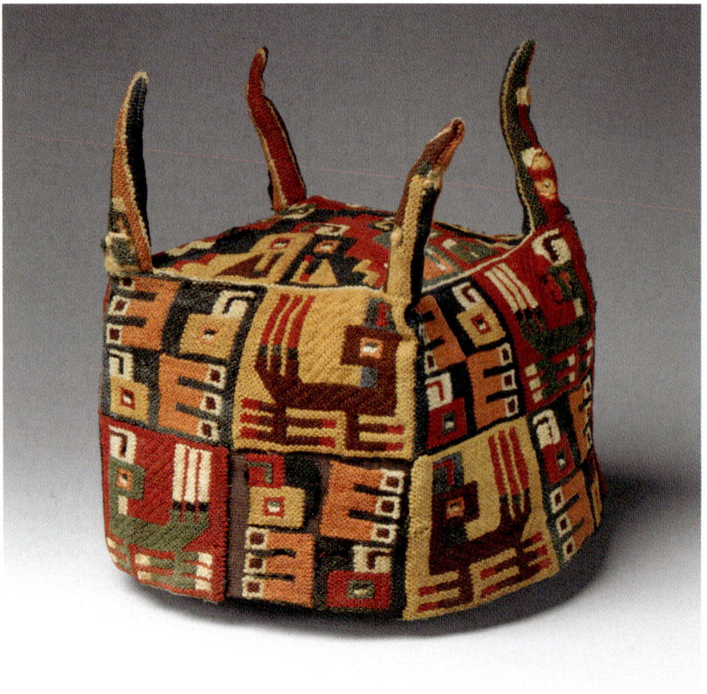

103 Four-cornered Hat, 500–900

fret motifs and from the creature's jaw stream down avian elements. The striking contrast between the sculpted animal with such naturalistic features as the long tail, along with the mythological creatures on the sides contributes to this vessel's aesthetic impact.

The awe-inspiring site of Tiwanaku would have been important to locals for its gathering and performance spaces as well as to others who would have sought it as a pilgrimage destination. Its location near Lake Titicaca, a primordial place of origin for some Andean societies, was significant for many. A plausible interpretation of the solar imagery is that Tiwanaku itself, on the eastern shores of Lake Titicaca, was where the sun, as personified by the solar staff deity, rose each day. There is also ample evidence from multiple faraway sites that people from Tiwanaku, or at least those allied with its rulers, settled in enclaves. In these regional centers, artists familiar with the milieu of the capital created similar material culture. One unique class of objects that exhibits a Tiwanaku
103 style is what are known as four-cornered hats. Textile artists created these distinctive garments from camelid fibers using pile weaving, in which looped yarns create three-dimensional

structures to project the identities of those wearing images of Tiwanaku origins. In this example, each side of the hat contains four avian creatures arching their heads upward, toward the projecting cones at each corner of the hat, echoing the running figures on the Gate of the Sun. The four corners and four directions of imagery recall the geometric divisions of the city itself and the *chakana*; in fact, the structure of the hat itself is similar to a cross draped across the head of the wearer and sewn at the edges. Such hats have also been associated with Wari weaving workshops, although Wari versions seemed to have been made in several pieces and sewn together, so the hats themselves might have been part of a more widespread sartorial trend.

Wari

104 Several hundred meters above Ayacucho, Peru, on the side of a mountain highway, the archaeological site of Wari hides in plain sight under a thick forest of prickly pear cacti. Touring the site is adventurous with the spiny plants all around, but one encounters certain architectural features almost suddenly, as if emerging from the mountainous landscape. The capital of Wari itself is huge. It truly covers a plateau, sprawling more than 6 square miles (more than 15 sq. km). There are multistory, terraced palace complexes, and everywhere the archaeologists have dug at Wari, barely scratching the surface, they uncover incredible feats of human engineering. There is a vast underground labyrinth composed of perfectly fitted

104 Wari, Peru

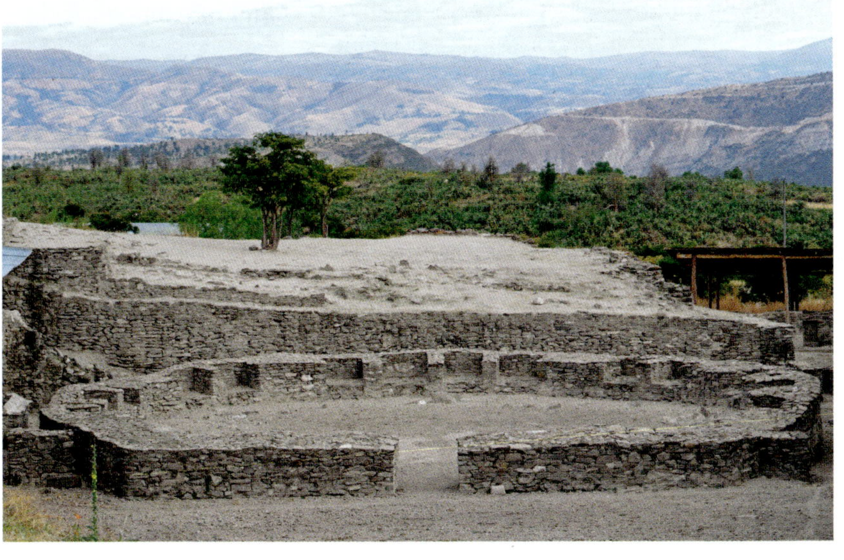

stone masonry, and multiple superimposed layers of large architectural complexes defined by D-shaped structures that formed restricted plazas surrounded by niche-filled walls. It seems impossible to determine where mountain ended and city began: the Wari quarried their construction blocks from the very crag and integrated their architecture in the depressions and outcrops, a practice later made famous by the Inka. In some of the quarries, Wari builders constructed multistory subterranean mausoleums, with megalithic blocks stacked to create airy burial chambers. When archaeology started up in earnest, however, these tombs had been long empty, looted in antiquity or the viceregal period.

Despite the excavation of multiple major tomb complexes and chambers, not one burial of an identified Wari leader has been found at the site itself. Without any known writing systems to shed light on Indigenous Wari concepts of time and history, researchers can only observe clues in the monumental precinct of the city, presumably the urban capital of a grand empire that flourished between about 500 and 1000. Separate neighborhood districts were connected by roads that extended across the city, and a sophisticated water management system drained both rainwater and wastewater away from the center. As perhaps the first true hegemonic empire in the Andes, it has no peers with which to compare it, except, perhaps, Teotihuacán in distant Mexico (see chapter 6). The disconnect between the oral traditions of the Wari and those of the later Inka means that it is impossible to know how the Wari characterized themselves and how their neighboring cultures conceived of this expansionist state. Architecture, imperial textiles, and other luxury arts represent an exciting visual culture with aesthetic innovations that changed the course of Andean art.

Drawing upon centuries of innovation by local cultures and coastal peoples, Wari society established one of the most widespread networks of artistic and political influence in the ancient world. As a result, works of art by Wari weavers, painters, potters, and sculptors are some of the most complex of any creations from the ancient Americas. The knowledge of Wari art and imperial ambitions often comes from far away from the capital itself. Near Cuzco, for example, the site of Pikillaqta has long fascinated archaeologists. A perfectly gridded compound seems to have been draped across the hilly landscape and constructed with all the hallmarks of large stone masonry walls similar to those at Wari itself. Excavations in the 1970s and 1980s also uncovered an extensive series of canals that led to the site, which was likely a Wari outpost and

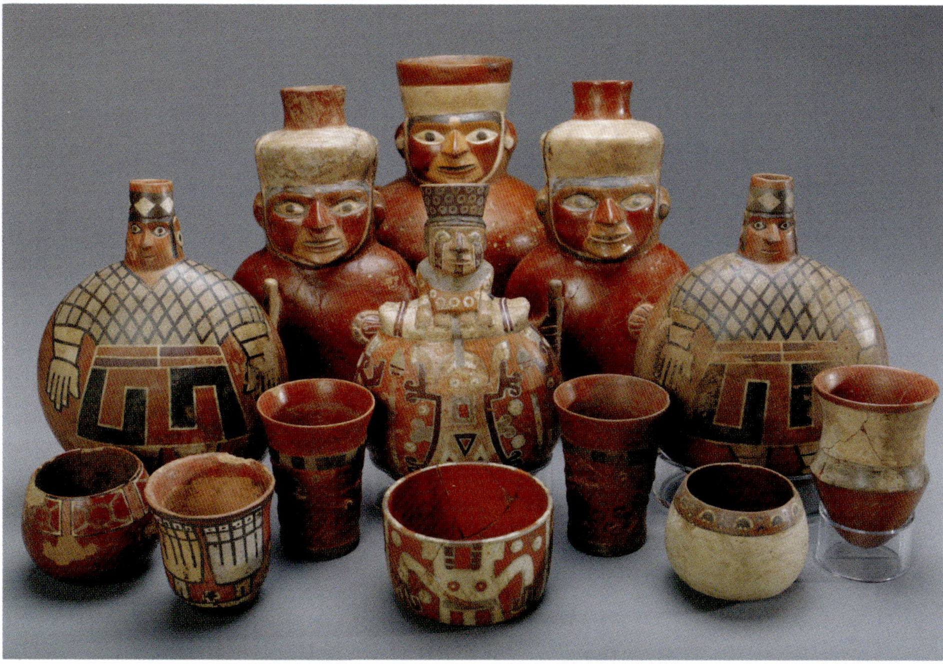

105 Ceramic Assemblage, 600–1050

destination for ceremony. Two sets of diminutive turquoise figurines found in an offering also signal the movement of luxury materials throughout the Wari Empire and the presumed wealth of the inhabitants of Pikillaqta.

In the opposite direction from Pikillaqta, another Wari outpost came into focus from excavations since 2013, about 600 miles (almost 1000 km) from the capital on the Pacific coast to the north of Lima. Excavations at the site of El Castillo de Huarmey uncovered the first untouched imperial tomb from the apex of Wari influence in the Andes, dating to the late eighth or early ninth century, opening new avenues for research into women rulers. The burials of three Wari royal women, two of whom were approximately fifty years of age, were surrounded by up to sixty other female or adolescent individuals, presumably sacrificed as funerary retainers.
105 Luxurious burial goods—an alabaster cup, brilliantly painted ceramic bottles, exquisite woodcarvings, and silver bowls—were miraculously preserved in the dry coastal environment. The Wari queens of Huarmey were buried with their finest regalia, including bimetallic earflares and boxes full of golden
44 weaving implements, similar to earlier assemblages of powerful

females in the Andes. One drinking vessel from the tomb contains a narrative scene that perhaps represents the arrival of the Wari people to the coast of Peru; in the painted scene, Wari warriors yield battle clubs against coastal fighters armed with spearthrowers. Several contemporaneous Wari outposts were present on the coast, for example, the coastal site of Cerro Baúl in the Moquegua Valley of southern Peru, where archaeologists also identified a brewery for *chicha*, a type of alcoholic beverage made from corn.

Feasting was also foundational at the capital of Wari. Ceramics show elaborate landscape mythologies with various anthropomorphic and animal figures, perhaps epic or historical heroes. For example, a category of large containers known as face-neck jars seem to be re-creations of funerary bundles, adorned with specific naturalistic portraits of ancestors, that were used, smashed, and deposited in burials. The largest set—up to almost thirty of these jars—was unearthed at the site of Conchopata, now located under the Ayacucho airport. They show some of the most evocative portraits of Wari nobility, including spectacular garments and painted designs on their faces and bodies. Painters at Conchopata also portrayed a similar staff deity to those found at Tiwanaku, accompanied by similar winged figures in profile. Other smaller jars with heads as their necks suggest that this class of containers was widely used throughout the empire.

Wari potters were extraordinarily gifted at both shaping clay into innovative forms and decorating the surface of vessels in exciting ways. All vessels were hand built by using either slabs or the coil technique, and some evidence for using ceramic molds for details like faces has been found. Pigments were largely mineral based, utilizing iron-based substances to achieve rich tans, browns, and dark reds. Intricate linework with black pigment outlined fields of white and brighter colors, and high polishing and finely controlled firing give the highest-quality vessels a very contemporary look. The finest pottery has been recovered from graves or dedicatory or ceremonial offerings. These include drinking or eating vessels with a variety of anthropomorphic and zoomorphic motifs.

Human figures depicted on pottery, like the face-neck jars,
tend to be very stylized. One ceramic portrait, dating between
the sixth and ninth centuries, depicts a small-scale humanlike
106 figure in a palanquin, or litter. The rectangular chamber
surrounded by heads of birds and mammals, similar to some
found in Tiwanaku art, contains the seated figure who faces
forward with hands raised; holes in the hands would have held
perishable materials, perhaps small-scale staffs or banners.

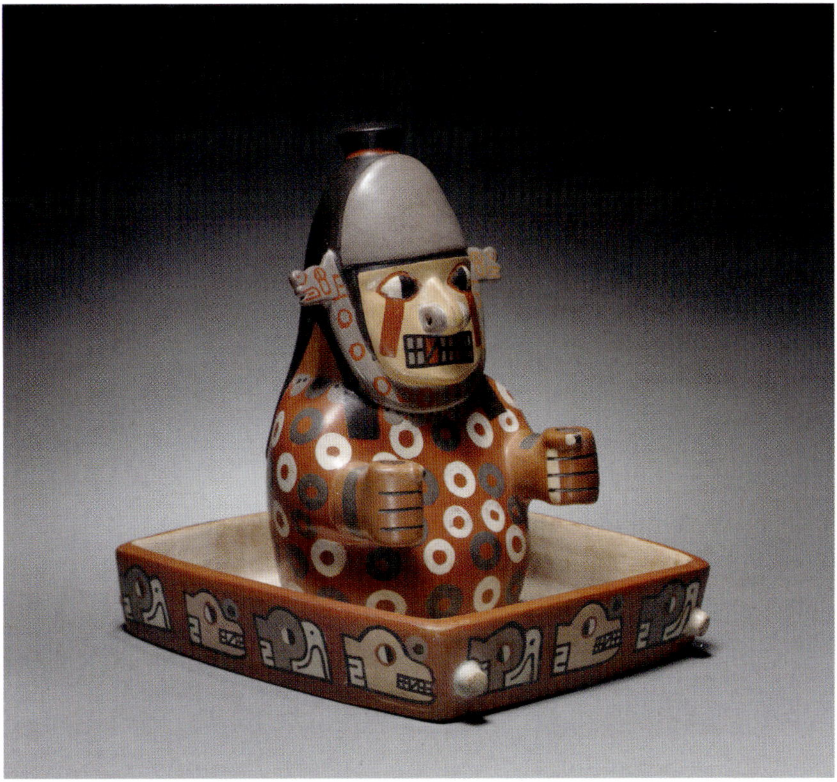

106 Anthropomorphic Figure, 500–900

The potter played with two and three dimensions as the figure's painted toes peek out from the garment, which is painted with a circular motif in white and gray, which may show a tie-dyed garment. The figure's elaborate headdress includes a conical cap with a dark panel hanging down from a circular element on top; the chin strap takes the form of a stylized two-headed feline with circular spots. The painter chose to mark the face of the individual with conventions that define supernatural figures: the large black-and-white pupils and red-colored fangs, echoing Chavín style, suggest either a divine being or a mask worn by the seated person. Or perhaps the figure here represents the funerary bundle of an important ancestor carried around by their descendants in a pilgrimage or procession.

107 Wari artists excelled at symmetrical, abstracted compositions of human figures in various media. One example in wood, though without a secure findspot and limited provenance,

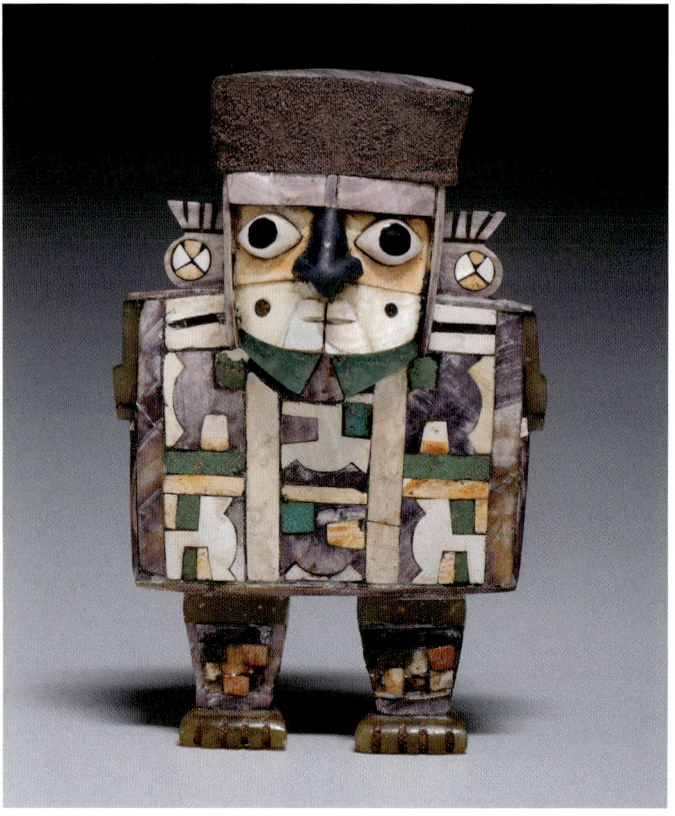

107 LEFT Anthropomorphic Figure, 600–1000
108 OPPOSITE Tunic, 600–850

also may underscore the powerful trade networks providing communities of artists with raw materials from far afield, as well as the bodily forms that personal regalia took. This wooden figure, made between the seventh and the tenth centuries, is inlaid with shell, stone, and silver and shows a standing individual wearing a square tunic, earflares, and a headdress. The variety of shells—including mother-of-pearl, *Spondylus* of both purple and orange color coming from faraway lands, and mussel—along with the silver and greenstone suggests long-distance procurement of luxury materials from the coasts and mountainous regions. The arms contain drilled holes that would have allowed it to be worn as a pendant, projecting its engaging gaze upon those who saw it. The small-scale depiction of a tunic with feline heads in alternating colors is also striking; the artists used valuable goods to represent a different valuable good in another medium.

In fact, Wari weavers were so talented that they achieved the highest thread count in the entire world before the Industrial Revolution. Perhaps the most valuable commodities for projecting the power of the Wari capital far and wide were elaborately woven textiles and feathered garments. Striking interlocking tapestry-woven tunics were garments for high-status males in the Wari realm. Wari tunics (sometimes known by the later Quechua term, *unku*), highly standardized in form and production, were also tools of empire building. They were, in a sense, wearable messages for nobility to proclaim their allegiance to the capital and the presumed rulers there, though the identities of such leaders remain unknown. The highest quality weavings would have been the pinnacle of luxury in the empire. They were probably commissioned, traded, taken, and ultimately many were buried with their wearers.

In one elaborate example from around 600 to 850, the colorful design appears to be entirely geometric from afar, perhaps linear or color blocks. Up close, a complex gathering of highly abstracted figures appears. Here the design includes stylized faces in profile interspersed with step-frets in undulating vertical columns.

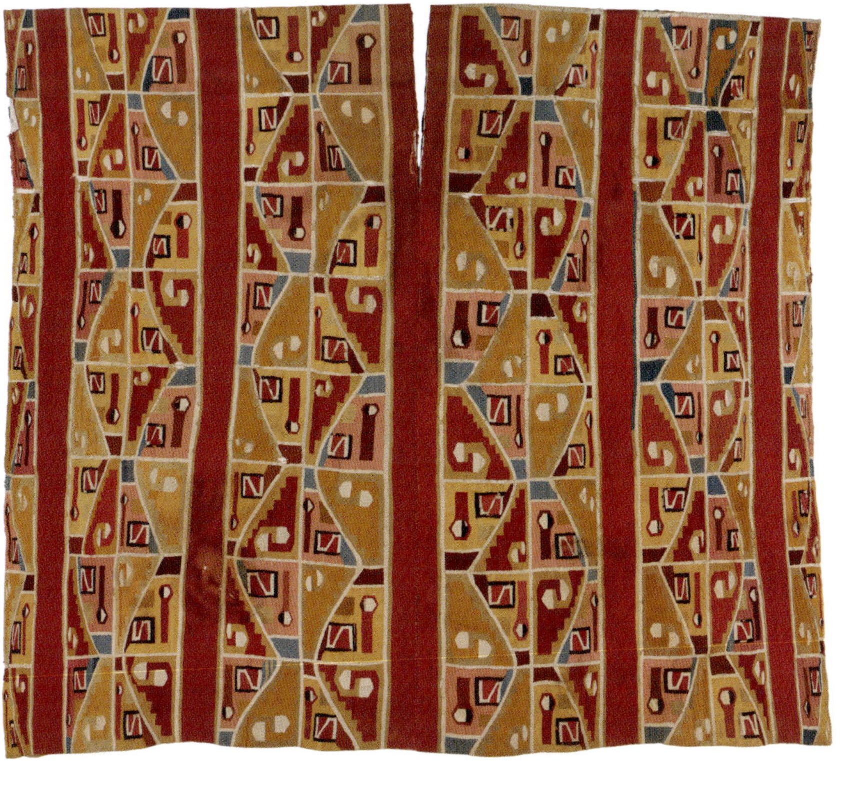

Similar to the figure in the litter above, the faces are characterized by a black-and-white pupil with tear-like face paint as well as crossed red fangs in their mouths. The motif is repeated vertically four times with different combinations of golden yellow, red, blue, white, and shades of tan and brown. Wari fiber artists began with two separately woven panels that were then stitched together, leaving room for the wearer's head and arms to pass through. The tunic was then likely belted at the waist. Makers imbued these garments with an almost ancient cubist sensibility, mixing planes of vision and distilling complex beings into geometric forms. A creative coda on either side includes a horizontally compressed version of the main visual elements.

One discovery in 1943 in southern Peru underscored the importance of textiles in Wari imperial strategies when operating far from the capital. In large ceramic jars, Wari
109 peoples had rolled up and cached ninety-six blue-and-yellow feathered panels, some measuring well over six feet in length, sometime in the seventh through ninth centuries. These stunning creations involved individually knotting thousands of feathers on cotton thread, which were then sewn together from bottom to top on a rectangular cotton panel so that the feathers overlaid each other in a luxurious, plush cascade. The feathers come from the Amazonian blue-and-yellow macaws, imported far from either the Wari capital or the coastal place these were recovered. The panels, now dispersed in various museum collections in Peru and around the world, contain braided cords on the upper sides, as though they were meant to be affixed to each other or to another scaffold or structure. The reconstruction shown here, however, is only a guess of how nine of these panels may have once enlivened a Wari architectural space. Perhaps Wari authorities traveled long distances, as a kind of peripatetic royal court, to exert political influence on regions far away from the capital. Such feathered panels and their bold aesthetic could induce a sense of awe in the Wari subjects.

In the absence of written records, although there certainly
134 were other systems of recording with textiles at this time, the corpus of Wari art comprises the remnants of imperial religious belief, economic systems, and governance. Similar to Tiwanaku, the leaders of Wari seemingly controlled a large swath of the Andes for centuries. The divergent visual strategies of Wari and Tiwanaku, while still sharing some motifs, may provide clues to different political strategies in the competing cities. For example, artists at Wari itself almost avoid figural sculpture in monumental stone while Tiwanaku is replete. The

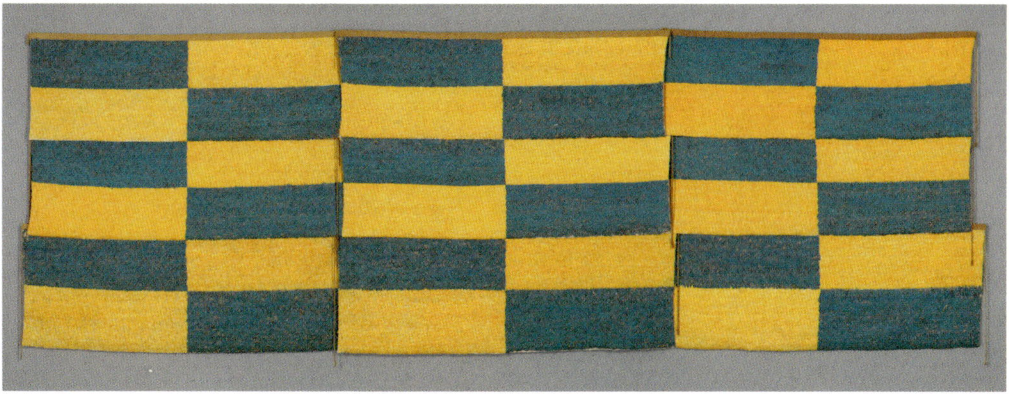

109 Feathered Panels, 600–900

leaders of these places were not peaceful overlords. Violence is especially evident in the capital of Wari, where several examples of desiccated trophy heads—sometimes with crania pierced to be suspended from a cord—have been excavated. Depictions of disembodied heads and prisoners also abound. These leaders traversed the mountains to establish political control over distant groups and obtain valuable raw materials such as metals and turquoise to create regalia for nobles.

Both places were centers of innovation in monumental megalithic architecture, perhaps sharing knowledge between communities of sculptors through long-distance interaction. There is even evidence that peoples identifying with both traditions interacted in certain places. The builders at both places extracted pieces of the mountainsides—which, at Wari, was the very interior of the city itself—in order to construct manmade spaces for ceremonial activities and the burial of important ancestors. When the Inka marched through this area centuries later, they likely encountered descendants of these great empires. They probably still told great epics from the oral histories and makers engaged in a uniquely Andean aesthetic foundation of abstraction. The legends were so salient in the minds of the locals, and therefore a threat to the Inka imperial control, that the Sapa Inkas may have erased the traces of these great powers in order to create a fictive origin from the shores of Lake Titicaca for their own wealth and legitimacy, described in chapter 9.

Chapter 8

East and West of the Rockies: Ancestral Native North America (200–1600 CE)

Ancestral Native North America

Chapters 6 and 7 detail two very distinct types of ancient American urbanism that engendered important artistic and architectural traditions in Mesoamerica and the southern Andes. This chapter describes contemporaneous developments in two case studies that represent the diverse material and visual cultures of Native North America. As best practices and scholarly ethics have evolved in recent years, non-Native archaeologists and art historians are charged to be aware of their subjectivities when studying the past of what is now the United States. Currently, the U.S. federal law known as the Native American Graves Protection and Repatriation Act (NAGPRA) requires consultation by museums and other institutions receiving federal funding about collecting and displaying any Native North American material. In the opinion of many artists, activists, and community leaders, it is inappropriate to illustrate certain sacred objects, funerary assemblages, or works considered cultural patrimony. The present discussion attempts both to incorporate these imperatives and honor the rich legacies of these creative makers from the ancient past that live on today in descendant communities of Native tribes and nations.

As mentioned in the introduction, makers in North America were present for millennia, sculpting stone, weaving fibers, and building ceremonial centers. These early societies traded far and wide for luxury materials, sponsoring artistic communities of practice who transformed such raw goods into personal regalia and ancestral representations. In the late first millennium CE several interconnected, complex political entities developed among what are known as mound-building peoples in the vast

Mississippi River Valley and Ancestral Puebloan peoples in the Southwest United States and northwestern Mexico. They built big settlements, such as those forming the archaeological sites of Cahokia and Chaco Canyon. This chapter draws attention to these major cities in diverse regions, which are sadly often unknown to nearby modern residents and barely taught in history, art history, or anthropology classes. Because of the historical context of European and American settlement and a relative lack of academic attention, the brilliant patrons and creators that lived in these ancient North American cities are rarely compared with their peers in Mesoamerica, Central America, and the Andes. These patrons and communities of practice were all interconnected by long-distance trade routes, however, so presenting a scholarly consensus on ancestral North American societies opens new avenues of inquiry on ancient American urban arts.

Mississippian Cities

7 Gathering places such as Poverty Point, Louisiana signal that rich networks of trade and artistic knowledge sharing were always a characteristic of Native North American societies. In the first millennium BCE, further developments in visual culture emerged among societies known as Adena and Hopewell, both characterized by construction of elaborate burial mounds in the fertile river valleys of the Midwest. The makers in these mound-builder cultures, who were peers of the Olmec, Chavín de Huántar, and early Maya-area artists farther south, transformed local and imported materials into ritual objects and stunning regalia. Pipes rendered naturalistically in the shape of humans, presumably rulers with elaborate headdresses and adornments like earspools and feathered bustles, indicate the importance of tobacco to social relations; the plant was originally used in Central and South America, in addition to other entheogenic cultivars. Burials contained assemblages of luxury goods made of pottery, bone, stone, and shell from the Gulf Coast; minerals such as mica; and even copper mined from the Great Lakes region.

For many centuries, builders throughout the eastern United States infused their complexes of mounds with sacred, celestial geometries and calendric significance, such as relational alignments of buildings with sightlines of the solar movements on the solstices or equinoxes. The implied emphasis on skywatching supports the interpretation of certain iconographies as being cosmological in nature. Supernatural creatures personified the earth and the sky, and these divine beings persisted into later visual and oral traditions. For

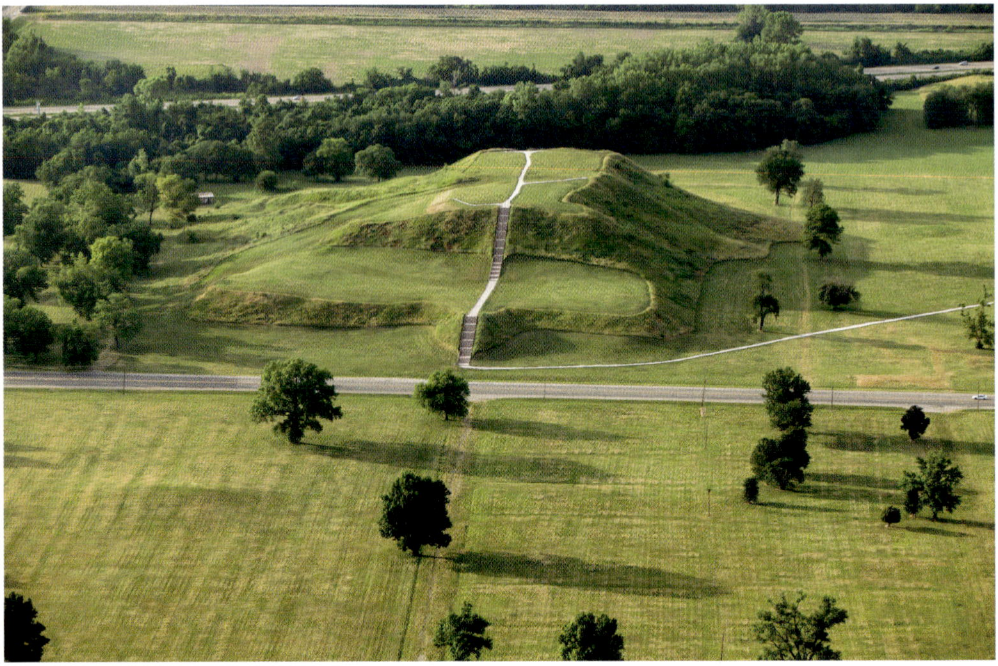

110 Cahokia, Illinois

example, Hopewell-period artists associated avian beings with features of birds of prey, such as eagles or hawks, with the sky, and they depicted watery creatures that combine reptilian and feline characteristics as denizens of land or underwater realms. These spiritual histories passed down for generations, long after peoples ceased building at such places as Adena or Hopewell around 500 CE.

Centuries later, on the east side of the Mississippi River, amid what is now the Illinois suburbs of St. Louis, residents constructed a much larger city composed of monumental earthen pyramids, causeways, and canals, known today as
110 Cahokia Mounds. Between about the tenth and fourteenth century, artists and builders of this Mississippian culture produced astonishing works of engineering and art. The largest structure at the site, known as Monks Mound, is one of the largest manmade buildings in the Americas, with a rectangular base of approximately 775 by 955 feet (235 × 290 m), larger than
84 the base of the Pyramid of the Sun at Teotihuacán. At its peak, the city boasted around 120 large mounds, about 80 of which survive to the present. The residents of Cahokia built these massive structures by hand, one basket load of earth at a time.

They structured the city with a conceptual four-quartered layout, with major east–west and north–south axes converging near Monks Mound. The Grand Plaza is thought to have held thousands of people for special occasions, and monumental circles of wooden posts would have served as solar or lunar calendrical monuments.

Throughout the vast Mississippian cultural region, sculptors of monumental works in stone focused their energies on
111 creating male-female Ancestral pairs. One such pair, from the fourteenth to sixteenth century, was reportedly discovered among a series of burial mounds in central Tennessee on the Cumberland River. Sculpted from sandstone at approximately one third life size, the pair depicts a nude male and female. The female (not shown here as it is the subject of an ongoing repatriation claim) is kneeling with each hand grasping her knees as she gazes slightly upward. She opens her mouth as if to speak. The male sits with his left knee folded under and his right foot facing forward, gently resting his hands on each knee. The details on the female's face, such as her brow, eyes and nose, are more delicately rendered, while the male's face is characterized by more bulging eyes and roughly shaped ears. Both individuals are depicted as having long hair pulled back over their shoulders. The differences in facture here may suggest that two different artists constructed these likenesses, or that they were not originally a pair, perhaps representing a male and

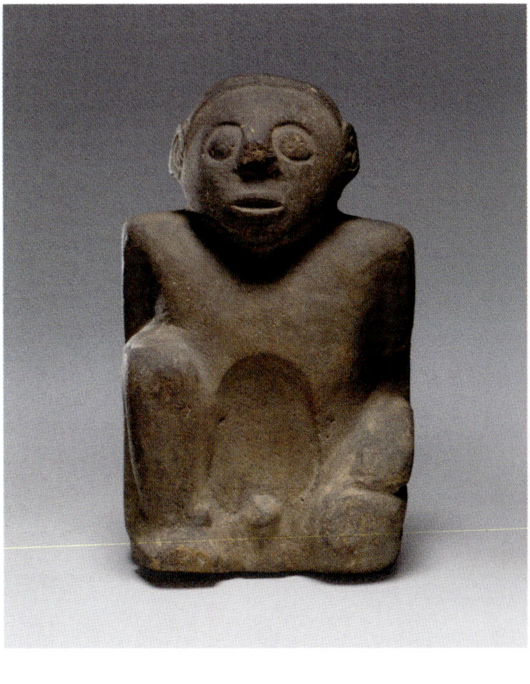

111 Anthropomorphic Sculpture (Ancestral Figure), 1350–1550

female from different lineages. Sixteenth-century accounts of Europeans visiting villages on the East Coast mention that similar sculptures made from wood were placed in mortuary buildings to watch over the recently deceased as their bodies were prepared for funerary rites.

112 Naturalistic depictions of epic characters also flourished among Mississippian communities of sculptural practice ranging from areas between Arkansas and Alabama. One striking twelfth-century example recovered from the Spiro Mounds, Oklahoma, is carved entirely of deep-red bauxite, and depicts a seated individual as a pipe bowl. This figure has been interpreted as an early version of an epic hero known as He-Who-Wears-Human-Heads-as-Earrings, or Redhorn, in Great Plains oral traditions, recorded in the early twentieth century. For descendant peoples, Redhorn is seen as a protagonist in sacred narratives related to the celestial underpinnings of human lives. In this depiction, he leans forward, nude except for a wide, beaded shell collar, feathered cape, earflares with stylized faces, and a headdress from which emerges a braided lock of hair over his left shoulder, cascading down his torso. Two drilled holes that meet at 90 degrees in

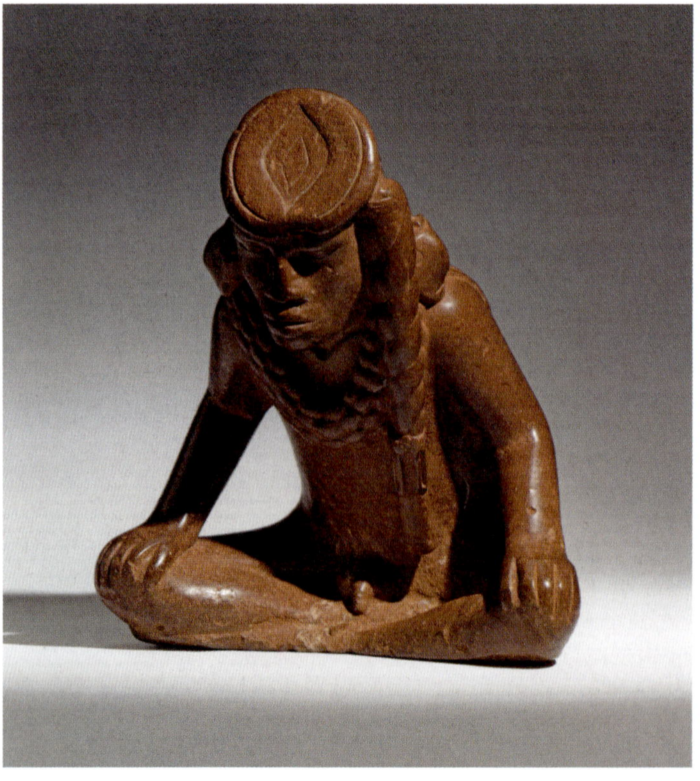

112 Anthropomorphic Pipe, 1100–1200

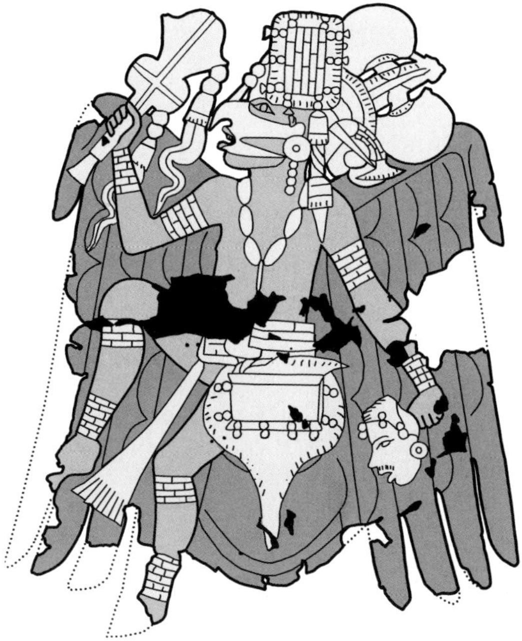

113 James A. Doyle, Drawing of Copper Plate, 1250–1350

the reverse of the figure once served as a pipe bowl, into which the user placed tobacco to be burned and inhaled through a perishable stem. Archaeologists found remains of a workshop of the red bauxite at Cahokia, suggesting that this and similar pipes may have been made there and shipped via riverine routes to places like Spiro.

More evidence supports the idea that patrons at Cahokia commissioned luxury goods that were then exported or gifted in diplomatic exchange. Across the southeastern states, peoples built such extensive mounded centers as Etowah Indian Mounds in Georgia during the time period from roughly 800 to 1600. There archaeologists recovered a series of important copper breastplates with extraordinary iconography dating to
113 around 1250 to 1350. One depicts a male holding a disembodied head, presumably of a captive or war victim, in his left hand, and a club or mace with feathered, beaded decoration in his right. The rich regalia represented includes a shell necklace, earspools, armlets, anklets, bracelets, and a graceful beaked mask reminiscent of a falcon or other raptor. The headdress contains beaded elements and a bi-lobed ornament, similar to

copper objects recovered archaeologically, along with a braided, adorned pendant that falls down the warrior's left side. Some have connected this image as well to Redhorn, also known as He-Who-Wears-Human-Heads-as-Earrings, like the pipe above, demonstrating both geographic and chronological continuity in this character's role in Mississippian cultures. Here, the hero wears a large cape or elegant backrack representing flight feathers. The metalworker skillfully layered the repoussé details to give the warrior figure a sense of motion in this triumphant dance. Holes pierced in the center of this plaque suggest it would have been suspended as a pectoral or affixed to a cotton garment worn by important leaders, parallel in
80, 95 style to metal plaques from Central and South America.

Mississippian rulers and their peers also connected themselves through commissioned artworks to powerful predatory cats, such as pumas. Although only rare North
11, 30 American examples survive to the present, carved wood figures also demonstrate how Native sculptors excelled at representing such supernatural beings as their peers have in Central and
114 South America and the Caribbean. One exceptional case is the well-known Key Marco feline sculpture carved between 700 and 1500, discovered in the late nineteenth century along Florida's Gulf Coast. Sculpted from a dense local hardwood, it depicts a slender kneeling figure with the head of a cat or wearing a catlike mask. The sculptor created graceful lines, seen in the figure's spiraled shoulders, suggesting either motion or the act of draping. The hands rest on the figure's lap, but the sculptor was ambiguous about details of the fingers or claws. The statue's reverse reveals a substantial tail, interpreted as that of a puma, a subspecies of which is native to Florida. The enlarged eyes are decorated with a feathered motif and a double line extends from the nose to the top of the head. The back of the head is incised with vertical lines, as if to represent hair. Perhaps this is the hair of the leader harnessing power of the apex predator puma by wearing this regalia or embodying a particular feline spirit.

Such falcon and puma predator imagery—combined with the head-taking by humans—suggests that conflict and sacrificial reciprocity was a feature of Mississippian societies, similar to what was present at other cities in the Americas at the time. Sculptors documented three-dimensional images of what have been called captives, but perhaps they are better described as
115 crouching figure pipes, dating to the fifteenth century. This male figure—nude except for the beaded bands on his upper arms, wrists, and calves—kneels and lowers his torso almost to the ground, grasping his shins while raising his head to

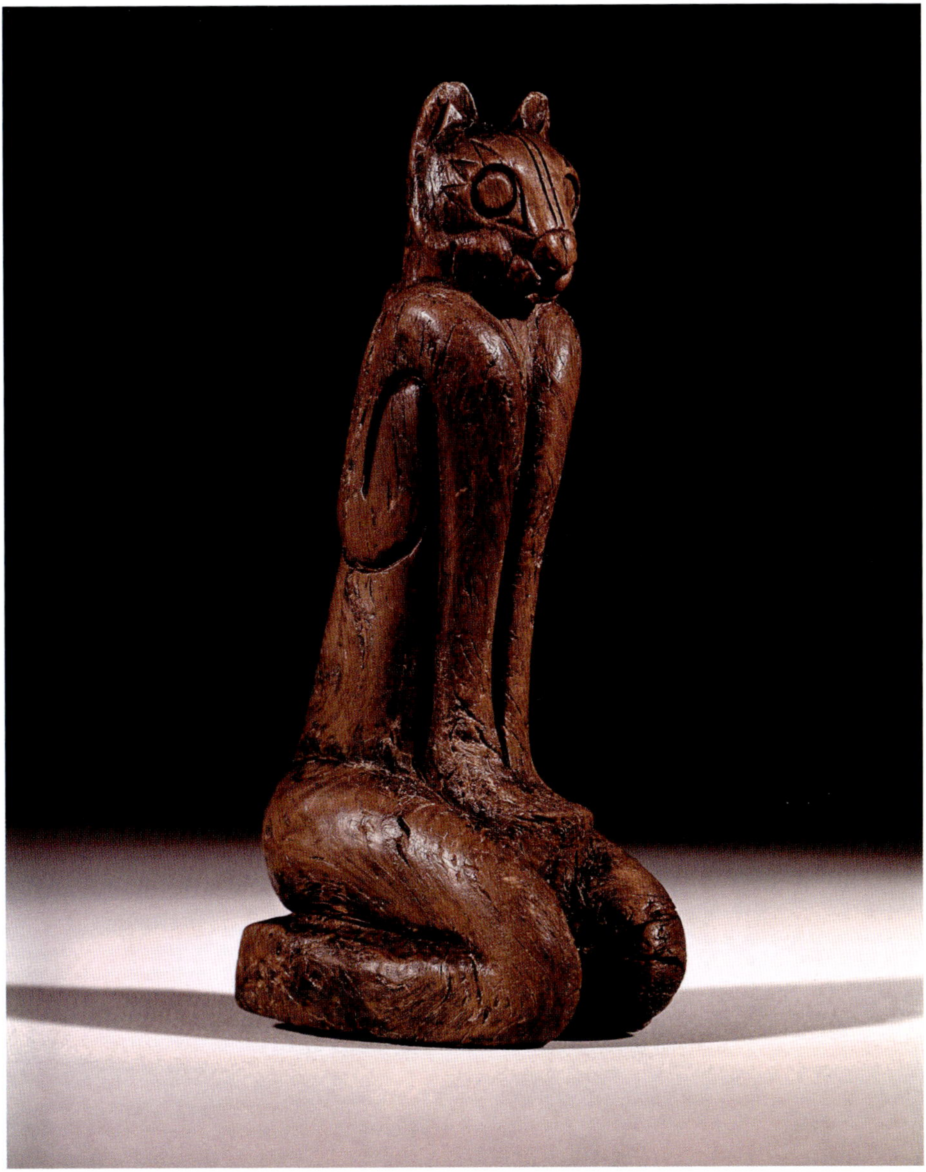

114 Zoomorphic Figure, 700–1500

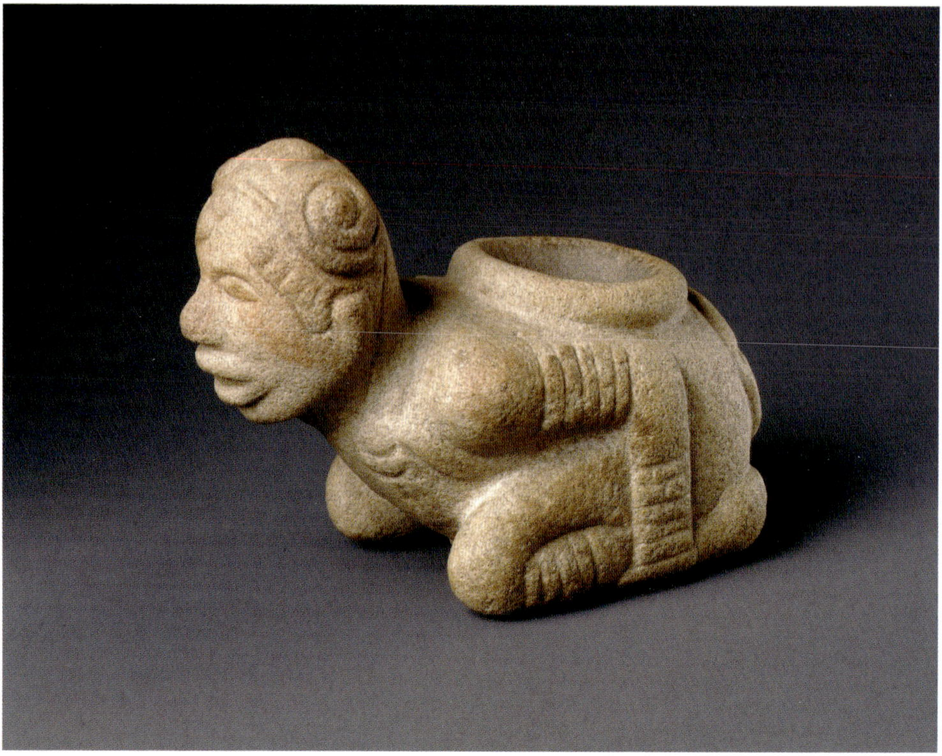

115 Anthropomorphic Pipe, 1400–1500

gaze forward. The sculptor lavished considerable attention on the head and hairline of the figure to shape two lateral spirals from which hair descends, and a lock containing spherical beads on the forehead. The parted lips of the figure reveal teeth, as if engaging the beholder in conversation. With similar beaded regalia as the dancing bird figure depicted in copper, it is possible that this particular character is depicted here in a different event in his epic history, or is a ritual specialist embodying another being altogether. Additionally, there may have been an element of humor or humiliation for the character in this submissive posture, as the user of the pipe smoked out
21, 48, of the rear end of the prone figure.

49, 145 Also similar to traditions in the Andes and Mesoamerica, Mississippian potters created vessels representing disembodied heads of divine figures, venerated ancestors, or defeated foes.
116 This example, created in Arkansas around 1450 to 1550, is a globular vessel with a level base in the form of what might be a deceased person. The potter skillfully rendered facial

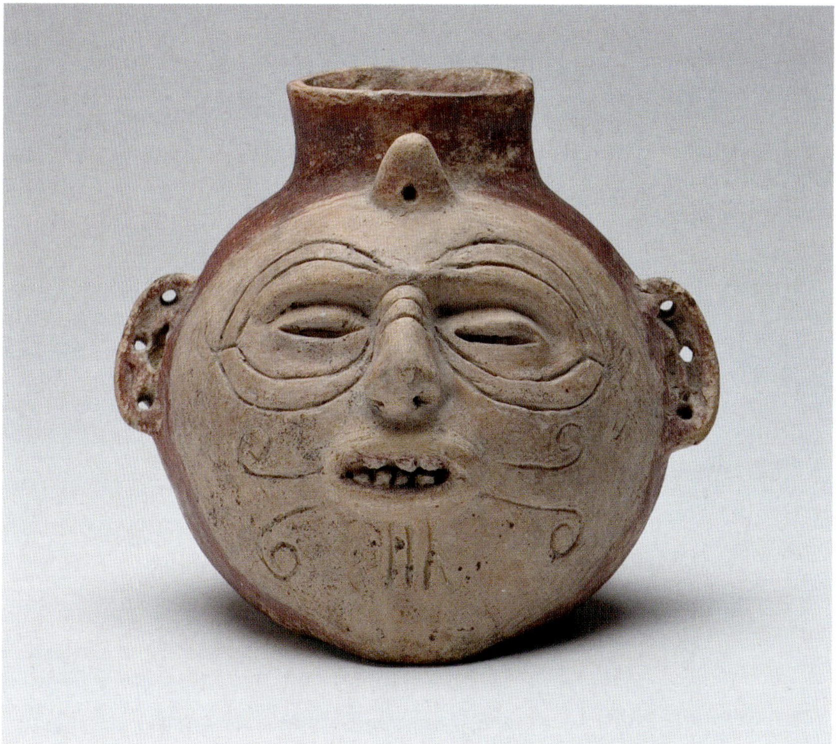

116 Vessel, c. 1450–1550

decoration recalling archlike shapes around the closed eyes. Volutes extending from both sides of the slightly open mouth, perhaps represent tattoos or scarification, or might symbolize breath or speech. The ears have three holes, which once may have held perishable ornaments. A hornlike projection from the forehead may indicate a particular headdress or hairstyle; the potter indicated hair with red and cream slip on the reverse of the head. These stylized portrait vessels could have served to allow the individuals depicted to be present in daily life or in offering or burial contexts.

By the end of the fourteenth century, the political power of Cahokia waned, and peoples had moved away from that powerful center. The long-term effects of this shift in cultural influence include changes in trade routes throughout the Mississippi and Ohio River Valleys as well as the strengthening of regional artistic traditions. These eastern peoples, descendants of those who built Cahokia, were those encountered first by the European invaders landing on the Atlantic coast in the sixteenth century from Canada to Florida, and probably by the Norse settlers in Newfoundland centuries prior. By the time the later colonizers reached far enough inland to observe the mounds built by the ancestral peoples, they saw only vestiges of these great cities. The thriving trade routes that connected eastern North America sadly brought with them the havoc of European diseases before any observers recorded the societies that were then subjected to orchestrated campaigns of violence and relocation. Descendant peoples, such as the Muskogean-speaking Indian tribes, have successfully gained possession of Mississippian ancestors and objects in recent years, signaling a sea change in the long-term housing of such collections in museums. Such collaborative exchanges in the coming years along with community archaeology will reveal new insights about the themes and protagonists of Mississippian compositions.

Ancestral Puebloan Cities

Driving north on the gravel road designated New Mexico State Road 57 is an isolating and beautiful journey leading through the arid landscape for more than 20 miles (32 km). Pausing at the top of a rise and looking in all directions, there are no other signs of modern life beyond the road ahead and behind. Suddenly, large mesas (flat-topped hills) begin slowly rising from the horizon and a subtle winding canyon appears as the road continues. The sandy desert landscape is covered in scrubby vegetation and the canyon walls appear bright as they continue to erode away with heavy rains. In this
117 striking setting, known as Chaco Canyon, powerful Puebloan leaders constructed a large series of great houses, the largest being known as Pueblo Bonito ("beautiful town"), which was occupied between the ninth and twelfth centuries by successive generations of people.

This large D-shaped complex served as a palatial compound for powerful families, a foundational spiritual space, and a venue for ceremonies and feasting. The house boasts hundreds of rooms in its multistory design, including subterranean chambers known as kivas. Builders used a combination of rubble fill, flat stone masonry, and timber to engineer tall walls with neatly aligned doorways, sometimes in T-shape form. The various rooms served ritual and functional purposes over several generations, and one room, known as Room 33, seems to have been reserved as a funerary space for the ruling family. There descendants of an important male in his forties buried him wearing elaborate beaded regalia composed of turquoise

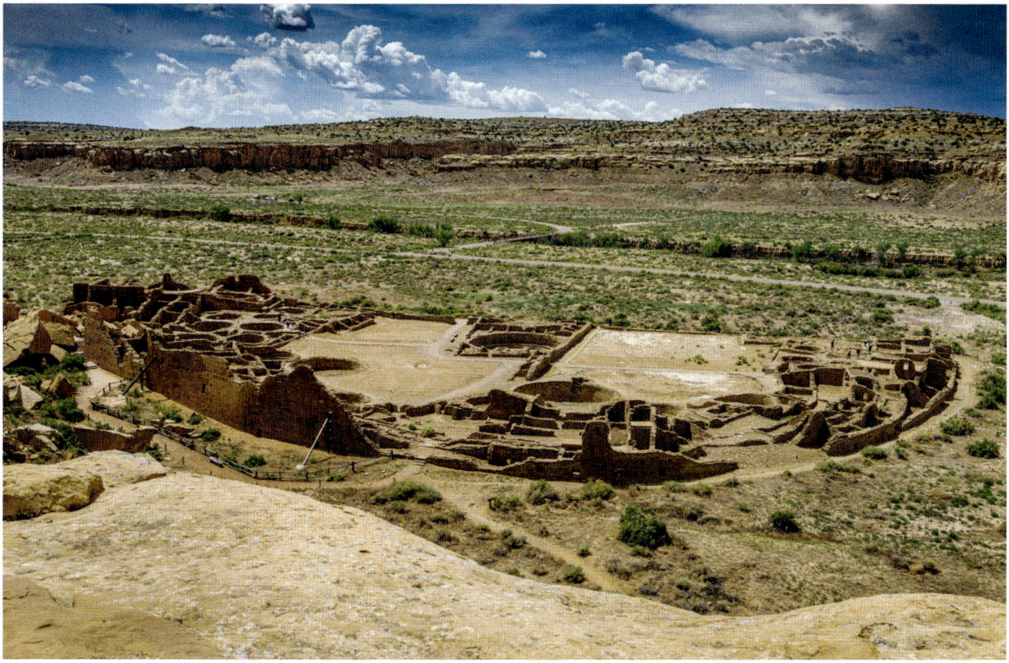

117 Pueblo Bonito, Chaco Canyon, New Mexico

and shell. Subsequently, thirteen other individuals of this family were buried there. New methods of archaeogenomics have demonstrated that the later burials all shared mitochondrial genomes, suggesting the primacy of matrilineal descent of this dynasty over generations. This is consistent with patterns of descent and inheritance reported by subsequent Indigenous peoples in the southwest.

Such elite compounds connected by low-density settlement form a different type of ancient American urbanism, in which most peoples lived in seasonal dwellings throughout a landscape punctuated by dynastic, courtly dwellings. Ancestral Puebloan leaders in other great houses also accomplished incredible feats of engineering in building great houses on
118 cliff sides, such as the Cliff Palace in Mesa Verde National Park, in Colorado. Built slightly later than Pueblo Bonito, between the late twelfth and early thirteenth centuries, the Cliff Palace contains dozens of kivas and multistory rooms that were remarkably preserved due to their location in the massive overhang of the cliff face. Access to this complex required wooden ladders, which could be removed in the case of unwanted visitors. Many Ancestral Puebloan stone buildings

were once covered with plaster and brightly painted, such as the Casa Blanca ("white house") in Canyon de Chelly, Arizona, which remains brightly painted today.

Archaeologists have recovered remarkable vessels from well-preserved courtly capitals like Cliff Palace. Creating pottery was as much a spiritual as a practical and artistic endeavor for Ancestral Puebloan potters. Hand built from local clays, the vessels come in a variety of forms for eating and drinking.
119 One notable series of 111 tall, elegant drinking vessels was recovered by archaeologists from Room 28 at Pueblo Bonito, near the Room 33 ancestral mausoleum. The vessels are shaped in organic, almost plantlike or gourdlike forms, with flat bases and small loop details for ease in handling, mounting, or lidding. The artists covered the surface of the vessels in white mineral slips and then painted elaborate geometric designs in black. A hallmark of the various types of black-on-white pottery is the play between the ground and the design, which for the viewer induces a dynamic experience in which the eye can focus on different fields from one moment to the next. Precise cross-hatching in some of the black-outlined fields adds to the visual impact of these drinking vessels when viewed from either up close or afar. Research has demonstrated that the Pueblo Bonito residents consumed chocolate, as residue testing on sherds of such vessels revealed the chemical signature of

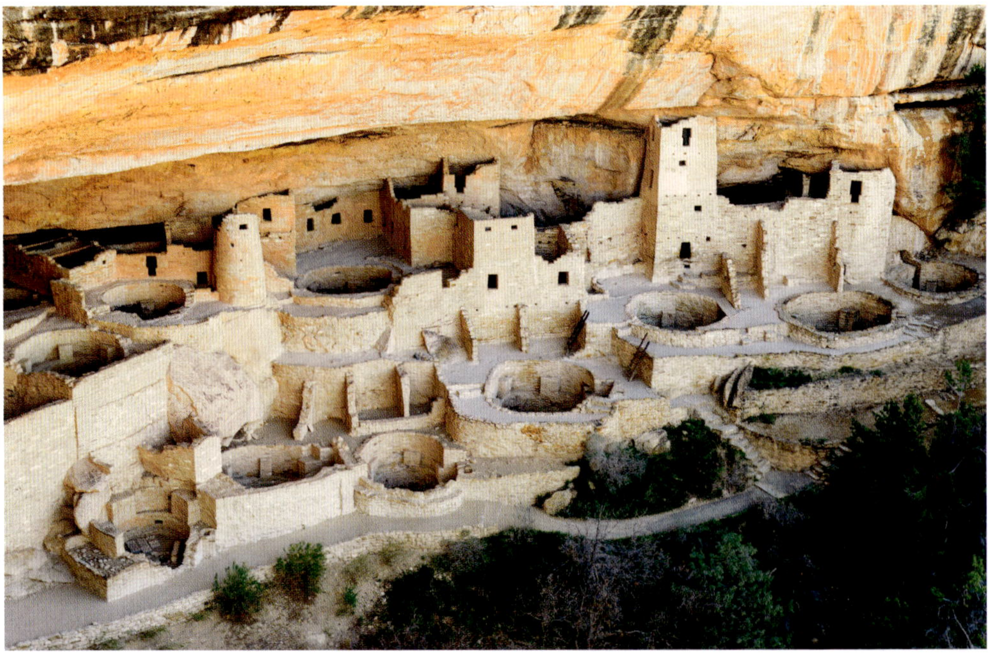

118 Cliff Palace, Mesa Verde, Colorado

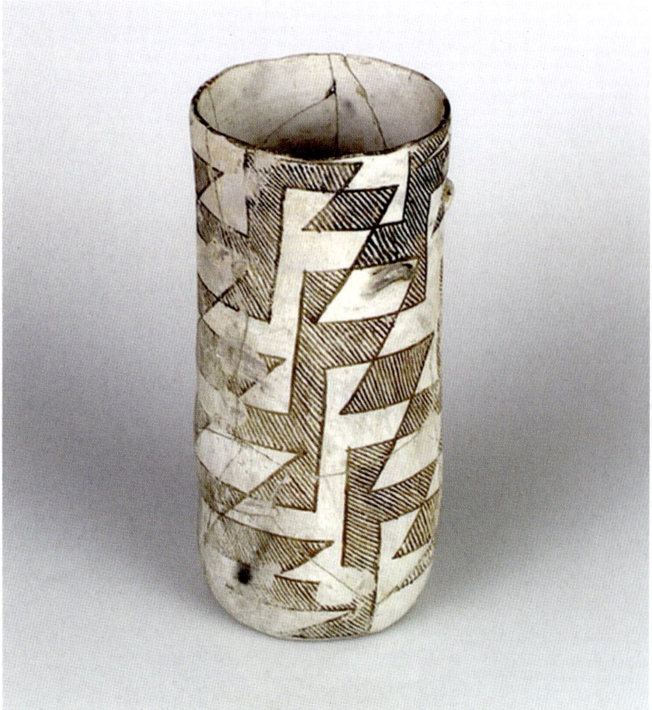

119 Cylinder Jar, 900–1130

theobromine, the active ingredient of cacao. This beverage, and perhaps the knowledge for producing the ideal types of vessels for its consumption, was a product of long-distance exchange with neighbors in Mesoamerica.

In fact, thriving trade routes leading into Chaco Canyon on an extensive road system brought long-distance luxury goods that were transformed into ritual objects and regalia. *Spondylus* shell, for example, was highly valued by peoples from Peru to Mexico, and Chaco artisans inlaid the marine bivalve with
120 a turquoise and jet micromosaic. This pendant, said to be from Pueblo Bonito, unites three different valuable materials, advertising the wearer's access to such preciosities. One could also imagine the design of the mosaic with its horizontal linearity once conveyed themes about the sacred landscape, symbolized by the orange shell, and the bright desert sky or body of water, depicted in turquoise.

A variety of social and environmental factors—such as drought, deforestation, or conflict between groups—led to the migration of peoples away from Chaco Canyon in the mid-twelfth century. Several regional artistic traditions emerged

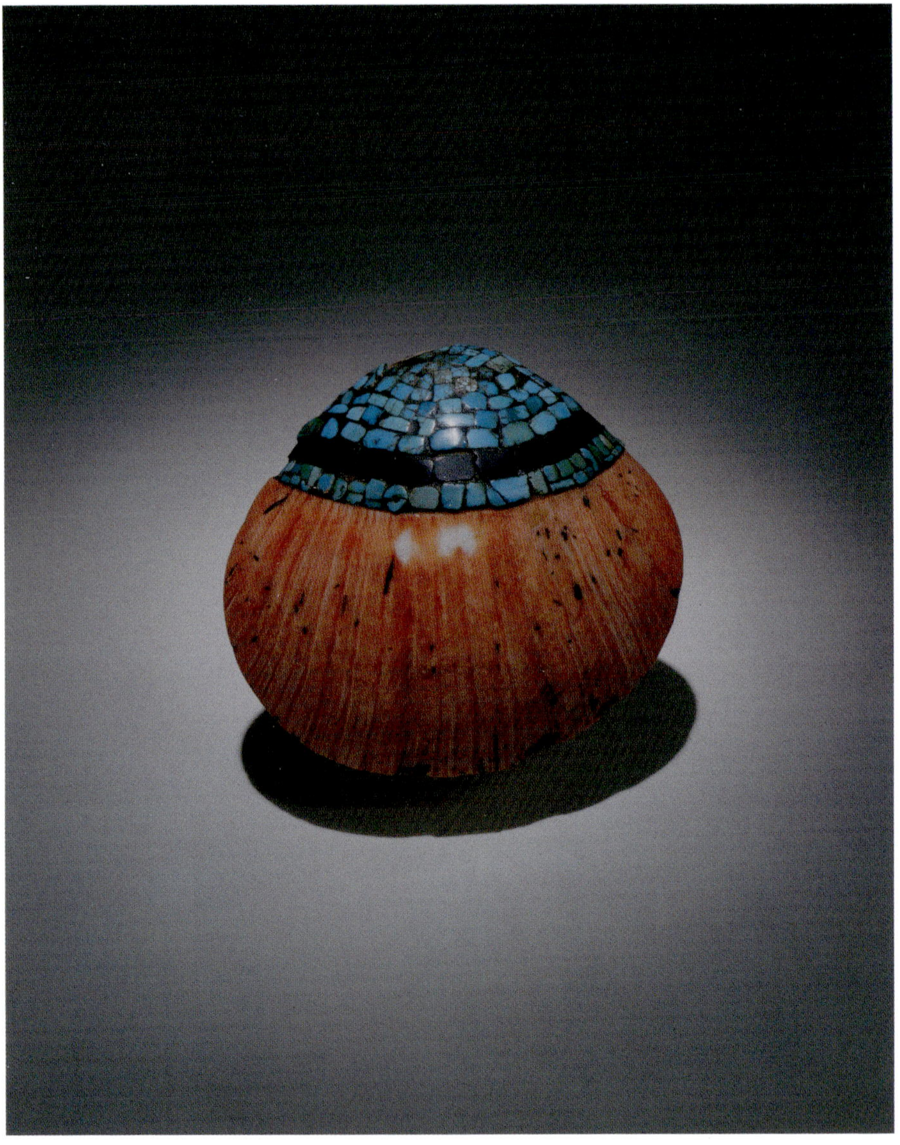

120 Mosaic Pendant, 900–1200

subsequently, such as the Mogollon cultures, renowned for their Mimbres pottery and other works. Mimbres painters innovated figural representations of people, plants, and animals that previous or subsequent artists avoided. One important feature of the objects now labeled Native American art in museum collections is that the original creators designed them for deposition in sacred places on the landscape, only
121 to be seen by non-mortal viewers. One such ancestral cache from the fourteenth century, recovered from a cave and now exhibited and published widely, contains representations of human and animal figures. The large figure, interpreted as a male, is carved in an upright position with arms folded across the torso. He wears a feathered necklace, bracelets, and brilliant garments or body paint, with the upper portion decorated in a black-and-turquoise zigzag pattern, and the lower portion containing horizontal rows of black-and-white rhomboids. The smaller figure, possibly a female counterpart, also wears a necklace and decorated garments. Both have striking horizontal face paint, indicating specific roles or embodied identities. Two serpents and a puma also bear

121 Ritual Assemblage, 1300–1400

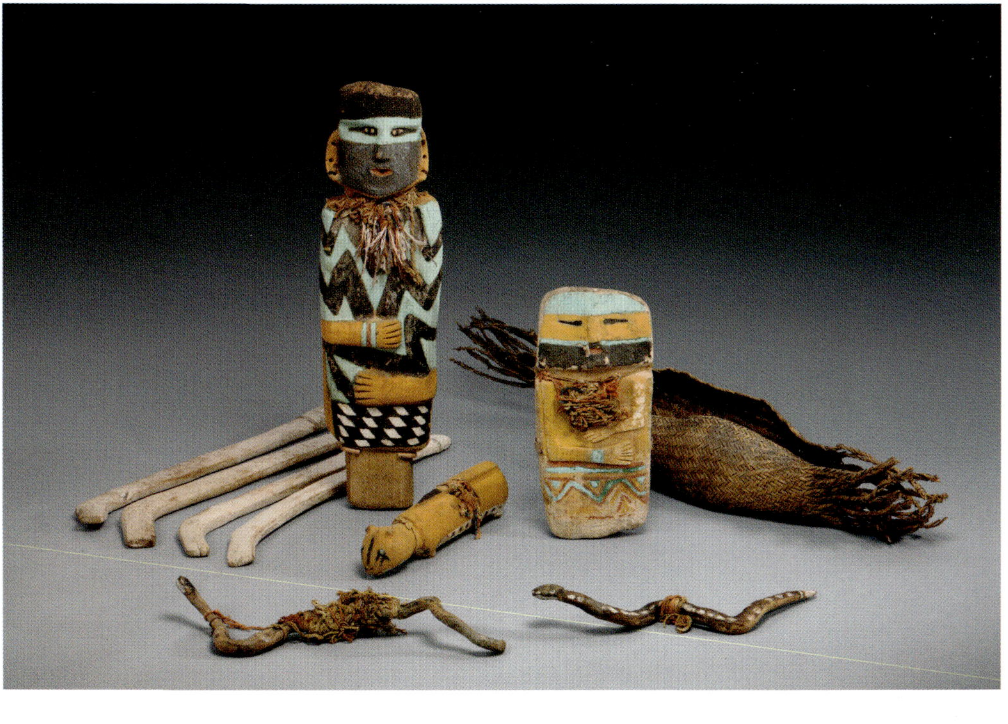

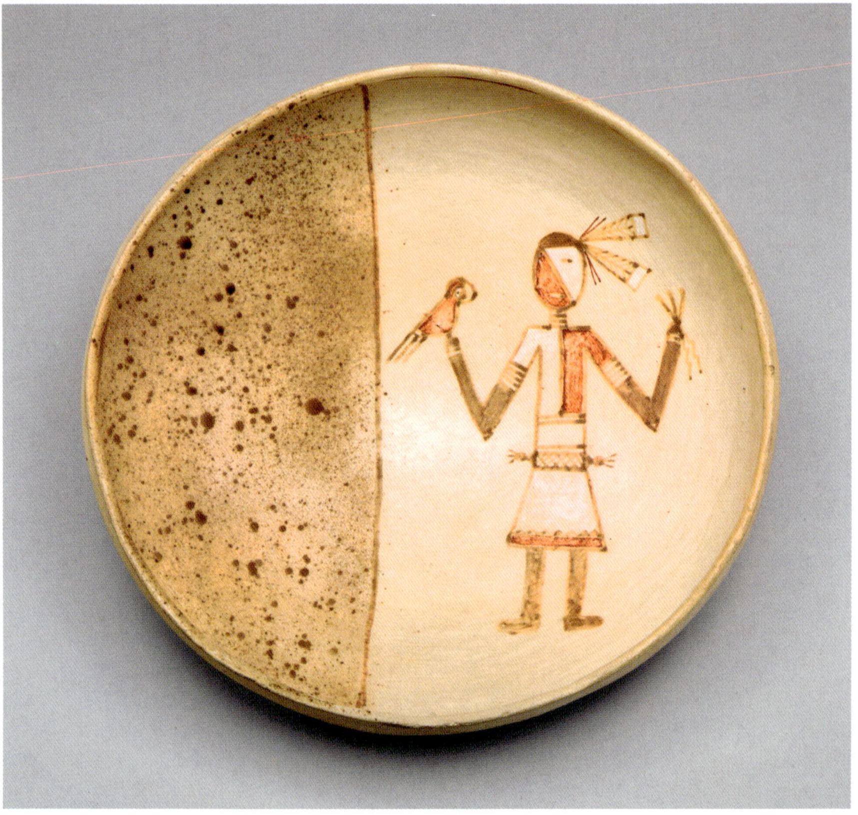

122 Bowl, 1400–1625

feathered and organic regalia, underscoring the importance of these animals to the peoples of this region.

Another animal featured widely in ancestral southwestern art is the scarlet macaw. These large parrots are native to southern and eastern Mexico, but were traded widely and possibly bred in Mogollon places as Paquimé, also known as Casas Grandes, located in the northwestern Mexican state of Chihuahua. There archaeologists recovered what appear to be breeding pens, along with eggshells and macaw remains. Like Casas Grandes artists, painters from the Sikyatki site, a center recognized by the Hopi as a place of their ancestors in what is now Arizona, featured macaws in scenes and abstract
122 designs. In this example, the painter represented an individual standing next to a darker field decorated with splattered paint, probably pigment blown through a reed tube. The vertical line that separates these zones might represent an architectural

element. The figure wears a textile skirt and their torso and
face are painted in alternating light and dark fields. Although
119, 121 not unique to this region, this technique of linear, geometric
abstraction with color blocking is a hallmark of Ancestral
Puebloan visual cultures. The regalia including two feathers,
along with the sticks held in the left hand and scarlet macaw in
the right, mark this individual as an important ritual specialist.

The general story of art among Mississippian and Ancestral Puebloan cities is one that is constantly evolving with new research. Importantly, the modern understanding of imagery and materiality from these diverse peoples is being enriched by the scholarship of Native curators, artists, and scholars, similar to Indigenous knowledge production in other regions of the Americas. These collaborative efforts allow a reassessment of past anthropological and art-historical framings of Native artistic communities that are problematic and a broader comparison to their peers further south. The recognition of movements of people, materials, and ideas in the centuries before European invasion now invites comparative research on broad concepts such as urbanism or rulership from within the ancient Americas, rather than searching for models from other parts of the global past.

Part IV
The Arts of Empires

In both Mexico and Peru, powerful dynastic families in the thirteenth and fourteenth centuries built on the existing traditions of royal and urban cultures to place themselves at the center of expansionist states that today we refer to as empires. Both empires were founded on the concept that the ruler, known as the Sapa Inka (the "only Inka" in Quechua) for the Inkas or the *huey tlatoani* ("great ruler" in Nahuatl) for the Mexica, had a direct connection to the divine as a basis for the right to rule. They drew this very ancient power from the mountains themselves, which historically had been considered ancestral forces and places of origin, as noted in previous chapters. They passed down their politico-religious authority coupled with associated bureaucratic institutions through patriarchal and sometimes matriarchal inheritance. Individual rulers in both contexts sought to outdo their predecessors, accumulating more territory through invasion. They placed their own loyal governors in charge of conquered areas and exacted tribute in the form of goods and labor, funneled toward the capitals of Tenochtitlán and Cuzco. By 1491, just before the Spanish invasion, their agents traded far and wide with peoples from all over the Americas, sharing foodstuffs, previous materials, finished objects, and ideas.

The concentration of power and wealth in these imperial contexts, especially the cosmopolitan capitals of Tenochtitlán and Cuzco, also elevated the role of the artists to essential players in the world of ancient American statecraft. Makers were charged to be innovative in their visual strategies to transform materials and to convey sacred concepts to imperial subjects, so they experimented with new media and different scales to make the political ambitions of their patrons manifest. This final section begins with the Inka Empire

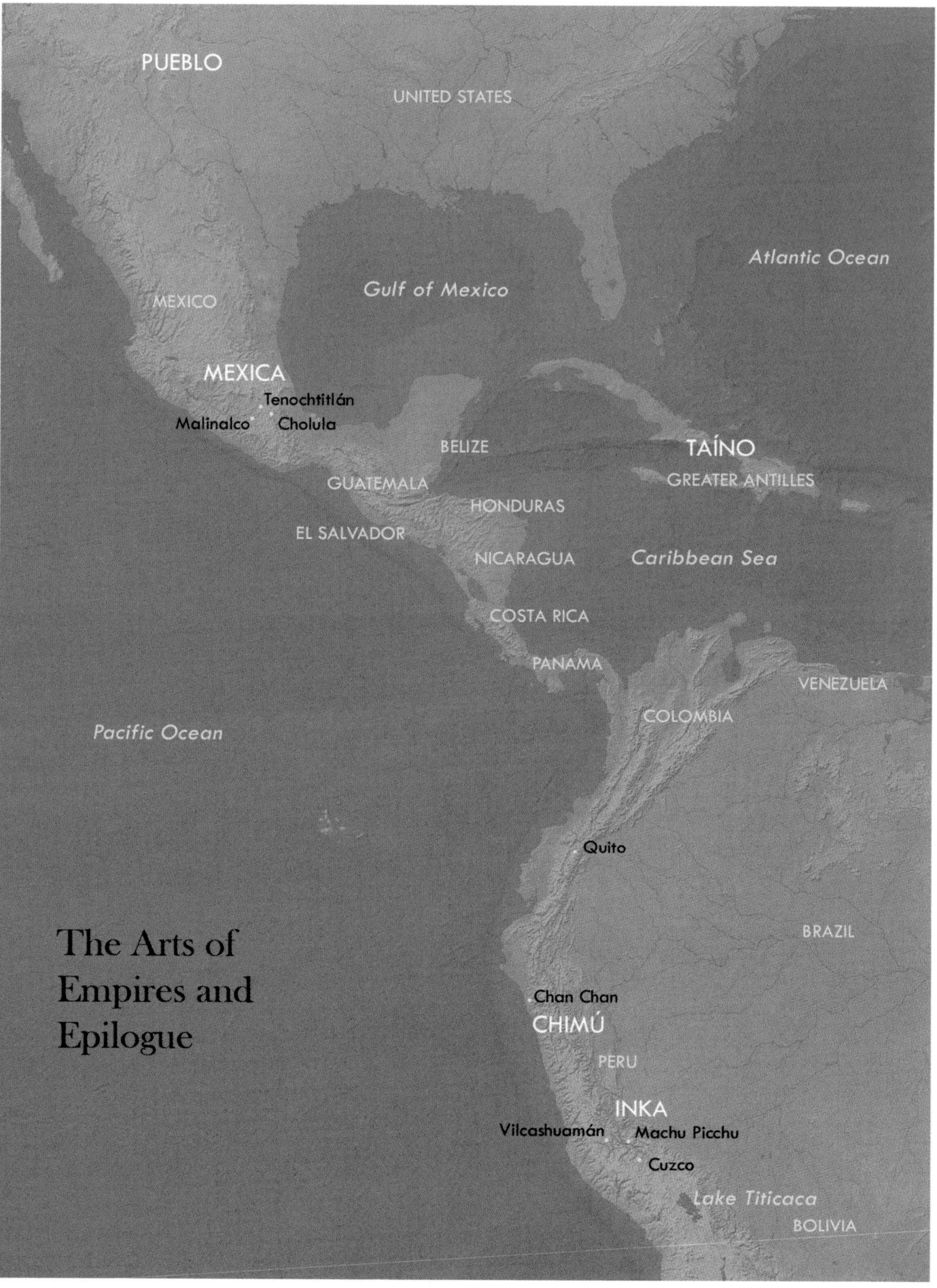

The Arts of Empires and Epilogue

and its greatest rivals, the north coast dynasties known as the Chimú or the Empire of Chimor, which were conquered in the late fifteenth century. The year 1532, when Spaniard Francisco Pizarro invaded Peru, is generally agreed to be the beginning of the end of Inka political domination in the Andes. The narrative of this final part of the book closes with the discussion of art in the Mexica Empire, founded around 1325, which reached its height at the same time as its Inka counterpart and most famously was toppled by the Spanish invaders, led by Hernán Cortés in 1521.

Chapter 9

Harnessing the *Wak'a*: Chimú and Inka (1000–1532 CE)

Chimú

123 The ancient city of Chan Chan, the seat of the Chimú Empire, near the center of Trujillo, a former Spanish colonial center on the north coast of Peru, is an impressive and unique site to behold. The dry desert coast is one of the harshest environments in the Americas and even today, communities struggle to eke a living out of the sandy soil through complex irrigation systems. Driving up to Chan Chan, which, at almost 8 square miles (20 sq. km), is such a large city as to

123 Chan Chan, Peru

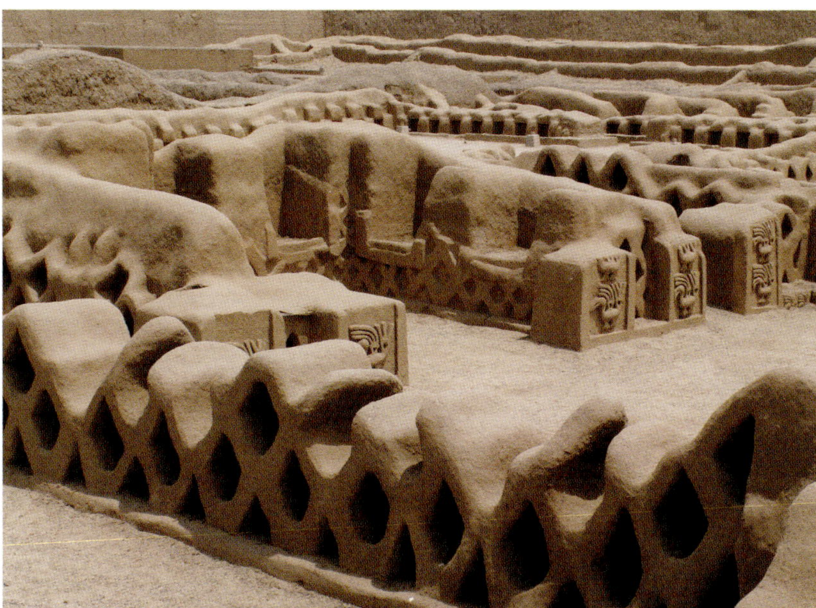

be split by the modern Panamerican highway, is an awe-inspiring experience, even compared to visiting other ruined 41 cities like Huacas de Moche. Viewing Chan Chan from afar does not reveal its majesty. High mud-brick walls conceal the extensive palace complexes and mega-scalar platforms; elaborate friezes with geometric, textile-like, and figural imagery of people and marine life; as well as some of the richest tomb complexes ever created. The experience of the Chimú residents was shaped by open plazas, sunken courts, and ramped pyramidal structures, which created differential access and prescribed movement throughout the great city, which may have held over 50,000 people at its peak. Nine enormous compounds dominate the city center, each surrounded by high adobe walls.

Once inside, winding corridors would have forced a visitor to a palace compound at ancient Chan Chan to meander their way around a disorienting pathway. The walls of all these halls were richly decorated with friezes sculpted out of adobe, long dried and baked by the hot sun, and many would have been brightly painted. Friezes show repeated portrayals of marine birds, hybrid supernatural creatures, ocean waves, *Spondylus* shell divers, and other highly abstracted depictions of the Chimú sacred landscape. Large woven tapestries could have also been hung over the walls to enliven such palatial spaces. The passages abruptly end at wide, awe-inspiring gateways that lead to massive level plazas. In the distance, the visitors would have seen lively polychrome wooden sculptures of standing male and female guardian figures holding ritual objects set into wall niches that stood watch over the ceremonies that occurred there. The sheer scale of these plazas suggests that very large crowds would have gathered here for special occasions. These compounds may have also functioned as funerary spaces after the death of the royals who inhabited them as palaces.

For most visitors, this plaza would have likely been the end of the journey. For a special set of ritual specialists or noble family members, the journey continued behind the presentation platform at the rear of the plaza. Restricted sectors at the most interior parts of the palace compounds of Chan Chan included rectangular reservoirs that ensured the royalty had water, tomb constructions, enormous complexes of storage cells, and possibly workshop areas for the famed artists of the royal court. The tombs were large subterranean hallways with niches and primary burials, reminiscent of those made 104, 43 of stone at the distant, ruined capital of Wari or earlier Moche pyramids. One can imagine that the Chimú rulers sought to create mud-brick mountains in the heart of their administrative

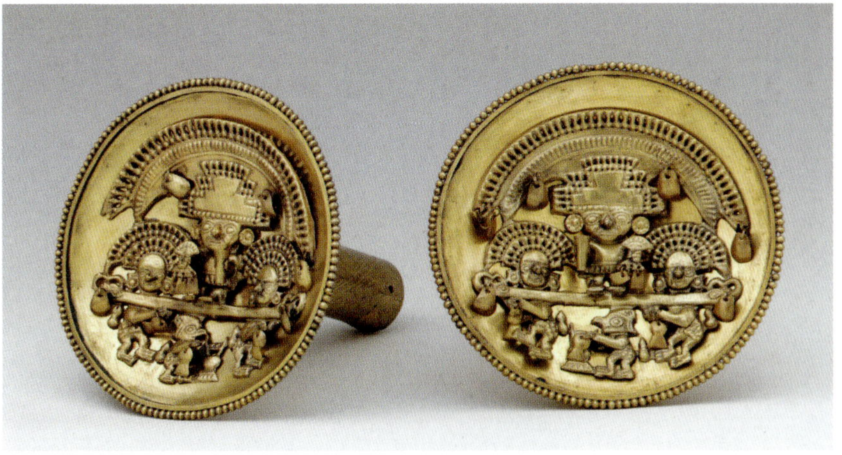

124 Ear Ornaments, 1350–1470

and ceremonial center to frame themselves as inheritors of ancient traditions that had come before them; they even buried important ancestors at sites like Huaca de la Luna. It is possible that between about 1250 and 1430 CE, the Chimú, who were accomplished sea traders, or their peers had contact with Polynesian peoples occupying Rapanui (Easter Island), over 2,370 miles (3,800 km) away. Needless to say, when the Inka Empire marched into northern Peru in the late fifteenth century, they faced a formidable foe in the Chimú dynasty.

The artists at Chan Chan were so talented that the Inka reportedly captured them and took them to their capital at Cuzco to put them into service of a new supreme ruler, the Sapa Inka. Despite the later conquest and probable sacking of Chan Chan at the hands of the Inkas and the Spanish, Chimú artists left behind their spectacular visions of idealized or actual events that occurred across the north coast of Peru. Rulers would have been carried around in processions as they
124 displayed their wealth and power, similar to a small-scale scene of a lord on a zoomorphic palanquin depicted on a set of spectacular earflares dating between 1350 and 1470. Gold workers meticulously crafted these ornaments from thinly hammered sheet metal, including the tiny hollow spheres that line the circular border and the rear cylindrical posts that would have been inserted into the ears and weighted in the back. Different techniques for shaping and joining the gold create a three-dimensionality and liveliness to the earflares, including a series of danglers that would have moved and created sound when worn, framing the face of the wearer.

Both mirrored scenes depict a central figure standing in frontal view, being borne on the palanquin by two attendants while a third person walks seemingly below the litter. The main character wears an enormous pyramidal headdress with feathered details that project in a wide arc along the upper edge of the composition. He also wears earflares that are surrounded by circular bosses, similar to the hollow spheres on the object itself, suggesting a meta-representation of the earflare. He carries a *kero* in one hand and a crescent-shaped
54 object that could be a fan, or perhaps a *tumi*, drawing parallels to that seen in slightly earlier Sicán art. The litter bearers wear similar fanned headdresses and earflares, and the third
24, 26 attendant is carrying a double spout-and-bridge bottle, a form long in use by Andean makers and popular among Chimú potters. These valuable parts of a ruler's assemblage would have created a striking image for any subjects observing the display, and these were likely included later as part of a funerary offering.

Because of the remarkable preservation of the coastal desert, evidence exists to demonstrate that such litter-bearing
125 scenes are not purely imaginary in nature. The carrying poles or even backrests of actual wooden litters survive, sometimes with extraordinary detail. This example is a wooden backrest painted and overlaid with metal and shell, radiocarbon dated to between 1185 and 1275. The border is carved in low relief with repeating, spiraled avian images. Five modeled figures emerge from the bright-red ground, which the artist painted with cinnabar. The largest figure in the center may represent a lord, similar to the one that would have been carried in the
106 litter, perhaps by the four others. Each figure wears a crescent headdress, a chinstrap terminating in two animal heads, as seen earlier in Wari imagery, and wide tunics covered with gold-alloy sheet. The arms are not indicated here but the legs with bare feet emerge from the bottom of the tunic. The faces of the figures are also painted bright red with cinnabar, with black lines descending from the nose to the chin, which contrasts sharply with the bright white eyes inlaid with shell. Such human-carried vehicles may have also been integral to processions of bundled ancestral remains on special occasions.

Rich narrative art had proliferated among the communities of practice on the north coast since Moche and Sicán/Lambayeque times (see chapter 3), and skilled metalworkers among the Chimú had worked to create drinking vessels with historical or mythological scenes. An example of this north coast tradition contemporaneous with the Chimú Empire is

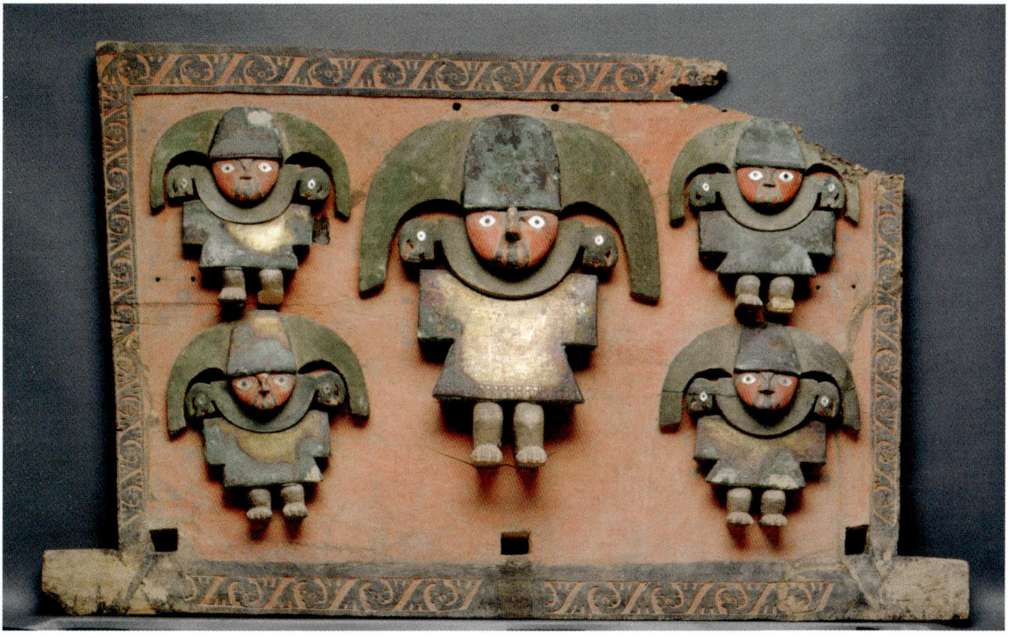

125 Litter Back, 1185–1275

126 a *kero*-shaped vessel with a subtle spout created of a single sheet of hammered silver. The vessel bears a low-relief scene wrapped around the entire surface, including the interior of the base, created using delicate repoussé (working metal from the reverse side) and chasing (working metal from the front side) techniques in the twelfth through fifteenth centuries. Visible only to the holder of the vessel when empty, the bottom of the beaker depicts an elaborate scene with a supernatural creature composed of the body of a scorpion and the head of a stylized person or deity. This principal character is surrounded by other animals including felines on the outer circular register.

Seemingly unconnected to the basal scorpion-deity scene, the outer walls of the beaker show registers of different figures engaged in what appear to be activities of the Chimú royal court. Figures on the lowest register, both mortal and supernatural, are depicted in crescent headdresses and different regalia holding a variety of ritual objects, such as *tumi*s, foodstuffs such as tubers, and *kero*s. The variation in the assemblages worn by the different individuals here may suggest different courtly roles or statuses. Above these characters are circular medallions that show scenes related to the sea, including depictions of reed boats and *Spondylus*

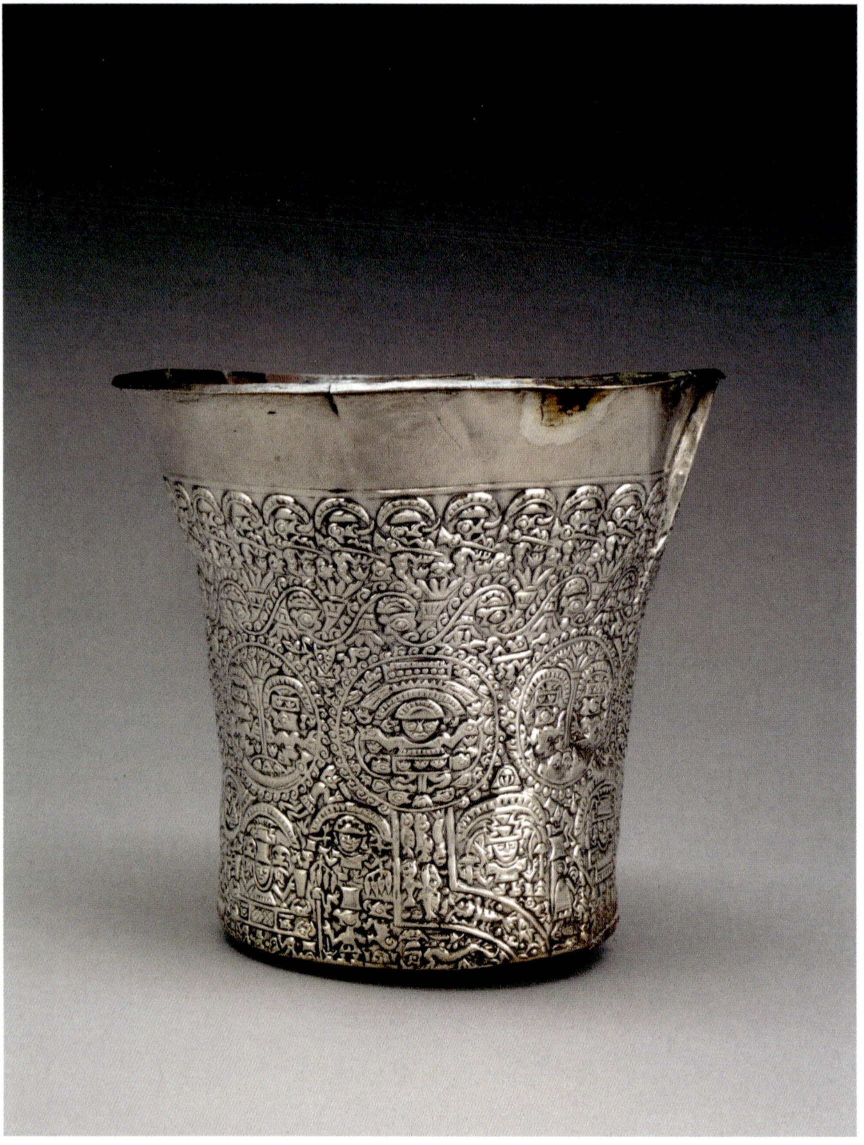

126 Vessel, c. 1100–1470

shells. Such shells were traded in very large quantities over very long distances for use by Chimú artists. The upper registers are repeated motifs of stylized waves and smaller zoomorphic figures holding staffs. Similar to other narrative drinking vessels, this elaborate scene may have been a mnemonic device for the performance of the epic history depicted there
63 as the holder turned the beaker in ceremony. Its remarkable preservation, especially considering the propensity of silver to corrode over time, suggests it ultimately formed a part of an important person's funerary offerings and may have been recovered from a dry, sealed tomb context.

Styles in Chimú metalwork are reminiscent of those created by Sicán/Lambayeque artists. Evidence suggests that upon gaining political control of the Lambayeque River region in the late fourteenth century, the Chimú leaders may have coopted the metalworkers into their own service. The artistic and multicultural community at the capital of Chan Chan gained great renown and was vital to producing the regalia and spiritually charged spaces that undergirded rulers' claims to power. The working of gold and silver in association with the duality of sun and the moon, the infusion of megascalar building projects with supernatural imagery, and the representation of male and female ancestral figures built on many centuries of oral and visual cultures dating back to Chavín de Huántar (1200–200 BCE). The ancient artistic energy, cultivated first in the north coast, was then put to use to fuel the ambitions of the Inka Tupac Yupanqui (mid-fifteenth century–1493). This ruler, holding the title of Sapa Inka and known as the Inka, expanded the empire's influence from Ecuador all the way to Chile, conquering the city of Chan Chan in the 1470s.

Inka

The succession of dynastic kings who governed what is known as the Inka Empire is perhaps best known for their perfection of the stunning megalithic, mortarless architecture, such as at Machu Picchu ("old peak" in Quechua). Perhaps known as Huayna Picchu ("young peak") to its original inhabitants
127 from around 1420 to 1532 CE, the ruined city has captivated the imagination of the world since the twentieth century, when its buildings were revealed to a global audience through photography. As one approaches the site today, cresting one of the terraced hillsides at 7,900 feet (over 2,400 m) above sea level, gazing at the misty mountaintop citadel engenders a sheer awe that certainly would have impressed fifteenth-century visitors to one of the Inka's highest cities as well.

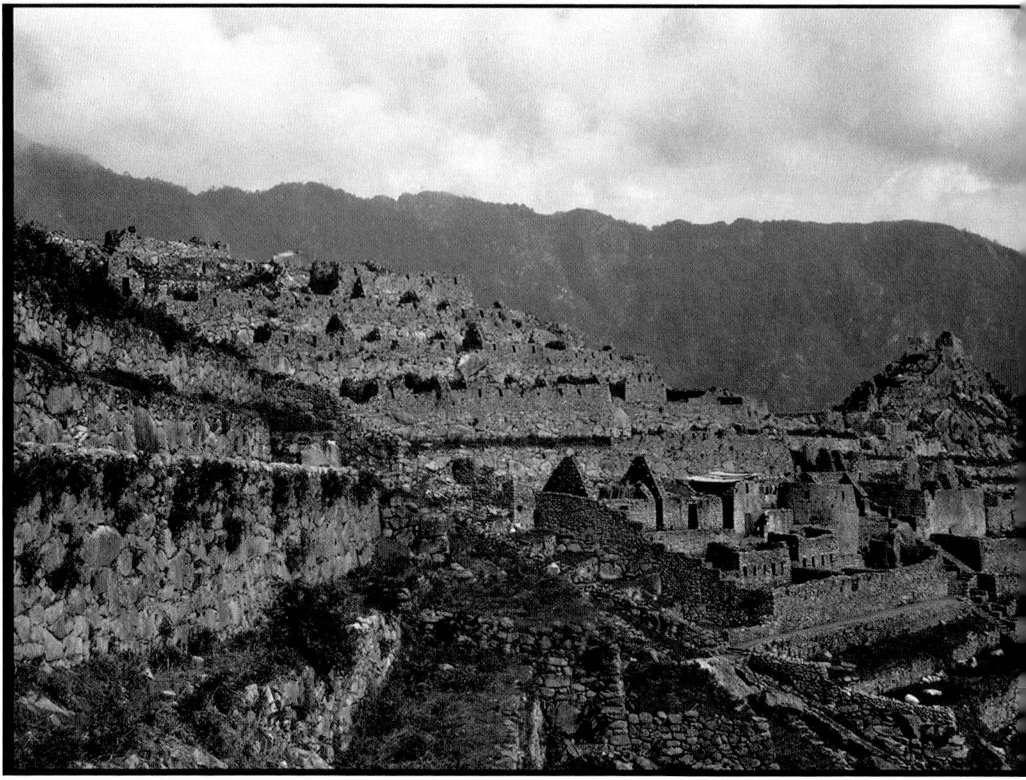

127 Martín Chambi, Panorama of Machu Picchu

The residential dwellings and ritual buildings seem to grow from the mountain's bedrock itself. Inka builders shaped the geology and added cut, beveled stone to create a whole. A relevant metaphor for this union of bedrock and cut stone comes from the Quechua term *kariwarmi*, "man-and-woman," in which complementary components merge harmoniously. In this way, the Inkas married the earth to their built environment. They employed a relational geometry as an overarching abstract principle founded on proportions, sightlines, and the movement of sunlight, as well as units of measurements based on the human body. Likely commissioned by the Inka Pachacuti (*c.* 1418–71), Tupac Yupanqui's father and who some consider to be the first emperor to expand the realm considerably beyond Cuzco, Machu Picchu may have served as a seasonal home for the royal court, abandoned upon the invasion of the Spanish.

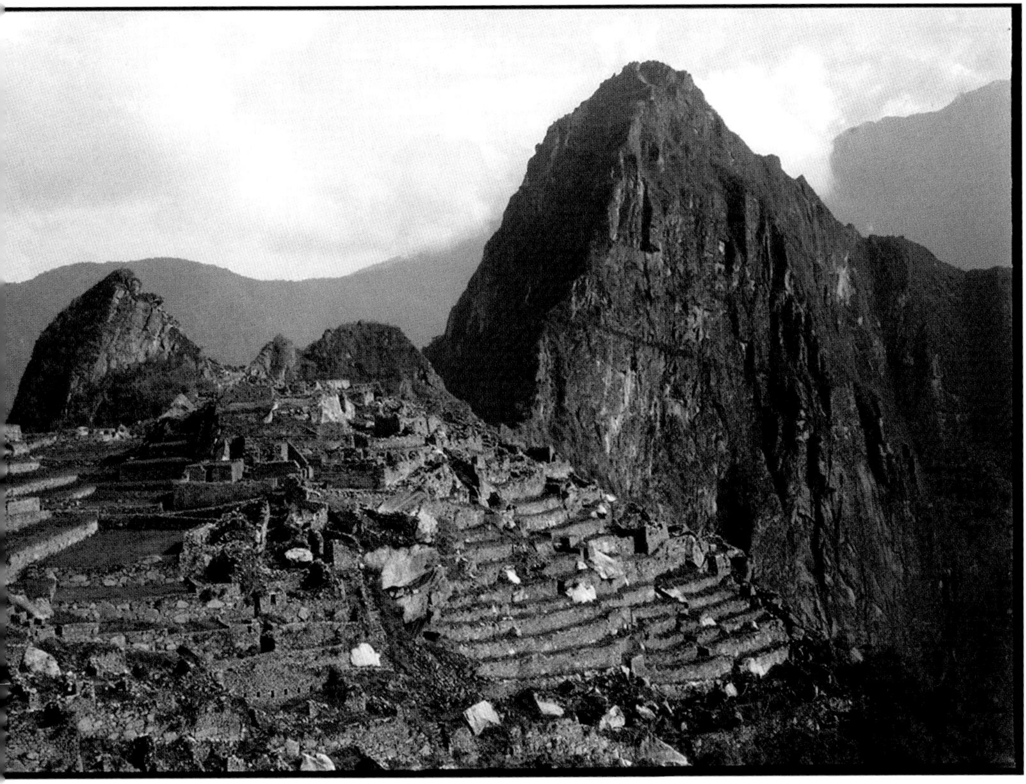

Surrounded by hundreds of agricultural terraces lined with stone walls, the royal estate itself lies at a terminus of a portion of the famed Inka trail, known as the *qhapaq ñan*, footpaths that crisscrossed the Andes and connected all corners of the empire, which was the largest in the ancient Americas stretching from what is now Colombia to Argentina. The court controlled access to the main plaza at Machu Picchu, royal residences, and temple area by erecting a large gated wall. Hydrology was an integral part of planning the city, and sophisticated waterworks channeled water for drinking and agricultural activities. The temple spaces were built precisely according to the alignments of the sun and other celestial bodies, similar to the building strategies around the imperial capital of Cuzco. Several large stone monuments sculpted by Inka artists retain their form and continue to hold significance for points of observation for the sun's movement or references to the surrounding mountainous landscape. The alignments still work and are observed by both local peoples and tourists today.

Several such sacred points on the urban landscape of Machu Picchu are known as *wak'a*s (or huacas) in Quechua, the lingua franca of the empire. This polyvalent term, difficult to define in other languages, encompasses sacred things and important natural or constructed places on the landscape (perhaps comparable to *k'uh* in the Maya region, *zemí* in the Antilles, or *teotl* in Central Mexico, see chapters 4, 5, and 11). *Wak'a* is an organizing concept when interpreting much of Inka stone sculpting. The inherent divinity in the stone itself also led sculptors to shape it in abstract and non-representational ways, or to not shape it at all, so many *wak'a*s were not figural and were often encountered in natural rather than constructed places. In these outdoor settings, Inka peoples visited *wak'a*s as shrines, leaving various types of offerings of foodstuffs, such luxury objects as shell or metals, or sacrificed animals.

Cuzco itself was the center of a vast network of *wak'a*s connected by the *qhapaq ñan*. The royal capital was conceptually the center of the Inka world, where the four quarters of the imperial realm created by Pachacuti, known as Tawantinsuyu ("the four parts together"), came together. The four regions were Chinchasuyu, Antisuyu, Qullasuyu, and Kuntisuyu, named after and based conceptually on the cardinal directions. Ritual conceptual pathways, known as the *ceque* ("line") system, radiated outward from Cuzco and spiritually connected *wak'a*s along the way, orienting the Inka lands. Noble lineages were responsible for honoring the *wak'a*s along the *ceque* lines throughout the year, unifying space and time. The deep-seated Andean duality also came into play in the spatial organization and social structure of Cuzco, which was physically halved into upper and lower sectors and symbolically halved among the elite families. These divisions were a large-scale expression of the complementarity between men and women, sun and moon, and other dualities (see chapter 1). The city today still maintains many of its astonishing Inka buildings, despite the Spanish appropriation of them for colonial foundations.

Although people had lived in the Cuzco valley for many centuries, during the fifteenth century, the Inka Pachacuti began a serious planning and rebuilding effort commissioning many important buildings and thoroughfares across the city. During this time the conventions for Inka mortarless stonework were established. The characteristics of the unique ashlar masonry, which is composed of rectilinear cut stone blocks,

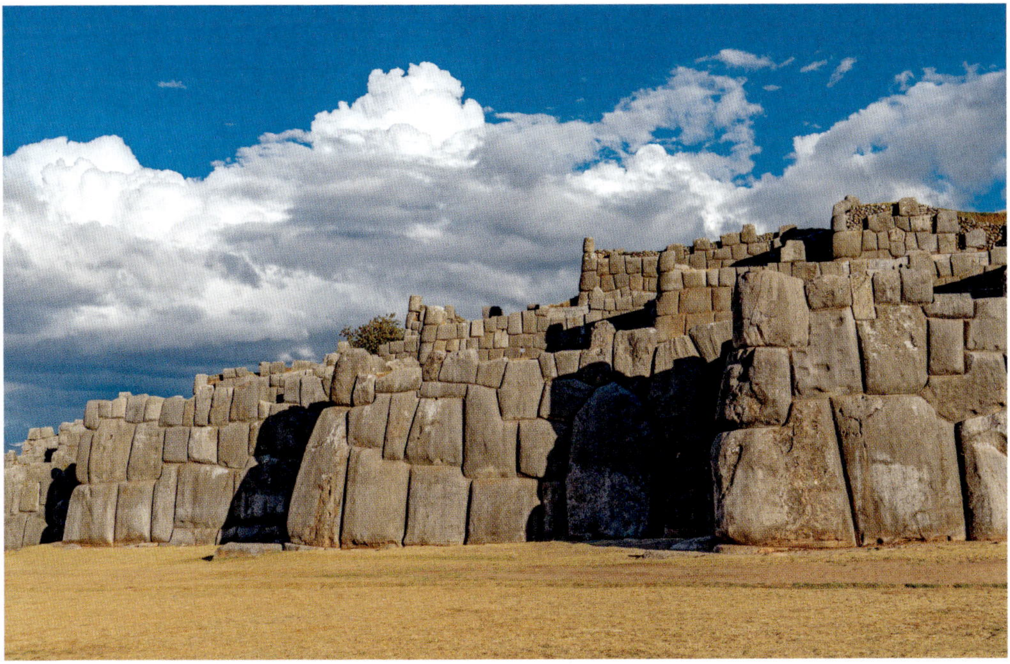

128 Sacsayhuamán, Peru

sometimes included a purposeful rounding of the external surfaces of stones, which the builders then polished to give the stones a living quality. One stone included a remarkable twelve angles, with the sides of varying length fitting perfectly with the surrounding blocks. Cuzco building aesthetics were often rectangular with the most important structures having trapezoidal doorways and windows. Cuzco's masons also demonstrated their prowess with rounded plans and sloping walls, such as the ones found in the various phases of the Qorikancha ("golden temple"), the spiritual center of the empire and the place from which the *ceque*s radiated.

Perhaps the largest stones ever moved by the Inkas were
128 placed on a ridge above the capital at a ceremonial, fortress-like structure known as Sacsayhuamán. Three colossal walls create terraces that line a large level plaza where important ceremonies were held. Today a speculative reenactment of the winter solstice celebration known as Inti Raymi is held in the archaeological park, though it may have originally been celebrated in the center of Cuzco during the Inka Empire. Several important *wak'a*s are near the main structures of Sacsayhuamán. One, known as Qenqo, is a natural rock

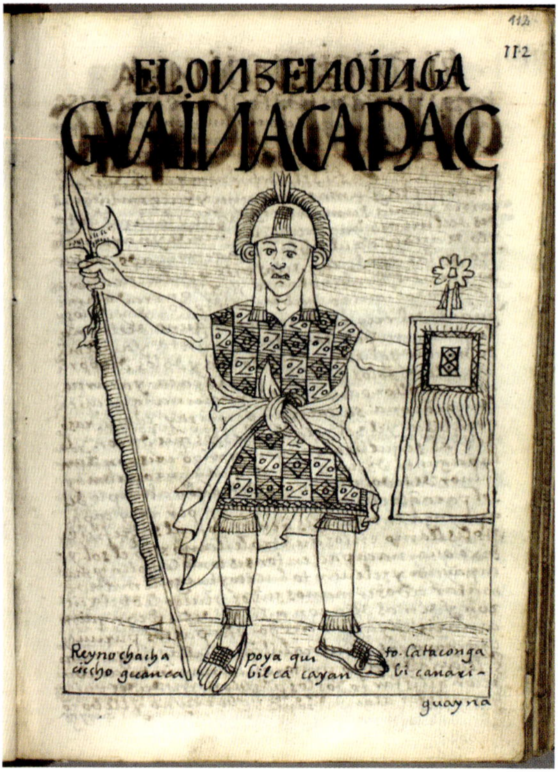

129 Felipe Guaman Poma de Ayala, *The Eleventh Inka, Huayna Capac*, 1615–16

formation shaped into a labyrinth with an underground chamber presumably used for important offerings. As at Machu Picchu, water was also a key part of Inka architectural practice at the *wak'a* known as Tambomachay, where builders channeled natural spring water into a series of stone fountains, cascades, and aqueducts. Few documentary sources testify to the precise uses of these *wak'a*s near Sacsayhuamán, and, unfortunately, many such important places were targets of early Spanish idolatry campaigns.

Knowledge of Inka political history and culture, as well as the many Indigenous terms for works in this chapter, comes
129, 130 from a variety of documentary sources, including a chronicle titled *El primer nueva corónica y buen gobierno* by the Indigenous author Felipe Guaman Poma de Ayala (*c.* 1535–after 1616), written around 1615–16. The handwritten manuscript relates the history of the Inka Empire and structure of Inka society as well as the actions of the Spanish and impact of colonialism on Tawantinsuyu. Illustrations in the document combine

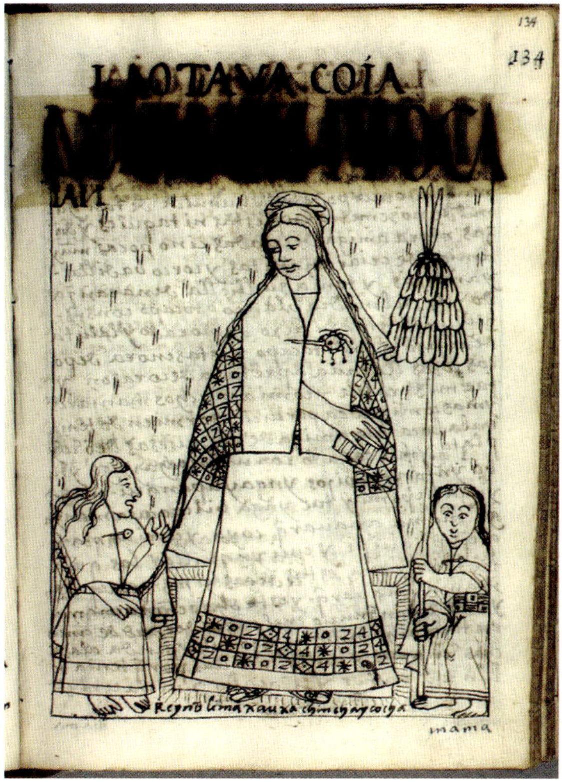

130 Felipe Guaman Poma de Ayala, *The Eighth Qoya, Mama Yunto Cayan*, 1615–16

Inka ways of thinking and representing with European techniques and materials introduced by the Spanish in the sixteenth century. In this pair of pages, the illustrator depicted Tupac Yupanqui's son, the Sapa Inka Huayna Capac (before 1487–1527) in a triumphant standing pose, holding a long staff with an axe head and a woven shield or standard. He wears a finely woven tunic, or *unku*, composed of square tiles (known as *tokapu*), tunic, sandals, and a feathered headdress along with earflares. According to the caption, the emperor, under whom Tawantinsuyu reached its greatest extent, conquered faraway regions such as Quito, now the capital of Ecuador, and Chachapoyas, on the eastern slope of the Peruvian Andes, before his untimely death in 1527, likely due to European diseases already introduced from colonizers.

The other page contains a portrait of an earlier Inka queen (*qoya*), the wife of Viracocha Inka (*c.* 1380–1438) and mother of Pachacuti, known as Mama Yunta (or Yunto) Cayan or Mama Runtu (*c.* 1400–mid-fifteenth century). She is accompanied by courtly attendants, depicted as people of short stature or non-standard bodies, whom Guaman Poma mentions on the following page the queen favored and, indeed, to whom she bequeathed her homestead (hacienda). In the image, she wears two sumptuous garments including an ankle-length wrap dress (*aksu*) and a rectangular shawl (*lliklla*). She also holds a bag (*chuspa*), perhaps for coca leaves. Like their Andean predecessors, the Inkas frequently used the coca leaf as an important substance in ceremonies. The attendant on the right of the scene holds up a feathered standard or parasol. Although these retrospective portraits were composed centuries after the subjects lived, certain details give insights into the courtly artistic production sponsored by the Inkas. The textiles were primary among the valued materials, with Inka weavers creating some of the finest tapestry cloth ever made, known in Quechua as *cumbi*.

Holding together the queen's *lliklla* in the manuscript is a
131, 132 metal pin known as a *tupu*. Andean metalworkers produced these simple but elegant pins beginning in the early first millennium CE or before. The two examples here from 1476 to 1532, were created by skillfully hammering metal to form a stem that would be inserted in the garment, and a rounded, flattened finial that would prevent the pin from falling through while in use. The perforation may have been used to add dangling adornments, similar to those seen in Maya Yunta Cayan's *tupu*, or to connect a paired *tupu* with a fiber cord. The two *tupu*s here are made of silver, with one having a slightly more golden hue, perhaps due to a distinct alloy or surface gilding. Women would also have worn two *tupu*s to fasten shawls or dresses made of camelid wool, so these two may have once been a complementary pair.

Returning to the portrait of the Sapa Inka, the *unku* that Huayna Capac wears in Guaman Poma's image is a specific type
133 of *cumbi* cloth, fashioned into a tunic that is entirely composed of *tokapu*s. This class of *unku* was reserved for the highest echelon of imperial authority and this is the only known example of an all-*tokapu* tunic that survives to the present. Inka weavers finely wove this garment around the year 1532 as a long rectangular tapestry with warps of natural cotton and wefts of spun and dyed camelid wool. A neck hole shows signs of wear—at least two incidents of damage were repaired in the past—and the sides were sewn up leaving room for the arms. It originally could have been belted at the waist, as shown in Guaman Poma's drawing. Sumptuary regulations dictated that such tunics were reserved for the emperor himself, whereas

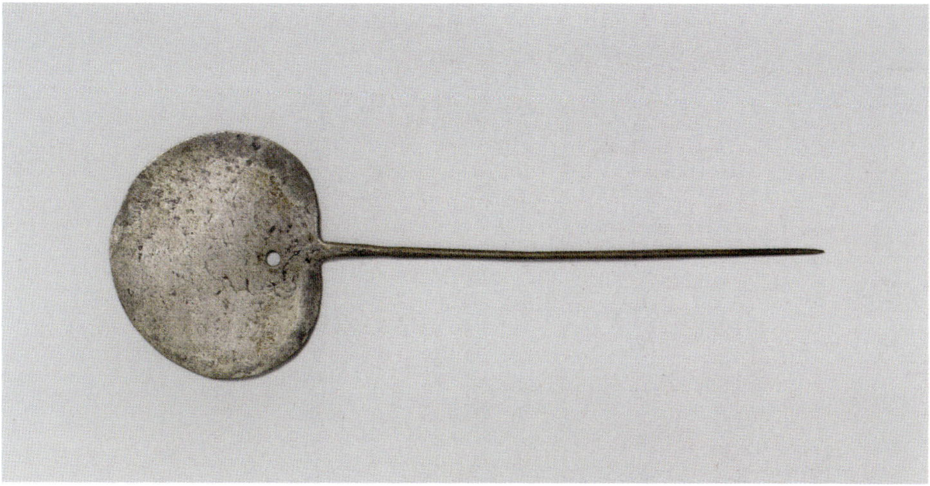

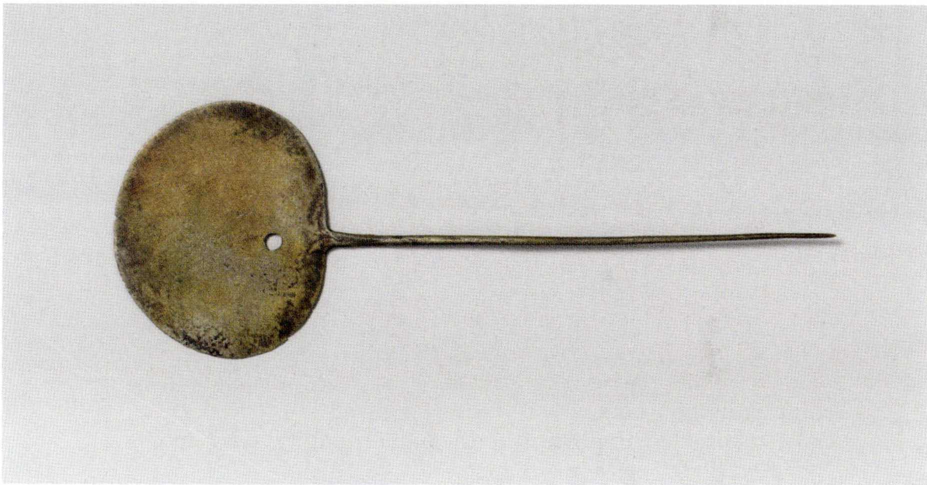

131 TOP *Tupu* (pin), 600–1500
132 ABOVE *Tupu* (pin), 600–1600

other tunics with *tokapu*s only on the waistband or collar could be worn by other nobles.

Recent studies of the royal tunic have proposed that the *tokapu* designs underscored to the Inka's subjects that he was the ultimate authority, embodying the empire itself. The most commonly featured *tokapu* design—unique to this tunic in the corpus of Inka textiles—is a small-scale representation of a checkerboard tunic. The full-sized checkerboard tunics, which have a red collar framed by black and white squares,

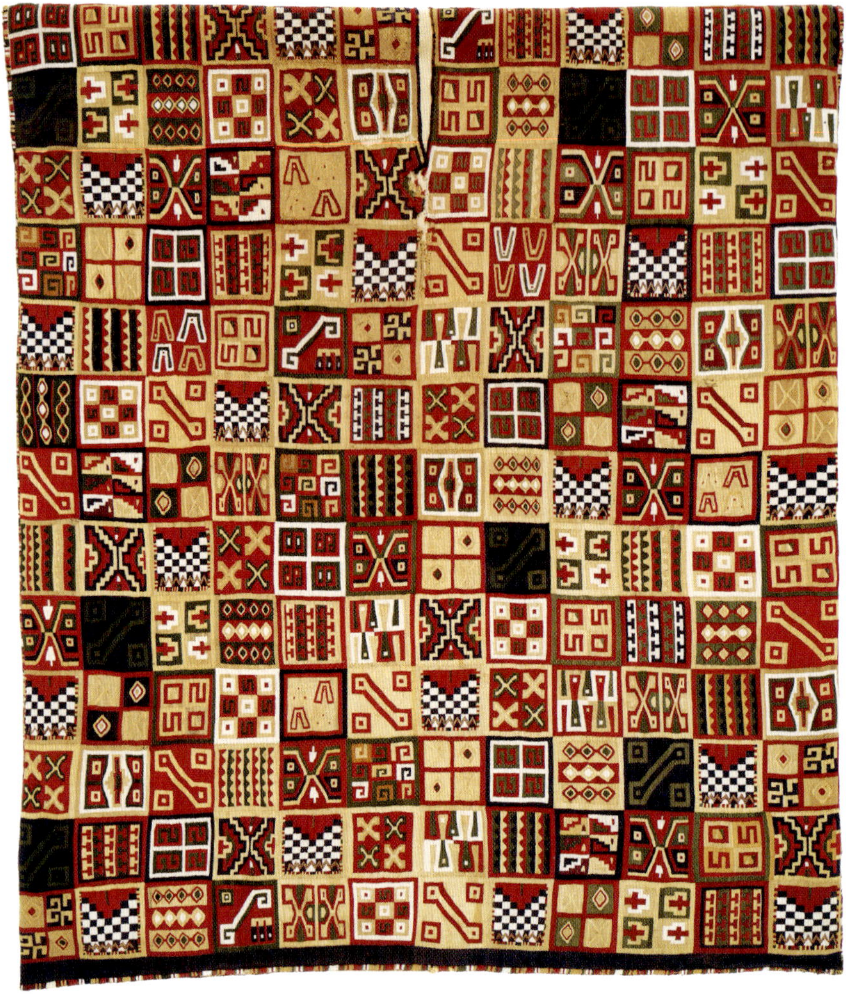

133 Royal Tunic, 1450–1540

were reportedly used by the Inka's personal squadron of royal bodyguards. Therefore one interpretation of the small tunic *tokapus* distributed around the surface of the *unku* is that they represent a supervisory military presence throughout the empire itself. In the absence of texts written in books or scrolls or carved into stone monuments, the Inkas conveyed their political might through their sartorial choices. Curiously, this tunic appears to be unfinished, as other Inka garments of this quality bear a brightly colored zigzag line across the dark band at the lower hem. Perhaps it was being produced for the Sapa

Inka Atahualpa (*c.* 1502–33), Huayna Capac's son, and he was executed by Spanish invaders before he could take possession of the garment. It could have been worn in the colonial period, explaining the evidence of wear in the neck area.

Textile production also engendered a unique form of
134 recordkeeping for imperial business: knotted cords joined on base strings, known as *khipu*s ("knot" in Quechua). The rulers and administrators of the largest empire in the Americas used *khipu*s as forms of taking census and inventory, and perhaps even for narrative or linguistic content, although the corpus of *khipu*s remains largely undeciphered. In fact, *khipu*s are also
105 known from Wari contexts, such as the royal mausoleum at Huarmey. An Inka official, known as the *khipucamayoc*, was the keeper of the *khipu*s, and served as a sort of exchequer or accountant. The number of strings from the base cord, the number of knots on each string, and even the types of knots recorded numerical information. Other aspects of the *khipu*s, such as the different colors of strings used, had other encoded information that is no longer known. Given the linguistic diversity across the vast territory in which *khipu*s were used, they served as trans-lingual communication systems. Thus, textile production, whether for garments or recording devices, was inextricably linked to tribute and imperial expansion.

The term *khipucamayoc* bears the root term *camayoc*, which is difficult to translate directly from Quechua but implies an

134 *Khipu*, 1476–1532

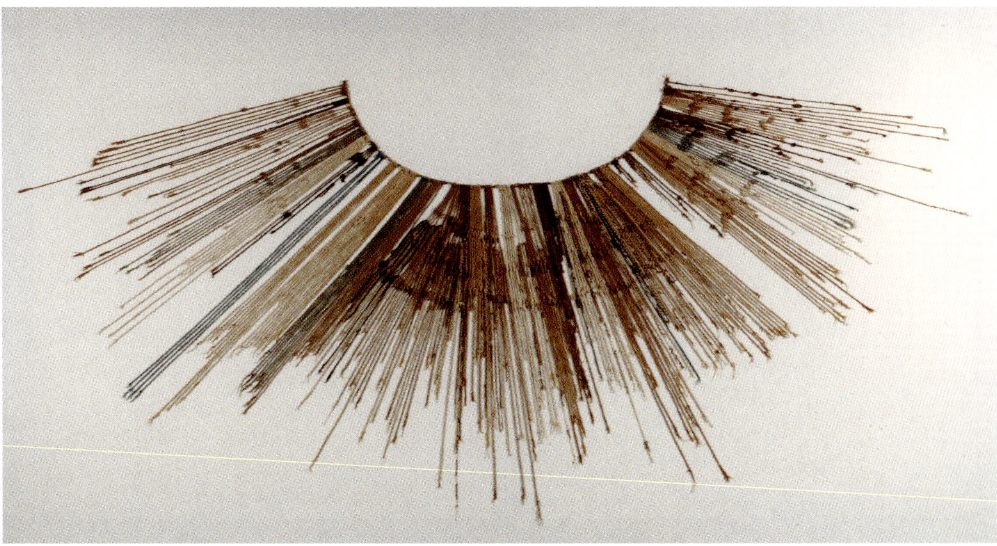

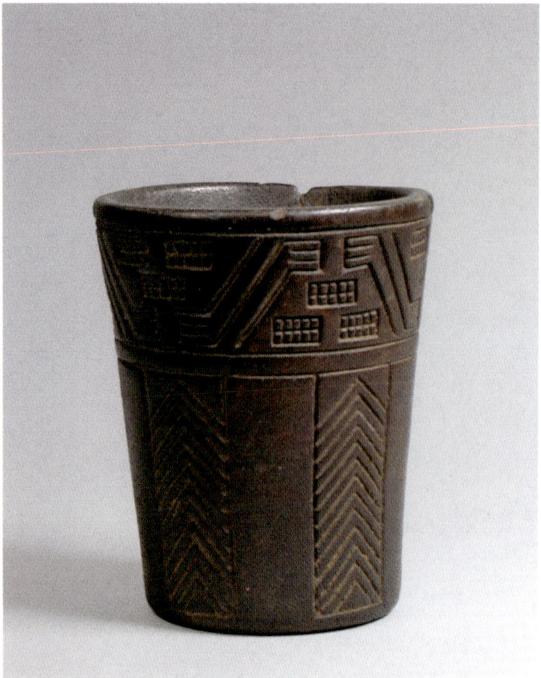

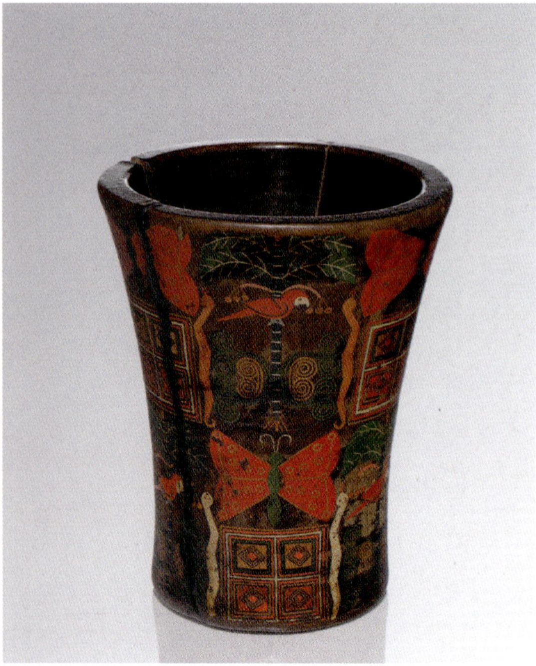

135 *Keros* (Vessels), *c.* 1500 and 1550–1800

individual who could manifest *camay* in objects. *Camay* is an inherent life force within matter that could be realized by the *camayoc*, who were the Inka artists. Inka makers innovated beautiful forms beyond the alteration of *wak'a*s or production of built environments and garments or regalia, especially in vessels used in important ceremonial feasts. Adopting the flaring vessel form from previous Andean societies, carvers
135 created wooden *kero*s that tended to be more stylized and geometric in decoration, but some created after the Spanish invasion depict elite individuals or figural motifs. *Kero*s were often made and used in unequal or asymmetrical pairs, expressing Andean duality and power dynamics within the social order in feasting contexts. The geometric *kero* dates to the fifteenth or early sixteenth century, and the *kero* with images of animals and trees was produced during Spanish rule after 1532.

A sculptor created the geometric *kero* with columns of upward-pointing chevron motifs around the body and a register around the rim that contains stylized faces and arms. *Kero*s frequently contain repeating motifs also found in textiles such as the *chakana* shape (see chapter 7). This contrasts with the brightly colored *kero* that features scarlet macaws perched in palm trees, framed by lighter-colored serpents and large red butterflies with incised spots. The animals are surrounded by square fields with four *tokapu*s, another reference to textiles. The passages in color here are not paint, but inlaid resins known as *mopa mopa* created from the plants in the *Elaeagia* genus, a material innovated in the northern reaches of the Inka
153 Empire. This material was still in use in the viceregal period, from the sixteenth to early nineteenth centuries.

Drinking, elaborate toasts, and offering liquids such as chicha, maize beer, were part of the empire building enterprise for the Inkas. Offerings appealed to *wak'a*s and especially the *apu*s, which were sacred mountain spirits or ancestors. These places were the sites of sumptuous sacrificial offerings
136 prepared and deposited in a ceremony known as *qhapaq hucha* (or *capacocha*), or "royal obligation". Beginning in Cuzco, the *qhapaq hucha* involved preparing specially selected juveniles as sacrifices, then ritually killing them and burying them with elaborate regalia and ritual objects such as small-scale metal figurines and textile garments. A metalworker constructed this example of a nude male wearing a headdress from sheet metal, even adding the detail of a puffed-out cheek, suggesting that this person was chewing coca. The figure was then wrapped in a tiny mantle and tunic along with a small version of a *chuspa*. This assemblage, created in the fifteenth or early sixteenth

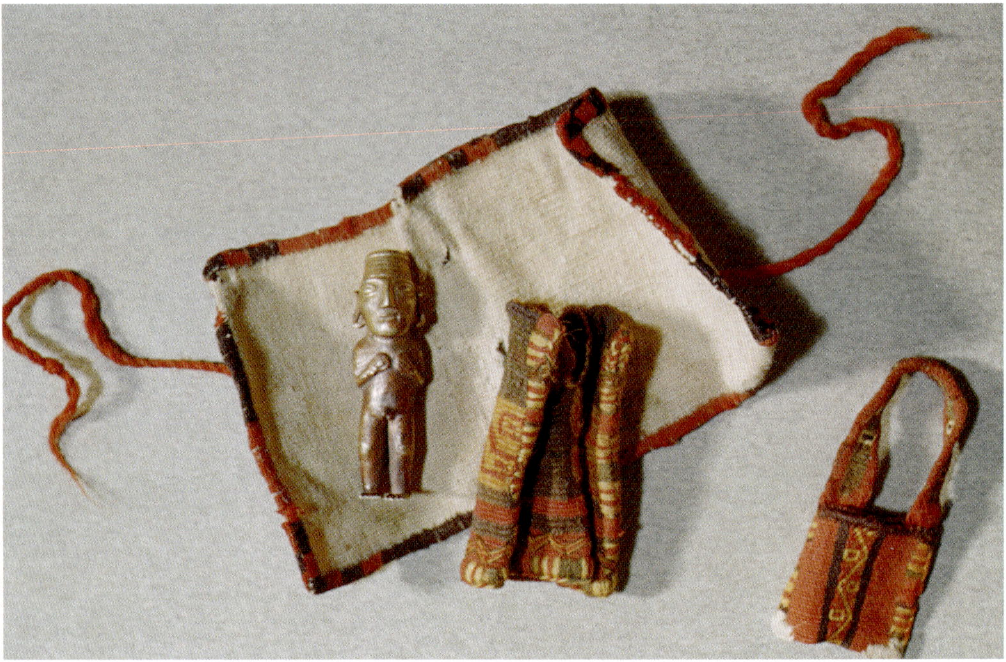

136 Ritual Assemblage, 1400–1532

century, could have formed part of a *qhapaq hucha* offering to an *apu* or *wak'a*.

Elaborate rituals of reciprocity with the sacred landscape such as the *qhapaq hucha* also necessitated new forms of containers for liquid offerings. Inka potters created libation vessels called *paccha*s, which allowed the user to pour chicha into one opening so it would then flow out another spout,
137 sharing the liquid with the earth. One *paccha* type from the fifteenth or early sixteenth century blends together the entire life cycle of maize and its products, underscoring the importance of rituals for agricultural fertility. The lower portion of this vessel is in the shape of a shortened digging stick, a tool that allows for the planting of maize, and it is crowned with a small corn cob. The upper portion is a small-scale version of a chicha storage vessel known as an *urpu*; it has a pointed base, handles, modeled adornments, and a tall neck with flaring rim. A painter decorated the *urpu* with vertical fields of red and featherlike designs, similar to the painting on large-scale versions, perhaps an abstraction of maize plants. As the patron of this vessel symbolically irrigated the earth with this offering, he or she would have been reenacting the

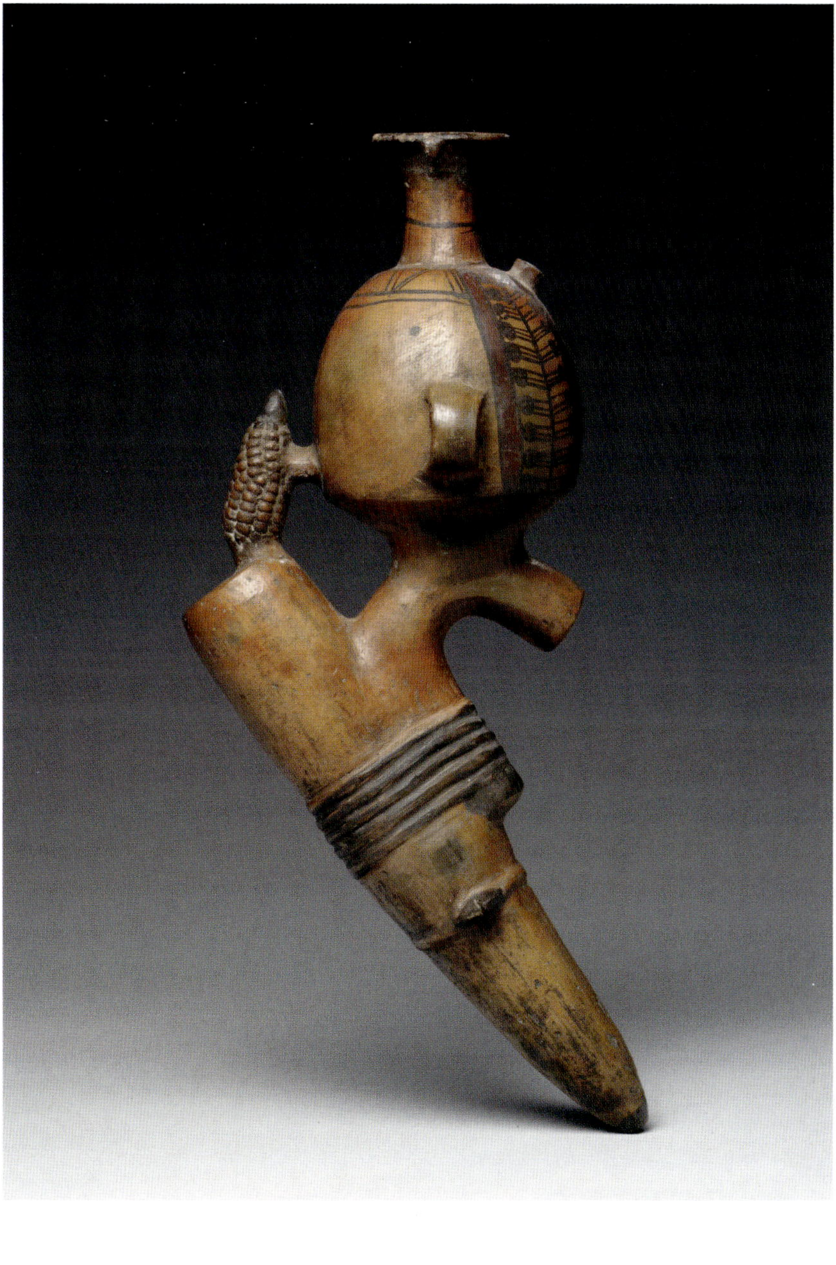

137 *Paccha* (Vessel), 1400–1532

beginning of the agricultural season. At its very core, the empire itself was built on the foundation of successful farming, manifested through artist-made offerings to *wak'a*s, *apu*s, and other parts of the divine Inka landscape.

Chapter 10

Altepetl, the Water Mountain: Mexica (1000–1521 CE)

The societies that organized themselves in Mesoamerica after about 1000 CE were the inheritors of deep-rooted beliefs in a divine landscape with a primordial mountain cave at its conceptual center. Beginning around the fourteenth century, peoples known widely as Nahuas, who had lived in the Basin of Mexico and had spoken the Nahuatl language for generations, began infusing their cities and political alliances in the area with sacred beliefs by constructing monumental ceremonial precincts in their capitals and commissioning stunning works of art and architecture. For the Nahuas, a central organizing principle was the term *altepetl*, "water mountain," which came to mean something equivalent to city-state. These autonomous political units were simultaneously viewed by their residents as spiritual and administrative centers. In the fourteenth and fifteenth centuries the leaders of three powerful *altepetl*s—Tenochtitlán, Tetzcoco, and Tlacopan—allied their forces to spread their politico-religious influence throughout what is now Mexico. Known as the Triple Alliance, they conquered other *altepetl*s and built their own mountain pyramids to inspire awe and engender loyalty among new subjects.

The Nahua rulers of the Triple Alliance referred to themselves as Mexica (later termed Aztec in the nineteenth century), from which comes the name of the country of Mexico. Throughout the empire, leaders constructed ceremonial centers, often upon existing sacred places, that brought the Mexica religion and military might to new peoples. One outstanding example of the power of Mexica builders to recreate origin places is found at a site known today as
138 Malinalco, located southwest of Tenochtitlán. The *huey tlatoani* (emperor) Axayacatl (*c.* 1449–81) conquered the area in the late fifteenth century and ordered the construction of new temples,

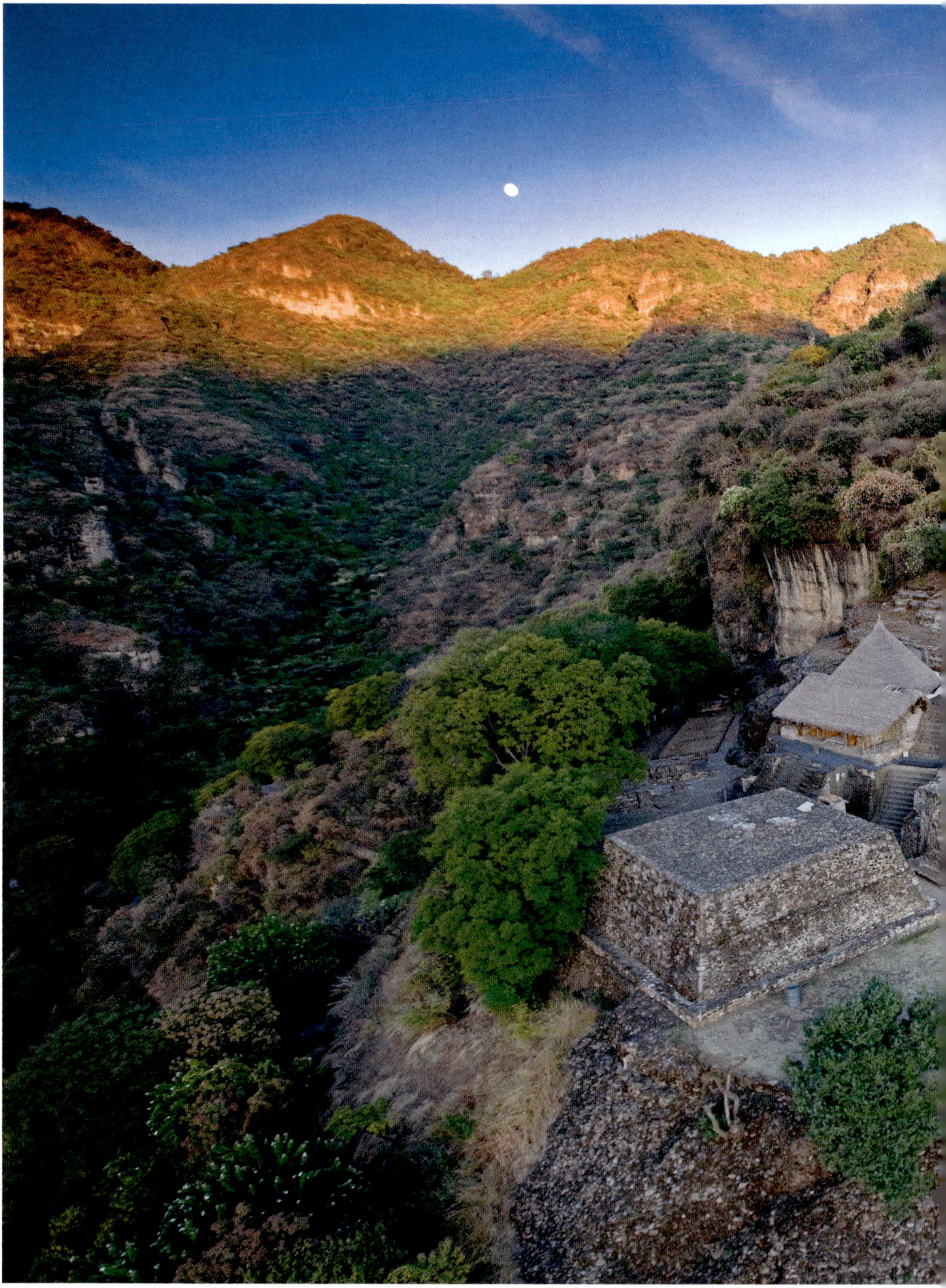

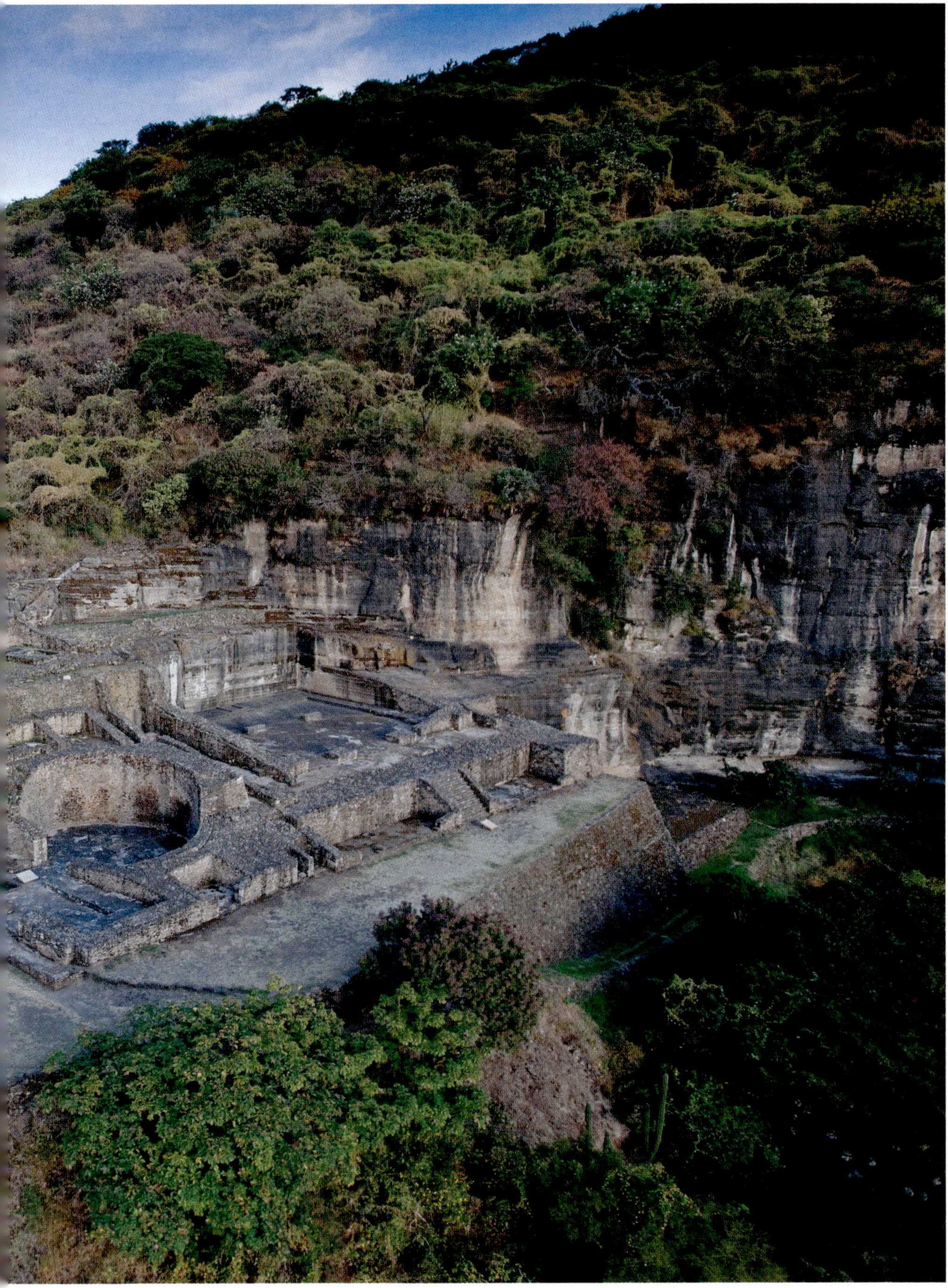

including three that are remarkably cut directly from bedrock, making this monolithic space literally built from the mountain cave itself. This architecture includes structural bases, stairways and balustrades, and figural sculptures of felines and other zoomorphic forms. These impressive feats may have been completed after 1501 by Axayacatl's brother, the *huey tlatoani* Ahuitzotl (*c.* 1450s–1502), who expanded the Mexica Empire considerably in the late fifteenth century. This mountain-cave complex was the setting of religious ceremonies such as autosacrifice (bloodletting) or captive sacrifice designed to bring propitious favor to the Mexica.

139 In the Triple Alliance capitals, builders also recreated sacred mountains by constructing agglomerative pyramidal structures, known in Nahuatl as *huey teocalli*, in Spanish as Templos Mayores (great temples). From available sources and recent archaeological work, it seems that these mountain pyramids like the one at Tenochtitlán faced west toward the setting sun and were crowned with two different temple buildings, with the southern one dedicated to the Mexica patron deity Huitzilopochtli and the northern one dedicated to the god of rain, known as Tlaloc. In this depiction of the Templo Mayor of Tenochtitlán from the 1580s, the Jesuit missionary Juan de Tovar (1543?–1626) depicted a pyramid platform with a twin staircase, with the stair risers and stepped terraces. He used European materials and conventions introduced by the Spanish colonizers, but infused the illustrations with Mexica imagery and concepts. The two temples at the summit of the pyramid have brightly painted jambs and lintels and large roof finials, known as *almenas*, that depict marine shells, projecting skyward. The temple on the right contains a representation of the seated figure of Huitzilopochtli and the temple on the left shows his counterpart, Tlaloc. They are flanked by seated banner-bearers, either human or stone. Below the stairs, the artist illustrated descending feathered serpents baring their fangs; these balustrades surround a field in which is written "Temple of the Image of Huitzilopochtli" in Spanish. The image to the right depicts a *tzompantli*, a wooden structure used to display human skulls; such constructions with actual or stone skulls have been recovered from near the Templo Mayor.

These two temple spaces may represent two primordial mountains, Coatepetl (dedicated to the solar Huitzilopochtli) and Tonacatepetl (dedicated to Tlaloc). Archaeology at the Templo Mayor of Tenochtitlán has demonstrated a series of elaborate dedicatory offerings along the axes of these temples with symbolism relating to each deity. Many of these offerings,

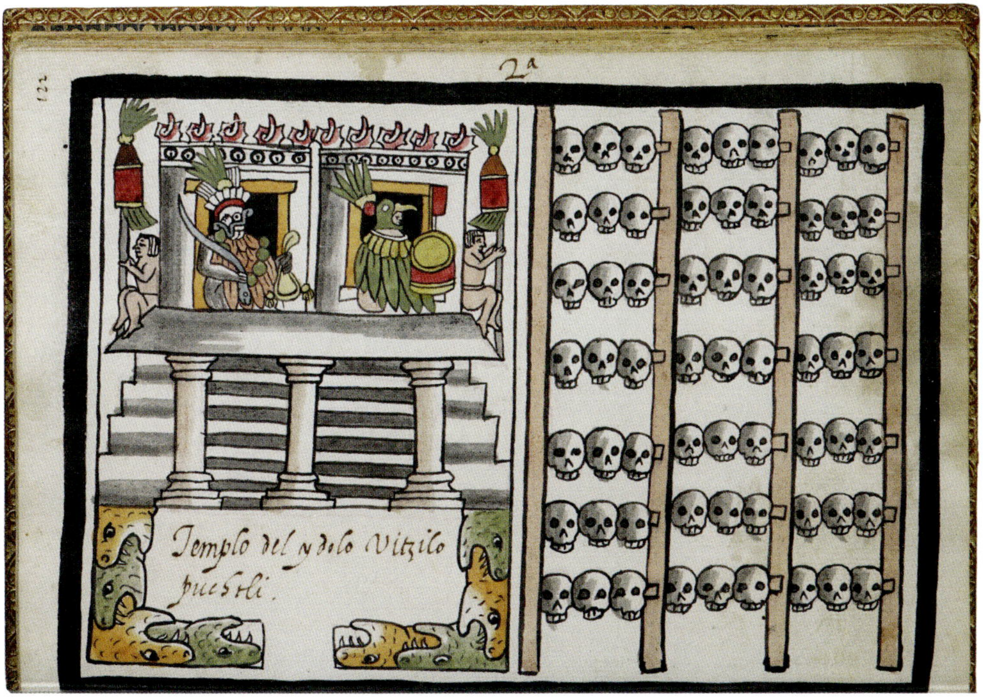

139 Juan de Tovar, *Tenochtitlan Templo Mayor*, from the *Tovar Codex*, 1582–87

deposited in elaborate stone boxes, contain highly valued materials brought from all corners of the Mexica Empire, including textiles, gold, shells, jade, and turquoise. They also sacrificed eagles, jaguars, and marine creatures such as starfish and coral, which had been remarkably transported from the faraway Gulf of Mexico and buried alive. These offerings perpetually recreated the origin stories of the peoples who arrived at Tenochtitlán and their legacy as the current incarnation of divine rulers.

Mexica lore drew power and aesthetic inspiration from an earlier society known as Toltecs, based at the large city of Tula, Hidalgo from the ninth to thirteenth centuries. The residents of Tula, who may have also spoken Nahuatl, were connected by trade and political relationships to the Maya peoples at Chichén Itzá, as evidenced by similar architecture and artistic
140 conventions (see chapter 4). At Tula, colossal sculptures of warriors held up the roof of the building as they stood watch over the main temple precinct. Standing at almost 16 feet (5 m) tall, this rigid warrior faces forward with an active expression, with parted lips and wide-open eyes, from which shell or

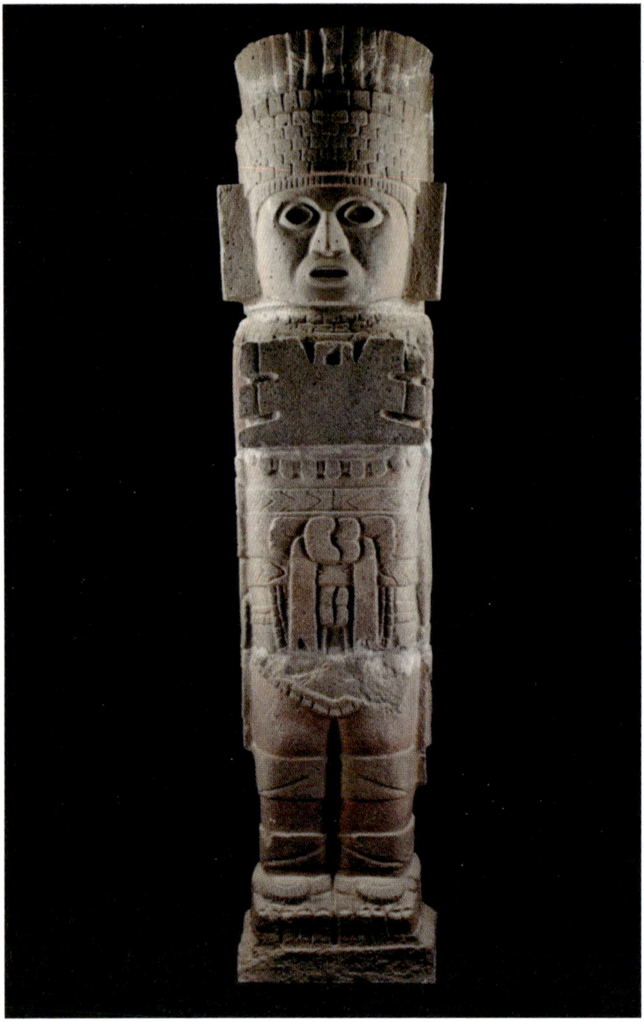

140 Anthropomorphic Sculpture (Tula Atlantean), 850–1250

stone inlays may have once reflected light. The barrel-shaped headdress is crowned with a row of feathers and the artists took special care to shape the rectangular earflares or flaps covering the ears. A large butterfly-shaped pectoral dominates the regalia, which also includes a collar, loincloth, and knotted belt that carries a large mirror disk on the figure's lower back. One the side of the sculpture, the warrior holds a spearthrower, known as an *atlatl* in Nahuatl, in his right hand, and darts in his left. The figure was architectural in nature, infusing the most visible platform at Tula with martial energies. The stony warrior was once brightly painted to inspire subjects or perhaps to instill fear in those who opposed. Such visual systems and depictions of militarism were built on traditions founded even earlier at Teotihuacán and then coopted by the Mexica for their ambitious purposes.

As the rulers of the Triple Alliance gained power through exacting tribute, Tenochtitlán became a mecca for artistic workshops, especially for sculptors of megalithic figures. Perhaps the best-known product of these artists is the
141 multivalent, 22-ton monument known as the Calendar Stone or Piedra del Sol, carved in the early sixteenth century, rediscovered in 1790 in Mexico City's main plaza, and currently the centerpiece of the Museo Nacional de Antropología. This iconic image serves at once as a stone for sacrifices or ritualized combat (known respectively as *cuauhxicalli* and *temalacatl*), a god image and solar representation, a calendric statement, and perhaps even a deified portrait of the Mexica ruler Moteuczoma II (*c.* 1466–1520), among others. Moteuczoma II is known for

141 Calendar Stone Sculpture, c. 1500–21

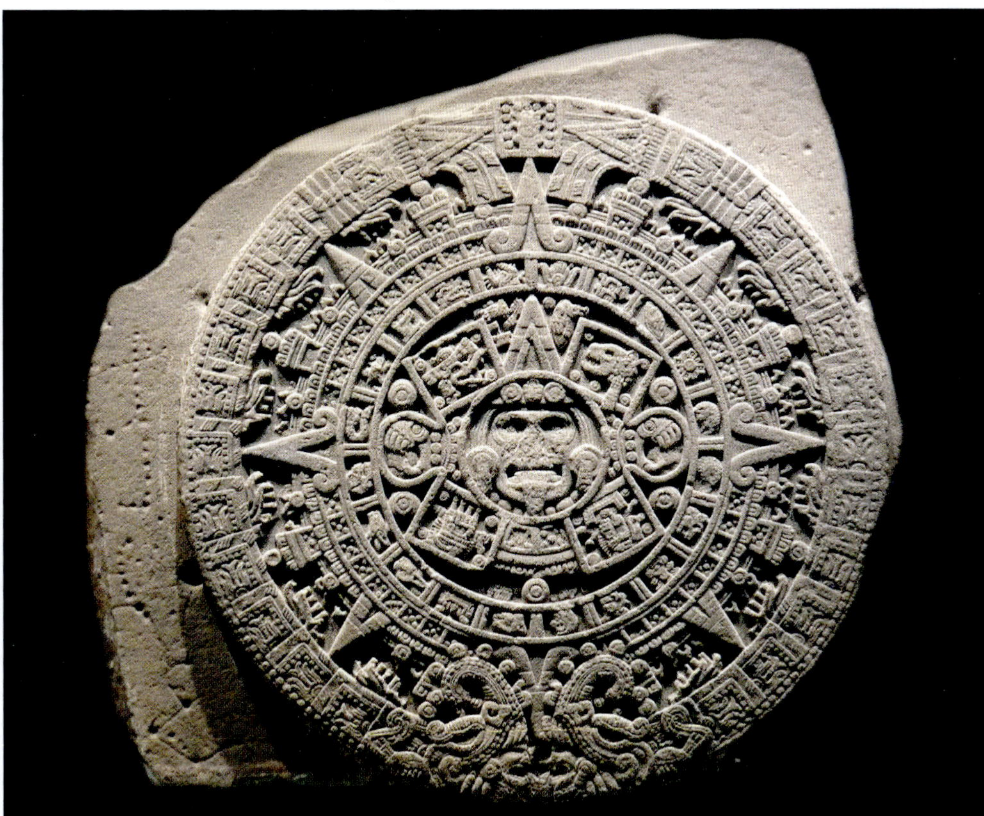

increasing the size of the Mexica Empire to its greatest extent and being a great patron of luxury arts in his royal court, before he was killed in 1520 during the Spanish invasion. The layering on the Calendar Stone of functional surfaces, mythic personages, historical characters, and oral histories is a hallmark of Mesoamerican art that truly reached its creative pinnacle among the sculptors in Tenochtitlán.

Originally facing skyward in the central precinct of Tenochtitlán, the Calendar Stone is celestial in meaning; the sculptors detailed the edge of the circular image with a band of sky-related hieroglyphs (*ilhuicatl*). Other hieroglyphs are present in the elaborate design of the surface, including the large hieroglyph for the 4-Motion (*Nahui Olin*), representing the fifth era of Nahua history, and four glyphs framing the central face: 4-Jaguar (*Nahui Ocelotl*), 4-Wind (*Nahui Ehecatl*), 4-Rain (*Nahui Quiahuitl*), and 4-Water (*Nahui Atl*). These are glyphic references to four previous eras in Mexica history, cycles of time in which other deities were said to have embodied the
39 sun. There are also twenty day signs of the cyclical calendar, which was present since the earliest hieroglyphic texts in Mesoamerica. Although the sculpture contains such calendric signs and textual elements, it was not necessarily intended to be read in a certain way, nor was it even a functional calendar despite its modern nickname. The outer concentric ring consists of two mirrored fire serpents (*xiuhcoatl*), surrounding a ring of solar rays and turquoise preciousness (*xihuitl*), which encloses the frame of the day signs around the central image.

The identity of the central figure has been a source of much debate since the nineteenth century, but a general consensus is that it represents the face of Tonatiuh, the deified sun at its zenith, or Yohualtecuhtli, a nighttime deity (or perhaps
144 Tlaltecuhtli). He is characterized by the grimacing mouth, flint knife-tongue, and claws grasping human hearts to either side. The embedded glyphs above the face may suggest that the image simultaneously records a portrait of Moteuczoma II embodying the Mexican patron deity Huitzilopochtli. Ultimately this massive image was destined to be set into a platform and serve as a place of presentation for Mexica subjects as they moved around the visual parable in ceremony. Today it is a primary symbol of identity in both ancient and contemporary Mexico.

Tonatiuh, the god likely present on the Calendar Stone, was one of many deities that served as vital subjects for Mexica sculptors. Three important female deities formed a core group in Mexica religious thought and artistic representations according to recorded mythologies, underscoring their

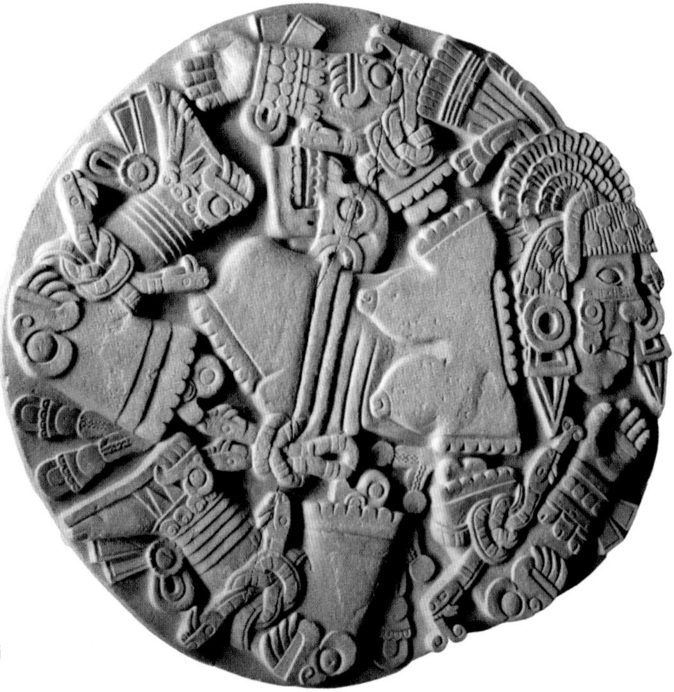

142 Coyolxauhqui
Sculpture, 1469

importance in relation to divine male counterparts or relatives.
142 One is the lunar goddess known as Coyolxauhqui, whose name refers to the bells pictured on her cheeks. This fifteenth-century representation of the goddess on a colossal lunar disk was discovered near the Templo Mayor in the late 1970s. Recorded oral histories indicate that Coyolxauhqui was beheaded by her brother, Huitzilopochtli, for betraying her mother, and her body ended up at the base of the mountain Coatepetl. Here the sculptors have emphasized the violence with which the goddess was dismembered and the chaos visible in her eventual deposition at the base of the mountain pyramid; the joints of her limb bones emerge from the torn flesh of the shoulders and hips. She wears a feathered headdress, circular and pointed ear pendants evoking the tail of Xiuhcoatl, the divine fire serpent, balls of feathers in her hair, and a trio of circular metal ornaments on her cheeks, the bells referenced in her name. A skull mounted to a knotted rattlesnake belt is the only other ornament on her body besides sandals and ropes around the calves and arms. The seeming motion and expression of the goddess suggests that the sculptors captured the moment of

her death, and other representations solely of her severed head depict her in postmortem repose.

The creator goddess mother of Huitzilopochtli and
143 Coyolxauhqui is known as Coatlicue ("serpent skirt") and was the subject of one of the most engaging works of Mexica sculpture in Tenochtitlán, possibly dating to the fifteenth century. Potentially placed at the summit of the pyramid along with a group of similar sculptures of Coatlicue and the related goddess Yolotlicue ("heart skirt"), this colossal image at more than eight feet (2.5 m) tall, is one of the most imposing works from the ancient Americas. The goddess is depicted nude from the waist up in a standing pose, though the deity is presented as decapitated and missing her hands. The sculptors focused their attention on the rich woven skirt composed of serpent bodies and serpent belt that also bears a skull at the waist knot in front and back. Where the goddess's head would have been are two serpents emerging from the torso, and simultaneously are depicted individually in profile and merge to give the impression of a monstrous being facing forward. She wears a necklace of disembodied hands and human hearts. The fierceness of Coatlicue is underscored by her giant talons emerging from feet that have themselves become zoomorphic beings.

Mexica sculptors in Tenochtitlán innovated a sculptural practice that infused multiple divine energies into god images such as this Coatlicue, by sculpting the image of a different earth deity on the underside of the statue, totally invisible to the beholder. Known as Tlaltecuhtli, this deity, interpreted as both male and female in different contexts, was associated with both generation and death, and appears under many iconic
144 Mexica works. She appears in colossal, full-figure form in one of the most important sculptures from ancient Mexico recovered archaeologically, a 13-ton monolith discovered near the Templo Mayor in 2006. The Tenochtitlán sculptors originally shaped the goddess from one giant slab of andesite, with the deity facing upward, arms and legs bent to 90 degrees in an active pose. The sculptors clearly disliked empty spaces, as the relief covers almost 90 percent of the surface of the stone.

This image, measuring some 13 by 11 feet (over 4 × 3.5 m), was purposefully or accidentally broken in antiquity; the four extant pieces would have surrounded the missing fragment. Investigators found no evidence of tool marks, however, suggesting that after a period of placement at the foot of the Templo Mayor, the sculpture was moved to its present location and became unstable. The central portion, which would have held a medallion with a mortal or divine standing figure, was

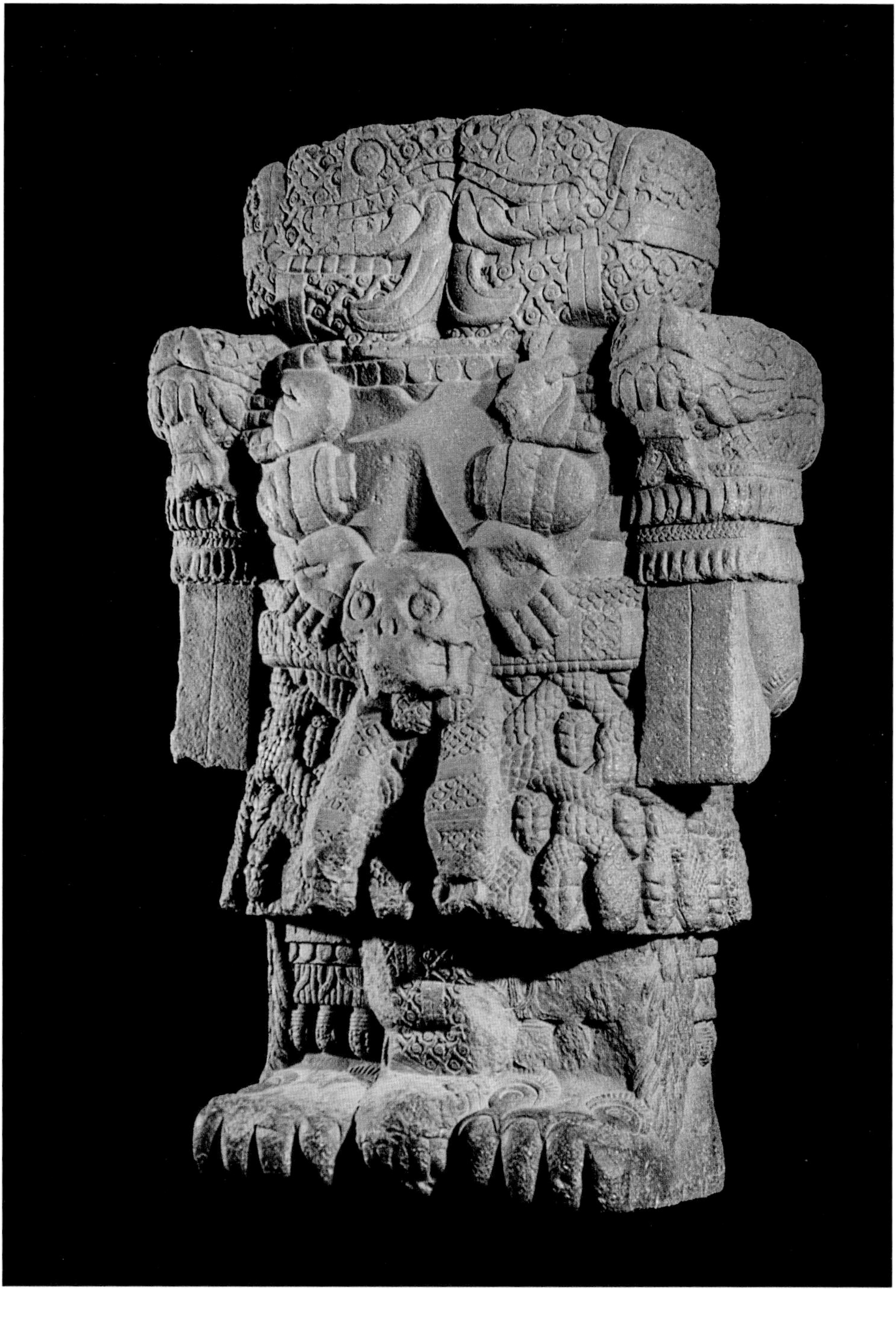

143 Coatlicue Sculpture, 1250–1521

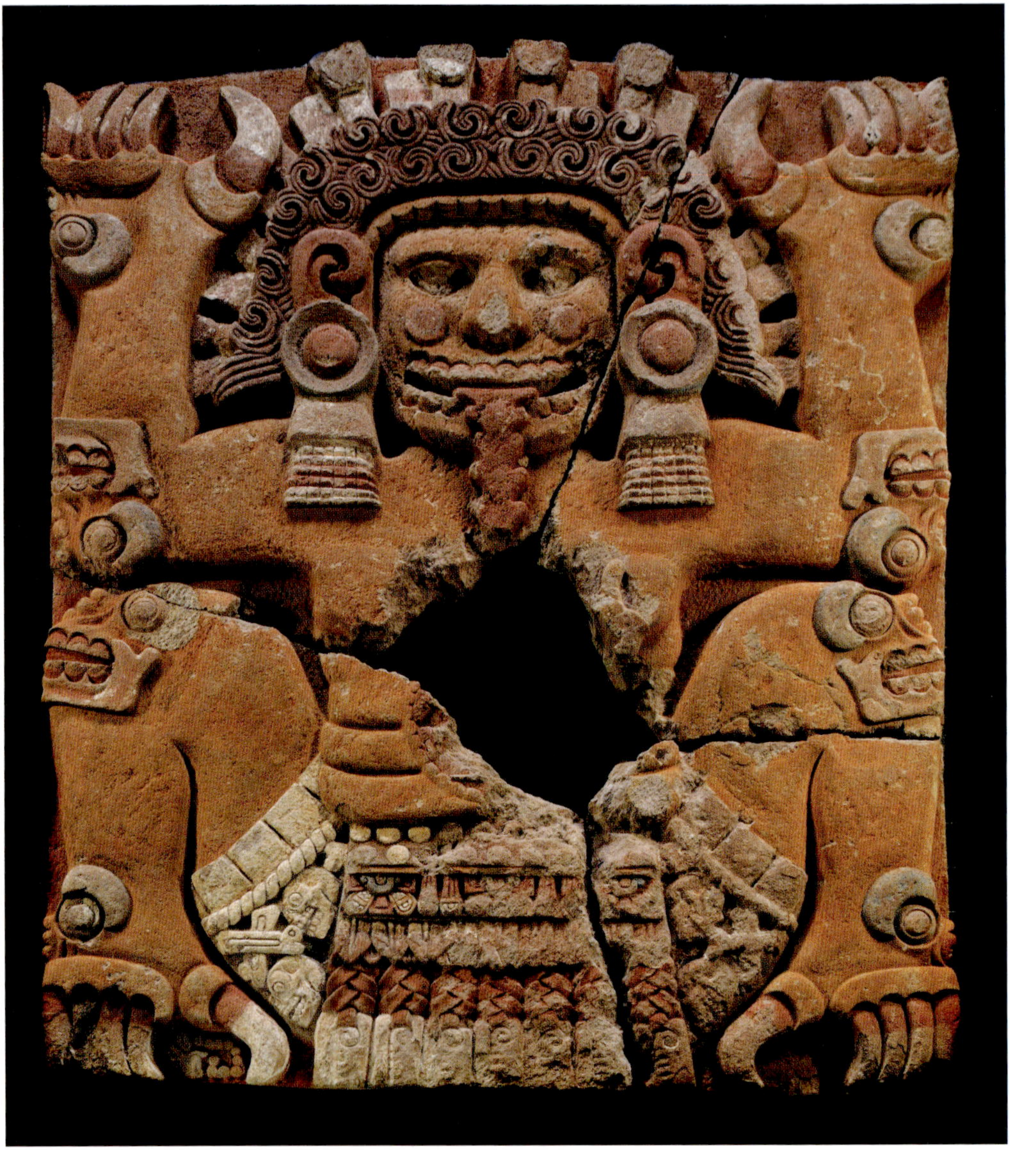

144 Tlaltecuhtli Sculpture, 1478–1502

removed at some point after the breakage and has yet to be found. Beneath the figure's right foot lies a day or year sign of 12-Rabbit, which could represent the year 1478 CE, a possible dedication date for the sculpture.

The well-preserved features of the anthropomorphic being display the talent of Mexica artists in embodying deities poised for action in the enduring medium of stone. The goddess has stylized curly hair, painted bright red, crowned by a series of strips of paper, symbolizing sacrifice. She wears earflares and a woven skirt and loincloth assemblage decorated with celestial and death-related imagery. Nude from the waist up, similar to the sculptures of Coyolxauhqui and Coatlicue above, she bears pendulous breasts and excess skin, interpreted as the physical attributes of an adult woman who has given birth and nursed children. Tlaltecuhtli stares forward from semicircular eyes and two bosses painted red with a blue circle frame her naturalistic nose. She slightly opens her fleshless mouth, exposing teeth and gums, and the tip of her tongue emerges to connect with a rippled stream of blood seemingly emerging from her own torso. The arms and legs of the goddess terminate in fearsome claws and the elbows and knees are covered with human skull elements that mirror each other and connect in this squatting position. The reconstituted fragments also illustrate how brightly painted the Mexica sculptures would have been in antiquity.

The creation of hidden sculptural programs through the carving of images on the underside mentioned above likely originated in the imperial workshops of Tenochtitlán in the fourteenth century. Images of Tlaltecuhtli appear frequently in this context, sometimes seemingly discontinuous with the primary subject, but usually engaging in productive dialogue with the visual surfaces. This allowed artists to infuse three-dimensional works with cosmological information that was known to only a select few. For example, if the upper surface of a monument included solar and stellar associations, it was vital to include the earth deity on the underside to make the meaning whole in the eyes of the patrons. Perhaps the carved undersides of sculptures could be analogous to the dedicatory caches; both actions were largely aimed at reaching a supernatural audience.

As mentioned above, the Mexica inherited and perpetuated a distinctly Mesoamerican religious tradition centered around maize agriculture and performing reciprocal acts with offerings to forces such as the sun and rain. Although rarer in colossal depictions than his peers, Tlaloc, to whom half of the summit of the Templo Mayor was dedicated, was an important subject

64 in Mexica arts. The characteristics of Tlaloc include goggle-
eyes, fangs, a braided or twisted element on the bridge of the
nose (similar to earlier deity portraits), and the color blue-
86 green, all of which were features of previous incarnations of a
storm deity that traces its origins back to Teotihuacán. Mexica
145 potters created masterful depictions of Tlaloc in offering
vessels, such as one excavated in Offering 56 at the Templo
Mayor of Tenochtitlán, dating between 1440 and 1469. The
original context of this vessel was a large deposit of materials
associated with water, including sawfish rostra, marine shells
and coral, greenstone sculptures and beads, and copal incense.
Tlaloc had watery and earthly associations as a progenitor of
rains and life-giving waters, distributed from a place called
Tlalocan, also a sacred mountain filled with sustenance.

Other important deities received the keen attention of
the Mexica sculptural workshops. Recovered from near the
base of the Iztaccíhuatl volcano which towers over Mexico
City today, one two-part sculpture stands out for its singular
virtuosity in technique and composition. The fourteenth-
146 to sixteenth-century work represents a deity known as
Xochipilli-Macuilxochitl seated atop a ceremonial platform.

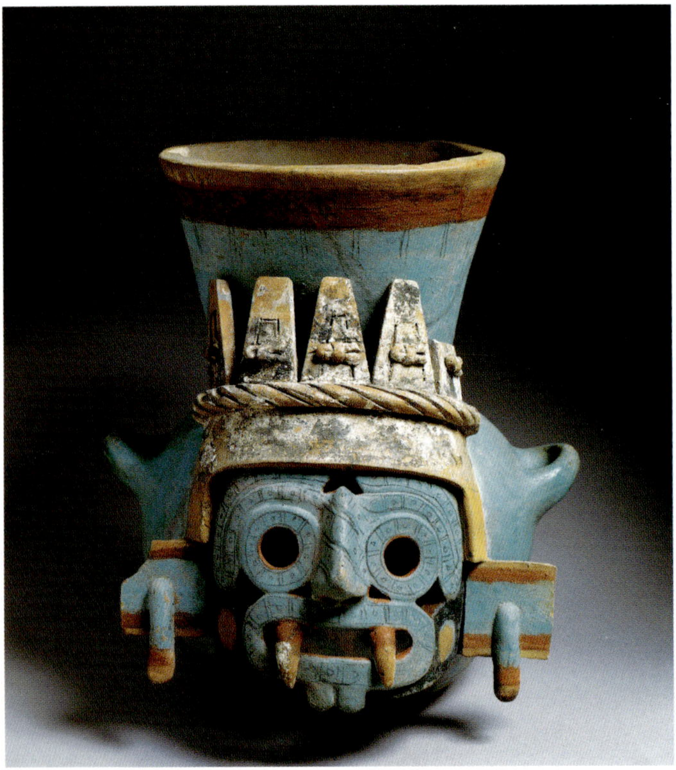

145 Tlaloc Vessel, 1440–69

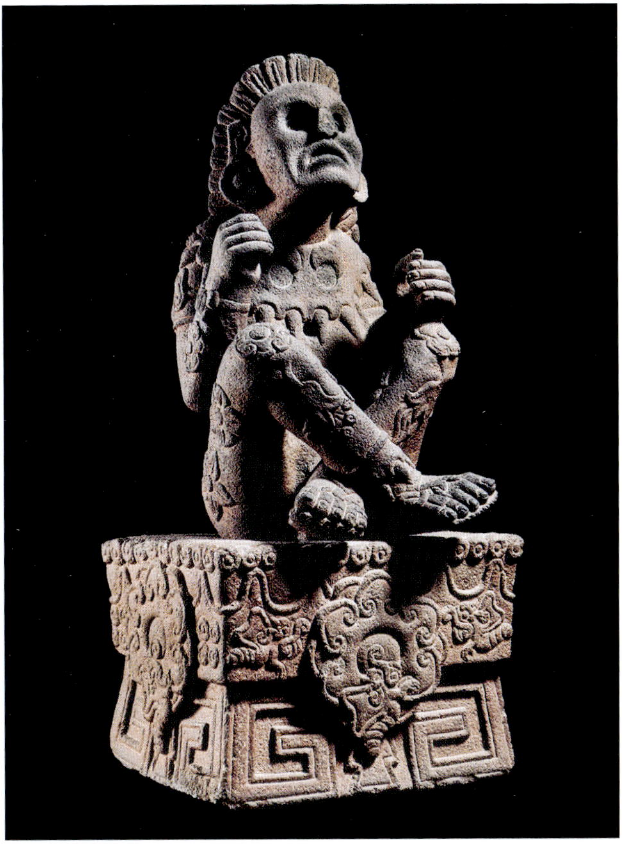

146 Xochipilli Sculpture, 1350–1520

The platform itself, similar in structure to the *talud-tablero*
86 buildings to earlier Central Mexican cultures, contains low-relief representations of celestial bodies, greenstone, and one large flower on each face being visited by a butterfly. This "Lord of Flowers, 5-Flower" deity was associated in Nahua thought with celebratory excess, especially music, singing, and dancing, as well as games and sexual pleasure.

The figure itself epitomizes the attentive renderings in three dimensions achieved by Mexica stone sculptors. The deity sits in an active cross-legged pose, resting his forearms on his thighs, facing slightly upward. The hands are realistically executed to have a cylindrical grip around something now missing, perhaps perishable objects that could be placed or removed for special occasions. His feathered headdress, mask, and earflares are complemented by an elaborate pectoral made of a feline pelt, perhaps a jaguar or puma. He also

wears armbands, bracelets, a loincloth, and knotted sandals. The sculptors took special care to emblazon representations of flowers and what may be psychedelic mushrooms in low relief on the deity's body, underscoring his preciousness and ceremonial importance. Sculptures such as this Xochipilli
95 may be considered god images, *ixiptla*, a word that also encompasses human embodiment of deities. This conceptual role of sculptures is related to the word *teotl*, which has come to be interpreted as god or sacred thing, as are *k'uh*, *zemí*, and *wak'a* in other languages.

Artists thus had the important role of making *teotl* manifest for their patrons through production of luxury goods. Information on the structure and organization of artistic workshops, which seems to have been largely based on the raw materials and end products, comes from the sixteenth-century work of the Franciscan friar Bernardino de Sahagún and Indigenous collaborators, titled the *Historia general de las cosas de Nueva España*, known commonly as the Florentine Codex. This important bilingual Spanish-Nahuatl text details the life of the Nahuas, including religion, politics, natural history, and the story of the Spanish invasion. In book 9, "Merchants, Artists of Gold, Precious Stones, and Rich Featherwork," the codex describes in rich detail how artists were organized; for example, there were two types of gold workers, various lapidary artists specializing in different valuable stones, and so on. The products of these workshop were also subject to what could be described as sumptuary laws under the *huey tlatoani*, reinforcing political and military hierarchy according to access to precious materials, such as gold, jade, turquoise, feathers, or cotton. The scribes of the Florentine Codex also associate these artistic practices with divine characters, underscoring the Mexica spiritual connections with the act of creating.

The collaborators on the Florentine Codex illustrations drew
96 from a long Indigenous legacy of illuminated manuscripts. Several pre-Hispanic Nahua religious and historical documents that were not destroyed during the Spanish invasion
147 demonstrate how Mexica painters recorded detailed chronicles in screenfold books. The painters of the codices, such as this example from the early sixteenth century, prepared the animal-skin base with a wash of gesso before rendering portraits of deities, origin narratives, and calendric cycles that may have been used for divination. On this page is a divinatory almanac featuring two back-to-back deities crouching or dancing above a stylized head of an underworld deity facing upward. The deity on the left is Mictlantecuhtli, a prominent deity of death, and on the right is Ehecatl, the god of wind. The death god's

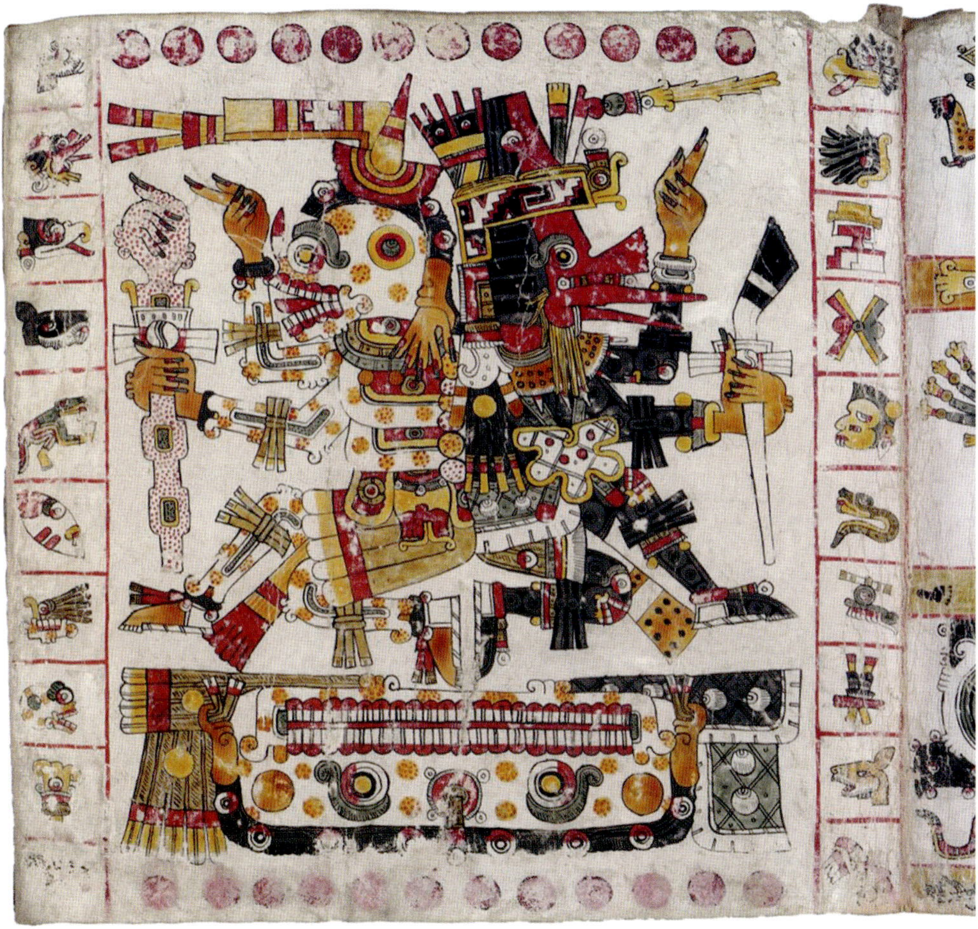

147 Page from Codex Borgia, c. 1500

attributes are the skeletal body and human-hand earrings, while the long-lipped wind god wears his characteristic half-conch pendant necklace. Both hold staffs or scepters in one hand—Mictlantecuhtli's is created from a human arm—and gesture with the other hand as if addressing the two corresponding columns of 10 day signs that line the left and right edges of the page. These day signs represent the 20 periods of 13 days in the Mesoamerican calendar. In this way, as with stone sculptures, manuscript painters layered calendric cycles that anchored historical events with supernatural knowledge to be read or recited in courtly ceremonies.

Perhaps the highest echelon of artists, as recorded in the Florentine Codex, were the *amantecah* (featherworkers), who

created feathered garments by tying and sewing bird feathers as well as stunning micro-mosaics in various forms made of cut and glued feathers. The key materials in this technique included orchid pseudobulbs, from which were extracted a vegetal adhesive known as *tzauctli*, and delicate bone tools known as *omihuictli* for composing the elaborate fields of
109 different-color feathers (this differs from other featherwork traditions of tying and sewing whole feathers). The birds themselves included hummingbirds, highland quetzals with famed bright green plumage, and even marine birds brought to the capital from faraway regions. A small group of Mexica featherworks survive, including four incredible feather mosaic
148 shields known as *chimalli*, created around 1500. These were less for use in combat than ritual processions or displays of power, but evidence suggests that these were also important objects created as tribute sent to the Mexica capital.

The *chimalli* now housed in Vienna is an extraordinary creation that began from a circular shield substructure made of leather, agave fibers, and cane reeds with leather straps, through which the owner could insert the forearm. The featherworkers then cut and glued thousands of feathers from the lovely cotinga (*Cotinga amabilis*), scarlet macaw, oriole (*Icterus gularis*), and roseate spoonbill, among others, onto the surface to compose the representation in profile of a canine standing on its hind legs. The shaggy body of the creature is bright blue from the cotinga feathers, and the creators of the shield delicately outlined patches of its hair in hammered gold sheet; gold also creates the eye with spoonbill feather lashes. This blue color, similar to the pigment slathered onto Tlaloc's effigy above, suggests that the subject is an aquatic creature, perhaps a coyote known as *ahuitzotl* or a name glyph ending in *coyotl*, which some have argued refers to the *huey tlatoani* of the same name who ruled until 1502. From the open mouth of the canine being comes a sharp tongue and two streams, one red and one blue, decorated with feathered-and-gold elements. This motif is actually a hieroglyphic representation of the Mexica concept of *atl-tlachinolli*, a metaphor for warfare referencing the violent combat between water and fire. As the patron of this shield wielded it in ceremony or supervising a courtly scene or conflict, the shield itself conveyed to observers a shimmering image of supernatural martial might, changing colors as it caught the light.

Another important class of artists that were incorporated into the Mexica imperial project were metalworkers, who created regalia and other materials from gold, silver, and
95 copper. Many such artists may have originally come from

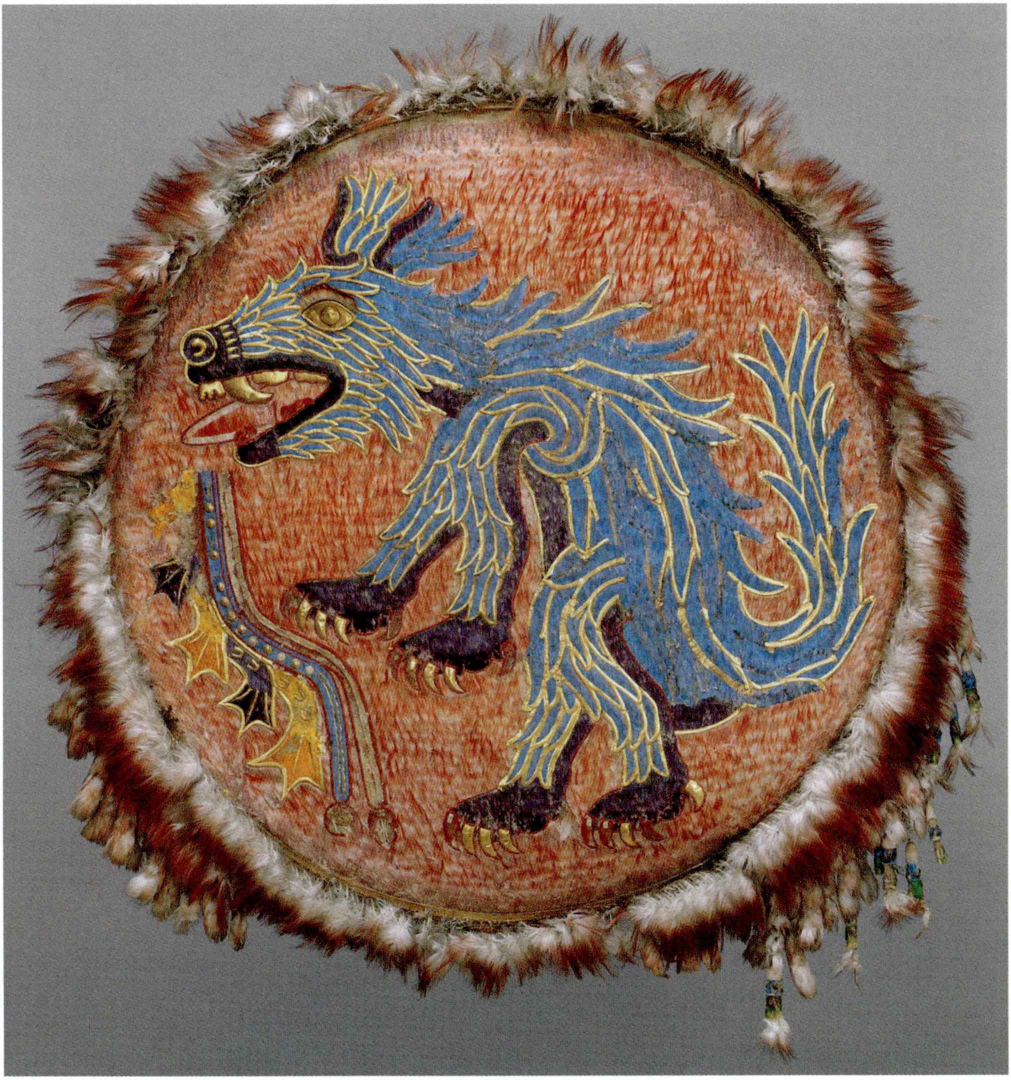

148 *Chimalli* (Feathered Shield), c. 1500

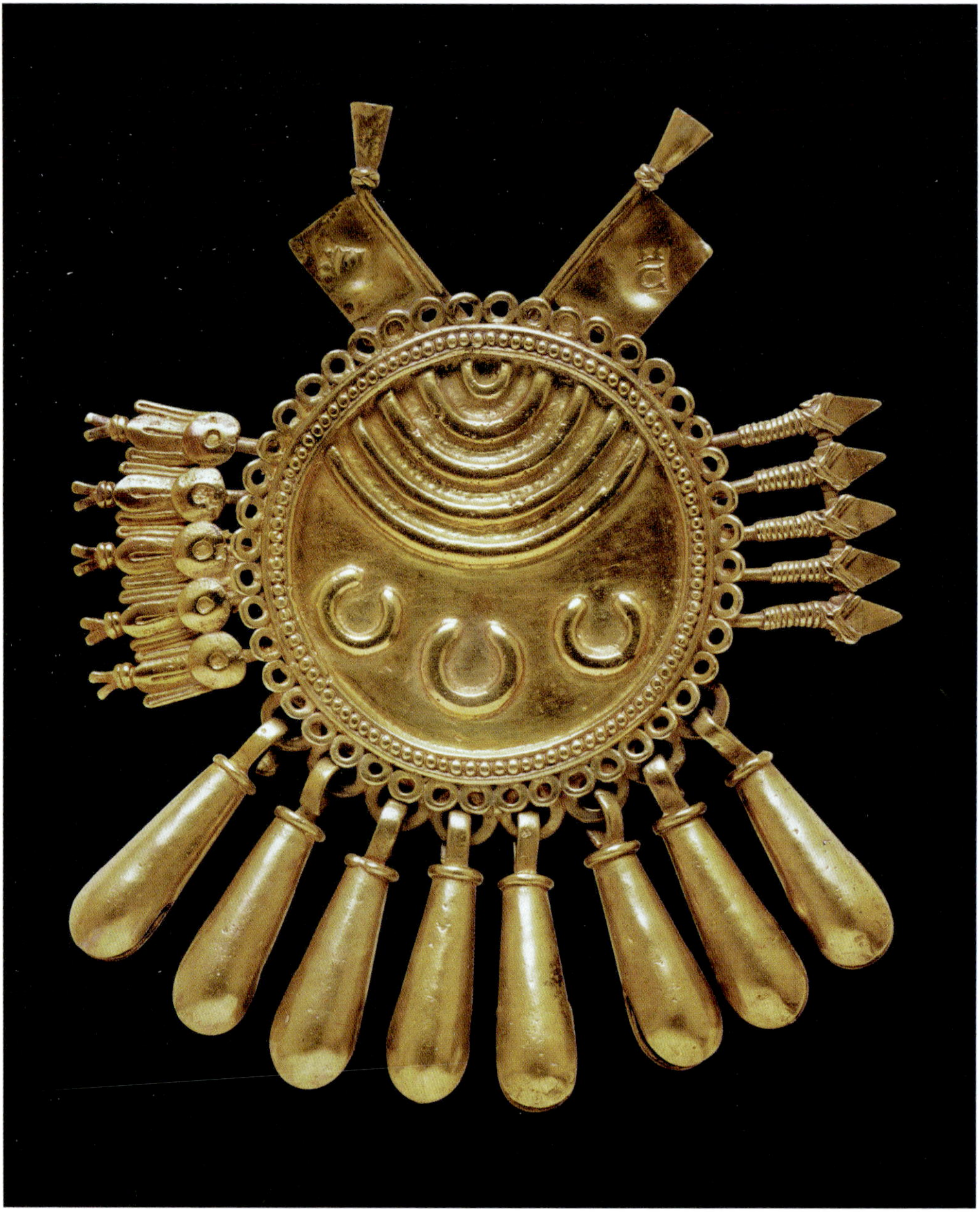

149 *Chimalli* Pendant, c. 1500

Oaxaca, a region that perfected techniques such as hammering and lost-wax casting centuries after it developed in Central and South America. Goldworkers conveyed military might at a small scale with expertly rendered pendants that would have adorned the body of rulers and created a sonic experience for
149 their subjects. One example is the rare survival of a *chimalli* pendant in gold, cast around 1500. The image is a circular shield surrounded by small spheres and rings made with false granulation and false filigree techniques, with descending concentric arches and three U-shaped elements meant to represent large-scale crescent ornaments in either gold or feathers. Below the shield, the artists attached eight elongated teardrop-shaped bells to infuse a musical aspect to the regalia. Five small-scale *atlatl* darts seem to cross behind the shield, underscoring the violence presumably threatened at the hands of the wearer.

This *chimalli* pendant was recovered in the Gulf of Mexico by a fisherman named Raúl Hurtado Hernández in the mid-1970s, thus earning its nickname as a part of the Tesoro del Pescador ("fisherman's treasure"). This context and the alloy composition high in copper suggest that the work was perhaps fashioned in Oaxaca for the Mexica royals along with the other bells and beads recovered in the same area. They were then presumably looted by Spanish invaders and lost to the sea in transit to the sixteenth-century Spanish court. A detail, added by the Spanish authorities who appropriated these ornaments, is visible on the two rectangular and tasseled flags at the top of this pendant. A small stamped "C" decorated with a crown indicates that this gold object was destined to the "Corona" (crown), part of the king's tax of one-fifth of the treasures stolen from Indigenous peoples in viceregal Mexico. After 1521, the year that Europeans seized control of Tenochtitlán, Mexica artists continued their sculptural, metallurgical, weaving, and featherworking practices. They were pressed into service for new purposes by the Spanish invaders and religious authorities as they expanded in the new colonial world, leaving in their wake a massive human toll.

Chapter 11
Epilogue: Final Considerations

This book is a celebration of the achievements of artists in North, Central, and South America who crafted traditions that developed independently from the rest of the world. The previous chapters, structured by regions within a loose chronological order, have been grouped in thematic parts. These sections relate earliest development of widespread visual cultures, the impact of rulers making claims to divinity who commissioned works from talented specialists, the effects of cities and how that closeness to others engendered new intentions and techniques of creating imagery, and the imposition of imperial rule over artists and their products. This epilogue describes the continuities and resonances of the arts of the ancient Americas from the year 1492, when the Spanish first invaded the Caribbean, until today. In many ways, the title *Arts of the Ancient Americas* is not ideal to describe the traditions emphasized here. The Inka and Mexica artists were contemporaries of Renaissance creators in Europe, who were decidedly not ancient in broader discussions of art history. Nor did the Indigenous ways of making and representing stop with the invasion of the Spanish and other Europeans, as many artists were put into service for new royals or even used ancestral art as resistance to colonial regimes. These traditions lived on as influences from Europeans, Africans who were originally enslaved, and Asians who were connected to the Americas through Pacific trade routes quickly spread throughout the region in the colonial period. Many modern and contemporary artists in multicultural descendant communities today have also drawn inspiration from ancestral arts.

Spanish religious authorities taught Indigenous peoples new
129, 130, artistic methods and introduced new Christian images of divine
139 beings through paintings and works on paper, beginning in the

sixteenth century. In another remarkable example, in the 1580s
and 1590s in what is now Pátzcuaro, Michoacán, Mexico, an
Indigenous artist by the name of Juan Bautista Cuiris (*c.* 1550–
150 1600) produced an image of the Virgin Mary. The mournful Mary
stares down, tears streaming from her eyes, as she is draped in
blue-green, purple, gold, and white garments. Her blue-and-gold
oval frame is surrounded by four winged cherubs with golden
curls and red and blue wings. This Virgin is inspired by European
models, perhaps prints in the possession of Augustinian monks
in what had become New Spain. This is no ordinary devotional
painting of Mary, however. The entire composition, including
the artist's signature and the stunning green background that
shimmers differently as the viewer moves, is composed of a
micro-mosaic of cut-and-glued bird feathers. This is perhaps
the best-preserved example of the products of colonial-period
148 *amantecah*, featherworkers making images of new deities during
the Spanish Empire, just decades after they worked in the court
of the Mexica emperor. This example and another featherwork
created by Cuiris depicting a youthful Jesus Christ were likely sent
to the royal court of Philip II (1527–98), king of Spain, eventually
ending up in the collections of the Habsburg royal family in
Vienna via his descendants. Visitors today view this image in the
religious galleries of the Austrian Imperial Treasury, along with
other astounding reliquaries and divine images composed of
such precious materials as ivory, gold, and silver.

"Curiosities" from American artists arrived in droves
through trans-Atlantic trade routes from the late fifteenth
century onward. In the early years of colonization, in which the
Spanish base was in the Antilles, Taíno artists merged their own
151, 152 creations with foreign materials to invent new types of zemís.
This composite object was once a zemí belt and headdress
or other regalia, and someone in the late fifteenth or early
sixteenth century mounted them to a European willow base to
make a colorful sculpture, perhaps for religious purposes. The
83 original beadwork could have been done in the same workshop
as the zemí belt now in Vienna. This reworking of ancestral
regalia for new purposes also involved adding a humanlike
face on the reverse of the zemí's head, remarkably carved from
African rhinoceros horn. This underscores the early African
presence in Antilles via the forced migration of enslaved peoples
and the creation of an Afro-Indigenous aesthetic that perseveres
into the present in the Caribbean. In many ways, this society
in the Caribbean islands was the first truly global moment in
modern history, in which peoples and materials from around
the world came together in new ways.

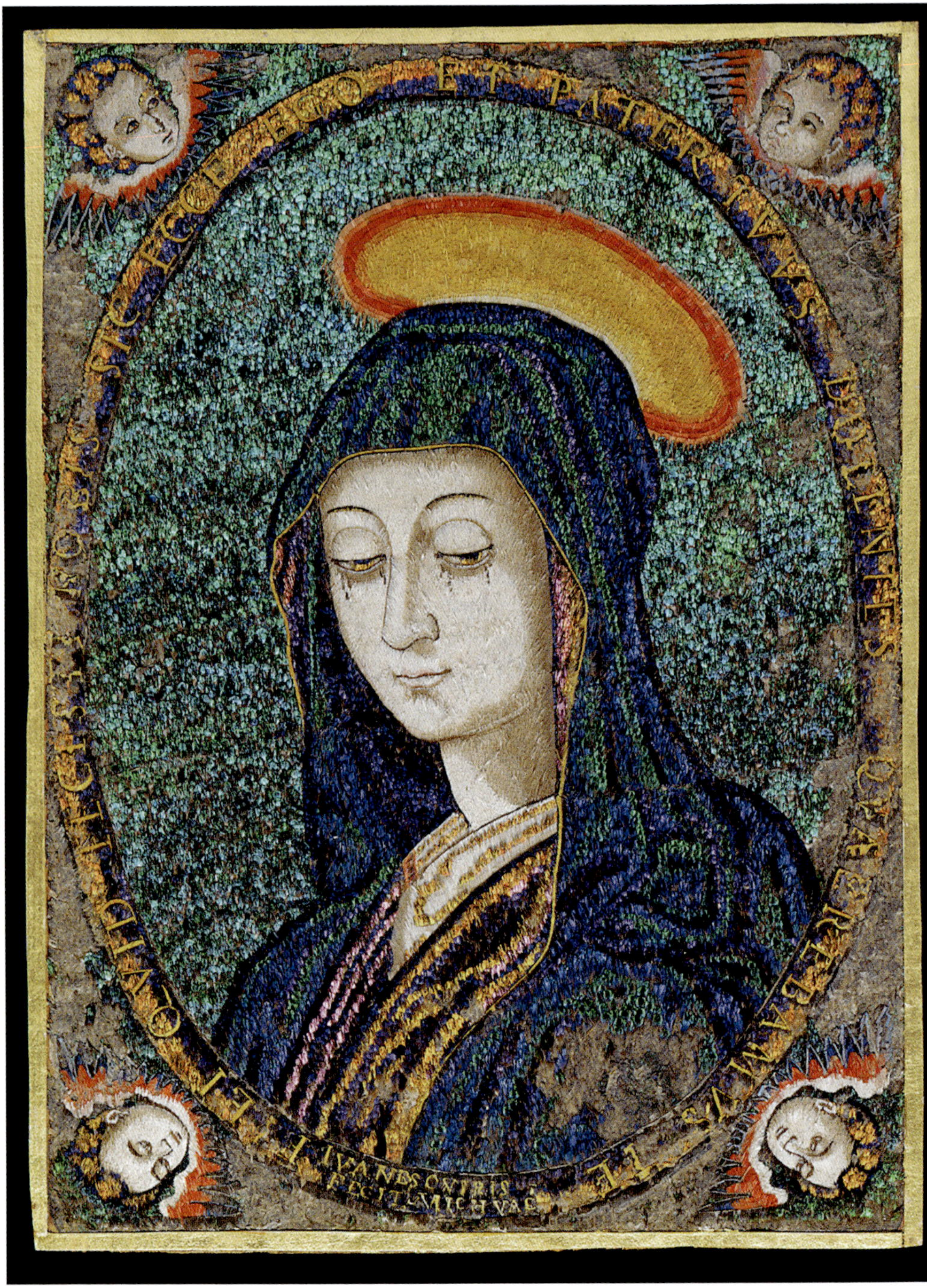

150 Juan Bautista Cuiris, *Portrait of the Virgin Mary*, 1590–1600

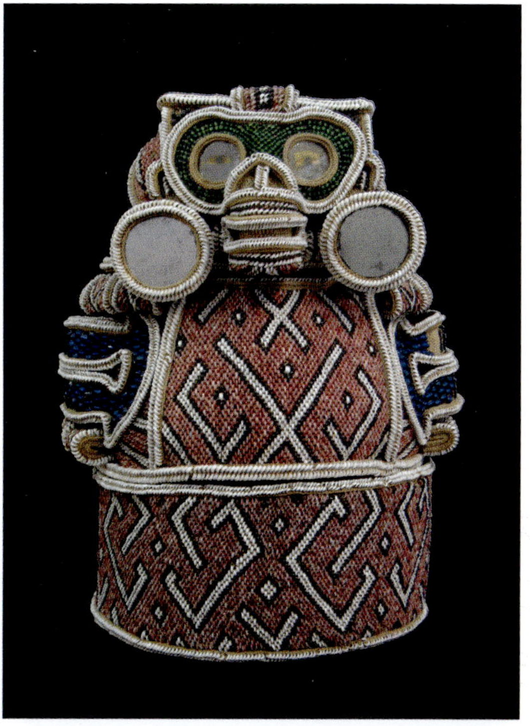

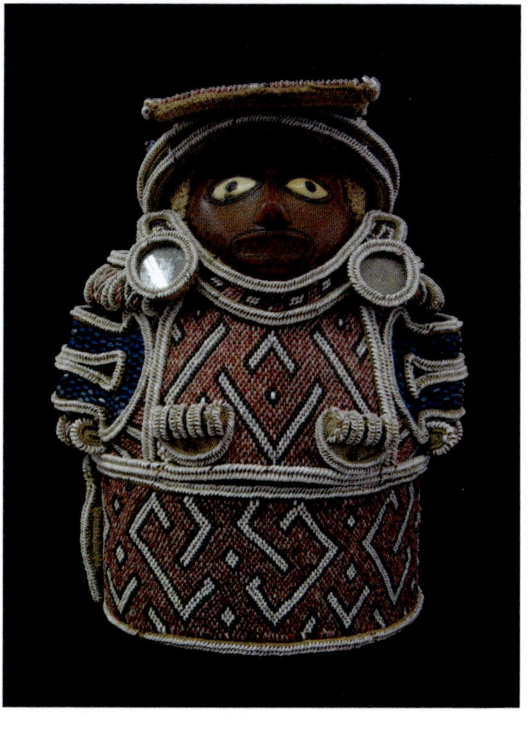

151, 152 TOP AND LEFT Reliquary Figure, obverse view and reverse view, 1492–1524

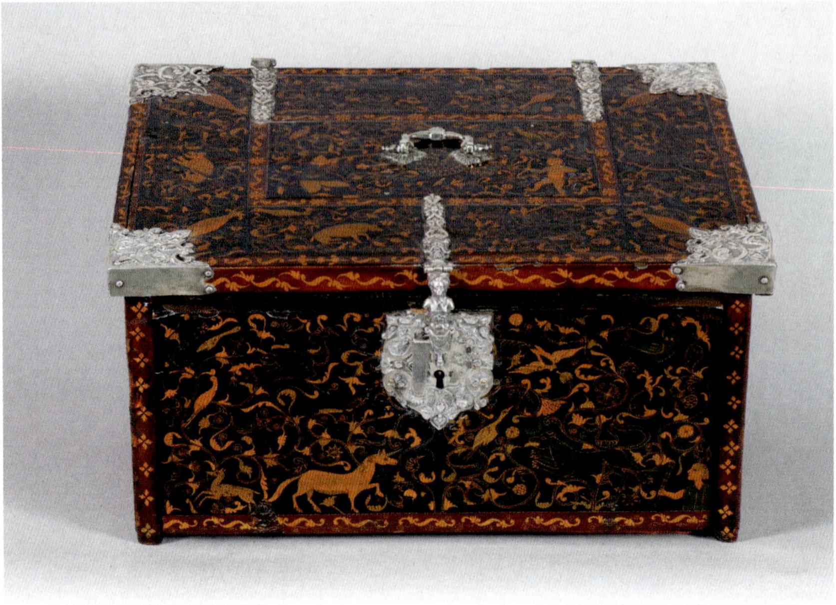

153 Portable Writing Desk, *c.* 1643

Many American artists applied pre-Hispanic techniques to the production of decorative arts that were subsequently used by the colonial elite or shipped back to Europe. In the northern Andes, a taste developed for a native tradition of
153 inlaid plant resins, known as *barniz de pasto* after the region of Pasto, Colombia, that perfected this treatment of the *mopa mopa* resin. This portable writing desk from the mid-seventeenth or eighteenth century exemplifies this American lacquer technique perfected during the Inka Empire. Made in the viceroyalty of New Granada, now Colombia, the travel desk demonstrates how artists stretched sheets of the inlaid varnish dyed in different colors, cut out designs, and heated the material to affix it to the wooden structure before adding the silver mounts. Produced for consumption in the colonies and in
135 Europe, such *barniz de pasto* objects incorporated new fanciful creatures and references to European tales rather than those of Indigenous American origin.

Perhaps the most aggressive act of redirecting Indigenous hands was in the construction of religious architecture. In many instances, Spanish authorities directly took over local sacred places and created new Catholic spaces to manipulate Indigenous thought toward Christianity. In the Andes,

authorities used the exceptional buildings created by the
Inkas as bases for new churches or colonial residences and
administration buildings. These wak'as, sacred spots on the
landscape venerated for generations, bccame sanctuaries
for worship for the Christian Holy Trinity, such as at
154 Vilcashuamán, near Ayacucho, Peru. There the Inkas had
constructed a monumental pyramid, known in Quechua as
an *ushnu*, that served as an elevated platform from which
the authorities, seated on megalithic thrones, would have
conducted important ceremonies. A large stepped platform
nearby, shown here, may have served as a temple to the sun.
The Spanish placed a chapel right on top of its large walls, and
the church is still in use today.

In Mesoamerica, a region in which sacred mountains were
revered and recreated as pyramids, the Spanish destroyed
temples to local deities and built churches in their stead. One
155 notable case is that of the Great Pyramid of Cholula, in the
modern Mexican state of Puebla. The building was constructed
over several centuries before about 900 CE to become one of
the largest pyramids in the world by volume, with a base of
over 1000 square feet (300 sq. m) and original height of more
than 80 feet (25 m), larger than Cahokia's largest mound and

154 Vilcashuamán, Peru

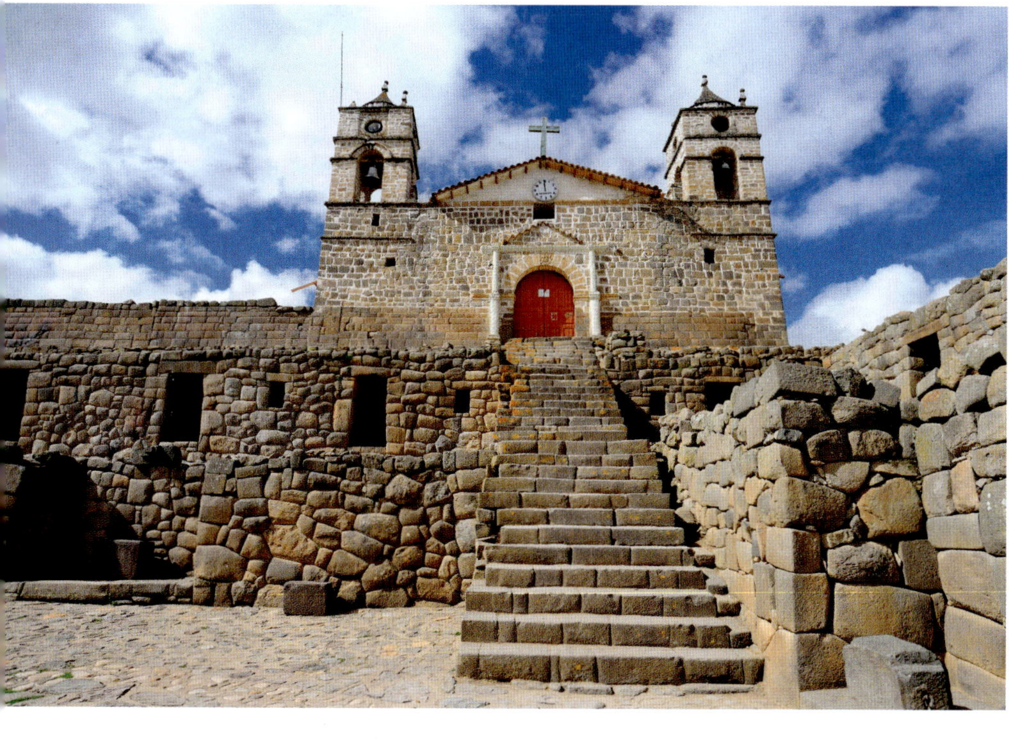

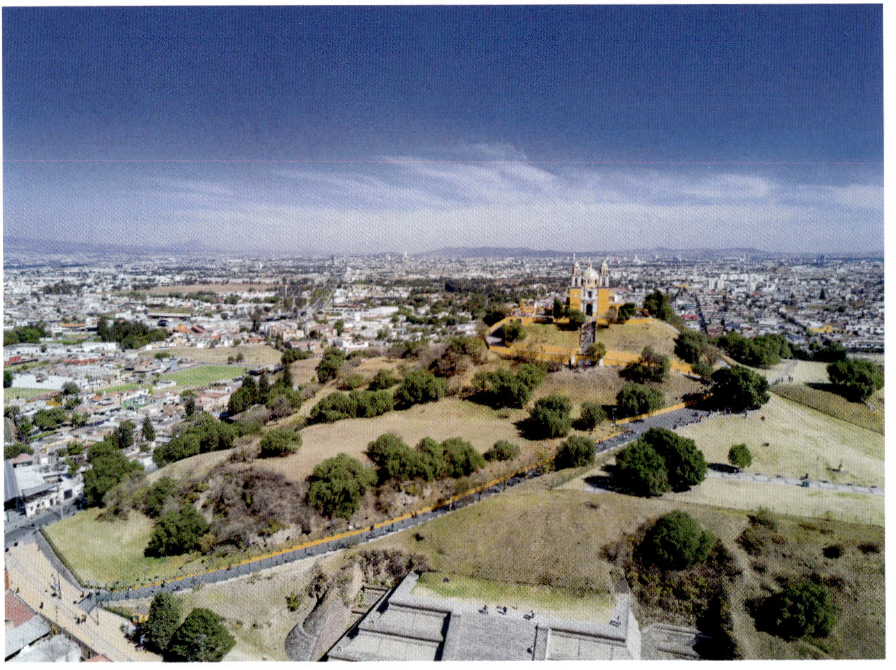

155 Cholula, Mexico

84, 110 the Pyramid of the Sun at Teotihuacán. The earthen pyramid's scale reflects the importance of the societies near Cholula, and the colonial enterprise coopted the summit of the pyramid mountain for religious purposes. The sixteenth-century Iglesia de Nuestra Señora de los Remedios still stands as a place of worship and important pilgrimage destination today. Other churches in the area around Cholula, especially the church of Santa María Tonantzintla, still display the syncretic artistic creations of Indigenous subjects in the New-Spanish baroque style, brightly painted in polychrome and gilded.

As the Spanish expanded their administration of colonial territories in the sixteenth century, they began importing imagery from Europe and parochial artists who began their careers in Europe, such as the Italian Jesuit painter Democrito Bernardo Bitti (1548–1610) who worked in Lima, began training Indigenous viceregal subjects in the techniques of early
156 modern art. A portrait of an Afro-Indigenous ruler and his two sons, painted in 1599 by Quito artist Andrés Sánchez Gallque (*c.* 1550s–1620s), exemplifies this new patronage of artistic workshops. It was commissioned by Juan del Barrio y Sepúlveda, a judge in Quito, for King Philip III (1578–1621).

Sánchez Gallque (referenced in Spanish documents with his brother as an Indigenous master painter, "*maestros pintores yndios*") may have been one of the first generation of local nobility to study art and writing with the Franciscans in Quito, which subsequently became an important painterly center in the viceregal period. His known works and documented commissions, including a contract to be master artist of an altarpiece in a regional church, confirm that his talent was recognized and, indeed, sought after. The title of his best-known work is *Don Francisco de Arobe and His Sons Don Pedro and Don Domingo*. This group portrait celebrated an alliance between the Spanish authorities and Don Francisco, who was charged with governing peoples in the coastal province of Esmeraldas, Ecuador, as proxy for the Crown.

The Afro-Indigenous subjects wear a striking combination of European and Indigenous regalia, including garments perhaps woven from Asian silks, as well as ruffled collars, while holding wide-brimmed hats that were fashionable in the
108, 133 day. Their woven tunics may be Andean in origin, similar to those woolen and cotton garments woven for many centuries before the Spanish invasion. Local regalia is present in the
73 gold nose and ear ornaments, shaped similarly to those found archaeologically in the northern Andes. Matching shell collars also speak to the Indigenous value systems that persisted in the face of colonialism. Sánchez Gallque delicately depicted these local leaders in a way that reveals his sensitivities for luxury materials and training in European forms of painting, such as the portrait in three-quarter view. The sons gaze respectfully

156 Andrés Sánchez Gallque, *Portrait of Don Francisco de Arobe and Sons Don Pedro and Don Domingo*, 1599

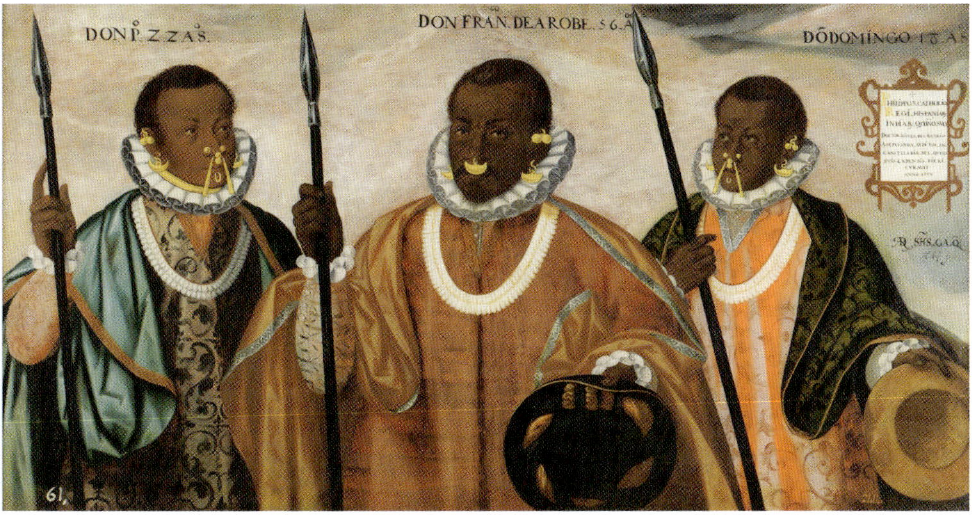

toward their father, who stares out confidently at the viewers of the painting, all three grasping their spears in a show of physical and political prowess. Judge del Barrio, the patron of the painting, sent it to Spain upon its completion, noting himself that it was "new and extraordinary."

Throughout the seventeenth and eighteenth centuries, artists in the colonies also began to produce devotional images for the expansive networks of religious orders both within the Americas and international. Several centers of artistic excellence emerged, such as Mexico City for altarpieces, Cuzco for paintings, and Guatemala for polychrome and gilded sculpture. By the early nineteenth century, the multicultural residents of the Americas formed new independent nations, largely rejecting further rule by European powers. Notable exceptions include French Guiana, still a department of France, and several Caribbean islands that still report to European administrators. Puerto Rico, which was one of the first places controlled by the Spanish, is currently a Commonwealth of the United States. Although not wholly separate from the modern nation-states that claim their land, Indigenous peoples have gained control of autonomous regions in Canada, the United States, Panama, and the Amazonian region, among others, although problems of settler violence and dispossession still persist. Given that these struggles for self-governance continue to this day, the present discussion of Ancestral traditions has avoided words like "conquest" or "conquered" or even "conquistador," given that, for many people, the resistance to colonial rule in the Americas is ongoing.

In this context of new forms of governance and new engagement with Indigenous descendants, a new global interest in the arts of the ancient Americas has emerged. Beginning especially with artists and architects in the late nineteenth and twentieth centuries, people have often revived and appropriated themes, imagery, and motifs from ancestral traditions. National museums across Latin America were formed, scientific archaeology began in earnest on ancient sites, and the study of imagery from pre-Hispanic monuments and books spurred on revolutions in scholarship and public awareness. Modernism as an artistic movement in the late nineteenth and early twentieth century also broke from previous traditions, concurrent with searches for new forms of self-expression, and painters and sculptors reached into the ancient Americas for inspiration. In the Caribbean region, to provide one example, greater recognition of both Indigeneity and African legacies heavily influenced the development of art in the twentieth century,

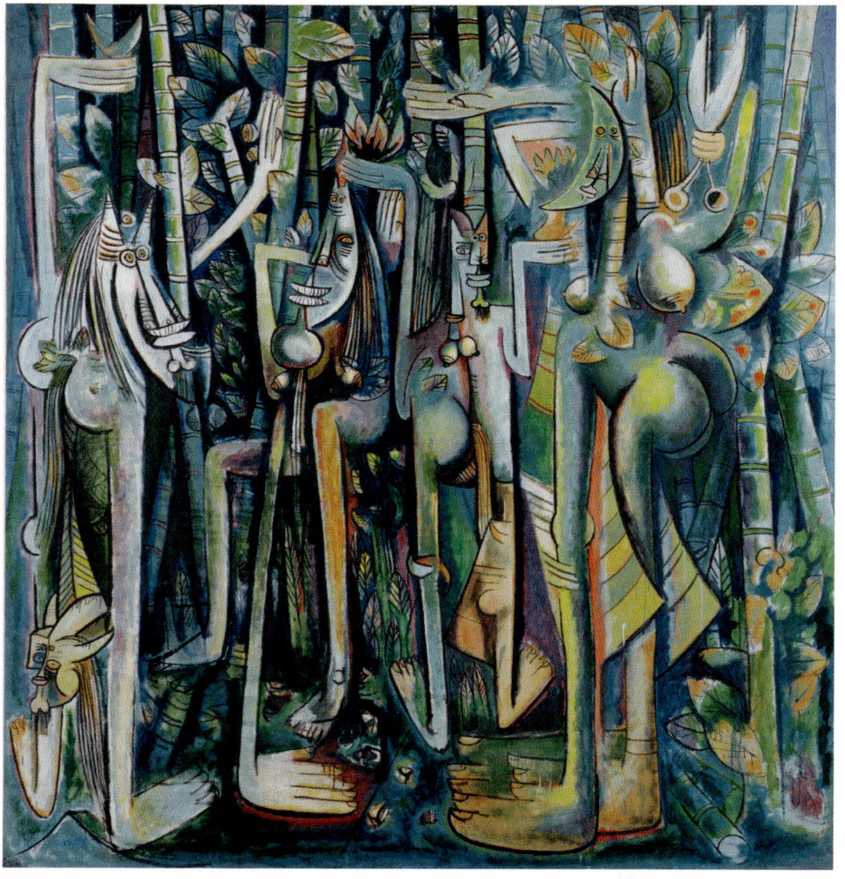

157 Wifredo Lam, *La jungla* (*The Jungle*), 1942–43

with such key figures as Wifredo Óscar de la Concepción Lam y Castilla (1902–82), better known as Wifredo Lam.

157 In one of his most well-known paintings, *La jungla* (*The Jungle*), Wifredo Lam referenced the Afro-Indigenous religious traditions such as Lucumí (also known as Santería) and Vodun. These religions incorporated Taíno beliefs in sacred landscapes, such as the power of zemí, and African practices, such as dance and reciprocal offerings when venerating ancestors, as they spread throughout the Antilles. Raised in Cuba, Lam spent time in European Surrealist circles, befriending Pablo Picasso, and even traveling to Mexico to stay with Frida Kahlo and Diego Rivera. During World War II he created his own vision for sacred Caribbean landscapes that had been dramatically transformed by colonialism

and the forced migration of enslaved peoples. In a forest of sugarcane in a moonlit or shadowy dreamscape, beings that share human and animal characteristics interact in a frenzy. Lam's work often references flying creatures and acts of ritual sacrifice, perhaps symbolized here by the large pair of shears in the upper right. He and others spurred on the important movements coming from Afro Caribbean, Afro Latinx, Afro Indigenous, and African American experiences that are now central parts of the discourse around art of the Americas.

Non-Indigenous builders and artists also drew great inspiration from ancient techniques as modern styles of architecture grew in popularity in the twentieth century. One such category, known as Mayan revival architecture, was popularized by the American architect Frank Lloyd Wright (1867–1959) at Ennis House, built in Los Angeles in 1924. Wright copied silhouettes of buildings from Palenque and Chichén Itzá and created his versions with poured concrete blocks that, when assembled, give the appearance of geometric textiles. These fanciful reinterpretations of ancient American architecture have also become the setting of critiques by contemporary artists. Brazilian artist Clarissa
158 Tossin (b. 1973), for example, filmed her 2017 work *Ch'u Mayaa* ("Maya blue" the pigment, in Yucatec Mayan) in one of Wright's houses with ancient-inspired choreography and music. She and other contemporary artists have drawn attention to these misrepresentations or appropriations of Ancestral

158 Clarissa Tossin, Still from *Ch'u Mayaa*, 2017

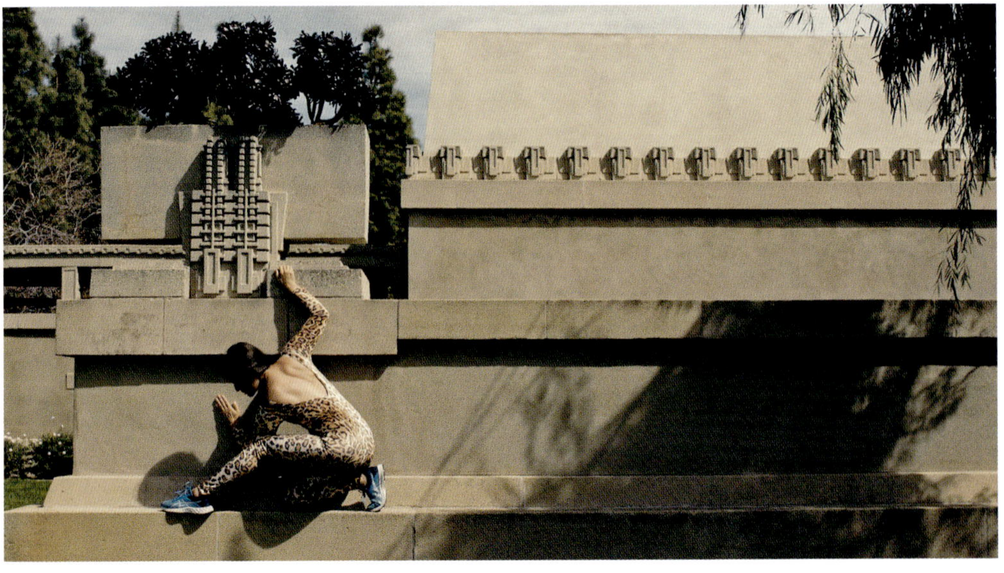

visual culture without proper consultation with descendant
communities that would be essential today.

Also in the early twentieth century, an interest in the
archaeology of ancestral Native American peoples in
the United States spurred expeditions to places like the
Southwest, where canyons and cliff faces were replete with
117, 118 historic Great Houses and other ceremonial places. Despite
ongoing disenfranchisement and relocation campaigns,
transcontinental travel after the establishment of permanent
European settlements gave Native Peoples access to a market
for selling pottery, baskets, and other creations. Pueblo artists
from New Mexico pueblos like Cochiti, Santo Domingo, Zia,
Acoma, San Ildefonso, Zuni, and many others, used art to
communicate their culture with non-Native peoples. For
traditional potters, the act of creating has a spiritual as well as
practical dimension and generations of certain families have
sustained themselves as full-time artists.

Nampeyo (1859–1942), a well-known potter of Hopi and
Tewa ancestry, revived ancestral methods of forming, firing,
and decorating pottery as early as the 1880s. She recovered
122 motifs from pottery from Sikyatki and other ancestral Hopi
159 settlements and incorporated them into a new style that
resonated with art collectors. Nampeyo composed this graceful
water jar with a wide, apple-shaped body and a relatively shorter
restricted neck. The rim and shoulder are painted with wide
black lines and a geometric, yet figural motif wraps around the
neck. The body of the vessel contains a finely painted design
alternating with an arched field containing floral motifs and a
stylized figure that references a bird in flight with outstretched
wings, flight feathers, and a tail feather, all decorated with
black semicircular designs and a reddish-brown wash. The jar
thus serves to depict figures from the sacred Southwestern
landscape and perhaps tell a story, to be "read" as the viewer
10 encounters the different motifs. After Nampeyo, scores of
Native artists continue to redefine the global contemporary art
scene by using ancestral art forms to tell new stories.

In the twenty-first century new archaeological discoveries continue to fuel great public interest in the arts of the ancient Americas, and many large-scale exhibitions, such as the *Golden Kingdoms: Luxury and Legacy in the Ancient Americas* (2017–18) (see Suggested Reading), have publicized the scholarly consensus on the great civilizations described in this book. At the same time, museums outside of source countries, such as the British Museum in London or the Metropolitan Museum of Art in New York, have also faced renewed scrutiny around the provenance of their collections and the appropriateness of displaying

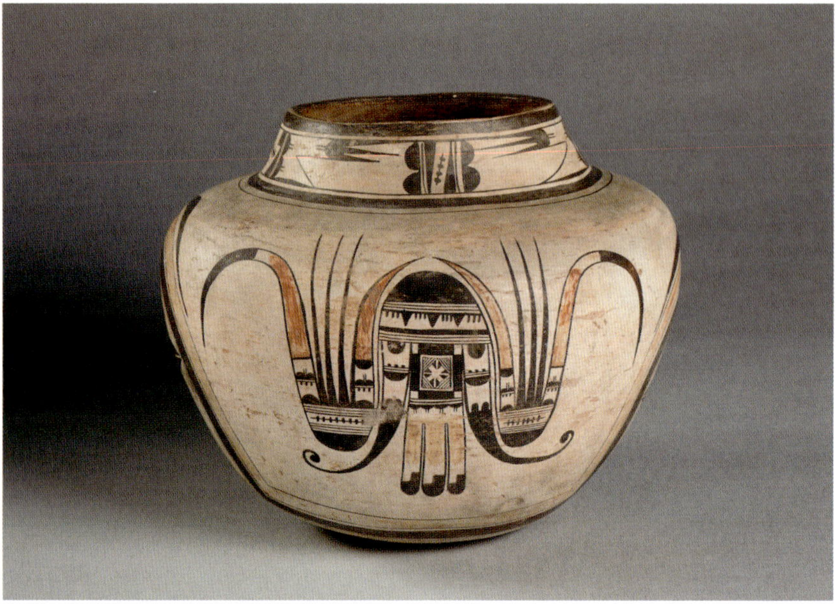

159 Nampeyo, *Jar*, 1900–15

assemblages governed by new national laws, such as the Native American Graves Protection and Repatriation Act (1990) in the United States. There have also been calls for new initiatives by museums to fulfill their mission of activating collections and engaging with key audiences, especially Latin American and Indigenous descendant and diaspora communities.

Contemporary artists are also incorporating museum archives, collections, and installations into their practice, critiquing the extraction and decontextualization of cultural patrimony. For example, Puerto Rican artist Miguel Luciano (b. 1972) collaborated with the Metropolitan Museum as a
160 Civic-Practice Artist in residence on a project called *Cemí-Libre* ("free zemí") in 2021. For a gallery installation of his work in
11 East Harlem, he created a bronze replica of the Met's Taíno cohoba stand, which was then on view in the exhibition *Arte del mar: Artistic Exchange in the Caribbean* (2019–21). Luciano's bronze zemí was freed from its plexiglass museum vitrine and welcomed into a community with a block party, including Taíno ritual practitioners, before being placed on view in a nearby gallery. Projects such as this have the potential to bridge ancestral themes and materials with contemporary concerns.

The goal for the preceding narrative is similar in scope: to underscore the contemporary relevance of all these wide-ranging, past cultures—connected by a uniquely ancient American story of the movement of people and ideas through the mountainous landscape—for audiences interested a truly global history of art. The objective here was to move away from describing the illustrated works with generalizations and investigate the thought process and technique of individuals artists. These amazing creations did not just emerge from societies, bubbling up from a cultural matrix. These makers are not mysterious, and, in some cases, as the ancient Maya, their names are known today. The actual sculptors or painters discussed herein made distinct choices that, even if far removed from a contemporary observer's worldview, resonate with those who appreciate beauty, culture, history, and beliefs. The highlights presented here only scratch the surface of the incredible corpus of art and architecture left behind by these artists. Hopefully this text is a jumping-off point for a journey to discover the arts of the ancient Americas, both through the Suggested Reading section that follows or by traveling directly to the wonderful sites and museums that now care for these important human achievements.

160 Miguel Luciano, *Cemí-Libre*, 2021

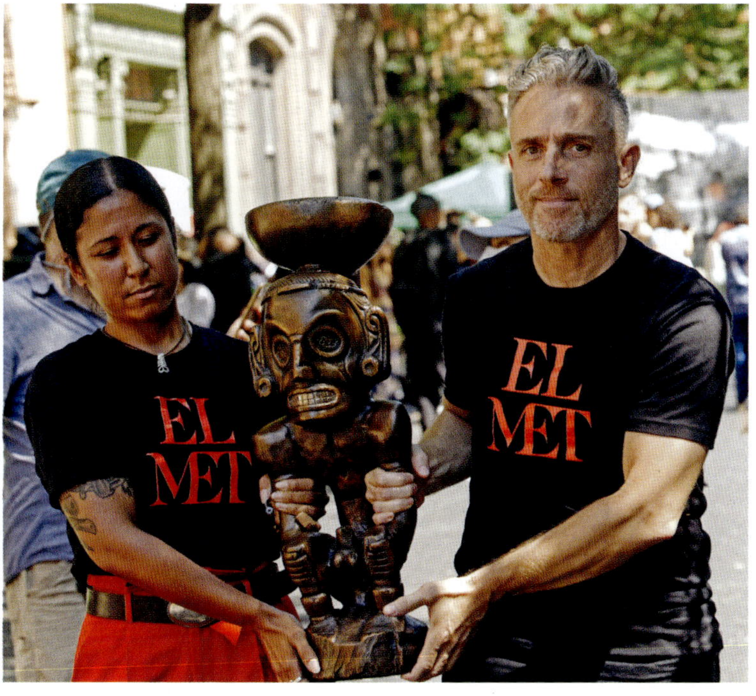

Suggested Reading

Abbreviations

AIC	The Art Institute of Chicago
AncM	*Ancient Mesoamerica*
BM	The British Museum, London
CIW	Carnegie Institution of Washington
CUP	Cambridge University Press
DAM	Denver Art Museum
DMA	Dallas Museum of Art
DO	Dumbarton Oaks Research Library and Collection
DUP	Duke University Press
FAMSF	Fine Arts Museums of San Francisco
FEPUCP	Fondo Editorial de la Pontificia Universidad Católica del Perú
INAH	Instituto Nacional de Antropología e Historia (Mexico)
JPGM	J. Paul Getty Museum
LACMA	Los Angeles County Museum of Art
MARI	Middle American Research Institute, Tulane University
MIA	Minneapolis Institute of Arts
MFAB	Museum of Fine Arts, Boston
MMA	Metropolitan Museum of Art
MNA	Museo Nacional de Antropología (Mexico)
NGA	National Gallery of Art
NMAI	National Museum of the American Indian, Smithsonian Institution
OUP	Oxford University Press
PMH	Peabody Museum of Archaeology & Ethnology, Harvard University
PNAS	*Proceedings of the National Academy of Sciences*
PUAM	Princeton University Art Museum
PUP	Princeton University Press
TH	Thames & Hudson
UAP	University of Arizona Press
UCLA	University of California, Los Angeles
UCP	University of Chicago Press
UNAM	Universidad Nacional Autónoma de México
UNMP	University of New Mexico Press
UOP	University of Oklahoma Press
UPC	University Press of Colorado
UPF	University Press of Florida
UTP	University of Texas Press
YUP	Yale University Press

A bibliography for all the research presented in this book would be a book in itself. As such, the bibliographic essays below provide annotated commentary on general sources and an abbreviated list of most recent specific studies (since 2014) corresponding to each of the chapters. Readers are highly encouraged to consult such sources for their own bibliographies and enter research rabbit holes as they so wish.

Preface

For a recent update on the Norse exploration of Canada and settlement at L'Anse aux Meadows, Newfoundland:

Ledger, Paul M., et al. 2019. "New horizons at L'Anse aux Meadows." *PNAS* vol. 116, no. 31, pp. 15341–43.

For discussions of contemporary issues facing archaeology and art history:

Flores, Tatiana, et al., eds. 2024. *The Routledge Companion to Decolonizing Art History*. New York: Routledge, Taylor & Francis Group.

Trever, Lisa, ed. 2023. "Uneasy Dialogues across Ancient Art History, Archaeology, and Contemporary Art Practice in the Americas." *21: Inquiries into Art, History, and the Visual*, special issue, pp. 165–88.

As an example of pseudo-archaeological interpretations of the American past and responses from scholars:

Hancock, Graham. 2019. *America Before: The Key to Earth's Lost Civilization*. New York: St. Martin's Press.

Society for American Archaeology. 2019. "Pseudoarchaeology, Scholarship, and Popular Interests in the Past in the Present." *SAA Archaeological Record* vol. 19, no. 5.

For information on the looting and sale of American antiquities:

Achim, Miruna, et al., eds. 2021. *Museum Matters: Making and Unmaking Mexico's National Collections*. Tucson: UAP.

Tremain, Cara G., and Donna Yates, eds. 2019. *The Market for Mesoamerica: Reflections on the Sale of Pre-Columbian Antiquities*. Gainesville: University of Florida Press.

Turner, Andrew D., and Megan E. O'Neil, eds. 2023. *Collecting Mesoamerican Art before 1940: A New World of Latin American Antiquities*. Los Angeles: Getty Research Institute.

Introduction

General Readings

Two recent general treatments on the Ancient Americas throughout time come from research on U.S. museum collections, including Michelle Rich, ed., *The Arts of the Ancient Americas at the Dallas Museum of Art* (Dallas: DMA, 2023); and Richard Townsend, *Indian Art of the Americas at the Art Institute of Chicago* (Chicago: AIC, 2016). The most comprehensive special exhibitions that included material from across regions are Joanne Pillsbury et al., eds., *Golden Kingdoms: Luxury Arts in the Ancient Americas* (Los Angeles: JPGM, 2017); and Richard Townsend, ed., *The Ancient Americas: Art from Sacred Landscapes* (Chicago: AIC, 1992). Foundational historical texts include Pál Kelemen, *Medieval American Art* (New York: Macmillan, 1943); and George Kubler, *The Art and Architecture of Ancient America, Third Edition: The Mexican, Maya and Andean Peoples* (New Haven: YUP, 1984). Publications on specific media or subjects include Johanna Minich et al., eds., *Ceramics of Ancient America: Multidisciplinary Approaches* (Gainesville: UPF, 2018); and Karen Olsen Bruhns and Karen E. Stothert, *Women in Ancient America*, 2nd ed. (Norman: UOP, 2014). Broad thematic volumes include Alessia Frassani, ed., *Visual Culture and Indigenous Agency in the Early Americas* (Leiden: Brill, 2022); Steve Kosiba, John Wayne Janusek, and Tom Cummins, eds., *Sacred Matter: Animacy and Authority in the Americas* (Washington: DO, 2020); Kenneth Hirth and Joanne Pillsbury, eds., *Merchants, Markets, and Exchange in the Pre-Columbian World* (Washington: DO, 2013); and Sarahh E. M. Scher and Billie J. A. Follensbee, eds., *Dressing the Part: Power, Dress, Gender and Representation in the Pre-Columbian Americas* (Gainesville: UPF, 2017).

Current sources for the arts of Native North America include multiauthor collaborative catalogs for museum collections and exhibitions, such as: Bruce Bernstein et al., eds., *Native American Art from the Thomas W. Weisel Family Collection* (San Francisco: FAMSF, 2023); Eric D. Singleton and F. Kent Reilly III, eds., *Recovering Ancient Spiro: Native American Art, Ritual, and Cosmic Renewal* (Oklahoma City: National Cowboy and Western Heritage Museum, 2020); and Jill Yohe and Teri Greeves, eds., *Hearts of Our People: Native Women Artists* (Minneapolis: MIA, 2019). General surveys include the 2nd edition of Janet Catherine Berlo and Ruth B. Phillips, *Native North American Art* (Oxford: OUP, 2014); and David Penney, *North American Indian Art* (London: TH, 2004). Several useful interventions in the history of U.S. and Native American relations also deserve mention, especially Ned Blackhawk, *The Rediscovery of America* (New Haven: YUP, 2023).

For focused texts on Mesoamerica there are numerous options, including Mary E. Miller, *The Art of Mesoamerica*, 6th ed. (London: TH, 2019); Michael D. Coe et al., *Mexico: From the Olmecs to the Aztecs* (London: TH, 2019); Susan T. Evans, *Ancient Mexico and Central America*, 3rd. ed. (London: TH, 2013); and David Carrasco, ed., *The Oxford Encyclopedia of Mesoamerican Cultures* (Oxford: OUP, 2001). The three-volume compendium of essays and descriptions of the Mesoamerican collection at the Dumbarton Oaks Museum also serves as generative resources: Karl Taube, *Olmec Art at Dumbarton Oaks* (Washington: DO, 2004); Susan T. Evans, *Ancient Mexican Art at Dumbarton Oaks* (Washington: DO, 2010); and Joanne Pillsbury et al., eds., *Ancient Maya Art at Dumbarton Oaks* (Washington: DO, 2012).

Recent decades have seen great advances in understanding Andean art, summarized in Rebecca Stone, *Art of the Andes: From Chavín to Inca*, 3rd ed. (London: TH, 2012); Jeffrey Quilter, *The Ancient Central Andes*, 2nd ed. (London: Routledge, 2022); Karen Olsen Bruhns, *Ancient South America*, 2nd ed. (Cambridge, CUP online, 2024); Michael E. Moseley, *The Incas and Their Ancestors: The Archaeology of Peru* (London: TH, 2001); and Elizabeth Hill Boone, ed., *Andean Art at Dumbarton Oaks* (Washington: DO, 1996), 2 vols. One of the most extensive catalogs of Andean art is published online by the Museo Larco, located in Lima, found at http://museolarco.org. Marco Curatola Petrocchi and colleagues have also published the edited volume in Spanish: Marco Curatola Petrocchi et al., *El arte antes de la historia: Para una historia del arte antiguo andino* (Lima: FEPUCP, 2020), which surveys the state of the field in Andean art history. Historical but useful summaries include Alan C. Lapiner, *Pre-Columbian Art of South America* (New York: Harry N. Abrams, 1976) and Wendell Bennett, *Ancient Arts of the Andes* (New York: Museum of Modern Art, 1954). Several sources for Andean textile arts stem from museum collections: Kristopher Driggers, *Cumbi: Textiles, Society, and Memory in Andean South America* (Tucson: Tucson Museum of Art, 2023); Rebecca Stone-Miller, *To Weave for the Sun: Ancient Andean Textiles in the Museum of Fine Arts, Boston* (Boston: MFAB, 1994); and her related text, Rebecca Stone-Miller, *The Jaguar Within: Shamanic Trance in Ancient Central and South American Art* (Austin: UTP, 2011). A recent set of essays about ancient Andean pottery at the Metropolitan Museum of Art, Hugo Ikehara-Tsukayama et al., *Containing the Divine: Ancient Peruvian Pots* (New York: MMA, 2023) complements the scientific studies in Michael Glascock, Hector Neff, and Kevin J. Vaughn, *Ceramics of the Indigenous Cultures of South America: Studies of Production and Exchange through Compositional Analysis* (Albuquerque: UNMP, 2019). Joanne Pillsbury, ed., *Guide to Documentary Sources for Andean Studies, 1530–1900* (Norman: UOP, 2008), 3 vols., details the available ethnohistoric sources for interpreting Andean art and history.

Regions that have received relatively less scholarly attention in art history and archaeology include the Isthmian countries of Nicaragua, Costa Rica, and Panama, and the northern Andean nations of Colombia and Ecuador. The same is true for the vast territory now covered by the Amazon rainforest and the Antilles archipelago. Slowly but surely the literature on the arts of these important ancient societies is expanding, including Colin McEwan and John W. Hoopes, *Pre-Columbian Art from Central America and Colombia at Dumbarton Oaks* (Washington: DO, 2021); and Colin McEwan and John W. Hoopes, *Pre-Columbian Central America, Colombia, and Ecuador: Toward an Integrated Approach* (Washington: DO, 2021); as well as the Denver Art Museum's symposium proceedings, Victoria I. Lyall, ed., *El Mar Caribe: The American Mediterranean* (Denver: DAM, 2024). Two important contributions for ancient Caribbean art are Lawrence Waldron, *Handbook of Ceramic Animal Symbols in the Ancient Lesser Antilles* (Gainesville: UPF, 2016) and Lawrence Waldron, *Pre-Columbian Art of the Caribbean* (Gainesville: UPF, 2019). Exhibition catalogs have also contributed to studies of pan-regional art, such as James Doyle, *Arte del mar: Artistic Exchange in the Caribbean* (New York: MMA, 2019); Rosemary A. Joyce, ed., *Revealing Ancestral Central America* (Washington: NMAI, 2013); and Colin McEwan et al., eds., *Unknown Amazon: Culture in Nature in Ancient Brazil* (London: BM, 2001).

Specific References

For general sources on the peopling of the Americas, Clovis culture, bannerstones, ancestral Arctic peoples, and early cave paintings:

Ardelean, Ciprian F., et al. 2023. "Oldest Art or Symbolic Expressions in North America? Pleistocene Modified Bones and a Human Remain at Sima de Las Golondrinas Cave, Zacatecas, Mexico." *L'Anthropologie* vol. 127, no. 2.

Aschero, Carlos, and Patricia Schneier. 2023. "Ese asunto de *Volver*: Producción y significación en el arte rupestre de Cueva de las Manos, Patagonia meridional andina." *Boletín del Museo Chileno de Arte Precolombino* vol. 28, no. 2, pp. 91–110.

Becerra-Valdivia, Lorena, et al. 2018. "Reassessing the Chronology of the Archaeological Site of Anzick." *PNAS* vol. 115, no. 27, pp. 7000–3.

Blume, Anna. 2021. "Bannerstones: An Introduction." *Smarthistory*. https://smarthistory.org/bannerstones/

Friesen, T. Max, and Owen K. Mason, eds. 2016. *The Oxford Handbook of the Prehistoric Arctic*. New York: OUP.

Meltzer, David J. 2015. *The Great Paleolithic War: How Science Forged an Understanding of America's Ice Age Past*. Chicago: UCP.

Prentiss, Anna Marie, et al. 2023. "Evolution of the Okvik / Old Bering Sea Culture of the Bering Strait as a Major Transition." *Philosophical Transactions of the Royal Society B* vol. 378, pp. 1–10.

Raff, Jennifer. 2022. *Origin: A Genetic History of the Americas*. New York: Twelve.

Sources on early American architecture:

González-García, A. César, et al. 2021. "The River and the Sky: Astronomy and Topography in Caral Society, America's First Urban Centers." *Latin American Antiquity* vol. 32, no. 1, pp. 154–72.

Inomata, Takeshi, et al. 2020. "Monumental Architecture at Aguada Fénix and the Rise of Maya Civilization." *Nature* vol. 582, pp. 530–33.

Kidder, Tristram R., and Seth B. Grooms. 2023. "Chronological Hygiene and Bayesian Modeling of Poverty Point Sites in the Lower Mississippi Valley, circa 4200 to 3200 cal BP." *American Antiquity* vol. 89, no. 1, pp. 98–118.

Triadan, Daniela. 2025. "Early Maya Monumentalism." *Annual Review of Anthropology* vol. 54, pp. 5.1–5.17.

For general sources on early figurines, pottery, fiber arts, and metal arts:

Beekman, Christopher, and Robert B. Pickering, eds. 2016. *Shaft Tombs and Figures in West Mexican Society: A Reassessment*. Tulsa: Gilcrease Museum.

Dillehay, Tom D. 2017. *Where the Land Meets the Sea: Fourteen Millennia of Human History at Huaca Prieta, Peru*. Austin: UTP.

Montt, Indira, et al. 2023. "Chinchorro Fibre Management in the Atacama Desert and Its Significance for Understanding Andean

Textilization Processes." *Journal of Anthropological Archaeology* vol. 71, pp. 1–16.
Pillsbury, Joanne, et al. 2015. *Design for Eternity: Architectural Models from the Ancient Americas*. New York: MMA.
Rice, Prudence. 2015. *Pottery Analysis: A Sourcebook*, 2nd ed. Chicago: UCP.
Splitstoser, Jeffery C., et al. 2016. "Early Pre-Hispanic Use of Indigo Blue in Peru." *Sciences Advances* vol. 2, no. 9, pp. 1–4.
Wright, Véronique, et al. 2015. "The origins of mural painting in Ancient Peru: Archaeometric Preliminary Study of the Ventarrón Mural Paintings, Valle de Lambayeque." *Heritage Science* vol. 3, pp. 1–10.

Chapter 1

General Readings

Since the publication of Elizabeth Benson's edited volume *Dumbarton Oaks Conference on Chavín* (Washington: DO, 1971), many advances have occurred in archaeology and art history, updated in a volume fifty years later, Richard Burger and Jason Nesbitt, eds., *Reconsidering the Chavín Phenomenon in the Twenty-First Century* (Washington: DO, 2023). This complements Peter Fux, ed., *Chavín: Peru's Enigmatic Temple in the Andes* (Zurich: Scheidegger & Speiss, 2013). These studies built upon Burger's own extensive work, published in Richard Burger, *Chavín and the Origins of Andean Civilization* (London: TH, 1993); and similar syntheses, such as William J. Conklin and Jeffrey Quilter, *Chavín: Art, Architecture, and Culture* (Los Angeles: Cotsen Institute of Archaeology, 2008). The most recent cogent analysis of the sculpture at the site of Chavín de Huántar comes from emerging scholars, e.g. Patricia Lagarde, "Sculpting with the Sun: Phenomenology of Light in Architectural Sculpture at Chavín de Huántar, Peru," *Latin American and Latinx Visual Culture* vol. 5, no. 3 (2023): pp. 32–49.

There are several recent volumes with new advances in Paracas research, including Kerstin Paradis Gustafsson's study of the Gothenburg textiles that were returned to Peru: Kerstin Paradis Gustafsson, *The Life Thread: Paracas Textiles and Culture* (New York: ACC Art Books, 2022); the catalog of the Museo Amano, Gabriel Herrera and Walter H. Wust, eds., *La trama ancestral: La colección textil del Museo Amano* (Lima: Wust Ediciones, 2019); in addition to foundational books such as Anne Paul, *Paracas Ritual Attire: Symbols of Authority in Ancient Peru* (Tulsa: UOP, 1990); and Anne Paul, *Paracas Art & Architecture: Object and Context in South Coastal Peru* (Iowa City: University of Iowa Press, 1991). Recent publications that relate Peruvian archaeological advances are Henry Tantaleán et al., eds., *La cerámica Paracas del valle de Chincha, costa sur del Perú* (Lima: Instituto Peruano de Estudios Arqueológicos, 2020); and Elsa Tomasto-Cagigao and Ann H. Peters, eds., *De Paracas a Nasca, interacción y transición: esferas geográficas, prácticas sociales y procesos históricos en la costa sur* (Lima: FEPUCP, 2019). Exhibition catalogs of Nasca materials are also useful sources, e.g. Cecilia Pardo and Peter Fux, eds., *Nasca* (Lima: Museo de Arte de Lima, 2017); Rosa Lasaponara, Nicola Masini, and Giuseppe Orefici, eds., *The Ancient Nasca World* (Cham: Springer, 2016) also contains a variety of chapters on the forefront of research on Nasca culture.

Specific References

On early Andean textiles and preceramic culture:
Pozorski, Thomas, and Shelia Pozorski. 2018. "Early Complex Society on the North and Central Peruvian Coast: New Archaeological Discoveries and New Insights." *Journal of Archaeological Research* vol. 26, pp. 353–86.
On the archaeoacoustics of Chavín de Huántar:
Kolar, Miriam A., 2017. "Sensing Sonically at Andean Formative Chavín de Huántar, Perú." *Time and Mind* vol. 10, no. 1, 39–59.
On Callango and Chavín-Paracas connections:
DeLeonardis, Lisa. 2023. "From the Inside Looking Out: Paracas Perspectives on Chavín." In *Reconsidering the Chavín Phenomenon in the Twenty-First Century*, ed. Richard L. Burger and Jason Nesbitt, pp. 271–98. Washington: DO.
On Cupisnique and Paracas ceramics:
Kriss, Dawn, et al. 2018. "A Material and Technical Study of Paracas Painted Ceramics." *Antiquity* vol. 92, no. 366, pp. 1492–1510.
DeLeonardis, Lisa. 2022. "Modeling the Sacred: The Pyramidal Form and Its Resonance in Paracas Sculptural Ceramics." *Latin American and Latinx Visual Culture* vol. 4, no. 2, pp. 10–28.
DeLeonardis, Lisa. 2016. "Encoded Process, Embodied Meaning in Paracas Post-Fired Painted Ceramics." In *Making Value, Making Meaning: Techné in the Pre-Columbian World*, ed. Cathy Lynn Costin, pp. 129–66. Washington: DO.
For sources on Nasca art and society:
Tierney, Meghan. 2022. "Beyond the San Pedro Cactus: Ancient Nasca Shamanism in Polychrome Ceramics." *Middle Atlantic Review of Latin American Studies* vol. 6, no. 2, pp. 1–28.

Chapter 2

General Readings

Comprehensive texts on Olmec art and archaeology include Christopher Pool, *Olmec Archaeology and Early Mesoamerica* (Cambridge: CUP, 2007); John Clark and Mary E. Pye, eds., *Olmec Art and Archaeology in Mesoamerica* (Washington: NGA, 2006); and Richard A. Diehl, *The Olmecs: America's First Civilization, Ancient Peoples and Places* (London: TH, 2004). Museum exhibitions have also gathered essays by leading international scholars: Kathleen Berrin and Virginia M. Fields, eds., *Colossal Masterworks of Ancient Mexico* (San Francisco: FAMSF, 2010); Michael Coe, *The Olmec World: Ritual and Rulership* (Princeton: PUAM, 1996); and Elizabeth P. Benson and Beatriz de la Fuente, eds., *Olmec Art of Ancient Mexico* (Washington: NGA, 1996). Recent exhibitions of Olmec art have been organized in Mexico, such as *Golfo: Mosaico Ancestral*, curated by Rebeca González Lauck at the Museo Nacional de Antropología, with a catalog under the same title, by Amalia Attolini Lecón (Mexico City: INAH 2019); and a version that traveled to Paris with its catalog, Dominique Michelet, ed., *Les Olmèques et les cultures du golfe du Mexique* (Paris: Musée du Quai Branly–Jacques Chirac, 2020).

Specific References

For more on Tlatilco, Tlapacoya, Las Bocas, El Manatí, Oxtotitlán and Chalcatzingo:

Pohl, Mary, and Christopher von Nagy. 2022. "Documenting and Dating Olmec-Style Cave Paintings, Guerrero, Mexico." Report: https://repository.lib.fsu.edu/islandora/object/fsu%3A791030

Santasilia, Catharina E., et al., eds. 2022. *Identities, Experience, and Change in Early Mexican Villages.* Gainesville: UPF.

For information on the excavations and offerings at La Venta:

Brittenham, Claudia. 2023. *Unseen Art: Making, Vision, and Power in Ancient Mesoamerica.* Austin: UTP.

Consult the following for more information on early scripts in Mesoamerica:

Carrasco, Michael D., and Joshua D. Englehardt. 2020. "Diphrastic Kennings on the Cascajal Block and the Emergence of Mesoamerican Writing." *Cambridge Archaeological Journal* vol. 25, no. 3, pp. 635–56.

Englehardt, Joshua D., et al. 2020. "Digital Imaging and Archaometric Analysis of the Cascajal Block: Establishing Context and Authenticity for the Earliest Known Olmec Text." *AncM* vol. 31, pp. 189–209.

Mora-Marin, David F. 2020. "The Cascajal Block: New Line Drawing, Distributional Analysis, and Orthographic Patterns." *AncM* vol. 31, no. 2, pp. 210–29.

Chapter 3

General Readings

Since the publication of Rafael Larco Hoyle, *Los Mochicas* (Lima: Rimac, 1939), Moche archaeology and art history have rapidly expanded. The many recent edited volumes and synthetic summaries include Joanne Pillsbury, ed., *Moche Art and Archaeology in Ancient Peru* (Washington: NGA, 2006); Steve Bourget, *Sex, Death, and Sacrifice in Moche Religion and Visual Culture* (Austin: UTP, 2006); and Bourget's *Sacrifice, Violence, and Ideology among the Moche: The Rise of Social Complexity in Ancient Peru* (Austin: UTP, 2016); Margaret Jackson, *Moche Art and Visual Culture in Ancient Peru* (Albuquerque: UNMP, 2008); Steve Bourget and Kimberly L. Jones, eds., *The Art and Archaeology of the Moche* (Austin: UTP, 2009); Jeffrey Quilter, *The Moche of Ancient Peru: Media and Messages* (Cambridge: PMH, 2010); and Elizabeth P. Benson, *The Worlds of the Moche on the North Coast of Peru* (Austin: UTP, 2012). Christopher Donnan's foundational *Moche Art and Iconography* (Los Angeles: UCLA, 1976) has now found a second life online at Dumbarton Oaks: https://www.doaks.org/research/library-archives/icfa/collections/moche-archive.

Specific archaeological studies have also flourished, such as Lisa Trever, *Image Encounters: Moche Murals and Archaeo Art History* (Austin: UTP, 2022); which followed *The Archaeology of Mural Painting at Pañamarca, Peru* (Washington: DO, 2017). An important volume is Jeffrey Quilter and Luis Jaime Castillo B., eds., *New Perspectives on Moche Political Organization* (Washington: DO, 2010), with a helpful overview in Christopher Donnan's essay, "Moche State Religion: A Unifying Force in Moche Political Organization" (pp. 47–69). Studies of individual royal dynasties and their funerary assemblages include Christopher Donnan, *La Mina: A Royal Moche Tomb* (Albuquerque: UNMP, 2022); Christopher Donnan, *Moche Tombs at Dos Cabezas* (Los Angeles: Cotsen Institute of Archaeology, 2007); and Christopher Donnan and Walter Alva, *Royal Tombs of Sipán* (Los Angeles: Fowler Museum of Cultural History, 1993). An English/Spanish study on the Huaca de la Luna complex is Santiago Uceda, Ricardo Morales, and Elias Mujica Barreda, *Huaca de la Luna: Moche Temples and Gods* (Lima: World Monuments Fund Perú, 2016).

Specific References

On iconography and styles of Moche art:

Muro Ynoñan, Luis A. 2023. "Moche Deathscapes: Performance, Politics, and the Creation of Myth in Huaca La Capilla–San José de Moro (650–740 CE)." *Journal of Social Archaeology* vol. 23, no. 3, pp. 243–63.

Rucabado, Julio. 2016. "(Re)Construyendo identidades: Los mochicas y sus vecinos." In *Moche y sus vecinos: Reconstruyendo identidades*, ed. Cecilia Pardo and Julio Rucabado, pp. 22–55. Lima: Museo de Arte de Lima.

Scher, Sarahh, 2020. "Destituir a los sacerdotes: La iconografía moche, la falsa ubicuidad y la creación de un canon." In Marco Curatola Petrocchi et al., *El arte antes de la historia: Para una historia del arte andino antiguo* (Lima: FEPUCP).

Weismantel, Mary. 2021. *Playing with Things: Engaging the Moche Sex Pots*. Austin: UTP.

Woloazyn, Janusz Z. 2014. *Los rostros silenciosos: los huacos retrato de la cultura Moche*. Lima: FEPUCP.

On metallurgy and metal objects:

Boswell, Alicia. 2021. "Metalwork in the Past and Present: Lord of Sipán and Tumi del Oro in Peru." *West 86th* vol. 28, no. 2, pp. 209–14.

Cesareo, Roberto, et al. 2016. "Analysis of the Spectacular Gold and Silver from the Moche Tomb 'Señora de Cao.'" *X-Ray Spectrometry* vol. 45, no. 3, pp. 138–54.

Kaulicke, Peter, and Doris Kurella. 2014. "Las máscaras doradas de la Huaca de la Luna: 'Efecto posterior' a los trabajos de Uhle." In Max Uhle, *Las ruinas de Moche*, pp. 79–116. Lima: FEPUCP.

For sources about the tombs of the Lords of Sipán:

Aimi, Antonio, et al. 2016. "Hacia una nueva cronología de Sipán." In *Lambayeque: Nuevos horizontes de la arqueología peruana*, ed. Antonio Aimi, Krzysztof Makowski, and Emilia Perassi, pp. 128–54. Milan: Lediziomi-Ledi.

For references on Sicán/Lambayeque art and culture:

Carcedo Muro de Mufarech, Paloma. 2014. "Los vasos en la orfebrería Sicán." In *Cultura Sicán: Esplendor preincaico de la costa norte*, ed. Izumi Shimada, trans. Gabriela Cervantes, pp. 107–46. Lima: Fondo Editorial del Congreso del Perú.

Shimada, Izumi, ed., 2014. *Cultura Sicán: Esplendor preincaico de la costa norte*. Trans. Gabriela Cervantes. Lima: Fondo Editorial del Congreso del Perú.

Wester La Torre, Carlos. 2016. *Chornancap: Palacio de una gobernante y sacerdotisa de la cultura Lambayeque*. Chiclayo: Ministerio de Cultura del Perú.

Chapter 4

General Readings

The following list should be considered a starting point for more in-depth study of the art and archaeology of the ancient Maya. For Classic Maya art and culture, the best introductory text is Michael Coe and Stephen Houston, *The Maya*, 10th ed. (London: TH, 2022). Other useful texts focused on Maya art and epigraphy include Oswaldo Chinchilla Mazariegos, *Art and Myth of the Ancient Maya* (New Haven: YUP, 2017); Mary Ellen Miller and Megan E. O'Neil, *Maya Art and Architecture*, 2nd ed. (London: TH, 2014); Andrea Stone and Mark Zender, *Reading Maya Art* (London: TH, 2011); and Simon Martin and Nikolai Grube's *Chronicle of the Maya Kings and Queens* (London: TH, 2008). Simon Martin's *Ancient Maya Politics* (Cambridge: CUP, 2022) is also a crucial explication of the political, historical, and spiritual implications of the content of the hieroglyphic texts from the Classic period. Traci Ardren, ed., *Ancient Maya Women* (Walnut Creek, CA: Altamira, 2002) also provides a broad perspective on gender from a variety of authors. Other sources on ancient Maya writing and decipherment include: Michael Coe, *Breaking the Maya Code*, 3rd ed. (New York: TH, 2012); Michael D. Coe and Mark Van Stone, *Reading the Maya Glyphs* (London: TH, 2005); Stephen Houston et al., eds., *The Decipherment of Ancient Maya Writing* (Norman: UOP, 2001); and Stephen Houston et al., *The Memory of Bones: Body, Being, and Experience among the Classic Maya* (Austin: UTP, 2006).

Ancient Maya art has also been the subject of museum exhibitions with illustrated catalogs, including: Oswaldo Chinchilla et al., eds., *Lives of the Gods: Divinity in Maya Art* (New York: MMA, 2022); Daniel Finamore and Stephen Houston, eds., *Fiery Pool: The Maya and the Mythic Sea* (New Haven: YUP, 2010); Miriam Judith Gallegos Gómora et al., eds., *Mayas: el lenguaje de la belleza* (Mexico City: INAH, 2015); Joanne Pillsbury et al., eds., *Ancient Maya Art at Dumbarton Oaks* (Washington: DO, 2010); Virginia Fields and Dorie Reents-Budet, eds., *Lords of Creation: The Origins of Sacred Maya Kingship* (Los Angeles: LACMA, 2005); Peter Schmidt et al., eds., *Maya* (New York: Rizzoli, 1998); Dorie Reents-Budet, *Painting the Maya Universe: Royal Ceramics of the Classic Period* (Durham, NC: DUP, 1994); and the catalog to the original blockbuster Maya art exhibition, Linda Schele and Mary Ellen Miller, eds., *Blood of Kings: Dynasty and Ritual in Maya Art* (Fort Worth: Kimbell Art Museum, 1986). Some earlier books that still prove useful include Herbert J. Spinden, *A Study of Maya Art: Its Subject Matter and Historical Development* (Cambridge: PMH, 1913); and, originally by Sylvanus Morley with subsequent editions by Robert Sharer and Loa P. Traxler, *The Ancient Maya* (Stanford: Stanford University Press, 1946) now in its 6th printing (2022).

Specific References

For publications on early Maya architecture:

Doyle, James A. 2017. *Architecture and the Origins of Preclassic Maya Politics.* New York: CUP.

Freidel, David A., et al., eds. 2020. *Maya E Groups: Calendars, Astronomy, and Urbanism in the Early Lowlands.* Gainesville: UFP.

For publications on Tikal, Yaxchilan, Palenque, Piedras Negras, and Copán, see:

Agurcia Fasquelle, Ricardo, et al. 2016. *Protecting Sacred Space: Rosalila's Eccentric Chert Cache at Copan and Eccentrics among the Classic Maya*. San Francisco: Precolumbia Mesoweb Press.

Brittenham, Claudia. 2019. "Architecture, Vision, and Ritual: Seeing Maya Lintels at Yaxchilan Structure 23." *Art Bulletin* vol. 101, no. 3, pp. 8–36.

Houston, Stephen. 2016. "Crafting Credit: Authorship among Classic Maya Painters and Sculptors." In *Making Value, Making Meaning:* Techné *in the Pre-Columbian World*, ed. Cathy Costin, pp. 391–431. Washington: DC: Dumbarton Oaks Research Library and Collection.

Houston, Stephen D., et al. 2021. "A Teotihuacan Complex at the Classic Maya City of Tikal, Guatemala." *Antiquity* vol. 95, no. 384.

On jade use among the ancient Maya:

Filloy Nadal, Laura. 2014. *Costume et insignes d'un gouvernant maya: K'inich Janaab' Pakal de Palenque.* Paris Monographs in American Archaeology 34. British Archaeological Reports Series 2590. Oxford: Archaeopress.

Filloy Nadal, Laura. 2017. "Forests of Jade: Luxury Arts and Symbols of Excellence in Ancient Mesoamerica." In *Golden Kingdoms: Luxury Arts in the Ancient Americas*, ed. Joanne Pillsbury, Timothy Potts, and Kim N. Richter. Los Angeles: JPGM.

Kovacevich, Brigitte. 2011. "The Organization of Jade Production at Cancuen, Guatemala." In *The Technologies of Maya Civilization: Political Economy and Beyond in Lithic Studies*, ed. Zachary X. Hruby, Geoffrey E. Braswell, and Oswaldo Chinchilla Mazariegos, pp. 151–63. Oakville, CT: Equinox.

For more information on Maya pottery and ceramic figurines, consult:

Aimers, James J., ed. 2014. *Ancient Maya Pottery: Classification, Analysis, and Interpretation.* Gainesville: UPF.

Aimi, Antonio, and Raphael Tunesi. 2017. "Notas sobre unos nuevos grandes artistas de los Sagrados Hombres de Chatahn." *Glyph Dwellers* 54, pp. 1–45.

Beliaev, Dmitri, and Albert Davletshin. 2014. "'It Was Then That That Which Had Been Clay Turned into a Man': Reconstructing Maya Anthropogonic Myths." *Axis Mundi* vol. 9, no. 2, pp. 2–12.

Brittenham, Claudia. 2019. "When Pots Had Legs: Body Metaphors on Maya Vessels." In *Vessels: The Object as Container*, ed. Claudia Brittenham, pp. 81–119. Oxford: OUP.

Doyle, James A. 2016. "Creation Narratives on Ancient Maya Codex-Style Ceramics in the Metropolitan Museum." *Metropolitan Museum Journal* vol. 51, pp. 42–64.

Halperin, Christina T. 2014. *Maya Figurines: Intersections between State and Household.* Austin: UTP.

Navarro-Farr, Olivia C., et al. 2020. "Expanding the Canon: Lady K'abel the *Ix Kaloomte'* and the Political Narratives of Classic Maya Queens." *Feminist Anthropology* vol. 1, no. 1, pp. 38–55.

O'Neil, Megan E. 2019. "The Painter's Line on Paper and Clay: Maya Codices and Codex-Style Vessels from the Seventh to the Sixteenth Centuries." In *Toward a Global Middle Ages: Encountering the World through Illuminated Manuscripts*, ed. Bryan C. Keene, pp. 125–36. Los Angeles: JPGM.

On later Maya art and Chichén Itzá:

Aldana y Villalobos, Gerardo. 2021. *Calculating Brilliance: An Intellectual History of Mayan Astronomy at Chich'en Itza*. Tucson: UAP.

Cockrell, Bryan, José Luis Ruvalcaba Sil, and Edith Ortiz Díaz. 2015. "For Whom the Bells Fall: Metals from the Cenote Sagrado, Chichén Itza." *Archaeometry* vol. 57, no. 6, pp. 977–95.

Milbrath, Susan. 2017. "Maya Astronomical Observations and the Agricultural Cycle in the Postclassic Madrid Codex." *AncM* vol. 28, no. 2, pp. 489–505.

Restall, Matthew, et al. 2023. *The Friar and the Maya: Diego de Landa and the Account of the Things of Yucatan*. Denver: UPC.

Stanton, Travis W., et al., eds. 2023. *When East Meets West: Chichen Itza, Tula, and the Postclassic Mesoamerican World*. Oxford: BAR. 2 vols.

Vail, Gabrielle, and Victoria R. Bricker. 2023. *Migration and Creation in Aztec and Maya Literature*. New York: Peter Lang.

Chapter 5

General Readings

Recent edited volumes addressing Ecuador, Colombia, Panama, and Costa Rica include Christopher Beekman and Colin McEwan, eds., *Waves of Influence: Pacific Maritime Networks Connecting Mexico, Central America, and Northwestern South America* (Washington: DO, 2022); and Jeffrey Quilter and John Hoopes, eds., *Gold and Power in Ancient Costa Rica, Panama, and Colombia* (Washington: DO, 2003). Past exhibition catalogs include Julie Jones, ed., *Jade in Ancient Costa Rica* (New York: MMA, 1998); Armand Labbé, *Shamans, Gods, and Mythic Beasts: Colombian Gold and Ceramics in Antiquity* (New York: American Federation of Arts, 1998); Detroit Institute of Arts, *Between Continents / Between Seas: Pre-Columbian Art of Costa Rica* (New York: Harry N. Abrams, 1981); and Elizabeth Kennedy Easby and John F. Scott, *Before Cortés: Sculpture of Middle America* (New York: MMA, 1970). An excellent source of research in Spanish on Colombian gold is the issues of the *Revista Boletín del Museo del Oro*, available on the Bogotá Gold Museum's website, https://www.banrepcultural.org/bogota/museo-del-oro.

Some of the key sources from the Spanish colonial period include various editions of Peter Martyr d'Anghera's work, such as his *De Orbe Novo: The Eight Decades of Peter Martyr d'Anghera* (1530), trans. Francis Augustus MacNutt (New York: B. Franklin, 1970), 2 vols. A helpful Spanish edition of Ramón Pané's late fifteenth-century work is Ángel Rodríguez Álvarez, ed., *Mitología Taína o Eyeri: Ramón Pané y la relación sobre las Antigüedades de los Indios; El primer tratado etnográfico hecho en América* (San Juan: Nuevo Mundo, 2008); for English, consult José Juan Arrom, *An Account of the Antiquities of the Indians: Fray Ramón Pané* (Durham, NC: DUP, 1999). Several editions and translations of the following sources are also useful for providing sixteenth-century context to these regions, including: Fernando Colón, *Historia del almirante don Cristobal Colón* (Madrid: Tomás Minuesa, 1892); the text by Gonzalo Fernández de Oviedo y Valdés, *Historia general y natural de las Indias* (Asunción: Editorial Guarania, 1944), 14 vols.; two texts by Fray Bartolomé de Las Casas: *Brevísima relación de la destrucción de las Indias* (Buenos Aires: Editorial Universitaria, 1966) and *Apologética historia sumaria* (Mexico City: UNAM, 1967), 2 vols.; and Francisco López de Gómara, *Historia general de las Indias* (Madrid: Calpe, 1922) 2 vols. Historical linguistic scholarship is also available, such as Adolfo Constenla Umana, *Las lenguas del Área Intermedia: Introducción a su estudio areal* (San José: Editorial de la Universidad de Costa Rica, 1991).

Specific References

For general sources on Ecuadorian and Colombian antiquity:

Falchetti, Ana María. 2018. *Lo humano y lo divino: Metalurgia y cosmogonía en la América antigua.* Bogotá: Ediciones Uniandes.

Lleras Pérez, Roberto. 2015. *Metallurgy in Ancient Ecuador: A Study of the Collection of Archaeological Metallurgy of the Ministry of Culture, Ecuador.* Oxford: Archaeopress.

McEwan, Colin, and Matthew Looper. 2021. "Seats, Seating, and Social Roles: Cross-Cultural Comparisons." In *Pre-Columbian Central America, Colombia, and Ecuador: Toward an Integrated Approach*, ed. Colin McEwan and John W. Hoopes, pp. 377–408. Washington: DO.

On the archaeology of San Agustín:

Drennan, Robert D., et al. 2018. *Regional Settlement Patterns in the Alto Magdalena: The San Agustín-Isnos Zone.* Pittsburgh: University of Pittsburgh Center for Comparative Archaeology.

On ancestral Costa Rica and Panama:

Fundación El Caño. 2015. *Guerreros de oro: Los señores de Río Grande en Panamá.* Panama: Caribe.

Gassman, Guntram, et al. 2023. "Investigating Pre-Columbian Gold and Copper in Costa Rica—Ores, Mines, and Artefact Production." *Metalla* vol. 27, no. 2, pp. 149–66.

Kuboyama-Haraikawa, Waka. 2023. *Celtiform Pendants from Pre-Columbian Costa Rica: Production, Distribution, and Experimental Replication.* Oxford: BAR.

Mayo Torné, Julia, et al. 2016. "La tumba T7 de la necrópolis de El Caño, tradición arqueológica Gran Coclé, Istmo de Panamá." *Arqueología Iberoamericana* vol. 30, pp. 30–43.

Mayo, Carlos, et al. 2025. "Analysis of Pigments Used in Ceramic Decoration from El Caño, Panama (600–1520 CE)." *Caribbean Journal of Science* vol. 55, no. 2, pp. 357–70.

On the art of the Amazonian region:

Cavalcante Gomes, Denise Maria, et al. 2023. "Archaeological Evidence of the Development of a Regional Society in Santarém (AD 1000–1600). Lower Amazon: A Path to Understanding Social Complexity." *Journal of World Prehistory* vol. 36, pp. 147–89.

Rolim de Souza Lima, Marcelle, et al. 2020. "História de vida de uma urna Marajoara: Reconectando contextos e significados." *Revista de Arqueología* vol. 33, no. 3, pp. 396–418.

On the art of the Antilles:
Hayward, Michele, H., et al. 2023. "Rock Art within the Indigenous Caribbean Physical and Cultural Landscape." *Revista de Arqueología Americana* vol. 41, pp. 23–111.

Chapter 6

General Readings

Several exhibition catalogs featuring Teotihuacán materials include Matthew Robb, ed., *Teotihuacan: City of Water, City of Fire* (San Francisco: FAMSF, 2017); Henri Stierlin, ed., *Teotihuacan: La cité des dieux* (Paris: L'Histoire, 2009); and Kathleen Berrin and Esther Pasztory, *Teotihuacan: Art from the City of the Gods* (San Francisco: FAMSF, 1993). Edited volumes exploring the influence of people from Teotihuacán throughout Mesoamerica include Claudia García-Des Lauriers and Tatsuya Murakami, eds., *Teotihuacan and Early Classic Mesoamerica: Multiscalar Perspectives on Power, Identity, and Interregional Relations* (Boulder: UCP, 2021); Kenneth Hirth, David M. Carballo, and Bárbara Arroyo, eds., *Teotihuacan: The World beyond the City* (Washington: DO, 2020); and Geoffrey Braswell, ed., *The Maya and Teotihuacan: Reinterpreting Early Classic Interaction* (Austin: UTP, 2004). Annabeth Headrick, *The Teotihuacan Trinity: The Sociopolitical Structure of an Ancient Mesoamerican City* (Austin: UTP, 2007); and Esther Pasztory, *Teotihuacan: An Experiment in Living* (Norman: UOP, 1997) provide useful summaries along with George L. Cowgill, *Ancient Teotihuacan: Early Urbanism in Central Mexico* (New York: CUP, 2015). For the Codex Nuttall, see Robert Lloyd Williams, *The Complete Codex Zouche-Nuttall: Mixtec Lineage Histories and Political Biographies* (Austin: UTP, 2013).

Specific References

For studies on Teotihuacán society, iconography, and writing:
Barnes, Trenton D. 2024. "Blood, Obsidian, and the Teotihuacan Cult of the Mirror." *AncM* vol. 35, pp. 451–71.
Carballo, David M. 2022. "Governance Strategies in Precolonial Central Mexico." *Frontiers in Political Science* vol. 4., pp. 1–13.
González Block, Miguel A. 2024. "From the Great Goddess to the Storm God: Cosmic Transformations at the Boundary between the Dry and Rainy Seasons in Classic Teotihuacan." *AncM* 35, pp. 839–64.
Hanson, Magnus Pharao, and Christophe Helmke. 2025. "The Language of Teotihuacan Writing." *Current Anthropology* vol. 66, no. 5, pp. 637–789
Helmke, Christophe. 2023. "Poetic Pairings and Lexical Calques at Teotihuacan: Forays in Historical Linguistics." *Ancient America* vol. 15.
Helmke, Cristophe, and Jesper Nielsen. 2021. "Teotihuacan Writing: Where Are We Now?" *Visible Language* vol. 55, pp. 29–73.
López Luján, Leonardo, and Michelle de Anda Rogel. 2019. "Teotihuacan in Mexico-Tenochtitlan: Recent Discoveries, New Insights." *The PARI Journal* vol. 19, no. 3, pp. 1–26.
Mandell, Elisa C. 2015. "A New Analysis of the Gender Attribution of the 'Great Goddess' of Teotihuacan." *AncM* vol. 26, pp. 29–49.
Rose, Timothy R., and Jane MacLaren Walsh. 2018. "The Stone Faces of Teotihuacan: Insights into Their Use, Manufacture, and Sources." *Journal of Archaeological Science: Reports* vol. 22, pp. 299–312.
For a summary of investigations into the Pyramid of the Moon and Feathered Serpent Pyramid:
Gómez Chávez, Sergio, et al. 2016. "AMS 14C Dating of Materials Recovered from the Tunnel under the Temple of the Feathered Serpent in Teotihuacan, Mexico." *Radiocarbon* vol. 59, pp. 1–13.
Sugiyama, Nawa. 2024. *Animal Matter: Ritual, Place, and Sovereignty at the Moon Pyramid of Teotihuacan*. Oxford: OUP.
For general sources on ancient Oaxaca and Monte Albán:
Finegold, Andrew. 2025. "Dreams of Gold: Mesoamerican Metalwork and the Question of Form." *Art History* vol. 48, no. 2, pp. 370–99.
Forde, Jamie E. 2016. "The Polychrome Ceramics of Tututepec (Yucu Dzaa), Oaxaca, Mexico: Iconography and Ideology." *AncM* vol. 27, no. 2, pp. 389–404.
Pérez Rodríguez, Verónica, Shanti Morell-Hart, and Stacie M. King. 2024. *Mesquite Pods to Mezcal: 10,000 Years of Oaxacan Cuisines*. Austin: UTP.
Robles García, Nelly M. 2019. *Oaxaca: Arqueología de una región mesoamericana*. Washington: Society for American Archaeology.
On ancient Veracruz:
Faust, Katherine A., and Kim N. Richter, eds. 2015. *The Huasteca: Culture, History, and Interregional Exchange*. Norman: UOP.
Stark, Barbara L. 2021. *The Archaeology of Political Organization: Urbanism in Classic Period Veracruz, Mexico*. Los Angeles: UCLA Cotsen Institute of Archaeology Press.

Chapter 7

General Readings

Two volumes provide updated syntheses of research on important Andean centers: Alexei Vranich and Charles Stanish, eds., *Visions of*

Tiwanaku (Los Angeles: Cotsen Institute of Archaeology Press, 2013); and Susan Bergh, ed., *Wari: Lords of the Ancient Andes* (Cleveland: Cleveland Museum of Art, 2012). The Denver Art Museum has also published a series of papers in Margaret Young-Sánchez, ed., *Tiwanaku* (Denver: Denver Art Museum, 2009); and the catalog Margaret Young-Sánchez, *Tiwanaku: Ancestors of the Inca* (Denver: DAM, 2004). In the latter, Paul Goldstein and Mario Rivera provide a helpful overview, "Arts of Greater Tiwanaku: An Expansive Culture in Historical Context," pp. 150–84. John Janusek, *Ancient Tiwanaku* (Cambridge: CUP, 2008) and his *Identity and Power in the Ancient Andes: Tiwanaku Cities through Time* (New York: Routledge, 2004) also provide useful background. And on Wari, Luis Guillermo Lumbreras, *El Imperio Wari: Del origen, expansión y legado del imperio milenario que hizo posible el surgimiento de los Incas* (Lima: Crítica, 2024); and José Ochatoma Paravicino and Martha Cabrera Romero, eds., *Wari: Nuevos aportes y perspectivas* (Ayacucho: Universidad Nacional de San Cristóbal de Huamanga, 2021).

Specific References

On Tiwanaku:

Caraguay, Favio. 2023. "Simbólica Andina y arte contemporáneo: Geometría de la *Chakana*." *Amarukan: Revista Andina de Ideas, Política y Cultura* vol. 1, no. 3, pp. 58–74.
Juengst, Sara L. 2023. *Cooperation and Hierarchy in Ancient Bolivia: Building Community with the Body.* Abingdon: Routledge.

For further sources on Huarmey, Pikillaqta, Conchopata, Cerro Baul, and Wari ceramic, fiber, and feather arts:

Deglin, Louise, et al. 2022. "Wari Imperial Motives: The Variety of Decorated Ceramics at Cerro Baúl." *Ñawpa Pacha* vol. 43, no. 1, pp. 1–26.
Giersz, Milosz, and Cecilia Pardo, eds. 2014. *Castillo de Huarmey: El mausoleo imperial Wari.* Lima: Asociación Museo de Arte de Lima.
Isbell, William Harris, et al. 2018. *Images in Action: The Southern Andean Iconographic Series.* Los Angeles: UCLA Cotsen Institute of Archaeology Press.
Jennings, Justin, and Stephen Berquist. 2023. "Ayllus, Ancestors and the (Un)Making of the Wari State." *Cambridge Archaeological Journal* vol. 33, no. 2, pp. 349–69.
Rosenfeld, Silvana A., et al. 2021. "Beyond Exotic Goods: Wari Elites and Regional Interaction in the Andes during the Middle Horizon (600–1000 CE)." *Antiquity* vol. 95, no. 380, pp. 400–416.
Stone, Rebecca R. 2023. "Representations of the San Pedro (*Trichocereus*, spp.) Cactus Flower and the *Anadenanthera Colubrina* Plant in Wari Textiles and Tiwanaku Art." *Boletín del Museo Chileno de Arte Precolombino* vol. 28, no. 1, pp. 221–46.
Williams, Patrick Ryan, et al. 2024. "Wari across the Andes: Modeling the Radiocarbon Evidence." *Quaternary International* vol. 703, pp. 49–66.
Young, Michelle, and Anita Cook. 2023. "Just Scratching the Surface: Post-Fire Engravings as Semasiographic Writing in the Ancient Andes." *Journal of Anthropological Archaeology* vol. 70.

Chapter 8

General Readings

Surveys of art and archaeology in Native North America include Heather L. Igloliorte and Carla Taunton, eds., *The Routledge Companion to Indigenous Art Histories in the United States and Canada* (New York: Routledge, 2023); and Timothy R. Pauketat, ed., *The Oxford Handbook of North American Archaeology* (New York: OUP, 2015). Art catalogs include John Lukavic et al., *Here Now: Indigenous Arts of North America at the Denver Art Museum* (Denver: DAM, 2022); Gaylord Torrence, *Art of Native America: The Charles and Valerie Diker Collection* (New York: MMA, 2018); Gaylord Torrence, *The Plains Indians: Artists of Earth and Sky* (Paris: Skira, 2014); and Richard Townsend, *Hero, Hawk, and Open Hand: American Indian Art from the Ancient Midwest and South* (New Haven: YUP, 2004). Some helpful recent archaeological edited volumes are Matthew E. Hill and Laren W. Ritterbush, eds., *People in a Sea of Grass: Archaeology's Changing Perspective on Indigenous Plains Communities* (Salt Lake City: University of Utah Press, 2022); and Brad Koldehoff and Timothy R. Pauketat, eds., *Archaeology and Ancient Religion in the American Midcontinent* (Tuscaloosa: University of Alabama Press, 2018).

The National Museum of the American Indian (NMAI) with locations in New York and Washington has published many important exhibition and collection catalogs with Native voices writing on Native arts: Emil Her Many Horses, ed., *Unbound: Narrative Art of the Plains* (2024); Suzan Shown Harjo, ed., *Nation to Nation: Treaties between the United States and American Indian Nations* (2014); Gabrielle Tayac, ed., *IndiVisible: African-Native American Lives in the Americas* (2009); Kathleen Ash-Milby, ed., *Hide: Skin as Material and Metaphor* (2009); Kathleen Ash-Milby, ed., *Off the Map: Landscape in the Native Imagination* (2007); George P. Horse Capture and Emil Her Many Horses, eds., *A Song for the Horse Nation: Horses in Native American Cultures* (2006); Karen Coody Cooper and Nicolasa I. Sandoval, *Living Homes for Cultural Expression: North American Native Perspectives on Creating Community Museums* (2006); Robert Joseph, ed., *Listening to Our Ancestors: The Art of Native Life along the North Pacific Coast* (2006); and Bruce Bernstein, *The Language of Native American Baskets: From the Weavers' View* (2003). The NMAI has also published explorations of individual modern and contemporary artists. Related to these exhibitions, the museum published the following volumes of symposium papers: *Vision, Space, Desire: Global Perspectives and Cultural Hybridity* (Washington: NMAI, 2006); and *Past, Present, and Future: Challenges of the National Museum of the American Indian* (Washington: NMAI, 2011).

Specific References

For sources on the art and archaeology of Cahokia and Mississippian art:

Baires, Sarah E. 2022. *Cahokia and the North American Worlds*. Cambridge: CUP.
Baires, Sarah E. 2022. *Land of Water, City of the Dead: Religion and Cahokia's Emergence*. Tuscaloosa: University of Alabama Press.
Bell, Austin J. 2021. *The Nine Lives of Florida's Famous Key Marco Cat*. Gainesville: UPF.
Bollwerk, Elizabeth A., and Shannon Tushingham, eds. 2016. *Perspectives on the Archaeology of Pipes, Tobacco and Other Smoke Plants in the Ancient Americas*. Cham: Springer.
Claassen, Cheryl, ed. 2023. *Landscapes of Ritual Performance in Eastern North America*. Oxford: Oxbow.
Cook, Robert A., and Aaron Richard Comstock, eds. 2022. *Following the Mississippian Spread: Climate Change and Migration in the Eastern US (ca. AD 1000–1600)*. Cham: Springer.
Dye, David H., ed. 2021. *Mississippian Culture Heroes, Ritual Regalia, and Sacred Bundles*: Lanham, MD: Rowman & Littlefield.
Dye, David H. 2017. "He-Who-Wears Human-Heads-As-Earrings: Mississippian Culture Heroes, Reincarnation, and Warfare." In *War & Peace: Conflict and Resolution in Archaeology*, ed. Adam K. Benfer. Calgary: University of Calgary.
Friberg, Christina M. 2020. *The Making of Mississippian Tradition*. Gainesville: UPF.
Giles, Bretton T., and Shawn P. Lambert, eds. 2021. *New Methods and Theories for Analyzing Mississippian Imagery*. Gainesville: UFP.
McNutt, Charles H., and Ryan M. Parish, eds. 2020. *Cahokia in Context: Hegemony and Diaspora*. Gainesville: UPF.
Milner, George R. 2021. *The Moundbuilders: Ancient Societies of Eastern North America*. New York: TH.
Steponaitis, Vincas P., et al. 2019. "Effigy Pipes of the Lower Mississippi Valley: Iconography, Style, and Function." *Journal of Anthropological Archaeology* vol. 55, pp. 1–25.

For recent sources on Chaco Canyon archaeology and Ancestral Puebloan art:

Anyon, Roger, and Steven A. LeBlanc. 2024. *Ancient Communities in the Mimbres Valley: Continuity and Change from AD 750 to 1350*. Tucson: UAP.
Berlant, Anthony, and Evan M. Maurer. 2018. *Decoding Mimbres Painting: Ancient Ceramics of the American Southwest*. Los Angeles: LACMA.
Creel, Darrell. 2022. *The Production and Distribution of Mimbres Pottery*. Albuquerque: UNMP.
Crown, Patricia, ed. 2020. *The House of the Cylinder Jars: Room 28 in Pueblo Bonito, Chaco Canyon*. Albuquerque: UNMP.
Gilman, Patricia A., and Steven A. LeBlanc. 2017. *Mimbres Life and Society: The Mattocks Site of Southwestern New Mexico*. Tucson: UAP.
Kennett, Douglas J., et al. 2017. "Archaeogenomic Evidence Reveals Prehistoric Matrilineal Dynasty." *Nature Communications* vol. 8.
Pinotti, Thomaz, et. al. 2024. "Picuris Pueblo oral history and genomics reveal continuity in US Southwest." *Nature* vol. 642, pp. 125–32.
Reyman, Jonathan E. 2024. *Pueblo Bonito and Chaco Canyon Revisited: The Published versus the Unpublished Record*. Albuquerque: UNMP.
Rother, Barbara J., et al., eds. 2024. *New Perspectives on Mimbres Archaeology: Three Millennia of Human Occupation in the North American Southwest*. Tucson: UAP.
Schwartz, Christopher W., et al. 2022. *Birds of the Sun: Macaws and People in the U.S: Southwest and Mexican Northwest*. Tucson: UAP.
Van Dyke, Ruth, and Carrie C. Heitman, eds. 2021. *The Greater Chaco Landscape*. Boulder: UPC.
Watson, Adam S., et al. 2015. "Early Procurement of Scarlet Macaws and the Emergence of Social Complexity in Chaco Canyon, NM." *PNAS* vol. 112, no. 27, pp. 8238–43.
Whiteley, Peter M., ed. 2018. *Puebloan Societies: Homology and Heterogeneity in Time and Space*. Santa Fe: School for Advanced Research Press.
Wright, Aaron M., ed. 2023. *Sacred Southwestern Landscapes: Archaeologies of Religious Ecology*. Salt Lake City: University of Utah Press.

Chapter 9

General Readings

There are some excellent general readings on the art of the Inka Empire, including Andrew James Hamilton, *Scale and the Incas* (Princeton: PUP, 2018); Andrew James Hamilton, *The Royal Inca Tunic: A Biography of an Andean Masterpiece* (Princeton: PUP, 2024); Sonia Alconini Mujica and R. Alan Covey, eds., *The Oxford Handbook of the Incas* (New York: OUP, 2018); Izumi Shimada, ed. *The Inka Empire: A Multidisciplinary Approach* (Austin: UTP, 2015); and Frances M. Hayashida, Andrés Troncoso, and Diego Salazar, *Rethinking the Inka: Community, Landscape, and Empire in the Southern Andes* (Austin: UTP, 2022). For texts that address general histories and sacred landscapes in the Inka Empire, see Craig Morris and Adriana Von Hagen, *The Incas: Lords of the Four Quarters* (London: TH, 2017); Brian S. Bauer, *The Sacred Landscape of the Inca: The Cusco Ceque System* (Austin: UTP, 1998); and Brian S. Bauer, *Ancient Cuzco: Heartland of the Inca* (Austin: UTP, 2004); Jessica Christie, *Memory Landscapes of the Inka Carved Outcrops* (Lanham, MD: Rowman and Littlefield, 2016); Adam Herring, *Art and Vision in the Inca Empire* (New York: CUP, 2015); Stella Nair, *At Home with the Sapa Inca: Architecture, Space, and Legacy at Chinchero* (Austin: UTP, 2015); Frank Meddens, Colin McEwan, and Nicholas Branch, *Inca Sacred Space: Landscape, Site, and Symbol in the Andes* (London: Archetype, 2014); Alan Kolata, *Ancient Inca* (Cambridge: CUP, 2013); and Carolyn Dean, *A Culture of Stone: Inka Perspectives on Rock* (Durham, NC: DUP, 2010). Some earlier texts that informed present work include Maria Rostworowski de Diez Canseco, *History of the Inca Realm* (Cambridge: CUP, 1999); Susan Niles, *The Shape of Inca History: Narrative and Architecture in an Andean Empire* (Iowa City: University of Iowa Press, 1999); Jean-Pierre Protzen, *Inca Architecture and Construction at Ollantaytambo* (New York: OUP, 1993); John Hemming, *Monuments of the Incas* (Boston: Little, Brown, 1982); and Graziano Gasparini and Luise Margolies, *Inca Architecture* (Bloomington: Indiana University Press, 1980).

Constance Classen, *Inca Cosmology and the Human Body* (Salt Lake City: University of Utah Press, 1993), complements the more recent book by Isabel Yaya, *The Two Faces of Inca History: Dualism in the Narratives of Cosmology of Ancient Cuzco* (Boston: Brill, 2012). On the multivalence of the term *wak'a*, see Tamara L. Bray, *The Archaeology of Wak'as: Explorations of the Sacred in the Pre-Columbian Andes* (Boulder: UPC, 2015); and on the Quechua language, see Bruce Mannheim, *The Language of the Inka since the European Invasion* (Austin: UTP, 1991). For general sources on the information encoded in the *khipus*, see Carrie J. Brezine et al., "A New Naming Convention for Andean *Khipus*," *Latin American Antiquity*, 2024); Sabine Hyland, "How *Khipus* Indicated Labour Contributions in an Andean Village: An Explanation of Colour Banding Seriation and Ethnocategories," *Journal of Material Culture* vol. 21 (2016): pp. 490–509); Rubén Urbizagástegui Alvarado, *La escritura inca: Quipus, yupanas y tocapus* (Lima: Hipocampo, 2014); Marcia Ascher and Robert Ascher, *Mathematics of the Incas: Code of the Quipu* (Mineola, NY: Dover, 2013); Frank Salomon, *The Cord Keepers: Khipus and Cultural Life in a Peruvian Village* (Durham, NC: DUP, 2004); and the now-dated study by Gary Urton, *Signs of the Inka Khipu: Binary Coding in the Andean Knotted-Strong Records* (Austin: UTP, 2003).

Specific References

On the Chimú Empire, the city of Chan Chan, and art of the north coast:

Carcedo de Mufarech, Paloma, 2017. "Reflexiones sobre la producción Sicán y Chimú de vasos tipo kero y discos en plata: Su iconografía y su relación con las miniaturas Chimú." *Bulletin de l'Institut Français d'Etudes Andines* vol. 46, no. 1, pp. 37–75.

Moreno-Mayar, J. Víctor, et al. 2024. "Ancient Rapanui Genomes Reveal Resilience and Pre-European Contact with the Americas." *Nature* vol. 633, pp. 389–97.

Pillsbury, Joanne, and Carol J. Mackey. 2020. "Lambayeque Silver Beakers: Further Considerations." *Ñawpa Pacha* vol. 40, no. 2, pp. 223–47.

Gabriel Prieto, et al. 2019. "A Mass Sacrifice of Children and Camelids at the Huanchaquito-Las Llamas Site, Moche Valley, Peru." *PLOS One* vol. 14, no. 3, pp. 1–29.

For sources on Inka history from the colonial period or Inka art and architecture:

Burger, Richard L., et al. 2021. "New AMS dates for Machu Picchu: Results and Implications." *Antiquity* vol. 95, no. 383, pp. 1265–79.

Femenías, Blenda. 2017. "Structure, Design, and Gender in Inka Textiles." In *PreColumbian Textile Conference VII / Jornadas de Textiles PreColombinos VII*, ed. Lena Bjerregaard and Ann Peters, pp. 341–48. Lincoln, NE: Zea.

Kusunoki, Ricardo, Cecilia Pardo and Julio Rucabado. 2023. *Los Incas. Más allá de un imperio.* Lima: Museo del Arte de Lima.

Chapter 10

General Readings

General books on the art and archaeology of the Mexica include Esther Pasztory, *Aztec Art* (Norman: UOP, 1998) and Michael E. Smith, *The Aztecs*, 3rd ed. (Hoboken, NJ: Wiley-Blackwell, 2011). Several art exhibition catalogs and edited volumes are excellent starting points, including Barbara Mundy et al., eds., *Mexico-Tenochtitlan: Dynamism at the Center of the World* (Washington: DO, 2025); Delia Cosentino and Adriana Zavala, *Resurrecting Tenochtitlan: Imagining the Aztec Capital in Modern Mexico City* (Austin: UTP, 2023); Barbara E. Mundy, *The Death of Aztec Tenochtitlan, the Life of Mexico City* (Austin: UTP, 2022); Martin Berger, Inés de Castro, and Doris Kurella, eds., *Aztecs* (Stuttgart: Linden-Museum, 2020); Deborah L. Nichols and Enrique Rodríguez-Alegría, eds., *The Oxford Handbook of the Aztecs* (New York: OUP, 2017); Elizabeth Morán, *Sacred Consumption: Food and Ritual in Aztec Art and Culture* (Austin: UTP, 2016); John M. D. Pohl and Claire L. Lyons, *The Aztec Pantheon and the Art of Empire* (Los Angeles: JPGM, 2010); Leonardo López Luján and Colin McEwan, eds., *Moctezuma, Aztec Ruler* (London: BM, 2009); and Elizabeth Brumfiel and Gary M. Feinman, eds., *The Aztec World* (New York: Abrams, 2008). Several older volumes that may be useful include Felipe R. Solís Olguín, *The Aztec Empire* (New York: Guggenheim Museum, 2004); Eduardo Matos Moctezuma and Felipe Solís Olguín, eds., *Aztecs* (London: Royal Academy of Arts, 2002); José Alcina Franch, et al., *Azteca-Mexica, las culturas del México antiguo* (Madrid: Sociedad Estatal Quinto Centenario, 1992); Henry B. Nicholson and Eloise Quiñones Keber, eds., *Art of Aztec Mexico: Treasures of Tenochtitlan* (Washington: NGA, 1983); and Richard Townsend, *State and Cosmos in the Art of Tenochtitlan* (Washington: DO, 1979). The leading sources in Spanish include Eduardo Matos Moctezuma and Leonardo López Luján, *Escultura Monumental Mexica*, 2nd ed. (Mexico City: Fondo de Cultura Económica, 2012); and in French, Leonardo López Luján et al., eds., *Mexica: Des dons et des dieux au Templo Mayor* (Paris: Musée du Quai Branly–Jacques Chirac, 2024).

One of the most important sources on the Mexica and the broader sixteenth-century world of Nahuatl-speaking peoples in Central Mexico is Bernardino de Sahagún, *Historia general de las cosas de la Nueva España*, known today as the Florentine Codex (1575–77). The Getty Research Institute has published a monumental digital version with multilingual content at https://florentinecodex.getty.edu/. Further sources include Elizabeth Hill Boone, *Descendants of Aztec Pictography: The Cultural Encyclopedias of Sixteenth-Century Mexico* (Austin: UTP, 2020); Diana Magaloni Kerpel, *The Colors of the New World: Artists, Materials, and the Creation of the Florentine Codex* (Los Angeles: Getty Research Institute, 2014); and Jeanette Favrot Peterson and Kevin Terraciano, eds., *The Florentine Codex: An Encyclopedia of the Nahua World in Sixteenth-Century Mexico* (Austin: UTP, 2019). Other editions of important chronicles include Diego Durán, *Historia de las Indias de Nueva España e Islas de la Tierra Firme* (Mexico City: Biblioteca Porrúa, 1967) and Alonso de Molina, *Vocabulario en lengua castellana y mexicana y mexicana y castellana* (Mexico City: Biblioteca Porrúa, 2004).

Specific References

On Mexica Art and archaeology:

Bassett, Molly H. 2015. *The Fate of Earthly Things: Aztec Gods and God-Bodies*. Austin: UTP.

Brittenham, Claudia. 2019. “What Lies Beneath: Carving on the Underside of Aztec Sculpture.” In *Conditions of Visibility*, ed. Richard Neer, pp. 43–73. Oxford: OUP.

Caplan, Allison. 2021. “Blowers of Sun-Excrement: Nahua Lost-Wax Gold Casting in the Florentine Codex Book 9, Chapter 16.” *West 86th* vol. 28, no. 2, pp. 215–31.

Caplan, Allison. 2020. “The Living Feather: Tonalli in Nahua Featherwork Production.” *Ethnohistory* vol. 67, no. 3, pp. 383–406.

Dupey García, Elodie, and Elena Mazzetto, eds. 2021. *Mesoamerican Rituals and the Solar Cycle: New Perspectives from the Veintena Festivals*. New York: Lang.

González López, Ángel. 2015. *Imágenes sagradas: Iconografía en esculturas de piedra del recinto sagrado de Tenochtitlan y el Museo Etnográfico*. Mexico City: INAH.

Hajovsky, Patrick Thomas. 2015. *On the Lips of Others: Moteuczoma’s Fame in Aztec Monuments and Rituals*. Austin: UTP.

López Luján, Leonardo, and José Luis Ruvalcaba Sil. 2015. “El oro de Tenochtitlan: La colección arqueológica del Proyecto Templo Mayor.” *Estudios de Cultura Náhuatl* vol. 49, pp. 7–57.

Russo, Alessandra. 2015. “Inventory of Extant Featherwork from Mesoamerica and New Spain.” In *Images Take Flight: Feather Art in Mexico and Europe, 1400–1700*, ed. Alessandra Russo, Gerhard Wolf, and Diana Fane, pp. 434–55. Munich: Hirmer.

Stuart, David. 2021. *King and Cosmos: An Interpretation of the Aztec Calendar Stone*. San Francisco: Precolumbia Mesoweb Press.

Chapter 11

General Readings

Several sources on the impact of the European invasion in the Americas have addressed the legacies of ancient American art in colonial and modern and contemporary art, e.g. Barbara Braun, *Pre-Columbian Art and the Post-Columbian World: Ancient American Sources of Modern Art* (New York: Harry N. Abrams, 1993); Susan E. Ramírez, *The World Upside Down: Cross-cultural Contact and Conflict in Sixteenth-century Peru* (Palo Alto: Stanford University Press, 1996); James Oles, *Art and Architecture in Mexico* (London: TH, 2013); and more recently, Megan O'Neil, *The Maya* (London: Reaktion, 2022); and Iria Candela and Joanne Pillsbury, "Weaving Abstraction in Ancient and Modern Art," special issue, *Metropolitan Museum of Art Bulletin* vol. 81, no. 2, 2023. Several exhibitions have examined colonial artistic production in New Spain, viceregal South America, and the Atlantic world more broadly, including Adriano Pedrosa and Tomás Toledo, eds., *Afro-Atlantic Histories* (São Paulo: DelMonico, 2021); Tatiana Flores and Michelle Ann Stephens, eds., *Relational Undercurrents: Contemporary Art of the Caribbean Archipelago* (Durham, NC: DUP, 2017); Ilona Katzew and Luisa Elena Alcalá, eds., *Contested Visions in the Spanish Colonial World* (Los Angeles: LACMA, 2011); and Elena Phipps et al., *The Colonial Andes: Tapestries and Silverwork, 1530–1830* (New York: MMA, 2004). Jorge Rivas has edited several important recent catalogs and symposia proceedings published by the Denver Art Museum on Spanish-American art, including *Appropriation & Invention: Three Centuries of Art in Spanish America: Selections from the Denver Art Museum* (2022); *Materiality: Making Spanish America* (2020); and *Circulación: Movement of Ideas, Art, and People in Spanish America* (2018). Carolyn Dean has contributed an important study with her *Inka Bodies and the Body of Christ: Corpus Christi in Colonial Cuzco, Peru* (Durham, NC: DUP, 1999).

Specific References

For sources on example works illustrated or mentioned in this chapter:

Alcalá, Luisa Elena, and Jonathan Brown, eds. 2015. *Painting in Latin America, 1550–1820: From Conquest to Independence*. New Haven: Yale University Press.

Batista de Costa, Everaldo, et al. 2022. "Decolonialidad originaria, barroco mestizo y territorio en América Latina (del Rosario de Puebla a Tonantzintla de Cholula, México)." *Anais do Museo Paulista* vol. 30, pp. 1–44.

Elmore, Steve. 2015. *In Search of Nampeyo: The Early Years 1875–1892*. Santa Fe: Spirit Bird Press.

Holohan, Kate E. 2023. "'If He Is Converted': A New Spanish Featherwork Ecce Homo in Southeastern Africa." *Religions* vol. 14, pp. 1–16.

Katzew, Ilona, ed. 2022. *Archive of the World: Art and Imagination in Spanish America, 1500–1800*. Los Angeles: LACMA.

Lerner, Jesse. 2023. "Ch'u Mayaa and the Appropriation of the Past." *21: Inquiries into Art, History, and the Visual* vol. 4, no. 2, pp. 245–58.

Newman, Richard, et al. 2023. "The Story of Elaeagia Resin (Mopa-Mopa) So Far." *Heritage* vol. 6, no. 5, pp. 4320–44.

Newman, Richard, et al. 2015. "Mopa Mopa: Scientific Analysis and History of an Unusual South American Resin used by the Inka and Artisans in Pasto, Colombia." *Journal of the American Institute for Conservation* vol. 54, no. 3, pp. 123–48.

Ostapkowicz, Joanna, et al. 2017. "Integrating the Old World into the New: An 'Idol from the West Indies.'" *Antiquity* vol. 91, no. 359, pp. 1314–29.

Pohl, John M. D. 2021. "The Flower World of Cholula." In *Flower Worlds: Religion, Aesthetics, and Ideology in Mesoamerica and the American Southwest*, ed. Michael D. Mathiowetz and Andrew D. Turner, pp. 222–42. Tucson: UAP.

Russo, Alessandra, et al., eds. 2016. *Images Take Flight: Feather Art in Mexico and Europe, 1400–1700*. Munich: Hirmer.

Wade, Edwin L., and Allan R. Cook. 2022. *The Call of Beauty: Masterworks by Nampeyo of Hopi*. Santa Fe: El Otro Lado.

Webster, Susan Verdi. 2014. "El arte letrado: Andrés Sánchez Gallque y los pintores quiteños de principios de la colonia." In *Andrés Sánchez Gallque y los primeros pintores de la Audiencia de Quito*, ed. Ximena Carcelén, pp. 21–97. Quito: Casa de la Cultura Ecuatoriana.

Wright-Carr, David Charles, and Francisco Marco Simón, eds. 2023. *From Ancient Rome to Colonial Mexico: Religious Globalization in the Context of Empire*. Boulder: UPC.

List of Illustrations

Dimensions are given in centimeters (inches), height before width before depth where relevant.

Abbreviations

AIC	The Art Institute of Chicago
BM	The British Museum, London
DO	Dumbarton Oaks, Pre-Columbian Collection, Washington, D.C.
LACMA	Los Angeles County Museum of Art
MET	The Metropolitan Museum of Art, New York
MFA	Museum of Fine Arts Boston
MNA	Museo Nacional de Antropología – INAH, Mexico City
NMAI	National Museum of the American Indian, Smithsonian Institution, Washington, D.C.
NMNH	Department of Anthropology, National Museum of Natural History, Smithsonian Institution, Washington, D.C.

1, 133 Royal Tunic, 1450–1540. Inca, Peru. Wool, cotton, 90.2 × 77.15 (35½ × 30⅜). DO (PC.B.518)
2 Denali National Park and Preserve, Alaska. Photo National Park Service/Tim Rains
3 Fluted Projectile Points, 9000–8500 BCE. Clovis, New Mexico. Edwards chert, 7.8 × 2.7 (3⅛ × 1⅛), 11.1 × 2.7 (4⅜ × 1⅛). Courtesy of the Penn Museum (36-19-16, 36-19-3)
4 Bannerstone, 3000–1000 BCE. Late Archaic Tradition, Indiana. Banded slate, 14 × 10 × 2 (5½ × 3⅞ × ⅞). NMAI (4/6786). Photo NMAI Photo Services
5 Zoomorphic Adze Handle, 100–500. Thule Tradition: Old Bering Sea Stage, Banks Island, Canada. Fossil ivory, 33 × 2.5 × 6 (13 × 1 × 2⅜). NMAI (2/4318). Photo NMAI Photo Services
6 Cueva de las Manos, Río Pinturas, Santa Cruz Province, Argentina, *c.* 7450 BCE. Photo Imago/Zoonar/SuperStock
7 LiDAR Image of Poverty Point World Heritage Site, Louisiana. Poverty Point Station Archaeology Program, University of Louisiana at Monroe
8 Anthropomorphic Figurine, 4000–1500 BCE. Valdivia, Ecuador. Clay, 9.7 × 3.5 (3⅞ × 1⅜). Museo de Arte Precolombino Casa del Alabado, Quito
9 Mantle, 450–175 BCE. Paracas, Peru. Camelid fiber plain weave embroidered with camelid fiber in stem-stitch, 142 × 241 (55⅞ × 94⅞). MFA. William Alfred Paine Fund (31.501). Photo MFA/Bridgeman Images
10 Kelly Church, Match-E-Be-Nash-She-Wish Band of Pottawatomi, *Sustaining Traditions—Digital Teachings*, 2018. Black ash, sweetgrass, copper and Rit dye; medicine pouch containing sage, tobacco, sweetgrass, and cedar; glass vial containing emerald ash borer and isopropyl alcohol; USB flash drive, 19.7 × 10.2 × 10.2 (7⅞ × 4⅛ × 4⅛). AIC. Mrs Leonard S. Florsheim Jr Fund (2020.389a-d). Photo AIC/Art Resource, NY/Scala, Florence. © Kelly Church
11 Zemí Cohoba Stand, 974–1020. Taíno, Dominican Republic (?). Guaiacum wood, shell, 68.5 × 21.9 × 23.2 (27 × 8⅝ × 9⅛). MET. The Michael C. Rockefeller Memorial Collection, Bequest of Nelson A. Rockefeller, 1979 (1979.206.380)
12 Crowns, 800–500 BCE. Chavín/Cupisnique, Peru. Gold, central crown 24 × 15.5 (9½ × 6⅛). NMAI (16/1972). Photo NMAI Photo Services
13 Richard Burger and Luis Caballero, Drawing of the Lanzón at Chavín de Huántar, Peru. Courtesy Richard Burger
14 Chavín de Huántar, Peru. Photo Daniel Ochoa/Adobe Stock
15 Tenoned Head, 1200–500 BCE. Chavín de Huántar, Peru. Stone. Museo Nacional de Chavín, Peru. Photo Peter Langer/Design Pics/SuperStock
16 Shell Trumpet, 1200–500 BCE. Chavín de Huántar, Peru. Museo Nacional de Chavín, Peru. Photo Dr Sarahh Scher
17 Bimetallic Effigy Spoon, 400–200 BCE. Chavín, Peru. Gold and silver, 11.1 × 2.6 × 3.6 (4⅜ × 1 × 1⅜). DO (PC.B.440)
18 Textile, 800–700 BCE. Chavín, Peru. Cotton, 90 × 63 (35⅜ × 24¾). DO (PC.B.544)
19 Stela, 1200–500 BCE. Chavín, Pacopampa, Cajamarca, Peru. Stone, 127 × 42 × 25 (50 × 16½ × 9⅞). Museo Larco, Lima, Peru (ML300025)

20 Mouth Mask, 800–550 BCE. Chavín/Cupisnique, Kuntur Wasi, Peru. Gold, 14.6 × 21.2 (5¾ × 8 ⅜). Museo Kuntur Wasi, San Pablo, Ministerio de Cultura del Perú (MKW-81223). Photo © Museo Kuntur Wasi
21 Stirrup-spout Bottle, 1200–500 BCE. Cupisnique, Peru. Ceramic, 24.3 × 12.8 × 13.4 (9⅝ × 5 × 5¼). Museo Larco, Lima, Peru (ML040218)
22 Frieze from Huaca Garagay, Peru, 1200–600 BCE. Photo Ewicho
23 Mantle, 450–175 BCE. Paracas, Peru. Camelid fiber plain weave with stem stitch and loop stitch embroidery, 145.4 × 249.2 (57¼ × 98⅛). LACMA. Los Angeles County Fund (67.4)
24 Vessel, 600–500 BCE. Paracas, Peru. Ceramic, polychrome slip, 16.5 × 11.7 × 11.7 (6½ × 4⅝ × 4⅝). Brooklyn Museum, New York. Frank L. Babbott Fund (59.197.1). Photo Brooklyn Museum
25 Hummingbird Geoglyph, Nasca, Peru, *c.* 200 BCE–600 CE. Photo Creative Pixels/Adobe Stock
26 Vessel, 350–500. Nasca, Peru. Ceramic and pigment, 17 × 14.6 (6¾ × 5¾). AIC. Kate S. Buckingham Endowment (1955.2166)
27 Colossal Head Number 4, 1200–900 BCE. Olmec, San Lorenzo, Mexico. Basalt, 170 × 105 × 102 (66⅞ × 41⅜ × 40⅛). Museo de Antropología de Xalapa, Mexico
28 Colossal Head Number 8, 1200–900 BCE. Olmec, San Lorenzo, Mexico. Andesite, 220 × 163 × 155 (86⅝ × 64⅛ × 61). Museo de Antropología de Xalapa, Mexico
29 Seated Figure, 1200–900 BCE. Olmec, Mexico. Ceramic, cinnabar, red ochre, 34 × 31.8 × 14.6 (13⅜ × 12⅝ × 5¾). MET. The Michael C. Rockefeller Memorial Collection, Bequest of Nelson A. Rockefeller, 1979 (1979.206.1134)
30 Anthropomorphic Bust, 1100–600 BCE. Olmec, El Manatí, Mexico. Wood, 48.9 × 20.2 × 14.5 (19¼ × 8 × 5¾). MNA (10-0581073). Secretaría de Cultura – INAH – MEX. Reproduction authorised by the Instituto Nacional de Antropología e Historia, Mexico
31 Zoomorphic Relief (Monument 9), 800–400 BCE. Olmec, Chalcatzingo, Mexico. Museo Chalcatzingo. Secretaría de Cultura – INAH – MEX. Reproduction authorised by the Instituto Nacional de Antropología e Historia, Mexico
32 Pyramid C, La Venta, Tabasco, Mexico. Photo Danita Delimont/Alamy Stock Photo
33 Seated Female Figure, 900–600 BCE. Olmec, La Venta, Mexico. 7.7 × 4.7 × 3.8 (3 × 1⅞ × 1½). MNA (10-0009652). Photo Jorge Pérez de Lara
34 Offering 4, 800–700 BCE. Olmec, La Venta, Mexico. Jadeite, cinnabar, and other materials, height of sixteen figures 15.3–20 (6–7⅞), six celts 23.6–25.5 (9¼–10). MNA (10-9650 0/22). Secretaría de Cultura – INAH – MEX. Reproduction authorised by the Instituto Nacional de Antropología e Historia, Mexico
35 Altar 4, 800–400 BCE. Olmec, La Venta, Tabasco, Mexico. Photo J. Enrique Molina/Alamy Stock Photo
36 Anthropomorphic Sculpture (El Luchador), 1300–600 BCE. Olmec, Mexico. Stone, 65 × 54.3 × 43.5 (25⅝ × 21⅜ × 17⅛). MNA (10-0003157). Photo Jorge Pérez de Lara
37 Ayax Moreno, Reproduction of the Oxtotitlán Cave Mural C-1. Olmec, Mexico. Courtesy the New World Archaeological Foundation
38 Michael D. Carrasco, Drawing of the Cascajal Block. Olmec, Mexico. Courtesy Michael D. Carrasco
39 Anthropomorphic Figure (Tuxtla Statuette), 162 CE. Epi-Olmec, Mexico. Jadeite, 15.4 × 9.3 (6⅛ × 3¾). NMNH (A222579-0)
40 Winged Pectoral, 900–400 BCE (carved), 100 BCE–100 CE (incised). Olmec/Maya. Quartzite or serpentine, 8.9 × 26.7 × 2.9 (3⅝ × 10⅝ × 1¼). DO (PC.B.538)
41 Frieze, Huaca de la Luna, 300–600. Moche, Peru. Photo courtesy World Monuments Fund
42 Mask, Huaca de la Luna, 300–400. Moche, Peru. Copper oxide, Titanostrombus galeatus snail, basalt, gold; hammered, gilded, 26 × 21 (10¼ × 8⅜). Linden-Museum Stuttgart. Photo © Linden-Museum Stuttgart/Anatol Dreyer
43 Huaca Cao Viejo, Peru. Moche. Photo Fundación Augusto N. Wiese
44 Bimetallic Nose Ornaments, *c.* 500. Moche, Huaca Cao Viejo, Peru. Gold, silver, turquoise, 3.1–4.9 × 5.4–7.7 (1¼–2 × 1¾–3⅛). Photos Fundación Augusto N. Wiese
45 Ritual garment, *c.* 500. Moche, Huaca Cao Viejo, Peru. Cotton, gilded copper, shell, feathers, 80 × 45 (31½ × 17¾). Photo Fundación Augusto N. Wiese
46 Ear Ornament, 640–680. Moche, Sipán, Peru. Gold, turquoise, wood, diameter 9.5 (3¾). Museo Tumbas Reales de Sipán, Lambayeque (MNTRS-77-INC-02; S/T1-O:2)
47 Stirrup-spout Bottle, 500–700. Moche, Peru. Ceramic, 28.7 × 15.4 × 15.4 (11⅜ × 6⅛ × 6⅛). Museo Larco, Lima, Peru (ML010847)
48 Stirrup-spout Bottle, 400–650. Moche, Peru. Ceramic, pigment, 34.9 × 20.7 × 21 (13¾ × 8⅛ × 8¼). Museo Larco, Lima, Peru (ML018883)
49 Stirrup-spout Bottle, 400–650. Moche, Peru. Ceramic, pigment, 31.5 × 22.2 × 17 (12⅜ × 8¾ × 6¾). Museo Larco, Lima, Peru (ML013572)

50 Stirrup-spout Bottle, 200–600. Moche, Peru. Ceramic, 19.2 × 27.5 × 12.4 (7½ × 10⅞ × 4⅞). Museo Larco, Lima, Peru (ML004214)
51 Pedro Neciosup Gómez, mural illustration, Pañamarca, Peru. Programa de Investigación Arqueológica (PRIA) "Paisajes Arqueológicos de Pañamarca"
52 Túcume, Peru. Sicán. Photo Christian/Adobe Stock
53 Funerary Mask, 900–1100. Lambayeque (Sicán), Peru. Gold, silver-copper alloy, cinnabar, 29.2 × 49.5 × 10.2 (11½ × 19½ × 4⅛). MET. Gift and Bequest of Alice K. Bache, 1974, 1977 (1974.271.35)
54 *Tumi* (Knife), 900–1100. Lambayeque (Sicán), Peru. Gold with turquoise inlay, 34 × 12.7 (13⅜ × 5). AIC. Ada Turnbull Hertle Endowment (1963.841)
55 Heather Hurst, North Wall Mural Illustration, San Bartolo, Guatemala. Maya. © Heather Hurst, 2004
56 Tikal, Guatemala. Maya. Photo WitR/Adobe Stock
57 Lintel (Yaxchilan Lintel 25), 723. Maya, Maya, Yaxchilan, Mexico. Limestone, 121 × 85.5 × 13.5 (47⅝ × 33⅝ × 5⅜). BM (Am1923,Maud.5). Photo The Trustees of the British Museum
58 Ian Graham, Drawing of Yaxchilan Lintel 25, underside. Maya. © President and Fellows of Harvard College, Peabody Museum of Archaeology and Ethnology (2004.15.6.5.22)
59 Lintel (Temple IV Lintel 3), 746–47. Maya, Tikal, Guatemala. Zapote wood, pigments, 176 × 205 (69¼ × 80¾). Museum der Kulturen Basel, Sammlung Carl Gustav Bernoulli (IVb 52.01). Photo Omar Lemke, 2020
60 Mosaic Vessel, 700–50. Maya, Tikal, Guatemala. Jade, height 24.2 (9⅝), diameter 10 (4). Museo de Arqueología y Etnología, Guatemala City. Photo akg-images/Andrea Baguzzi
61 Mosaic Funerary Mask, 683. Maya, Palenque, Mexico. Jade, shell, obsidian, 25.6 × 18.8 × 10.6 (10⅛ × 7⅜ × 4⅛). MNA (10-0001300). Photo akg-images
62 Relief Panel (detail), 700–800. Maya, Temple XIX, Palenque, Mexico. Stone. MNA. Photo DeAgostini Picture Library/Scala, Florence
63 Attributed to the Metropolitan Painter, Cylinder Vessel, 700–800. Maya. Ceramic, slip, 14 × 10.2 × 10.6 (5⅝ × 4⅛ × 4¼). MET. The Michael C. Rockefeller Memorial Collection, Purchase, Nelson A. Rockefeller Gift, 1968 (1978.412.206)
64 Incense Burner, 600–800. Maya, Palenque, Mexico. Ceramic, 66 × 37 × 16 (26 × 14⅝ × 6⅜). MNA. Photo Jorge Pérez de Lara
65 Whistle with Anthropomorphic Figure (Maize God), 600–900. Maya. Ceramic, pigment, 21 × 5.4 × 4.3 (8¼ × 2⅛ × 1¾). Brooklyn Museum, Dick S. Ramsay Fund (70.31). Photo Brooklyn Museum
66 Anthropomorphic Sculpture (Maize God), 715. Maya, Temple 22, Copán, Honduras. Limestone, 89 × 56.5 × 30 (35 × 22¼ × 11¾). BM (Am1923,Maud.8). Photo The Trustees of the British Museum
67 Wajaat Na Chahk and collaborator, *Relief Panel (Panel 3), c.* 782–95. Maya Piedras Negras, Guatemala. Dolomite, 50 × 100 × 25 (19¾ × 39⅜ × 9⅞). Museo Nacional de Arqueología y Etnología, Guatemala City, Ministerio de Cultura y Deportes de Guatemala. Photo Juan Trujillo, courtesy of MET
68 Chichén Itzá, Yucatán. Maya, Mexico. Photo a_medvedkov/Adobe Stock
69 Pages from Dresden Codex, 1250–1524. Maya, Mexico. Amate paper, pigment, height 25 (9⅞). SLUB Dresden (Mscr.Dresd.R.310)
70 Throne, 500–1500. Manteño-Huancavilca, Cerro Jaboncillo, Ecuador. Stone, 40 × 68 × 75 (15¾ × 26¾ × 29½). NMAI (1/6380). Photo NMAI Photo Services
71 Anthropomorphic Figure, 350 BCE–350 CE. La Tolita, Ecuador. Ceramic, 45.2 × 35 (17¾ × 13¾). Museo de Arte Precolombino Casa del Alabado
72 Ciudad Perdida, Sierra Nevada de Santa Marta, Colombia. Photo causeway/Adobe Stock
73 Mouth Mask, 100 BCE–300 CE. Calima-Malagana, Colombia. Gold, 28 × 25.5 (11 × 10). Museo del Oro, Banco de la República, Bogotá (O33312). Photo Clark Manuel Rodríguez
74 Zoomorphic Lime Container, 100 BCE–800 CE. Calima-Yotoco, Colombia. Gold, platinum, 6.6 × 13.5 (2⅝ × 5⅜). Museo del Oro, Banco de la República, Bogotá (O33156). Photo Clark Manuel Rodríguez
75 Anthropomorphic Sculpture, 1–900. San Agustín, Colombia. Stone, 102 × 36 × 20 (40⅛ × 14⅛ × 7⅞). BM (Am1899,1012.1). Photo The Trustees of the British Museum
76 Votive Figure, 600–1600. Muisca, Colombia. Gold-copper alloy, 10.1 × 10.2 × 19.5 (4 × 4 × 7⅝). Museo del Oro, Banco de la República, Bogotá (O11373). Photo Clark Manuel Rodríguez
77 Metate, 100–500. Central Region, Costa Rica. Stone, 73.6 × 46.4 × 48.3 (29 × 18¼ × 19). MET. The Michael C. Rockefeller Memorial Collection, Bequest of Nelson A. Rockefeller, 1979 (1979.206.426)
78 Zoomorphic Pendant, 300–500. Central Region, Costa Rica. Jadeite, 20.3 × 5.9 (8 × 2⅜).

Museo Nacional de Costa Rica (MNCR), San José (1.5 TR 2C(34))
79 Anthropomorphic Vessel, 500–800. Guanacaste-Nicoya, Costa Rica. Ceramic, pigment, 27.7 × 21 × 20.5 (11 × 8⅜ × 8⅛). Museo Nacional de Costa Rica (MNCR), San José (14505). Photo © Dirk Bakker. All rights reserved 2026/ Bridgeman Images
80 Funerary Assemblage, 700–900. Coclé, Sitio Conte Grave 26, Panama. Gold, greenstone, emerald, quartz, plaque 22 × 24 × 0.5 (8¾ × 9½ ×¼). Peabody Museum Expedition, 1933. Courtesy of the Peabody Museum of Archaeology and Ethnology, Harvard University (33-42-20/1613, 33-42-20/1674.4, 33-42-20/1685, 33-42-20/1745.1, 33-42-20/1777)
81 Plate, 700–900. Coclé, Sitio Conte, Panama. Ceramic, pigment, diameter 34.5 (13⅝). Courtesy of the Penn Museum, Philadelphia. Panama, Cocle Expedition; J. Alden Mason, 1940 (40-16-1581)
82 Funerary Urn, 400–1400. Marajoara, Brazil. Ceramic, height 81 (32). Museu Nacional, Rio de Janeiro. Photo © 2017 Museu Nacional/UFRJ
83 Belt, 1475–1635. Taíno. Cotton, shell, jet, brass, mirror, height 11 (4⅜), length 115 (45⅜). Weltmuseum Wien. Photo © KHM-Museumsverband, Weltmuseum Wien
84 Teotihuacán, Mexico. Photo Dina/Adobe Stock
85 Mosaic Figure, 200–250. Teotihuacán, Pyramid of the Moon, Mexico. Serpentine, greenstone, and shell, 25.4 × 10.5 × 4.8 (10 × 4⅛ × 1⅞). MNA (10-615743). Photo Jorge Pérez de Lara
86 Façade of the Feathered Serpent Pyramid, Teotihuacán, Mexico, 200–650. Stone, pigment. Photo Archive Image/Alamy Stock Photo
87 Mural, Teotihuacán, Mexico, 200–650. Pigment, stucco. Secretaría de Cultura – INAH – MEX. Reproduction authorised by the Instituto Nacional de Antropología e Historia, Mexico
88 Anthropomorphic Sculpture (Water Goddess), Teotihuacán, Mexico, 200–650. Stone, 316 × 165 × 165 (124⅜ × 65 × 65). MNA (10-0001163). Photo Jorge Pérez de Lara
89 Anthropomorphic Mask, 200–650. Teotihuacán, Mexico. Stone, 12.9 × 12.7 × 6.4 (5⅛ × 5 × 2½). Museo de la Cultura Teotihuacana, INAH (359_022). Secretaría de Cultura – INAH – MEX. Reproduction authorised by the Instituto Nacional de Antropología e Historia, Mexico
90 Zoomorphic Mask, 100 BCE–200 CE. Monte Albán, Mexico. Jade, shell, slate, 17 × 15 × 10.9 (6¾ × 6 × 4⅜). MNA (10-0009646). Photo Jorge Pérez de Lara
91 Funerary Urn, 200 BCE–200 CE. Zapotec, Monte Albán, Mexico. Ceramic, shell, pigment, 20.3 × 13.2 × 11.7 (8 × 5¼ × 4⅝). MNA (10-0061331). Photo Jorge Pérez de Lara
92 Anthropomorphic Figure (Sonriente), 600–800. Veracruz, Mexico. Ceramic, slip, paint, 47.5 × 29.9 × 15.9 (18¾ × 11¾ × 6¼). MET. The Michael C. Rockefeller Memorial Collection, Bequest of Nelson A. Rockefeller, 1979 (1979.206.1211)
93 Zoomorphic Sculpture (Yoke), 300–600. Veracruz, Mexico. Stone, 12 × 37.5 × 40 (4¾ × 14⅞ × 15¾). LACMA. Purchased with funds provided by Camilla Chandler Frost (M.2010.115.692)
94 Frieze, El Tajín, Veracruz, Mexico, 700–900. Photo Suzuki Kaku/Alamy Stock Photo
95 Pectoral, 1200–1520. Mixtec, Tomb 7, Monte Albán, Mexico. Gold, 11.4 × 8.6 × 0.2 (4½ × 3⅜ × ⅛). Museo de las Culturas de Oaxaca, INAH (10-0222116). Secretaría de Cultura – INAH – MEX. Reproduction authorised by the Instituto Nacional de Antropología e Historia, Mexico
96 Pages from Codex Zouche-Nuttall, 1200–1521. Mixtec, Mexico. Deer skin, gesso, pigment, closed 19 × 23.5 (7½ × 9⅜). BM (Am1902,0308.1). Photo The Trustees of the British Museum
97 Tiwanaku, Bolivia. Photo F1online digitale Bildagentur GmbH/Ritterbach/Alamy Stock Photo
98 Gate of the Sun, Tiwanaku, Bolivia, 500–950. Stone, 300 × 400 (118⅛ × 157½). Library of Congress, Prints and Photographs Division, Washington, D.C. (LC-DIG-ds-01943)
99 Anthropomorphic Sculpture (Ponce Stela), Kalasasaya, Tiwanaku, Bolivia, 600–1000. Stone, height 350 (137⅞). Photo Atlantide Phototravel/ Getty Images
100 Textile, 250–450. Tiwanaku, Peru. Camelid fiber, 48.9 × 77.5 (19¼ × 30½). MFA. Charles Potter Kling Fund (1994.203). Photo MFA/Charles Potter Kling Fund/Bridgeman Images
101 *Kero* (Vessel), 656–822. Tiwanaku or Wari. Wood, 17.1 × 14 (6¾ × 5½). Fine Arts Museums of San Francisco. Museum purchase, David I. Clayton Acquisition Fund and Virginia Patterson Fund (2003.3). Photo Joseph McDonald, courtesy of the Fine Arts Museums of San Francisco
102 Zoomorphic Incense Burner, 500–1000. Tiwanaku, Bolivia. Ceramic, pigment, 45 × 15 × 29 (17¾ × 5⅞ × 11⅜). NMAI (23/7095). Photo NMAI Photo Services
103 Four-cornered Hat, 500–900. Tiwanaku or Wari. Camelid fiber, height 17.8 (7⅛), circum. 57.8 (22⅞). MET. Bequest of Arthur M. Bullowa, 1993 (1994.35.158)
104 Wari, Peru. Photo imageBROKER/Peter Giovannini/Alamy Stock Photo
105 Ceramic Assemblage, 600–1050. Wari, Castillo de Huarmey, Peru. Ceramic, pigment,

dimensions variable. Photo © Miłosz Giersz/ Castillo de Huarmey Archaeological Project
106 Anthropomorphic Figure, 500–900. Wari, Peru. Ceramic, pigment, 26.3 × 21.6 × 24.8 (10⅜ × 8½ × 9¾). The Cleveland Museum of Art. Leonard C. Hanna Jr. Fund (1997.1)
107 Anthropomorphic Figure, 600–1000. Wari, Peru. Wood with shell-and-stone inlay and silver, 10.2 × 6.4 × 2.6 (4 × 2½ × 1). Kimbell Art Museum (AP 2002.04). Photo Kimbell Art Museum/ Bridgeman Images
108 Tunic, 600–850. Wari, Peru. Wool and cotton interlocked tapestry weave, length 219.7 (86½). Rhode Island School of Design Museum. Mary B. Jackson Fund and Edgar S. Lownes Fund (40.007)
109 Feathered Panels, 600–900. Wari, Peru. Feathers, cotton, camelid fiber, 73.7 × 213 (29⅛ × 83⅞). MET. The Michael C. Rockefeller Memorial Collection, Bequest of Nelson A. Rockefeller, 1979 (1979.206.467)
110 Cahokia Mounds State Historic Site, Illinois. Photo Kent/Adobe Stock
111 Anthropomorphic Sculpture (Ancestral Figure), 1350–1550. Mississippian, Tennessee. NMAI (7277). Photo NMAI Photo Services
112 Anthropomorphic Pipe, 1100–1200. Mississippian, Caddo Nation of Oklahoma. Bauxite, height 22.5 (8⅞). The University of Arkansas, Fayetteville, Museum Collections (47-2-1). Photo John Lamberton
113 James A. Doyle, Drawing of Copper Plate, 1250–1350. Mississippian, Etowah Mounds, Georgia. Copper, height 27.9 (11). NMNH (A91117)
114 Zoomorphic Figure, 700–1500. Calusa, Key Marco, Florida. Wood, 15.1 × 4 × 6.5 (6 × 1⅝ × 2⅝). NMNH (A240915-0)
115 Anthropomorphic Pipe, 1400–1500. Mississippian. Stone, pigment, 12.2 × 17 × 8.6 (4⅞ × 6¾ × 3½). Brooklyn Museum, New York. Frank Sherman Benson Fund and the Henry L. Batterman Fund (37.2802PA). Photo Brooklyn Museum
116 Vessel, *c.* 1450–1550. Mississippian, Arkansas. Ceramic, pigment, 18.4 × 17.8 × 19.7 (7¼ × 7 × 7¾). Saint Louis Art Museum (67:2005)
117 Pueblo Bonito, Chaco Culture National Historical Park, New Mexico. Photo Mschneider/ Adobe Stock
118 Cliff Palace, Mesa Verde National Park, Colorado. Photo Jeff/Adobe Stock
119 Cylinder Jar, 900–1130. Ancestral Puebloan, Room 28, Pueblo Bonito, Chaco Canyon. Pottery, clay slip, paint, 12 × 11 × 24.5 (4¾ × 4⅜ × 9⅝). NMAI (5/2104). Photo NMAI Photo Services
120 Mosaic Pendant, 900–1200. Ancestral Puebloan, Chaco Canyon. Spondylus shell, turquoise, jet/lignite, 17.9 × 18.2 × 2.5 (7 × 7⅛ × 1). NMAI (7/1615). Photo NMAI Photo Services
121 Ritual Assemblage, 1300–1400. Salado (Mogollon), New Mexico. Wood, stone, plant fibers, cotton, feathers, hide, and pigment, height (male figure) 64 (25¼), height (female figure) 36 (14¼). AIC. Major Acquisitions Centennial Endowment (1979.17.1-11)
122 Bowl, 1400–1625. Ancestral Hopi (Sityatki), Arizona. Ceramic and pigment, 11.5 × 31.6 × 31 (4⅝ × 12½ × 12¼). AIC. Gift of Edward and Betty Harris (2004.1152)
123 Chan Chan, Huanchaco, Peru. Photo gaelj/ Adobe Stock
124 Ear Ornaments, 1350–1470. Chimú, Peru. Gold, 13.7 × 13.7 × 12.7 (5½ × 5½ × 5). MET. Jan Mitchell and Sons Collection, Gift of Jan Mitchell, 1991 (1991.419.67)
125 Litter Back, 1185–1275. Chimú, Peru. Wood, gold alloy, pigment, shell inlay, 60.4 × 95 (23¾ × 37⅜). The Cleveland Museum of Art. John L. Severance Fund (1952.233)
126 Vessel, *c.* 1100–1470. Chimú, Peru. Hammered silver, 17.8 × 19.1 (7⅛ × 7⅝). Denver Art Museum. Gift of the Collection of Frederick and Jan Mayer (1969.303). Photo © Denver Art Museum
127 Martin Chambi, Panorama of Machu Picchu, Peru, 1930s. Archivo Fotográfico Martin Chambi, Cusco, Peru. © Martin Chambi
128 Sacsayhuamán, Cusco, Peru. Photo SL-Photography/Adobe Stock
129 Felipe Guaman Poma de Ayala, *The Eleventh Inka, Huayna Capac*, from *El primer nueva corónica y buen gobierno*, 1615–16. Ink on paper. Det Kongelige Bibliotek, Copenhagen
130 Felipe Guaman Poma de Ayala, *The Eighth Qoya, Mama Yunto Cayan*, from *El primer nueva corónica y buen gobierno*, 1615–16. Ink on paper. Det Kongelige Bibliotek, Copenhagen
131 *Tupu* (pin), 600–1500. Wari or Inca, Peru. Silver, 6.1 × 17.1 (2⅜ × 6¾). MET. Gift of Mr and Mrs Nathan Cummings, 1964 (64.228.703)
132 *Tupu* (pin), 600–1600. Wari or Inca, Peru. Silver, 6 × 17.1 (2⅜ × 6¾). MET. Gift of Mr and Mrs Nathan Cummings, 1964 (64.228.702)
133 see entry **1**
134 *Khipu*, 1476–1532. Inca, Peru. Cotton, 80 × 168 × 5 (31½ × 66⅛ × 2). Museo Larco, Lima, Peru (ML600004)
135 above *Kero*, *c.* 1500. Inca, Peru. Wood, height 15.6 (6¼), diameter 12.1 (4⅞). MET. The Michael

C. Rockefeller Memorial Collection, Bequest of Nelson A. Rockefeller, 1979 (1979.206.1074)
135 below *Kero*, 1550–1800. Inca, Peru. Wood, pigments, vermilion/cinnabar, tree pitch/gum, varnish, 24 × 24.1 × 18.8 (9½ × 9½ × 7⅜). NMAI (15/2412). Photo NMAI Photo Services
136 Ritual Assemblage, 1400–1532. Inca. Gold, camelid fiber, tunic 6.6 × 5.7 (2⅝ × 2¼), bag 3.2 × 3.8 (1⅜ × 1½), figure 5.7 × 1.5 × 1.4 (2¼ ×⅝ ×⅝), mantle 13.9 × 8.4 (5½ × 3⅜). American Museum of Natural History, New York (41.2/902, 41.2/903, 41.2/904, 41.2/905). Photo MET/Art Resource/ Scala, Florence
137 *Paccha* (Vessel), 1400–1532. Inca, Peru. Ceramic, pigment, 42.3 × 22.6 × 13.6 (16⅝ × 8⅞ × 5⅜). BM (Am1947,10.39). Photo The Trustees of the British Museum
138 Malinalco, Mexico. Photo Cavan Images/ Peter Essick/Alamy Stock Photo
139 Juan de Tovar, Tenochtitlan Templo Mayor, from the *Tovar Codex*, 1582–87. Paper, pigment. John Carter Brown Library (Codex Ind. 2)
140 Anthropomorphic Sculpture (Tula Atlantean), 850–1250. Toltec, Tula. Stone, 483 × 120 × 100 (190⅛ × 47¼ × 39⅜). MNA (10-0081772). Secretaría de Cultura – INAH – MEX. Reproduction authorised by the Instituto Nacional de Antropología e Historia, Mexico
141 Calendar Stone Sculpture, *c.* 1500–21. Mexica, Mexico. Stone, diameter 358 (141). MNA. Photo Image Asset Management/World History Archive/ SuperStock
142 Coyolxauhqui Sculpture, 1469. Mexica, Templo Mayor, Mexico. Stone, pigment, 225 × 205 × 37 (88⅝ × 80¾ × 14⅝). Museo del Templo Mayor, INAH (10-0001123). Photo Frank Nowikowski/Alamy Stock Photo
143 Coatlicue Sculpture, 1250–1521. Mexica, Mexico. Stone, 350 × 130 (137¾ × 51⅛). MNA (10-0001153). Photo Jorge Pérez de Lara
144 Tlaltecuhtli Sculpture, 1478–1502. Mexica, Templo Mayor, Mexico. Stone, pigment, 400 × 370 × 38 (157½ × 145⅝ × 15). Museo del Templo Mayor, INAH. Photo © Kenneth Garrett/GEO Image Collection/Bridgeman Images
145 Tlaloc Vessel, 1440–69. Mexica, Templo Mayor, Mexico. Ceramic, pigment, 32.5 × 32.5 (12¾ × 12¾). Museo del Templo Mayor, INAH. Photo De Agostini/A. De Gregorio/Superstock
146 Xochipilli Sculpture, 1350–1520. Mexica, Mexico. Stone, 115.5 × 55.5 (45½ × 21⅞). MNA. Photo Jorge Pérez de Lara
147 Page from Codex Borgia, *c.* 1500. Hide, gesso, pigment, 26.5 × 27 (10⅜ × 10⅝). Biblioteca Apostolica Vaticana (Borg.mess.1)
148 *Chimalli* (Feathered Shield), *c.* 1500. Mexica, Mexico. Feathers, gold plate, cane, leather. Weltmuseum Wien (43380). Photo © KHM-Museumsverband, Weltmuseum Wien
149 *Chimalli* Pendant, *c.* 1500. Mixtec, Mexico. Gold, 10.5 × 8.5 (4⅛ × 3⅜). Museo Baluarte de Santiago, Veracruz (10-213084). Secretaría de Cultura – INAH – MEX. Reproduction authorised by the Instituto Nacional de Antropología e Historia, Mexico. Photo Michel Zabé/Art Resource, NY
150 Juan Bautista Cuiris, *Portrait of the Virgin Mary*, *c.* 1590–1600. Michoacán, Mexico. Feather mosaic, wood, paper, 25.4 × 18.2 (10 × 7⅛). Kunsthistorisches Museum, Vienna (Schatzkammer, GS Kap 322)
151, 152 Reliquary Figure, 1492–1524. Taíno. Wood, bone, cotton, shell, rhinoceros horn, height 32 (12⅝). Museo delle Civiltà, Rome
153 Portable Writing Desk, *c.* 1643. Barniz de Pasto lacquer on Spanish cedar (Cedrela odorata), with silver mounts, 20.2 × 39.4 × 35 (8 × 15½ × 13¾). Courtesy of the Hispanic Society of America (LS2446)
154 Vilcashuamán, Peru. Photo imageBROKER/ Peter Giovannini/Alamy Stock Photo
155 Great Pyramid of Cholula, Mexico. Photo Kit Leong/Adobe Stock
156 Andrés Sánchez Gallque, *Portrait of Don Francisco de Arobe and Sons Don Pedro and Don Domingo*, 1599. Oil on canvas, 92 × 175 (36¼ × 68⅞). Museo del Prado, Madrid (P004778)
157 Wifredo Lam, *La jungla* (*The Jungle*), 1942–43. Oil and charcoal on paper mounted on canvas, 239.4 × 229.9 (94¼ × 90½). The Museum of Modern Art, New York. Inter-American Fund (140.1945). © 2026 Wifredo Lam Estate, ADAGP, Paris and DACS, London
158 Clarissa Tossin, *Ch'u Mayaa*, 2017. HD single-channel digital video. Choreography/Performer: Crystal Sepúlveda. Courtesy Clarissa Tossin
159 *Nampeyo*, Jar, 1900–15. Painted ceramic, height 25.1 (10), diameter 29.8 (11¾). Denver Art Museum. Gift of C.W. Douglas (1929.72). Photo © Denver Art Museum
160 Miguel Luciano, *Cemí-Libre*, 2021. Pictured: Aya Rodríguez-Izumi and Miguel Luciano with Cemí. Photo Argenis Apolinari

Index

Page numbers in italics indicate the pages on which figures appear

A

abstraction: Amazonian *143,* 144; Ancestral Puebloan *205,* 208–09; as artistic choice 9, 30, 40; Calima-Malagana 133; Chimú *213,* 214; Inka 220, 222, 232, *233*; Mexica 247; Mixtec 169; Moche *81,* 82; Nasca 50–51, *52*; Olmec 56, 63–64; Paracas *24,* 48, *48*; Teotihuacán 155, *156*; Tiwanaku 173, 181–82; Tlatilco 58; Veracruz 166–67, *167*; Wari 186, 187–88, *187–89,* 189–90

Africans 256, 257, 264–65, 266

agriculture: cotton 23–24, 33; fertility and 108, 118, *232,* 232–33; Inka terraces and *220–21,* 221; irrigation and 33, 77, 213, 232. *See also* maize

Ahuitzotl 238, 252

Amazonia 26, 35, 40, 127, 142–45, *143,* 190, 264

ancestors: depiction of 23, 68, *68,* 127–28, *128,* 162, *163,* 187, *187*; mountain burials of 163, 191; mountains as 12–13, 210, 231; paired 195; political power and 44, 127–28, *128,* 140; textiles and 47

Ancestral Puebloan cities 202–09, *203–08*

Andes: Andes mountains 11, 33, 173; artistic conventions 34, 35, 38, 44–45, 144, 181, 191 (*see also* complementarity; duality); camelids and 24, 33, 47, 173, 179, 181, 182–83, 226; chakana motif 176, 183, 231; inlaid resin work *230,* 231, 260, *260*; worldview of 34–35, 222, 231, 233–34. *See also individual cultures*

Antilles Archipelago 145–46, *146,* 257, *259*

architecture: adobe 50, 77–78, *78,* 80, *81,* 81–82, 93, *94–95, 213,* 214; Ancestral Puebloan 202, 203–04, *203–04*; astronomy and 34, 100, 122, 176, 193, 221, 238; Chavín 35, *36–37,* 37–38, *39*; colonial 260–62, *261–62*; Inka 220, *220–21,* 222–23, *223,* 261, *261*; Maya 100, 101, *102–03,* 110, 122; Maya revival 266, *266*; Mexica 235–39, *236–37, 239,* 243, 244, 247–48; Moche 77–78, *78,* 80, *81,* 81–82; Olmec 56–57, 63, *63*; sculptural 176–77, *177*; seasonal 16, 18, 19, 203; Taíno 145, 147; Tairona *130–31,* 131; Teotihuacán 151, *152–53,* 154, 155, *157,* 157–58, 249, *249*; Wari *183,* 183–84; wooden 76. *See also* mounds, Mississippian; platforms; plazas

astronomy: architecture and 34, 100, 122, 176, 193, 221, 238; Maya codices and 123; star motifs and 160; stone monuments and 221–22, 242

Axayacatl 235, 238

B

ball game, the 122, 147, 166–67, *167*

basketry 24–25, *25,* 179

beading 146, *146,* 257, *259*

books: Codex Zouche-Nuttall *170–71,* 171–72; Dresden Codex 123, *126*; Florentine Codex (Sahagún and Indigenous collaborators), 250, 251–52; Mexica 250–52, *251*

C

Calima-Malagana 131–33, *132*

Calima-Yotoco *133,* 133–34

camelids 24, 33, 47, 173, 179, 181, 182–83, 226

Caral 20, 34

caves: architecture as 46; architecture from 235–38, *236–37*; cave painting 16–17, 68–69, *69*; cenotes and 110, 123; offerings in 134, 207; as places of origin 61–62, *62,* 99, *100–01,* 154, 235; sculpture depicting 61–62, *62,* 66–67, *67*

Cemí-Libre (Free Zemí, Luciano) 268, *269*

ceramics: Ancestral Puebloan 204–05, *205, 208,* 208–09; Costa Rican 139; Cupisnique 44–45, *45*; early development 21–23, *22*; Ecuadoran *129,* 129–30; Gran Coclé 140, *141,* 142; Marajoara 142–44, *143*; Maya 111, *113,* 113–16, *115*; Mississippian 200–01, *201*; Moche 82, 84, *87–90,* 87–91; modern Native North American 267, *268*; molds and 23, 87, 93, 116, 129, 186; Monte Albán 164–65, *165*; Nasca 50–51, *52*; Olmec 58–60, *59*; Paracas 48–50, *49*; Santarém 145; Sicán/Lambayeque 93; slip decoration and 23, 49, 50–51, 58, 87, 186, 201, 204; stirrup spouts and 45, *45,* 87, *87, 88–89,* 89, *90*; urn burials and 144, 164–65; Veracruz 165–66, *166*; Wari *185,* 186–87, *187*

Chalcatzingo 61–62, *62,* 66–67

Chambi, Martín: *Panorama of Machu Picchu, 220–21*

Chan Chan *213,* 213–14, 215, 219

Chavín/Chavín de Huántar 33–46; architecture 35–38, *36–37*; influence and legacy *41,* 41–46, *43–46,* 49, *49,* 87, 91, 177, 187, 219; metalwork 38, 40, *40*; stone sculpture *36,* 37–38, *39*

Chichén Itzá 122–23, *124–25,* 239, 266

Chimú *213*, 213–19, *215*, *217–18*
Ch'u Mayaa (Maya Blue, Tossin) 266, *266*
Church, Kelly: *Sustaining Traditions—Digital Teachings* 25
Cliff Palace 203–04, *204*
coca 133–34, 226
codices. *See* books
Colombia *27*, *130–33*, 130–36, *135–36*, *269*
colonial period 256–64, *258–63*
colonialism 8, 9, 225, 266
complementarity 34, 35, 220, 222, 226, *226*. *See also* duality
Copán 116, 117–19, *118*, 122
copper 48, 78–79, *79*, 84, 93, 193, *197*, 197–98, 252–55
Costa Rica 70, 123, 136–39, *138–39*, 170. *See also* Panama
Cuiris, Juan Bautista: *Portrait of the Virgin Mary* 257, *258*
Cupisnique 44–45, *45*, 91
cups. *See keros*

D
duality 34–35, 38, 42, 45, 82, 219, 222, 231. *See also* complementarity

E
earthworks: Marajoara 144; Mississippian mounds 18–19, *19*, 192–95, *194*, 196, 197, 202; Nasca Lines 50, *51*
Ecuador 21, *22*, 127–30, *128*, *129*
El Castillo de Huarmey *185*, 185–86, 229
El Perú-Wak'a *107*, 107–08, 116
El primer nueva corónica y buen gobierno (Guaman Poma) *224–25*, 224–26
El Tajín 167–68, *168*
Etowah Indian Mounds *197*, 197–98

F
feasting 23, 120, 144, 147, 180–81, *181*, 186, 202, 231
featherwork 69, 190, *191*, 251–52, *253*, 225, 257, *258*
fertility: agriculture and 108, 118, *232*, 232–33; jade symbolism and 108, 119; Moche erotic pottery and 90–91; shells and 26; Valdivia figurines and 21, *22*
fiber arts. *See* basketry; textiles
first Americans 11–26; ceramics 21–23, *22*; dramatic arts 20–21; fiber arts 23–25, 26; metalworking 26, 28; migration into the Americas 11–13; rock art 16–18, *18*; shelter and architecture 16–20, *19*; weaponry and implements 13–16, *14–15*, *17*; wood working 25–26
Florentine Codex (Sahagún and Indigenous collaborators) 250, 251–52
fresco, 159–60, *160*. *See also* mural painting

G
Gallque, Andrés Sánchez: *Portrait of Don Francisco de Arobe and Sons Don Pedro and Don Domingo* 262–63, *263*
Garagay 45–46, *46*
gender. *See* women
gold: Calima-Malagana 131–33, *132*; Calima-Yotoco *133*, 133–34; Chavín 38; Chimú *215*, 215–16, *217*; colonial 263; Costa Rican 138–39; Gran Coclé 140, *141*; Kuntur Wasi 28, *28*, 43–44, *44*; Mexica 239, 250, *254*, 252–55; Mixtec *169*, 169–71; Muisca 134, 136, *136*; Panamanian in general 130–31, 142; Sicán/Lambayeque 93–95, *96–97*; solar association of, 28, 38, 82, 219
gourds 21, 34, 98, 99, *100*, 204
Gran Coclé 139–42, *141*
greenstone: Calima-Malagana 133; Costa Rican 139, 140; Maya 73, 108, *110*, 110–11; Mexica 248, 249; Monte Albán 162–63, *164*; Olmec 56, 60, 63, 64, *65*, 70, *72*; Santarém 145; Teotihuacán 155, *156*, 157, 160, 162, *163*; Wari 188, *188*. *See also* jade
Guaman Poma de Ayala, Felipe: *El primer nueva corónica y buen gobierno* *224–25*, 224–26

H
Huaca Cao Viejo *81*, 81–84, *83*, *85*
Huaca Prieta 24, 33–34
Huacas de Moche 77–78, *78*, 80, 81, 215
Huayna Capac *224*, 225, 226, 228–29

I
incense 111, 114–16, *115*, 123, 128, 181, *181*, 248
indigo 33–34, 116, 179
Inka 219–34; architecture 219–23, *220–21*, *223*, 261, *261*; ceramics 232–34, *233*; Cuzco 210, 215, 221, 222–23, 231, 264; feasting and *230*, 231; Felipe Guaman Poma de Ayala and *224*, 224–26, *225*; Machu Picchu 219–22, *220–21*; metalwork 226, *227*, 231, *232*; *qhapaq ñan* 221, 222; religion 221, 222, 223–24, 231; rulers (Sapa Inka) 191, 210, 215, 219, 225, 226; sacrifice and 222, 231–32, *232*; Sacsayhuamán 223, *223*; textiles 226–29, *228–29*, 231, *232*

J
jade: Costa Rican 138, *138*; green feathers and 69; maize imagery and 56, 108, *109*; Maya 105, 108–11, *109–10*, 122, 123; Mexica 239, 250; Monte Albán 163, *164*; offerings of 123; the sacred landscape and 53; Teotihuacán 162; trade networks and 70, *72*, 73, 108, 119, 122, 138. *See also* greenstone
Jar (Nampeyo) 267, *268*
jewelry: ear rods 140, *141*; earspools 84, *86*, *215*, 215–16; necklaces/collars *72*, 73, *254*, 255; nose ornaments 43–44, *44*, 82, *83*, 84, 132, *132*, 136; sound-making 43–44, *44*, 215, *254*, 255

K

keros *180,* 180–81, 216–19, *218, 230,* 231

L

La jungla (*The Jungle,* Lam) 264–66, *265*
La Tolita *129,* 129–30
La Venta *62–63,* 62–69, *65–69*
Lady K'abal Xook *104–05,* 105–07
Lam, Wifredo: *La jungla (The Jungle)* 264–66, *265*
landscape, sacred: architecture as 116, 131; cenotes 110, 123; colonial appropriation of 261; depiction of 205, 214; Native North American 267; origin stories and 123, 235; perspectivism and 26; ritual offerings in 134, 207, 231–32; supernatural beings in 11, 146, 186, 222; zemís and 146, 268. *See also* earthworks; mountains
Las Bocas 58, *59,* 60
looting 9, 62, 114, 131, 184, 255
Lord 8 Deer Jaguar Claw *170–71,* 171–72
Luciano, Miguel: *Cemí-Libre* (Free Zemí) 268, *269*

M

Machu Picchu 219–22, *220–21*
maize: Inka and 231, 232–34, *233*; Maya and 60, *61,* 73, 99, *100,* 108, 116, *117–18,* 118; Mexica and 247; Mixtec and *169,* 169–70; Olmec and 56, 57, 60, *72,* 73; Teotihuacán and 162, *163*
Malagana. *See* Calima-Malagana
Malinalco 235–38, *236–37*
Mama Yunto Cayan *225,* 225–26
Manteño 127–28, *128*
Marajoara 142–44, *143*
masks: Calima-Malagana *132,* 132–33; Kuntur Wasi, 43–44, *44*; Maya 108, *110,* 110–11; Monte Albán 163, *164*; Sicán/Lambayeque 93, 94, *96*; Teotihuacán 158, 162, *163*
Maya, 98–126; the ball game and 122; books (codices), 111, 114, 123, *126*; calendar system 71, 98, 101, 106, 123; Central Mexican influence on 122, 158–59; ceramics 111, *113,* 113–16, *115*; Chichén Itzá 122–23, *124–25,* 239, 266; Copán 116, 117–19, *118,* 122; El Perú-Wak'a *107,* 107–08, 116; hieroglyphic script 100–01, *104–05,* 105, 106, 108, 110, 111, *113,* 114, 119–21, *120–21,* 123; jade sculpture 105, 108–11, *109–10,* 118–19, 122, 123; music 116, *117*; Olmec influence on 98–99, *100–01,* 108; Palenque 108, *110,* 110–11, *112,* 114–16, *115,* 266; Piedras Negras 119–21, *120–21*; political organization 98, 100, 101, 108, 110–11, 116, 119–22, 158; Quiriguá 119, 122; religion 98–99, *99–100, 104–05,* 105–06, 108, 111, 112–16, *113, 115,* 116–18, *117–18,* 123, 126; San Bartolo 98–99, *99–100*; stone sculpture *104,* 105–07, 111, *112,* 116, 118, *118*; Tikal 100, *102–03, 107,* 107–08, *109,* 121, 158; Yaxchilan *104–05,* 105–07, 121
Maya revival 266–67, *266*
Mesoamerica: the ball game and 122, 147, 166–67, *167*; calendar system 170–71, 241, 242, 247, 250, 251; rain gods and 111, 113, *113,* 158, 238, 247–48, *248*; worldview 56, 176 (*see also* caves; maize). *See also individual cultures*
metalwork: casting 28, 130–31, 134, 136, *136,* 169, *169,* 252–55; Colombia and 130–31, *132–33,* 132–34; colonial 260, *260,* 263; duality and 38, *39,* 82, *83,* 219, 226, *227*; early metallurgical development 26, 28; platinum *133,* 134. *See also* copper; gold; silver
Mexica 235–55; *altepetl*s and 235; architecture 235–39, *236–37, 239,* 243, 244, 247–48; artistic culture of, 250, 252; books 250–52, *251*; ceramics 248, *248*; featherwork 251–52, *253,* 255; hieroglyphic script 166, 242, 247, 252–55; Malinalco 235–38, *236–37*; metalwork 252–55, *254*; religion 151, 169, 238–39, 241, *241,* 242–52, *243, 245–46, 248–49, 251*; rulers *(huey tlatoani)* 210, 235, 237, 241–42, 250, 252; stone sculpture *241,* 241–47, *243, 245–46,* 248–50, *249*; Tenochtitlán 210, 238–39, 241–48, 255; Toltecs and 239–41, *240*
Mississippian cities 18–19, *19,* 192–202, *194, 196–97, 199–201*
Mixtec 168–72, *169, 170–71*
Moche 77–91; architecture 77–78, *78,* 80, *81,* 81–82; artistic/cultural connections to 93, 94, 177, 214, 215; ceramics 82, 84, *87–90,* 87–91; Chavín influence and 87, 91; Huaca Cao Viejo *81,* 81–84, *83, 85*; Huacas de Moche 77–78, *78,* 80, 81, 215; metalwork 78–79, *79,* 82, *83,* 84, *85–86*; mural painting and architectural relief 77–78, *78,* 91, *92*; Pañamarca 91, *92*; political organization 80, 81–82, 84, 87, 88, 91; religion 77–78, *78,* 80, 82, *87,* 87–88, 90–91; Sipán 84, *86,* 87
modern and contemporary art *25,* 264–66, *266,* 266–67, *266,* 268, *269*
Mogollon *207,* 207–08
Monte Albán 162–65, *164–65,* 168–69. *See also* Mixtec
mosaic: architectural 157; depiction of *157,* 158; feather 252, 257, *258*; greenstone 63–64; jade 108, *109–10,* 110–11; shell 155, *155*; turquoise 84, *86,* 169, 205, *206*
Moteuczoma II 241–42
mounds, Mississippian 18–19, *19,* 192–95, *194,* 196, 197, 202
mountains: ancestor burials and 163, 191; as ancestors

12–13, 210, 231; Andes mountain range 11, 33, 173; architecture incorporating 77, *183,* 183–84, 220, *236–37,* 238; architecture reproducing 18, 63, *63,* 99–100, *102–03,* 110, 116, 151, 154, 214–15, 238, *239,* 243, 261–62, *262*; as conceptual centers 12–13, *13*; deities emerging from 98, 154; deities ruling over 246; as living beings 13, 98, 99, *100–01,* 113, 116; metals as essence of 28; origin stories and 62, 63, 116, 210, 235, 238; stone sculpture symbolizing 66–67, *67,* 221–22; transportation of stone from 57, 157
Muisca 134, 136, *136*
mural painting: early Andean development of 24; Maya 98–99, *99–100*; Moche 91, *92*; Olmec style 68–69, *69*; Teotihuacán 159–60, *160*
musical instruments: drums 50, 114; flutes 20, 114; rattles 38, *39,* 84, 116, 144, 166; trumpets 38, *39,* 42, 114; whistles 116, *117*

N
Nampeyo: *Jar* 268, *268*
Nasca 50–52, *51–52*
Native North America, in general 192–93, 209, 266–67, 267, *268. See also* Ancestral Puebloan cities; Mississippian cities
naturalism: as artistic choice 9, 30, 40; Calima-Malagana 133; Ecuadoran 129–30; Maya 105–06, 108, *109,* 111, *112,* 114, 120, *120–21*; Mexica 247, 249; Mississippian 193, 196, *196*; Mixtec 169; Moche 78, 87, 88–89, *88–90,* 93; Nasca 51–52; Olmec 53, *54–55,* 56, 58, 66; Teotihuacán 155; Tiwanaku *181,* 181–82, 249; Wari 186

O
Olmec, 53–73; colossal heads 53, *54–55,* 57, 64; influence on Maya art 98–99, *100–01,* 108; La Venta *62–63,* 62–69, *65–69*; legacies of 56, 57, 69–73, *71–72*; religion 57, 58, 59–60, 61, 63–64; San Lorenzo and the highlands 53–62, *54–55, 59, 61*

P
Pachacuti 220, 222, 225
Pacopampa 42, *43,* 45
Pakal (K'inich Janaab Pakal I) 108, *110,* 110–11
Palenque 108, *110,* 110–11, *112,* 114–16, *115,* 266
Panama 123, 136–38, *137,* 139–42, *141,* 170, 264. *See also* Costa Rica
Pañamarca 91, *92*
Panorama of Machu Picchu (Chambi) *220–21*
Paracas 46–50, *48–49,* 50
Piedras Negras 119–21, *120–21*
pigments: adobe sculpture and 46; artists' access to 23; burial goods and 14; cinnabar 48, 60, 64, 93, 110, 111, 164–65, *165,* 216, *217*; copper-based 48; hematite 60, 64, 159; iron oxide 159; Maya blue 116, 123, 129, 266; slip decoration and 23, 49, 50–51, 58, 87, 186, 201, 204
Pikillaqta 184–85
platforms: Chavín de Huántar 35, 37; Chimú 214; early Andean 34; first American 19; Inka 261, *261*; Mexica 238, *239,* 242, 248–49, *249*; Moche 77, 80; Olmec 56–57, 63; Panamanian 137; Taíno 145; Teotihuacán 154; Tiwanaku 173, 175, 176; Toltec 240–41
plazas: Chavín 35, 37, 38; Chimú 214; European 241; Inka 221, 223; Maya 98, 99–100; Mississippian 195; Moche 77, 78; Olmec 62; Teotihuacán 155–56, 158, 159; Tiwanaku 173, 176, 180; Wari 184
Portrait of Don Francisco de Arobe and Sons Don Pedro and Don Domingo (Gallque) 262–64, *263*
Portrait of the Virgin Mary (Cuiris) 257, *258*
pottery. *See* ceramics
Poverty Point 18–19, *19,* 193
Pueblo Bonito 202–03, *203,* 204–05, *205*
pyramids: depiction of 177, *177,* 179, *179*; Great Pyramid of Cholula 261–62, *262*; Maya 100, 101, *102–03,* 122; Mexica 238; Moche 81–82; Olmec 63, *63*; Sicán/Lambayeque 93, *94–95*; Teotihuacán 151

Q
Quiriguá 119, 122

R
realism. *See* naturalism
religion: Ancestral Puebloan 202, 209; Chavín 34, *36,* 37, 49; cosmologies and 26, 193–94, 247; the feathered serpent and 58, 61–62, 99, *99–100,* 108, 155, *157,* 157–58, 159, 238; Inka 221, 222, 223–24, 231; maize and 60, *72,* 73, 99, 108, 116–18, *117–18,* 162, 231, 232–34, *233*; Maya 98–99, *99–100, 104–05,* 105–06, 108, 111, 112–16, *113, 115,* 116–18, *117–18,* 123, 126; Mexica 151, 169, 238–39, 241, *241,* 242–52, *243, 245–46, 248–49, 251*; Mississippian 193–94, 196, *196–97,* 197–98, 199, *199*; Mixtec *169,* 169–71; Moche 77–78, *78,* 80, 82, *87,* 87–88, 90–91; Monte Albán 164–65, *165*; Olmec 57, 58, 59–60, 61, 63–64; Paracas 49; rain gods and 111, 113, *113,* 158, 238, 247–48, *248*; Sicán/Lambayeque 93, 94–95; Spanish 123, 256–57, 261–62, *261–62,* 264; Taíno *27,* 145–47, *146,* 257, *259,* 265, 268, *269*; Teotihuacán 154, *157,* 157–58, 159–62, *160–61,*

163; Tiwanaku 177, *177–79,* 179–80; Veracruz 167–68, *168*; *wak'a*s and 35, 222, 223–24, 231, 260–61; Wari 186, 190; zemís and *27, 146,* 146–47, 257, *259,* 265, 268, *269*. *See also* caves; ritual
ritual: archaeological evidence for 38, 82, 84; architecture and 20, 63, 82, 91, *92, 152–53,* 155, 176, 202, 220; *ceques* and 222, 223; dedicatory offerings and 63–64, 66, *66,* 78, 108, 134, 155, 157, 166, 186, 238–39; depicting *87,* 87–88, *104–05,* 105–07; divine embodiment and 84, 96, 106, 107, 177, 198, 200, 207, 250; feasting and 180; fertility and 232–34, *233*; geoglyphs and 50; incense and 111, 114–16, *115,* 123, 128, 181, *181,* 248; pipes and 193, 200 (*see also* tobacco); psychoactive substances and 38, *40,* 48, 134, 144, 179, 226, 250; regalia for 26, 64, 84, *85,* 205, *206,* 252–55, *253*; sacrificial substitution and 60; sound and 114, 116, *117*; violence and 52, 241, 252 (*see also* sacrifice). *See also* feasting; religion; sacrifice

S

sacrifice: Inka 222, 231–32, *232*; Maya *104–05,* 106; Mexica 238, 239, 241, 247; Mississippian 198; Moche 82, *87,* 87–88; modern art and 265–66; Monte Albán 162; Paracas burials and 47; Sicán/Lambayeque 93–94, 95; substitution and 60; Teotihuacán 155, 157; Veracruz 167–68, *168*
Sacsayhuamán 223, *223*
Sahagún, Bernardino de: Florentine Codex (with Indigenous collaborators) 250, 251–52
San Agustín 134, *135*
San Bartolo 98–99, *99–100*
San Lorenzo 53–62, *54–55, 59, 61,* 70
Santarém 145
screenfold books. *See* books
sculpture: adobe 45–46, *46, 213,* 214; agency of 57; artist training and 119; celts, 65, *66,* 138, 163; colossal heads 53, *54–55,* 57, 64; greenstone 60, 63, *65,* 70, *72,* 73, 145, 160, 162, *163,* 248; stelae *36,* 37, 42, *43,* 45, 64, 100, 116, 119, 177–79, *178*; stone in the round 53, *54–55,* 57, 66–68, *67–68,* 116, *118,* 118–19, 134, *135, 137,* 137–38, 160–62, *161,* 166–67, *167,* 177–79, *178, 195–96,* 195–97, 198, 200, *200,* 239–41, *240,* 244, *245,* 248–49, *249*; stone relief *36,* 37, 38, 42, *43,* 61–62, *62,* 66–67, *67, 104–05,* 105–07, 111, *112,* 119–21, *120–21,* 167–68, *168,* 176–77, *177, 241,* 241–43, *243,* 244, *246,* 247; stone *wak'a*s and 222, 223–24; tenoned heads 37–38, *39,* 176; thrones 66–67, *67,* 127, *128*; wood *27,* 60, *61, 107,* 107–08, 145–46, 180–81, *181,* 187–88, *188,* 198, *199,* 207, *207,* 214, 216, *217, 230,* 231
shells: beads 146, *146,* 147, 202–03, 263, *263*; conch 38, *39,* 42, 122, 252; depiction of 42, *43,* 158, 159, *160,* 214, 217–19, *218,* 238, *239, 251,* 252; fertility and 26; inlay of 78, *79,* 110, *110,* 155, *156,* 162–63, *164,* 188, *188,* 205, 216, *217*; as offerings 38, 123, 222, 239, 248; *Spondylus* 111, 155, *156,* 188, *188,* 205, *206,* 214, 217–19; trade networks and 7, 26, 38, 158, 193, 205, 219
Sicán/Lambayeque 91, 93–97, *94–97,* 216, 219
Sikyatki *208,* 208–09, 267
silver: Chavín 38; Chimú 216–19, *218*; colonial 260, *260*; Inka 226, *227*; lunar association of 28, 38, 82, 219; Wari, 188, *188*
Sipán 84, *86,* 87
Sitio Conte 140, *141*
Spanish Empire: colonial violence and 123, 202, 255; hunt for gold and 28, 134, 255; religion and 123, 145–46, 256–57, 261–62, *261–62,* 264. *See also* colonial period
Spiro Mounds *196,* 196–97
Sustaining Traditions—Digital Teachings (Church) *25*

T

Taínos *27,* 145–47, *146,* 257, *259,* 268, *269*
Taironas *130–31,* 131
Templo Mayor of Tenochtitlan (Tovar) 238, *239*
Teotihuacán 151–62, *152–53, 156–57, 160–61, 163,* 168, 241, 248
textiles: architectural decoration and 77, *78,* 214; Chavín *41,* 41–42; cotton 34, 41, *41,* 146, *146,* 190, 198, 226; geoglyph planning and 50; Huaca Prieta 24, 33–34; Inka 226–29, *228*; Maya 105, 120; Moche 84; Paracas *24,* 47–48, *48*; sculptural motifs and 176; Tiwanaku *179,* 179–80, *182,* 182–83; Wari 185–86, 187, *187, 189,* 189–90
Tikal 100, *102–03, 107,* 107–08, *109,* 121, 158
Tiwanaku 173–83, *174–75, 177–82,* 190–91
Tlatilco/Tlapacoya 58, 59–60
tobacco 134, 144–45, 193, 197
Toltecs 239–41, *240*
Tossin, Clarissa: *Ch'u Mayaa* (Maya Blue) 266, *266*
Tovar, Juan de: *Templo Mayor of Tenochtitlan* 238, *239*
trade networks: Amazonian 144, 145; ancestral Native North American 192, 193, 197, 201, 202, 207–08; Antillean 145; bannerstones and 16; birds/feathers and 7, 190, 207–08; chocolate and 204–05; emeralds and 131–32, 140; European 256, 257; goldwork and 123, 142; greenstone and 56, 63, 139, 145, 188; jade and 70, *72,* 73, 119; Panamanian 139; politics and 64, 119, 191, 239;

shells and 7, 26, 38, 158, 193, 205, 219; spear points and 14–15; Toltec 239
turquoise: beads 202–03; figurines 185; inlay 94–95, *97*; Mexica culture and 239, 242, 250; mosaic 84, *86*, 169, 205, *206*; trade networks and 7, 191, 239

U
urbanization: Ancestral Puebloan cities 202–09, *203*, *204–05*, *206*, *207–08*; beginnings of 20; definition of 148; Inka *220–21*, 220–22; Mississippian cities 193–200, *194–97*, *199–201*; Moche 80; Monte Albán 162–65, *164–65*, 168–69; Wari 184. *See also* Teotihuacán

V
Valdivia 21, *22*
Veracruz 165–68, *166–68*
violence: colonial 123, 202, 255; mythological *243*, 243–44, *245*; regalia for 84, *85* (*see also* weapons); rulership and 81–82, 88, 106, *107*, 107–08, 134, *134*, 158, *224*, 225; trophy heads and 52, 191, 198; warfare 34, 81–82, 155, 162; warrior depiction 84, *86–87*, 87, 134, *135*, 186, 198, 239–41, *240*. *See also* sacrifice; weapons

W
Wajaat Na Chahk 119–20, *120–21*
wak'as (huacas) 35, 222, 223–24, 231, 260–61
Wari 183–91, *183*, *185*, *187–89*, *191*, 216, *217*, 229
weapons: axes as 134, *135*, *224*, 225; ceremonial 93–94, *97*, 252, *253*, 255; clubs 82, 88; darts 15, 82, 240, 255; spears 13–14, *14*, *104–05*, 106, 107, 264; spearthrowers 15–16, 26, 82, 88, 177, 186, 240. *See also* violence
weaving. *See* textiles
women: female deities 42, *43*, 160–62, *161*, *243*, 243–47, *245–46*; Marajoara society and 144–45; political power and 42, 82–84, 91, 96, *104–05*, 105–07, 145
written script: individual glyphs 166, *166*, 170–71, 242, 247, 251–52, 255; Isthmian 70–72, *72*; Maya 100–01, *104–05*, 105, 106, *107*, 108, 110, 111, *113*, 119–20, *120–21*, 123; Olmec 56, 70, *71*

Y
Yaxchilan *104–05*, 105–07, 121
Yik'in Chan K'awiil *107*, 107–08, *109*

Z
Zapotecs. *See* Monte Albán
zemís *27*, *146*, 146–47, 257, *259*, 265, 268, *269*

World of Art

'The single most influential series of art books ever published' *Apollo*

'Outstanding ... exceptionally authoritative and well-illustrated' *Sunday Times*

'World of Art delivers real knowledge with crisp, useful clarity' *Guardian*

Comprehensive in coverage and accessible to all, the World of Art series explores both the newest and the perennial in all the arts, covering themes, artists and movements that straddle the centuries and the gamut of visual culture around the globe.

You may also like:

Art and Architecture in Mexico
James Oles

The Art of Mesoamerica From Olmec to Aztec
Mary Ellen Miller

Black Art A Cultural History
Richard J. Powell

Caribbean Art
Veerle Poupeye

Latin American Art Since 1900
Edward Lucie-Smith

North American Indian Art
David W. Penny
Foreword by George Horse Capture